Business Plan for Artists

++

Business Plan for Artists

**Copyright © 2016 Some Rights Reserved
Latimer Publishing, LLC
Box 94040, Cleveland, Ohio, 44101 USA**

Business Plan for Artists

About the Author - John Latimer

As a songwriter, entrepreneur and music business professional, John Latimer has over 30 years' experience in various aspects of the entertainment and music industry. He has been a talent buyer, booking agent, event and concert promoter, Artist developer, record label owner, manager, video director, record producer, publicist, publisher and consultant.

Latimer began his career in the entertainment business as a talent buyer and booker, promoting events and concerts. After graduating from The Ohio State University, Latimer's first real gig in the entertainment business was booking and promoting performances and events for the Pirates Cove Nightclub located in the Flats Entertainment District of Cleveland, Ohio. After a few years, Latimer became an agent with Energy Talent Agency to book local and regional talent. Later, Latimer turned his attention back to talent buying and promoting concerts for the Limelight Entertainment Complex. Latimer then formed Bullseye Booking Agency, where booked and promote acts throughout the Eastern U.S.

As a producer, Latimer's works with audio as well video. Latimer formed Play Records which released 13 albums. Latimer also co-produced and co-directed, two television shows: "Good Rockin' Tonight" and "Alternate Beat." In 2011, Latimer co-hosted a weekly podcast, "The Music Biz Workshop," to explore the business side of music. Latimer also produces the Undercurrents Radio Show.

Undercurrents, Inc., is one of Latimer's companies and began as an annual music industry conference & showcase. It has since evolved into a niche marketing and promotion company. Latimer regularly consults with Artists and entertainment professionals about their specific projects.

In addition to providing consulting services to musicians, songwriters, bands and independent labels, Latimer teaches music business courses and regularly participates as a speaker and panelist at entertainment conferences, seminars and workshops.

Latimer's books, "Event and Concert Promotion," "Forget the Majors, Launch The Artist's Own Record Label," "Music Industry Tips and Tats," "Record Label Marketing in the Digital Age," "Business Plan for Artists" and "Artist Development in the Music Business" are available through Latimer Publishing.

For more information about John Latimer, visit his website http://JohnLatimer.us

++++++++++++++++++++++++++++++

Business Plan for Artists
Copyright © 2016
by John Latimer

Printed and bound in the United States of America. Some Rights Reserved. No part of this book may be reproduced in any form or by any electronic or mechanical means including information storage and retrieval systems without permission in writing from publisher, except by a reviewer, who may quote brief passages in a review.

Published by:
Latimer Publishing, LLC
Box 94040
Cleveland, Ohio 44101
(440) 331-0700
http://www.LatimerPublishing.com

First Edition

ISBN: **978-0-9814934-9-7**

Printed in the U.S.A.

To my children Kathryn and Patrick

Business Plan for Artists
Table of Contents

Introduction

CHAPTER 1   (pages 1 – 14)
1.01 **Introduction to Business Plans**
1.02 Plan the Plan
1.03 Determine Objectives
1.04 Goals & Objectives Checklist
1.05 Financing Goals
1.06 How Will You Use Your Plan?
1.07 Assessing Your Co.'s Potential
1.08 Updates
1.09 Managing the Major Revisions
1.10 Ingredients

CHAPTER 2   (Pages 15 – 18)
2.01 **Executive Summary**
2.02 About Artist & Mission Statement
2.03 Artist's Company Summary
2.04 Management Summary
2.05 Products & Services Summary
2.06 Marketing Summary
2.07 Customer Summary
2.08 Promotion Summary
2.09 Advertising Summary
2.10 Competition Summary
2.11 Sales Summary
2.12 Intellectual Property Summary
2.13 Technology Summary
2.14 Finance Summary
2.15 Resources Summary
2.16 Appendix Summary

CHAPTER 3   (Pages 19 – 50)
3.01 **Company Overview**
3.02 Company Description
3.03 Company Structure
3.04 Organizational Structure
3.05 Operations Plan
3.06 Company Location
3.07 Company Layout
3.08 Company Objectives
3.09 Artist Summary
3.10 Income Sources
3.11 Keys to Success
3.12 Milestones
3.13 Contingency Planning
3.99 Short-Term Plan

CHAPTER 4   (Pages 49 – 68)
4.01 **Personnel Overview**
4.02 Management Team
4.03 Musicians
4.04 Singers
4.05 Songwriters
4.06 Producers
4.07 Audio Engineers
4.08 Agents
4.09 Publicists
4.10 Publishers
4.98 Administrative
4.99 Sourcing

CHAPTER 5   (Pages 69 – 94)
5.01 **Products & Services**
5.02 Product Development
5.03 Product Strategy
5.04 Product Mix
5.05 Live Performances
5.06 Producing
5.07 Recorded Audio
5.08 Mixing & Editing Audio
5.09 Mastering Audio

5.10 Recorded Video
5.11 Manufacturing Process
5.12 Pressing Vinyl
5.13 Packaging Process
5.14 Non-Audio Merchandise
5.99 Future Products & Services

CHAPTER 6   (Pages 95 – 134)
6.01 **Marketing Plan Overview**
6.02 Marketing Plan
6.03 Marketing Goals & Objectives
6.04 Market Analysis
6.05 Market Potential
6.06 Market Segmentation
6.07 SWOT Analysis
6.08 Marketing Mix
6.09 Branding Strategy
6.10 Creditability
6.11 Product Testing
6.12 Targeted Market Strategy
6.13 Pricing Policy
6.14 Packaging Strategy
6.15 Online Marketing Plan
6.16 Social Media Plan
6.17 Monitoring and Evaluation

CHAPTER 7   (Pages 135 – 146)
7.01 **Customer Overview**
7.02 Customers - Fans
7.03 Entertainment Industry
7.04 Customer Niches
7.05 Customer Profiles
7.06 Customer Demographics
7.07 Customer Service Plan

CHAPTER 8   (Pages 147 – 186)
8.01 **Promotion Plan Overview**
8.02 Promotion Analysis
8.03 Promotion Objectives
8.04 Promotion Potential
8.05 Promotion Strategy
8.06 Communication Strategy
8.07 Co-Op Promotions
8.08 Radio Promotions
8.09 Video Promotions

8.10 Performances Promotion

CHAPTER 9   (Pages 187 – 218)
9.01 **Advertising Plan**
9.02 Advertising Strategy
9.03 Advertising Analysis
9.04 Advertising Objectives
9.05 Advertising Potential
9.06 Advertising Budget
9.07 Advertising Mix
9.08 Co-Op Advertising
9.09 Creative Talent
9.10 Offline Advertising
9.11 Online Advertising

CHAPTER 10   (Pages 219 – 226)
10.01 **Competition Overview**
10.02 Industry Analysis
10.03 Industry Participants
10.04 Competitive Research
10.05 Competitive Comparisons
10.06 Main Competitors
10.07 Competitive Strategy

CHAPTER 11   (Pages 227 – 274)
11.01 **Sales Plan Overview**
11.02 Sales Management
11.03 Sales Objectives
11.04 Sales Strategy
11.05 Pricing Strategy
11.06 Profit Sources
11.07 Sales Forecast
11.08 Growth Strategy
11.09 Sales Programs
11.10 Sales Affiliates
11.11 Merchandise Sales Strategy
11.12 Online Sales Strategy
11.13 Recordings Sales Strategy
11.14 Performances Sales Strategy
11.15 Publishing Sales Strategy
11.16 Distribution – Overview
11.17 Content Licensing
11.18 Ticket Sales Strategy

CHAPTER 12 (Pages 275 – 298)
12.01 Intellectual Property
12.02 Copyrights
12.03 Patents
12.04 Trademarks
12.05 Discography
12.06 Performing Rights Orgs
12.07 Registration
12.08 Content Development
12.09 Content Clearances
12.10 Digital Rights Management

CHAPTER 13 (Pages 299 – 312)
13.01 Technology Overview
13.02 Office Technology
13.03 Promotion Technology
13.04 Recording Technology
13.05 Equipment Technology
13.06 Software Technology

CHAPTER 14 (Pages 313 – 352)
14.01 Financial Plan Overview
14.02 Start-up Summary
14.03 Use of Funds
14.04 Important Assumptions
14.05 Key Financial Indicators
14.06 Break Even Analysis
14.07 Projected Profit & Loss
14.08 Projected Balance Sheet
14.09 Goodwill
14.10 Accounting
14.11 Independent Accountant's Report
14.12 Forecasted Financial Statement
14.13 Forecasted Balance Sheet
14.14 Forecasted Statement Cash Flow
14.15 Forecasted Operating Expenses
14.16 Forecasted Assumptions
14.17 Forecasted Revenue
14.18 Risk Reduction
14.19 Risk Management
14.20 Exit Strategy
14.21 Spending Strategy
14.22 Return on Investment
14.23 Budgets
14.24 Financial Ratios
14.25 Accounts Receivable
14.26 Accounts Payable

CHAPTER 15 (Pages 353 – 364)
15.01 Resources Overview
15.02 Related Statistics
15.03 Industry Involvement
15.04 Legal Resources
15.05 Web Related Sources
15.06 Research, Stats & Demographics
15.07 Trade Publications
15.08 Databases

CHAPTER 16 (Pages 365 – 368)
16.01 Appendix Overview
16.02 Forward Looking Statements
16.03 Personal Income Statement
16.04 Resumes of Team

Forms (Pages 369 – 3848)
Agreement – Band Member
Agreement – Artist / Mgmt.
Agreement – Artist / Producer
Agreement – Artist / Publisher
Agreement – Artist / Record

Glossary (Pages 385 – 404)

Index (Pages 405 – 407)

Business Plan for Artists
Introduction
Creating a Successful Business Plan (for the Artist)

The following document was created strictly for those interested in understanding the different aspects of an Artist's Business Plan. There are several models for creating business plans and as such, this is only one possible model. Make sure that the business plan that is written best reflects the Artist and the Artist's music.

Just a reminder: The Artist's business combines the Artist's music, the Artist's band and all of the promotion and marketing that an Artist does so that they are successful in this industry.

What is a Business Plan?
The business plan outlines the Artist's professional goals, how the goals will be achieved and the resources needed to get in order to achieve those goals. It is basically the story of the Artist's career and the Artist's business. The business plan takes the Artist from the "idea stage" to the "action stage." A good business plan helps the Artist focus on their business as well as their art.

Why Write a Business Plan?
At the very basic level (and perhaps the most important level), the business plan allows the Artist to focus on their business, set a realistic plan with realistic goals, and get them moving forward with their career. Additionally, the business plan can be used to bring in key players who the Artist would like to have as a part of their team. These key players might include prospective managers, agents, labels, musicians, etc. The Artist's business plan shows these people that the Artist has thought about their career, planned how they want to achieve the Artist's goals and treat the Artist's career seriously. Finally, the business plan is often used to obtain financing from grants, loans, investors, banks, venture capitalists, government, etc.

Prepare to Write the Business Plan:

- Consider the reader and objectives
- Research all elements for each section of the business plan
- Write the business plan yourself
- Develop an outline of key sections
- Use realistic financial projections
- Make sure the business plan looks professional and the tone is professional
- Try to be positive and upbeat
- Always use third person, never first person (I, we)
- Always be honest and show how you arrived at the conclusions
- Always check spelling and grammar
- Get someone to read it over and provide feedback.

Chapter 1
Introduction to Business Plans

A business plan for Artists is a written description of their business's future. It's a document that tells them what plan to do and how they plan to do it. If you jot down an idea on the back of an envelope describing your business strategy, you've written a plan, or at least the seed of a plan.

> **If you're making any money doing anything,
> you're doing business.**
>
> **If you're selling recordings to fans or performances to concert promoters,
> you're doing business.**
>
> **If you want to start doing this or keep doing this…**
>
> **You Need a Plan.**

Business plans are inherently strategic. You start here, today, with certain resources and abilities. You want to get to there, a point in the future (usually three to five years out) at which time, your business will have a different set of resources and abilities as well as greater profitability and increased assets. Your plan shows how you will get from here to there. Without a plan, you may never get there.

Whether the Artist Business Plan is long, short, elaborate or simple, they still contain the same basic elements that they always have. Typically, most business plans have an executive summary, a marketing plan, sales plan, promotion plan, a management team description and financials (income, cash-flow and balance sheet projections).

About the only person who doesn't need a business plan is one who's not going into business. Artists don't need a plan to start a hobby or to moonlight from their regular job. But anybody beginning or extending a venture that will consume significant resources of money, energy or time, and is expected to return a profit. These artists should take the time to draft some kind of plan.

Not all business plans are written by starry-eyed musicians and bands. Many are written by and for Artists that are long past the startup stage. Either way, a plan is necessary for an Artist to increase their chances of success.

> **If you don't have a plan,
> you will never get there.**

Established or middle-stage enterprises may draft plans to help them find funding for projects or growth just as the startups do. They may feel the need for a written plan to help manage an already rapidly growing business. Or a plan may be seen as a valuable tool to be used to convey the mission and prospects of the business to investors, customers, suppliers or others.

> **A business plan is a fluid document; it changes as the business grows.**

1.02
Plan the Plan

Congratulations. You've decided to write a business plan, and you're ready to get started. You've just greatly increased the chances that your business venture will succeed. But before you start drafting your plan, you need to plan the plan. That's what this book is all about.

One of the most important reasons to plan your plan is that you may be held accountable for the projections and proposals it contains. That's especially true if you use your plan to raise money to finance your art and your company. A business plan can take on a life of its own, so thinking a little about what you want to include in your plan is obvious.

Second, as you'll soon learn if you haven't already, business plans can be complicated documents. However, the more you prepare your plan, the easier it will become. As you draft your plan, you'll be making lots of decisions on serious matters, such as what marketing strategy you'll pursue or the projects that you intend to get involved with such as recording or touring. Thinking about these decisions in advance is an important way to minimize the time you spend planning your business and maximize the time you spend generating income.

To sum up, planning your plan will help control your degree of accountability and reduce time-wasting indecision. To plan your plan, you'll first need to decide what your goals and objectives in business are. Yes, every artist wants to be successful. That's great, but what's the plan to do so.

As part of that, you'll assess the business you've chosen to start, or are already running, to see what the chances are that it will actually achieve those ends. Finally, you'll take a look at common elements of most plans to get an idea of which ones you want to include and how each will be treated.

> **To plan your plan you'll first need to decide what your goals and objectives are in your art and in your business are.**

1.03
Determine Objectives

Close your eyes. Imagine that the date is five years from now. Where do you want to be? Will you be running a business that hasn't increased significantly in size? Will you command a rapidly growing empire?

Answering these questions is an important part of building a successful business plan. In fact, without knowing where you are going, it is not really possible to plan at all.

> **AGAIN:**
> **If you don't have a plan,**
> **you will never get there.**

Now is a good time to let your mind roam, exploring every avenue that you'd like your business to go down. Try writing a personal essay on your business goals. It could take the form of a letter to yourself, written from five years in the future, describing all you have accomplished and how it came about.

Getting a firm handle on your goals and objectives is a big help in deciding how you'll plan your business.

1.04
Goals and Objectives Checklist

If you're having trouble deciding what your goals and objectives are, here are some questions to ask yourself:

- How determined am I to see this succeed?
- Am I willing to invest my own money and work long hours for no pay, sacrificing personal time and lifestyle, maybe for years?
- What's going to happen to me if this venture doesn't work out?
- If it does succeed, how many employees will this company eventually have?
- What will be its annual revenues in one year? Five years?
- What will be its market share in that time frame?
- What are my plans for geographic expansion? Local? National? Global?
- Am I going to be a hands-on manager, or will I delegate a large proportion of tasks to others?
- How comfortable am I taking direction from others? Could I work with partners or investors who demand input into the company's management?

1.05
Financing Goals

It doesn't necessarily take a lot of money to make a lot of money, but it does take some. That's especially true if, as part of examining your goals and objectives, you envision very rapid growth.

Energetic, optimistic artist-entrepreneurs often tend to believe that sales growth will take care of everything, that they'll be able to fund their own growth by generating profits.

> **Don't be Delusional**
>
> **Be Realistic**

This cash flow conundrum is the reason so many fast-growing companies have to seek bank financing or equity sales to finance their growth. They are literally growing faster than they can afford.

Start by asking yourself what kinds of financing you're likely to need--and what you'd be willing to accept. It's easy when you're short of cash, or expect to be short of cash, to take the attitude that almost any source of funding is just fine. But each kind of financing has different characteristics that you should take into consideration when planning your plan.

Financial Characteristics
1. First, there's the amount of control you'll have to surrender. An equal partner may, quite naturally, demand approximately equal control. Venture capitalists often demand significant input into management decisions. Record labels are like banks and want to see a return on their investment. Angel investors may be very involved or not involved at all, depending on their personal style.
2. Also consider the amount of money you're likely to need. This is true for the start-up as well as for each project that the Artist gets involved with such as recording, merchandising or touring.
3. The third consideration is cost. This can be measured in terms of interest rates and shares of ownership as well as in time, paperwork and the hassle of getting it done.

1.06
How Will You Use Your Plan?

Believe it or not, part of planning your plan is planning what you'll do with it. No, we haven't gone crazy--at least not yet. A business plan can be used for several things, from monitoring your company's progress toward goals to enticing key collaborators to join you in your quest for stardom and fame. Deciding how you intend to use your business plan is an important part of preparing to write it.

Do you intend to use your plan to help raise money? In that case, you'll have to focus very carefully on the executive summary, the management, and marketing and financial aspects. You'll need to have a clearly focused vision of how you plan to make a profit.

Do you intend to use your plan to attract talented collaborators such as musicians, agents or producers? Then you'll want to emphasize such things as possible stock options and other aspects of compensation as well as location, work environment, corporate culture and opportunities for growth and advancement.

Do you anticipate showing your plan to record labels or distributors to demonstrate that you're a worthy Artist? A solid business plan may convince a booking agent of some reason to favor you over your rivals.

> **A solid business plan may convince a booking agent, concert promoter or record label of a reason to begin collaborating.**

1.07
Assessing Your Co.'s Potential

For most of us, unfortunately, our desires about where we would like to go aren't as important as our businesses' ability to take us there. Put another way, if you choose the wrong business, you're going nowhere.

Luckily, one of the most valuable uses of a business plan is to help an Artist decide whether the venture they have their heart set on is really likely to fulfill their dreams.

Test your idea against at least two variables. First, financial, to make sure this business makes economic sense.

Second, lifestyle, because there are certainly long hours and long days.

Answer the following questions to help you outline your company's potential. There are no wrong answers. The objective is simply to help you decide how well your proposed venture is likely to match up with your goals and objectives.

Financial:
- What initial investment will the business require?
- How much control are you willing to relinquish to investors, partners or collaborators?
- When will the business turn a profit?
- When can investors, including you, expect a return on their money?
- What are the projected profits of the business over time?
- Will you be able to devote yourself full time to the business, financially? If not now, when?
- What kind of salary or profit distribution can you expect to take home?
- What are the chances the business will fail?
- What will happen if it does?

Lifestyle:
- Where are you going to live?
- What kind of work are you going to be doing?
- How many hours will you be working?
- Will you be able to take vacations?
- What happens if you get sick?
- Will you earn enough to maintain your lifestyle?
- Does your family understand and agree with the sacrifices you envision?

Now that you understand why you need a business plan and you've spent some time doing your homework gathering the information you need to create one, it's time to roll up your sleeves and get everything down on paper. The following pages will describe in detail the essential sections of a business plan: what you should include, what you shouldn't include, how to work the numbers and additional resources you can turn to for help.

```
┌─────────────────────────────┐
│    Business Plan Uses       │
│         Internal            │
│         External            │
└─────────────────────────────┘
```

1.08
Updates

A business plan is a fluid document and should be updated every month, every week and every day; whenever things change, you should update the plan. Things always change.

While this might seem like more work, it's actually the opposite; the constantly-updated business plan is what helps an Artist organize and makes order out of chaos. It becomes a long-term planning process that sets up your strategy, objectives and the steps you need to take by constantly being aware of the results of these steps.

The Annual Update
Update your plan thoroughly at least once a year. You can start with an old plan and revise, but make sure you're taking a fresh look--distance yourself from the trees and look at the forest.

Accounting and financial analysis normally works in months since the books close after every month. Make sure you have a monthly review of the difference between planned results and actual results for your sales, profits, balance and cash.

You must also review the activities, deadlines and planned results that don't fall into the financials. A good plan is full of milestones, assumptions and tasks, all of which should be measurable. Make sure you review and update these measured results every month.

1.09
Managing the Major Revisions

The business planning process involves an important paradox. Strategy works only when consistently applied over a long period, which means that you can't implement strategy without following a long-term plan. However, blindly following a long-term plan can also kill a company that stubbornly insists on following a plan that isn't working.

Resolution of the paradox is called management. It involves judgment. The owners, operators and managers of the business have the responsibility of distinguishing between consistently applying long-term strategy and blindly following a failing plan. There are no easy rules for this, but the first place to look for clues is in false assumptions. Has the real world proven wrong the assumptions on which your strategy is based? This kind of subjective judgment is what makes business management so important. The planning process, with its regular review, is critical.

A Good Business Plan is Never Done

1.10
Ingredients

Although the cover letter and executive summary are written last, they are the first part of a business plan. For the rest of this chapter, review what goes into a business plan but don't write any of the executive summary until all others sections if the plan are completed.

In addition to the primary use of a business plan to keep the Artist focused, many times the business plan is used by the Artist to attract collaborators and entertainment industry funding. When that is the case, the Artist will need an introduction letter.

Cover Letter

1. Introduction – Cover Letter

As with any other forms of business communication, the writer must enclose a cover letter describing the request as well as the Artist's background. The cover letter reveals the main purpose behind the Artist's concept and why you believe it will be successful. Keep in mind that business plans are used for projects as well as for companies.

Plan to keep the cover letter to one or two pages. The actual plan contains complete details but the cover letter summarizes with the most important points of the plan. The cover letter should provide enough information to entice the reader to open the business plan itself.

Identify the Artist in the first lines of the business plan cover letter. Provide the Artist's name and company name, title, and a little background on the business. Demonstrate to the reader that that the Artist is well connected or established. If you have met the other party before and they specifically requested more information from you about the Artist's business, refresh their memory in the opening paragraph.

Describe the reasons why you decided to embark on this new business idea. For instance, you saw a need in the entertainment business for a new style or new niche of music.

Identify the benefits or advantages you have over others when it comes to this business concept. For instance, if you have many years of experience as an Artist, a customer list of fans and entertainment industry professionals, or you own copyrights to help the business thrive, this is important information to hold the interest of an investor, partner or collaborator.

Discuss briefly how you plan to manage and compete. Tell the reader why this Artist is superior to that of the competition.

Mention a few key statistics, demographics data, focus group responses, or results of marketing research you've done on the idea. This shows that you've done the Artist's homework while writing the plan and you're not simply relying on assumptions or dreamed up projections.

Close the Artist's Business Plan letter with an upbeat and optimistic short paragraph that reiterates the Artist's confidence in the idea. Ask the reader to contact you after reviewing the information for questions or to set up an in-person meeting to discuss the Artist and their project / business.

The introduction of an Artist's Business Plan can be one of the most crucial parts of making the presentation. The goal is to have the reader want to read the next part: The Executive Summary.

Executive Summary

2. Executive Summary
The Executive Summary should, at the very least, introduce the Artist and their business, describe the project briefly, overview the goals, provide a synopsis of the marketing plan and briefly describe the sales possibilities and finances.

Although at the beginning of the Artist's actual business plan, the Executive Summary is always written last!

An Executive Summary is written last but read first.

It is normally 10% in size of the Artist's Business Plan or one page.

In section two of the Artist Business Plan, include:
- 2.01 – Executive Summary
- 2.02 - About Artist & Mission
- 2.03 - Artist's Company Summary
- 2.04 - Management Summary
- 2.05 - Product & Serv. Summary

- 2.06 - Marketing Summary
- 2.07 - Customer Summary
- 2.08 - Promotion Summary
- 2.09 - Advertising Summary
- 2.10 - Competition Summary
- 2.11 - Sales Summary
- 2.12 - Intellectual Prop. Summary
- 2.13 - Technology Summary
- 2.14 - Finance Summary
- 2.15 - Resources Summary
- 2.16 – Appendix Summary

- 3.05 – Operations Plan
- 3.06 - Company Location
- 3.07 - Company Layout
- 3.08 - Company Objectives
- 3.09 - Artist Summary
- 3.10 - Income Sources
- 3.11 - Keys to Success
- 3.12 - Milestones
- 3.13 - Contingency Planning
- 3.99 - Short-Term Plan

Company Summary

3. **Company Summary**

In this section of the Executive Summary of the Artist Business Plan, summarize the company of the Artist. Include the company description, structure, operations, location and layout. In addition, consider the company objectives, the Artist summary, income sources, keys to success, miles stones, a contingency plan and a short term plan.

Indicate in this area the Artist's goals for the next 6 months, 1 year, 3 years and 5 years.

Include goals and objectives that the Artist wants to achieve; when they want to achieve them and how they will measure their success.

In section three of the Artist Business Plan is the Company Summary and includes:
- 3.01 - Company Overview
- 3.02 - Company Description
- 3.03 - Company Structure
- 3.04 - Organizational Structure

Management & Personnel Summary

4. **Management & Personnel**

The Management and Personnel Summary section of the Executive Summary of Artist Business Plan explains who is involved with the Artist and the Artist's company.

This includes a brief bio of the Artist and, if not present within the bio itself, a history of the Artist or band.

Other Key Players (Optional)

If the Artist is working with other key players who are necessary and/or important to the Artist's success, this section introduces them and indicates their role. For example, this section may introduce the Artist's band members, manager, agent, producer, publisher, accountant, booker, etc.

This section is especially important if you are working with someone who isn't well known and you are trying to establish their credibility. Or, this gives you a chance to celebrate someone who is well known and working on the Artist's project.

If you want to include longer bios of these people, place that information in the Appendix and referencing to it.

The section of the Management and Personnel section of the Artist Business Plan includes:
- 4.01 - Personnel Overview
- 4.02 - Management Team
- 4.03 - Musicians
- 4.04 - Singers
- 4.05 - Songwriters
- 4.06 - Producers
- 4.07 - Agents
- 4.08 - Publicists
- 4.09 - Publishers
- 4.10 - Administrative
- 4.99 - Sourcing

Product & Services Summary

5. **Product & Services Summary**
   What is the Artist selling? The Artist may be able to sell their talents as a service to event promoters or may be able to sell their merchandise to their fans. Either way, or both, the Artist's company should identify these products and/or services.
   In this section of the Executive Summary, the Artist-Entrepreneur should identify current products and/or services they are offering to customers. In addition, they should state the plan for future projects, which may or may not turn into products.
   Summarize the recordings, the merchandise, the live shows, and the song catalog for licensing.

In addition, identify the manufacturers who are working with the Artist.

The Products and Services section of the Artist Business Plan includes:
- 5.01 - Products & Services
- 5.02 - Product Development
- 5.03 - Product Strategy
- 5.04 - Product Mix
- 5.05 - Live Performances
- 5.06 - Producing
- 5.07 - Recorded Audio
- 5.08 - Mixing & Editing Audio
- 5.09 – Mastering Audio
- 5.10 - Recorded Video
- 5.11 – Manufacturing Process
- 5.12 - Packaging Process
- 5.13 - Pressing Vinyl
- 5.14 – Non-Audio Merchandise
- 5.99 - Future Products & Services

Marketing Plan Summary

6. **Marketing Plan Summary**
   Another plan within the pan is the Marketing Plan. The Marketing Summary is in section six of the Executive Summary. It consists of multiple segments.

   This also gives a chance to list key past successes and milestones that the Artist has already surpassed.

   Get the reader excited about the project, the Artist and what the Artist has already done.

   This gives you a chance to show the Artist's track record – you could show past sales (if they have been strong), successful tours, key gigs, awards and honors, etc.

The Marketing Plan of the Artist Business Plan includes:
- 6.01 - Marketing Plan Overview
- 6.02 - Marketing Plan
- 6.03 - Marketing Goals & Obj.
- 6.04 - Market Analysis
- 6.05 - Market Potential
- 6.06 - Market Segmentation
- 6.07 - SWOT Analysis
- 6.08 - Marketing Mix
- 6.09 - Branding Strategy
- 6.10 - Creditability
- 6.11 - Product Testing
- 6.12 - Targeted Market Strategy
- 6.13 - Pricing Policy
- 6.14 - Packaging Strategy
- 6.15 - Online Marketing Plan
- 6.16 - Social Media Plan
- 6.17 - Monitoring and Evaluation

Customer Summary

7. Customer Summary

As discussed in the customer section of the Artist Business Plan, there are two main types of customers for every Artist: fan customers and music industry customers. The summary about the Artist's customers is in this section of the Executive Summary.

In this section is a summary of each of those customers; their demographics as well as their lifestyles.

State why a fan-customer buys a ticket to your performances or a download of your recordings. State why talent buyers are eager to book the Artist for an upcoming gig.

The Customer Summary section of the Artist Business Plan includes:
- 7.01 - Customer Overview
- 7.02 - Customers - Fans
- 7.03 - Customers - Industry
- 7.04 - Customer Niches
- 7.05 - Customer Profiles
- 7.06 - Customer Demographics
- 7.07 - Customer Service Plan

Promotion Plan Summary

8. Promotion Plan Summary

Another important section of the Artist Business Plan is their focus on promotion. Promotion is the ongoing effort made by an Artist and their team, to keep the Artist's brand in the face of fans, customers and music industry professionals. In addition to news releases, there are plenty of strategies that an Artist can utilize to accomplish their promotion goals. These are defined in the Promotion Plan.

The Promotion Plan section the Artist Business Plan includes:
- 8.01 - Promotion Plan Overview
- 8.02 - Promotion Analysis
- 8.03 - Promotion Objectives
- 8.04 - Promotion Potential
- 8.05 - Promotion Strategy
- 8.06 - Communication Strategy
- 8.07 - Co-Op Promotions
- 8.08 - Radio Promotions
- 8.09 - Video Promotions
- 8.10 - Performance Promotions

Advertising Plan Summary

9. Advertising Plan Summary
The summary of the Advertising Plan identifies the potential as well as the means for the Artist working with newspapers, magazines, TV and other media in order to better reach customers and fans. The Advertising Summary is in section 9 of the Executive Summary.

The Advertising Summary of the Artist Business Plan includes:
- 9.01 - Advertising Plan
- 9.02 - Advertising Strategy
- 9.03 - Advertising Analysis
- 9.04 - Advertising Objectives
- 9.05 - Advertising Potential
- 9.06 - Advertising Budget
- 9.07 - Advertising Mix
- 9.08 - Co-Op Advertising
- 9.09 - Creative Talent
- 9.10 - Offline Advertising
- 9.11 - Online Advertising

Competition Summary

10. Competition Summary
The Competition Summary helps the Artist understand their competitors including the analysis, research and those in their niche.

This section of the Executive Summary explains why the Artist is better than their competition.

The Competition Summary section of the Artist Business Plan includes:
- 10.01 - Competition Overview
- 10.02 - Industry Analysis
- 10.03 - Industry Participants
- 10.04 - Competitive Research
- 10.05 - Competitive Comparisons
- 10.06 - Main Competitors
- 10.07 - Competitive Strategy

Sales Plan Summary

11. Sales Plan Summary
How is the Artist's CDs and merchandise getting to the end consumer? How is the Artist planning on getting their bookings? How is the Artist going to have their songs used in recordings?

Identify any sales activities that you have planned for the bookings, licensing, and music recordings. Summarize the strategies to accomplish the sales objectives and place them in this section of the Executive Summary.

The Sales Plan of the Artist Business Plan includes:
- 11.01 - Sales Plan Overview
- 11.02 - Sales Management
- 11.03 - Sales Objectives
- 11.04 - Sales Strategy
- 11.05 - Pricing Strategy
- 11.06 - Profit Sources
- 11.07 - Sales Forecast
- 11.08 - Growth Strategy
- 11.09 - Sales Programs
- 11.10 - Sales Affiliates
- 11.11 - Merchandise Strategy

- 11.12 - Online Sales Strategy
- 11.13 - Recordings Sales Strategy
- 11.14 - Performances Sales
- 11.15 - Publishing Sales Strategy
- 11.16 - Distribution
- 11.17 - Content Licensing
- 11.18 - Ticket Sales Strategy

Intellectual Property Summary

12. Intellectual Property Summary

In this section of the Executive Summary identify the intellectual property of the Artist. Include copyrights, patents and trademarks.

State the collaborators involved with the ownership of this intellectual property. If songs have been licensed to a music publisher, put that here as well.

The Intellectual Property Plan of the Artist Business Plan includes:
- 12.01 - Intellectual Property
- 12.02 - Copyrights
- 12.03 - Patents
- 12.04 - Trademarks
- 12.05 - Discography
- 12.06 - Performing Rights Orgs
- 12.07 - Registration
- 12.08 - Content Development
- 12.09 - Content Clearances
- 12.10 - Digital Rights Management

Technology Summary

13. Technology Summary

A technology strategy explains how technology should be utilized as part of an Artist's overall business strategy as well as the strategies utilized for each of the Artist's projects. If an Artist is planning a tour, they would consider the types of technologies they would need on the road.

In this section of the Executive Summary, identify and summarize the various types of technology needed for the Artist's company such as office technology as well as the technology used, and needed, for promotion, recording, performances and sales.

The Technology Summary of the Artist Business Plan includes:
- 13.01 - Technology Overview
- 13.02 - Office Technology
- 13.03 - Promotion Technology
- 13.04 - Recording Technology
- 13.05 - Equipment Technology
- 13.06 - Software Technology

Finance Plan Summary

14. Financial Plan Summary

The summary of the Artist's finances identifies the ways and means of how the Artist will fund the various projects. Include that information in this section of the Executive Summary.

This includes financial analysis as well as forecasts and strategies.

Sections of the Finance Plan include:
- 14.01 - Financial Plan Overview
- 14.02 - Start-up Summary

- 14.03 - Use of Funds
- 14.04 - Important Assumptions
- 14.05 - Key Financial Indicators
- 14.06 - Break Even Analysis
- 14.07 - Projected Profit and Loss
- 14.08 - Projected Balance Sheet
- 14.09 - Goodwill
- 14.10 - Accounting
- 14.11 - Accountant Report
- 14.12 - Forecasted Finances
- 14.13 - Forecasted Balance Sheet
- 14.14 - Forecasted Cash Flows
- 14.15 - Forecasted Operating Exp
- 14.16 - Forecast Assumptions
- 14.17 - Forecasted Revenue
- 14.18 - Risk Reduction
- 14.19 - Risk Management
- 14.20 - Exit Strategy
- 14.21 - Spending Strategy
- 14.22 - Return On Investment
- 14.23 - Budgets
- 14.24 - Financial Ratios
- 14.25 - Accounts Receivable
- 14.26 - Accounts Payable

Resources Summary

15. **Resources Summary**
    This section of the Executive Summary shows the summary of resources available to the Artist, and more importantly, which ones the Artist plans to use. Resources may be related to the music industry, legal participants, as well as web stats and trade publications.

The Resources section of the Artist Business Plan include:
- 15.01 - Resources Overview
- 15.02 - Related Statistics
- 15.03 - Industry Involvement
- 15.04 - Legal Resources
- 15.05 - Web Related Sources
- 15.06 - Research, Stats & Demog.
- 15.07 - Trade Publications
- 15.08 - Databases

Appendix Summary

16. **Appendix Summary**
    All the Artist's appendices come at the end of the document,

    They should be used to provide supplemental information, however the business plan should be able to stand alone. They take care of the nice to know but not the necessity to know. They should be neat, professional and well-organized.

    A detailed timeline should also be included in the appendix. Make sure you reference to it in the Business Plan. The best format for this is a calendar or a chart where you can plot all the Artist's dates and what you need to have achieved by then.

    In the Appendix section of the Artist Business Plan includes:
    - 16.01 - Appendix Overview
    - 16.02 - Forward Looking Statement
    - 16.03 - Personal Income Statement
    - 16.04 - Team Members Resumes

Notes

Chapter 2
Business Plan for Artists
Executive Summary – Sample

2.01
Executive Summary Introduction

An Executive Summary is a synopsis of the entire business for the Artist. It must be concise and compelling. The nice thing about Executive Summaries for Artists, it that is not only keeps the Artist focused on their business and career, it also provides a document for any potential collaborators such as managers, agents, investors and record labels executives.

The Executive Summary is the introduction of the Artist and the Artist's business. It is not a promo kit but, in a essence, functions to entice potential collaborators to pay attention. The first page of the proposal is the most important section of the entire document. It's the introduction. Here is where the reader will glimpse a snapshot of what is to follow. Specifically, it summarizes all of the Artist's key information and is a sales document designed to convince the reader that this project should be considered for support.

After the introduction and cover letter to any potential collaborator, an Executive Summary for an Artist is much like any other summary. The main goal is to provide a condensed version of the content of a longer report.

The executive summary is usually no longer than 10% of the original document. It can be anywhere from 1-10 pages long, depending on the report's length. Executive summaries are written literally for others who most likely DO NOT have the time to read the original. If the Executive Summary convinces the reader that the business or project is viable, they then will read the rest of the document. Sometimes, they request the Artist to only send the Executive Summary. If they are interested, they then will request the rest of the business plan.

For any business, Artist or non-Artist, the executive summary is often the initial face to a potential collaborator or investor, so it is critically important that the right first impression is created right away.

2.02
About One-Great-Artist (OGA) Artist & Mission Statement Example

Our business model is fully aligned and synchronized with the interests of the Artist and the fan. One-Great-Artist is active in a number of areas, including; performing, recording, publishing, touring, licensing and merchandising. The Artists' brands will drive the business, and the win-win-win economics between Artist, Artist's company, and fan will make the risk more tolerable and the return on investment more predictable.

2.03
Artist's Company Summary Example

One-Great-Artist (OGA) is a multimedia entertainer who creates and supplies profitable, positive, audio and visual entertainment to a diverse, international consumer group. OGA is committed to wholesome entertainment across the board and firmly believes that quality and palatable entertainment can be realized without compromising commercial appeal. OGA distinguishes itself through the commitment it undertakes with each of its creative projects. Contrasting the typical scenario in which an entertainment group spends more money producing the music than they do in its marketing and promotion, OGA will utilize a stable of experienced and resourceful producers to ensure the highest quality product within established production budgets. This in conjunction guarantees the impetus necessary to create "winning" products in the marketplace.

OGA is composed of three internal divisions: music & songwriting, live presentations, and recording audio & video. The company will compete and earn revenue immediately through the creation of several lucrative profit centers, beginning with publishing, live performances and then extending into recorded music and video.

Each of the recordings that OGA produces and owns will create valuable short-term streams of revenue. Owning and controlling the rights to each of its albums will enable OGA to grow its music catalog into a valuable asset, one of several-hundred revenue producing titles.

The talented group of individuals who have united to form this innovative company, combined with industry affiliations and highly esteemed Board of Directors, will catapult OGA into the future as one of the industry's leading entertainment companies.

2.04
Management Summary Example

Currently, OGA is self-managed and has plans to hire a manager once the finance warrants this investment. The primary member of the Artist's team is John Latimer and he is performing all the management duties.

One-Great-Artist is slow to hire new people, and very loyal to those who are hired. Immediate personnel plans call for increases from 4 people this year to 10 one year from now. The increase is needed as the overall fan base expands. Most of the new personnel will go into concert production, promotion and sales. The company will also work with part time people and volunteers to handle mail, phone back up, street teams, etc.

2.05
Products & Services Summary Example

There are a variety of products associated with One-Great-Artist. The first is the live show. The second is the recorded music. The third is the publishing. The fourth is the merchandising.

2.06
Marketing Summary
Example

The overall marketing plan is again, two-fold. One-Great-Artist is marketing to key industry personnel such as promoters, agents, and festival directors which will enhance the marketing to fans who respond to the industry's pitch. The marketing toward fans is targeted through upcoming performances as well as through the use of the Internet.

2.07
Customer Summary
Example

One-Great-Artist has three types of customers. The first type of customer purchases music and merchandise. This customer is the general public who purchases music downloads, tickets to the Artist's performances, compact discs, t-shirts, etc. The second type of customer purchases services of the Artist via performances and bookings or musicianship on recordings.. The third type of customer for OGA licenses songs, trademarks and recordings via endorsements and recordings.

2.08
Promotion Summary
Example

Exposing One-Great-Artist to our customers is two fold. The best way is to get fans to get to know the Artist is in a live performance setting. The second is through music channels such as the internet, radio, and video outlets. The promotion for each live performance is defined on local, regional and national levels. While the promotion through music channels includes an ongoing presence on social media sites and targeted e-blasts.

2.09
Advertising Summary
Example

The advertising strategy for One-Great-Artist to our customers is two-fold since we have two types of customers. We plan to continue adverting our shows and recordings to our fans via print and online media. We set aside 10% of every live performance to further promote upcoming engagements. Our advertising plan to attract talent buyers for festivals and night clubs is via email, direct mail and telephone calls.

2.10
Competition Summary
Example

The musical niche that OGA has chosen to pursue of its Artist is one with few competitors. Granted, there are thousands of wanna-be bands competing for fans, OGA is unique because of our live show and unique songs. Competition is ongoing and can be fierce. OGA plans to reduce this competition by being better prepared and producing only quality shows, recordings and merchandise.

2.11
Sales Summary
Example

The sales of One-Great-Artist's products / services will be generated by our team of agents, distributors, merchandisers and publishers to grow and build a sustainable entertainment career.

In the past year, OGA has performed in 12 cities surrounding their home base. The plan is to increase this number by 6 new markets by year's end.

In addition, OGA currently has 15

recordings available online with plans to release one new recording per month.

2.12 Intellectual Property Summary Example

John Latimer is OGA's primary songwriter and he owns and e controls the copyrights, via his publishing company, to all but three of his musical compositions. In addition, OGA has other co-writers within the band who own their own copyrights.

In addition, OGA and One-Great-Artist are registered trademarks with the US Trademark office.

The Artist holds no patents at this time.

2.13 Technology Summary Example

The technology that OGA utilizes while running the business include a laptop computer with various software programs, a color-printer and scanner as well as a cell phone.

In addition, OGA also has recording equipment capable of making demo recordings and videos.

OGA also has sufficient stage gear to perform a quality live concert.

2.14 Finance Summary Example

OGA anticipates 2 phases of capital funding. Initially we will raise $100,000 in seed capital. The second phase requires $1 Million of which $750,000 will be needed immediately and the rest as the company grows. We anticipate revenues of $350,000 at the end of the first year with gross profits of $175,000. Conservatively, our net income should increase to $425,000 by the end of the second year. See Financial Reports at the end of the One-Great-Artist Business Plan for details.

One-Great-Artist. P.O. Box 0000, Any Town, USA 44101 info@One-Great-Artist.com (800) 555-1212

2.15 Resources Summary Example

The music business is ALL about networking. Reaching out to fans, as well as music industry professionals, is a key to the success of One-Great-Artist. OGA has built relationships with agents, publicists and key ex-record label executives as a part of One-Great-Artist's team building.

2.16 Appendix Summary Example

The appendix to the Financial Plan summarizes the results of the economic forecasts including the historical and projected economic condition of OGA's target market. It provides tables that summarize, at a minimum, population, employment, personal income and inflation forecasts 20 years into the future. The financial plan is supported by a current regional economic forecast report.

In addition, the resume of the owners of the company are posted in the appendix,

Chapter 3
Business Plan for Artists
The Company

After contemplating the plan of the plan, it's time to begin working on the nuts and bolts of the Artist's Business Plan. The details of the summary are addressed in each section of the plan.

As mentioned above, the executive summary is completed last. How can you summarize something if the details have not been identified first?

Company Style, Type & Detail

In the Company Summary, Artists need to identify more specifics and details about their company. Those details include information about the company, description, structure, organization, operations, location, layout and objectives as well as an Artist summary, income sources, keys to success, milestones, contingency plans and short-term plans.

Successful Artists have Successful Companies

There are many sub-topics, as shown below. The Company Overview section of an Artist's Business Plan is the first part.

- 3.01 Company Overview
- 3.02 Company Description
- 3.03 Company Structure
- 3.04 Organizational Structure
- 3.05 Company Operations Plan
- 3.06 Company Location
- 3.07 Company Layout
- 3.08 Company Objectives
- 3.09 Artist Summary
- 3.10 Income Sources
- 3.11 Keys to Success
- 3.12 Milestones
- 3.13 Contingency Planning
- 3.99 Short-Term Plan

****

Company Overview

3.01 Company Overview

The Company Overview section of an Artist's Business Plan is a brief description of the Artist. Included in this

paragraph is the name of the Artist, the number of members involved with the Artist (if a band), other significant participants such as co-writers, the style of music that the Artist performs and the current status of the Artist such as: preparing songs, rehearsing sets, preparing for recording, etc.
  A. Name of the Artist
  B. Names and number of members
  C. Other significant collaborators
  D. Style of music
  E. Current status

****

3.01   Task

Write a paragraph or two about: The Artist's Company Overview.

****

Company Description

3.02
Company Description

When writing the Artist Business Plan, the company description section describes how the Artist's business ownership is structured. People reading the business plan will be looking to see how the company is structured and who owns what.

In the Company Description of an Artist's Business Plan, the Artist should state one of three different company types that they are or that they plan to be: sole proprietorship, partnership or corporation. This section describes the legal structure of the business. It may be a single sentence if the business is a sole proprietorship. If the business is a partnership or a corporation, it may be longer as it needs to identify the various partners. Be sure that it is explained who holds what percentage of ownership in the company.

****

3.02 Task

Describe the company. Perhaps the company is only the Artist as a soloist. The company may be the Artist as a band. The Artist's company may be the Artist and the Artist's investor. This depends on the Artist and what is best for the Artist's career. Many beginning Artists are either a sole proprietorship or a partnership. As Artists start to understand the business, they usually form an LLC: Limited Liability Corporation.

If the Artist performs live, then put that in the company description. If the Artist does not perform live but plans to, put that in the company description.

If the Artist is a songwriter, mention that in the company description. If the Artist is also a recording Artist, put that in the description.

If the Artist is not performing, not recording and not ready for product development, state the intentions of the Artist. Remember, this is a plan, so what's the plan? Write it down.

****

Company Structure

3.03
Company Structure

The structure of the Artist's company depends upon the choice of the Artist. This is what the Artist has selected as a business type. If it's a sole proprietorship, the structure is simple as it's just the Artist and no other. However, the Artist may have selected that their business be a partnership or a corporation. It is one of the three.

In addition to the business type of the company, there then comes the issue of who's in charge. Once again, as a sole proprietorship, it's obvious who the boss is. However, if the company's structure is that of a partnership or corporation, then someone must be running the ship.

If the Artist's company is set up as a partnership, perhaps the direction is determined by a majority vote. This should be defined in this section of the Artist's Business Plan.

If the Artist's company is a corporation, then there will be a president of the company. Perhaps the Artist has multiple members, and they all own a piece of the company. They should elect someone to run the corporation. Another option would be for the Artist to hire a person to run the company. Either way, someone has to be in charge. Who is it? Write it down.

What are the roles of the other owners and participants? Provide a short but concise description.

****

3.03 Task

Write a paragraph about the Artist's company structure. This depends on the Artist's business type. If it's a sole proprietorship, the structure is simple as it's just the Artist and no other. However, if the business is a partnership or corporation, then write about the structure of leadership. Who's in charge? What are the roles of the other participants? Provide a short but concise description.

****

Organizational Structure

3.04
Organizational Structure

The organizational structure of a business plan shows a simple and effective way that the Artist's company is organized. The easiest way to show the structure of an organization is to create a chart of the organization with a description of each of the levels of functions within the company.

An organizational structure spells out the business's tasks as well as coordination and supervision. An Artist's organization can be structured in many different ways, depending on its goals and objectives. For example, if the Artist is a band, perhaps one member organizes and runs the rehearsals while another coordinates the publicity for upcoming gigs. Another example might be a touring band utilizing a good logistics person and one who advances shows.

Organizational structure affects the Artist's organizational action in two big ways. First, it provides the foundation for standard operating procedures and routines. Second, it determines which individuals participate in which decision-making processes.

> **Organizational Structure**
>
> 1. **Provides foundation for operations**
>
> 2. **Determines decision makers**

If an Artist's company is owned by the members, then this section of the business plan may show who is responsible for the graphics of a certain promotion or who is responsible for scheduling recording sessions or who decides on the set list for live performances.

Organizational Structure Types
1. Entrepreneurial structures (pre-bureaucratic) - Entrepreneurial structures lack standardization of tasks because this type of structure is most common in smaller organizations and is best used to solve simple tasks. This type of organizational structure is totally centralized. This type of structure is usually when an Artist is a soloist or owns the whole business and hires side-musicians to assist. The strategic leader makes all key decisions and most communication is done by one on one conversations. It is particularly useful for a new entrepreneurial business as it enables the founder to control growth and development.

2. Bureaucratic structures - This type of organizational structure of an Artist's business is suited for more complex or larger scale organizations and may involve have many individuals from the president of the company down to the lowest paid worker. In this type of structure there are clear defined roles and responsibilities, a hierarchical structure of authority and respect for merit. When an Artists deals with a large record label, this is there structure.

3. Post-Bureaucratic Structure - Post-bureaucratic organization attempts to describe an organization that is fundamentally non-bureaucratic and in which decisions are based on dialogue and consensus rather than authority and command. In this case, decision making by consensus is often used by Artists when deciding which new songs to record or which dates to tour.

4. Functional Structure - A functional

organizational structure consists of activities such as coordination, supervision and task allocation for the Artist. The organizational structure determines how the organization performs or operates. The term organizational structure refers to how the people in an organization are grouped and to whom they report. One traditional way of organizing people is by function. Other than knowing which of the Artist's musicians are playing what instrument, some other common functions within an Artist's organization include promotion, production, marketing, and accounting.

****

3.04 Task

Write a paragraph or two about: Organizational Structure of the Artist's Business.

****

Operations Plan

3.05 Operations Plan

Many Artists and their small businesses are running at the speed of sound, struggling with all the "hats' they wear while trying to become successful. Not only are Artists trying to write or perform their next hit, they often are recording, touring, or planning their next project or promotion, not including grappling with prospecting, building a fan base, tweaking product mixes, updating their website, managing employees and paying their bills. With social media, there are even more tasks to handle on a daily basis. But wait: What about the big picture?

Artists and their companies benefit greatly from developing an actionable Operations Plan. This plan is updated frequently and details the company's goals, strategies and processes. Another way to think about an operations plan: It's the how-to book for fulfilling the Artist's goals and objectives.

Remember, everything in the entertainment business is a project. Therefore, the smart move is to refine your project management skills.

Many Artists have great content and charisma and may have great ideas, but as they go out into the market and gain traction, and sales start accelerating, operations don't keep up. When that happens, the Artist's company will have cash flow problems, customer satisfaction issues, and then the quality of the Artist's brand will suffer.

An operations plan may cover the Artist's strategy and processes for a variety of issues including band members, technology, finance, sales and marketing. At a minimum, an Artist's company should document all support processes, such as rehearsals, payroll, human resources, and accounting.

Artists should begin with a detailed

assessment of the company's processes; from development to marketing to fans and customer relationships. This exercise helps highlight any break-downs in the chain, and produces an action plan. Perhaps, the Artist should meet with their team regularly to review sales, and at the same time, create a forward-looking 12-month rolling plan to help guide the Artist through the desired process.

---

3 Step Operations Plan

1. **Current State**
2. **Future State**
3. **Initiatives**

Many Artists approach operations planning using a three-step process that analyzes the company's current state, future state and the initiatives. For each initiative, such as launching a new recording, the company will examine the related financials, talent and operation's needs, as well as target customers. When this approach is used, the Artist or the Artist's manager can estimate the cost of the project and then calculate the return on investment and predict revenues. The question of "Is this project worth the time and money?" readily gets answered.

Instead of documenting day-to-day processes, such as bookkeeping and payroll, Artists should work toward a higher-level document. It is recommended that Artists have two plans: one for day-to-day operations and another for the longer view. Then they should integrate the two plans together. By not linking the two, Artists run the risk that expenses may run too high. There will be too much firefighting, and growth of the business won't be sustainable over the long run.

Keys Business Operations

Location
Equipment
Labor
Process

Operations may seem like the ugly stepchild compared to the glamour of product or service development and marketing, yet operations are the lifeblood to any business, especially those in the arts. Operations are just as critical as sales. Sometimes the market moves too fast to do business as usual and Artists need to continually probe and be prepared to shift with the times. For example, what happens if an Artist's new recording goes viral and everybody on the planet wants a copy? Is the Artist's company prepared to handle the demand?

Business Operations Typically include Four Key Areas:

1. **Location: Where does the Artist do business — physically and online?**
2. **Equipment: What tools does the Artist need to get the job done?**
3. **Labor: Who is going to do the work?**
4. **Process: What is the way that business will get done?**

The operations plan of an Artist's Business Plan describes the processes and resources that the Artist will use to produce the highest quality products or services as efficiently as possible.

The importance of each of these areas depends on the nature of the Artist's company. For example, physical location is important for the members to commute for rehearsal. The equipment used by the Artist may be their instruments but it's also their amps, vans, and computers used for mixing and/or promotion. The labor is the members of the Artist's group as well as the many collaborators involved with the Artist. The process is how they all work together.

In the operations plan, Artists should include a description of how they plan for each of the four key operational areas. As Artists become more established, operational changes are necessary to achieve the new goals and objectives detailed in the Artist's Business Plan. This is where the Artist will plan to implement and fund a new project (recordings) or expand services (performances) to their established markets.

****

3.05 Task

Write a paragraph or two about: Company Operations for the artist's company.

****

Company Location

3.06
Company Location

Choosing a business location for an Artist is perhaps the most important decision their small business or startup will make, so it requires precise planning and research. The reason it's so important is that it involves looking at fan demographics, assessing the proper venues to perform, developing music industry connections, scoping the competition, staying on budget, understanding state laws and taxes, and much more.

Here are some tips to help an Artist choose the right location for their business.

Most businesses choose a location that provides exposure to customers: fan customers as well as music industry professionals. Additionally, there are other factors and needs to consider.

1. Brand Image – Is the location consistent with the image that the Artist wants to maintain? For example, an Artist who fit the "avant garde" niche may be better located in New York City than Kansas City as their style may attract more fans in New York City than in Kansas City.
2. Competition – Is the Artist business in the area where they are complementary or competing? Competition is fierce in bigger cities. Perhaps an Artist would be better locating their business in an area where they can develop their

art a little more fluently and then expand into a bigger market.
3. Local Labor Market – Does the area have potential experienced employees and collaborators? Every Artist needs a team of the best people they can find. Perhaps a small town may not have the necessary individuals to help the Artist grow and succeed.
4. Future Growth – If an Artist anticipates further growth, they may look for an office and rehearsal space that has extra space in case it's needed. In addition, perhaps the Artist has a plan to move to a new location once they have honed their skills. It's better to plan ahead than to have no plan at all.
5. Proximity to Collaborators – This includes music stores, studios, performance venues as well as print media and radio stations. Once again, the bigger the market that an Artist is located in, the larger the possibility for quality collaborators. In addition, larger cities have larger media outlets.
6. Safety – Consider the crime rate. Will the Artist's equipment and instruments, as well as their employees, be safe in the building or walking to their vehicles?
7. Zoning Regulations – Some zoning laws prohibit certain types of business in certain properties or locations. Noise can be a problem as well. Artists can find out how a property is zoned by contacting the local planning agency.

Location Factors

1. **Brand Image**
2. **Competition**
3. **Local Labor Market**
4. **Future Growth**
5. **Proximity to Collaborators**
6. **Safety**
7. **Zoning Regulations**

Besides determining what the Artist can afford for setting the location of their business, they should be aware of other financial considerations:

- Hidden Costs – Very few spaces are business ready. There may be costs like renovation, sound-proofing, decorating, IT system upgrades, and so on.
- Taxes – What are the income and sales tax rates for the state, county or city? What about property taxes? Could taxes be reduced by locating the business across a nearby state line?
- Minimum Wage – While the federal minimum wage is set by the federal government, many states have a higher minimum.
- Government Economic Incentives – The business location can determine whether the business may qualify for government economic business programs, such as state-specific small business loans and other financial incentives
- Is the area business friendly?

Understanding laws and regulations imposed on businesses in a particular location is essential. As Artists look to grow their business, it can be advantageous to work with a small business specialist or counselor. Check what programs and/or support that the state government and local community may offer to small businesses. Many states offer online tools to help small business owners start up and succeed. Local community resources such as SBA Offices, Small Business Development Centers, Women's Business Centers, and other government-funded programs specifically support small businesses.

****

3.06 Task

Write a paragraph or two about: Company Location.

****

Company Layout

3.07
Company Layout

A part of any business plan is a description of the office layout. For Artists, they need to consider where they are going to be doing administrative business as well as rehearsal business; each of which has specific concerns. Office layouts are arranged so that staff can work together in departmental and team groupings, providing the best opportunity for efficient work flow, communication and supervision. Much of this depends on the amount of work an Artist undertakes as opposed to hiring third-party collaborators to help them with their business.

If the Artist designs their own flyers and posters, perhaps they will need a place in their office for graphic work. If the Artist prepares their own direct mail promotion pieces, perhaps they need an area for word processing and photocopying. If the Artist is more than a solo-Artist, perhaps a large rehearsal room with sound baffling and electrical outlets is necessary.

Items that are addressed when considering a company layout include: workspace per staff member; fire safety arrangements; lighting levels; signage; ventilation; temperature control, parking and welfare facilities.

Office layout designs should provide an environment suitable for the business needs of the organization. Modern office layouts are frequently planned using CAD (Computer-aided design) drawing software. This way an Artist can plan ahead when looking at their company layout.

Desks in an office may be needed for computers or space for a lap-top. Open plan offices are often divided up into smaller offices by using partitions. When this happens the designer has to take into account several factors including:
    Heating/cooling zoning
    Ventilation
    Lighting and light switches

Emergency lighting
Small power
Voice and data cabling
Fire alarms
Fire escape routes
Noise/acoustics

In addition, offices need to have access to basic welfare facilities such as toilets and drinking water. Consideration may also be given to vending, catering or a place where the Artist can relax and take a break from their desk or rehearsal.

****
3.07 Task

Write a paragraph or two about: Company Layout.

****

Company Objectives

3.08
Company Objectives

The first part of setting up an Artist's company should now be completed and now it's time to explore the company objectives. To get to this point in an Artist's Business Plan, the company was described, the structure was established, the operations were defined, the location was set, and the office layout was planned.

Now it's time to set the Objectives.

An Artist with well-chosen goals and objectives point their new business in the right direction and keep their company on the right track. Just think about what a performance would be without instruments or what the Billboard charts would be without a bullet. Goals and objectives keep an Artist focused.

When establishing goals and objectives, Artists should try to involve everyone who will have the responsibility of achieving those goals and objectives after they are identified.

Goals vs. Objectives

- Goals tell an Artist where they want to go; objectives tell them exactly how to get there.

- Goals can increase an Artist's effectiveness; objectives back their goals and make the Artist more efficient.

- Goals are typically described in words; objectives often come with numbers and specific dates.

Goals
Goals establish the what, where and why: What an Artist is doing, where they're going, and why will it be completed. Goals help Artists improve their overall effectiveness as a company — whether to start gigging, or to get more gigs, or to

write better songs, or to record an album. The more carefully an Artist defines their goals, the more likely they are to do the right things and achieve what they wanted to accomplish in the first place.

Objectives
Objectives are the how as well as the when. Objectives provide the specific steps Artists and their company need to take in order to reach each of their goals. They specify what must be done — and when. The "when" is crucial. Set a deadline.

Together, goals and objectives form the road map for an Artists company's future. Without them, Artists risk making wrong turns and wasting precious energy.

Steps to establish goals and objectives
The first approach to specifying goals and objectives begins with a review of the Artist's mission statement. Using key phrases from the mission statement to define their major goals leads into a series of specific business objectives.

The connections between goals and the Artist's mission are easy to visualize if a flowchart is used. Key phrases in the Artist's Mission Statement lead to major goals, which lead to specific business objectives.

If the Artist's mission statement doesn't suggest a list of goals, they may want to re-evaluate it to see whether it really captures what their business is about.

Example:
Suppose that a goal of an Artist is to double the number of people downloading their newest recording. The objectives may be as follows:

- Gain awareness by placing print ads in four regional markets and by airing radio ads in two major markets (by June 10)

- Attract first-time customers by offering an online giveaway of a free t-shirt (by July 1)

- Cultivate prospective fans by implementing a permission-based weekly e-mail to 2,500 targeted contacts (by July 10)

- Convert 10 percent of fans to customers, using e-mail reminders (beginning July 25)

Artists should always make sure their goals are measurable. By establishing metrics goals, Artists can gauge their progress and recognize immediately when their efforts are going off track.

Secondly, most goals define positive outcomes that Artists want their business to achieve, but sometimes an Artist will also want to set goals to avoid pitfalls and to eliminate a few weaknesses.

To help develop goals that cover all the bases for an Artist, consider the following key questions:

1. Achieve: What does the Artist want to attain in the future? More gigs, more recordings? More downloads from fans?
2. Conserve: What does the Artist want to hang on to? Current fans? Image?
3. Eliminate: What does the Artist want to get rid of? Late rehearsals? Being unprepared? Sloppy bookkeeping?
4. Avoid: What does the Artist want to avoid? Losers? Haters?

---

5 Goal Categories
1. Day to day goals
2. Problem solving goals
3. Development goals
4. Innovation and creative goals
5. Profitability goals

One more way to think about business goals is for an Artist to consider each of the five categories into which most goals fall:

1. Day-to-day work goals are directed at increasing an Artists company's everyday effectiveness. They may involve things like promotion planning, tour routing, order tracking, office management, or customer follow-up. As a start, Artists should name at least one change that they can make in their day-to-day operations that will make a difference in their overall effectiveness. Write it down as a business goal.

2. Problem-solving goals address specific challenges that confront an Artist's business, such as low bookings, funding, team building or quality of show issues. List the two biggest problems that face the Artist's company, and then write goals that can solve them.

3. Development goals encourage the education of new skills and expertise, whether learning new songs, business set-up, or helping an Artist's employees. Consider formulating at least one development goal for the Artist or their company?

4. Innovation goals help an Artist find new ways to improve the following: original songs, cover versions of other's songs, licensing, web site, promotion timing or products or services that an Artist's company offers, how they market their company, and how they distribute and deliver what their company sells. Artists have multiple income sources and therefore strategies may need to be planned for each project. Identify any innovative approaches that could make the Artist's business more effective in the future? If so, formulate an appropriate goal.

5. Profitability goals set an Artist's sights on where they want their bottom line to be. When all is said and done, profit is the No. 1 goal for profit-making companies. How can an Artist eat if there is no profit? The art will not survive if the Artist does not eat. Remember, this is the music BUSINESS.

These goal-setting approaches lead to a respectable list of goals and maybe more goals than is practical for one business plan. Artists should select the five goals that they think are absolutely, positively essential to their business success.

After an Artist decides on their list of goals, they need to fine-tune each one:
- Keep each goal clear and simple.
- Be specific.
- Be realistic.
- Push and think big.
- Keep goals in sync with the mission.

As discussed further in Section 6.07 of an Artist's Business Plan, a SWOT analysis the Strengths and Weaknesses as well as Opportunities and Threats. This information allows Artists to develop strategies that are relevant and realistic to their organization. It also helps keep their goals in check. Plenty of Artists are delusional. Don't be one of them.

Short-terms goals should be achievable in less than one year, while long-term goals take over a year to accomplish. Artists should evaluate long-term goals annually and adjusted for changes in societal trends, fan acquisition, competitive landscape, technical innovations and the music industry in general.

Artists should ask themselves where they want to be in three months, one year, and five years. The vision that an Artist may have for their organization should be reflected in their company's objectives. Organizational objectives can be a mixture of both short term and long term goals. A great tip is to start with 5 year goals. Where does the Artist see their company in five years? What do they want to have achieved by then? What strategies do they want to pursue in order to achieve those goals? These strategies are an Artists one year objectives. What does an Artist have to do right now to support their business strategies for their quarterly or monthly goals?

For example, suppose an Artist's five year goal is to have one million listeners hear their recordings. To get to that goal, Artists may want to expand their promotion internationally. Their 1 year goal can be "Establish an online presence in two new social networks." Then break it down further to set a quarterly goal such as "Conduct a needs analysis for the US and European market."

Artists should use the SMART model to set their organizational objectives. Smart Artists make objectives through key results: Specific, Measurable, Attainable, Relevant and Timely.

SMART Objectives

Specific
Measurable
Attainable
Relevant
Timely

For example, an Artist may have a start-up company in Cleveland and their long term goal is to be recognized as the best live performer in the industry. Instead of setting an organizational objective as "Being recognized as the best live performer," the Artist may want to apply the SMART model to their objectives and ask these following questions:

Specific – What type of performance does the Artist want to be the best at? On what scale do they want to compete? Does the Artist want to be the best live performer in their area or in the world?

Measurable – How will the Artist know when they have achieved their objective? What benchmarks is the Artist going to use to measure their success?

Attainable – Is this objective achievable given an Artist's resources? What are the obstacles that they are going to encounter and can they get past the hurdles?

Relevant – How relevant is this objective to the goals of the Artist, their company and employees? Will it benefit the organization?

Timely – When does the Artist want to achieve this objective? Be specific.

****

3.08 Task

Write a paragraph or two about: Company Objectives.

****

Artist Summary

3.09

Artist Summary

As a part of the Artist Business Plan, there is a summary of what the Artist is about. This section is also reflected in various sections of Artist Development Plan including sections such as content creation, attitude and image. This summary should also be a part of the biography of the Artist found in the Artist Promo Kit.

****

3.09 Task

For this part of the Artist Business Plan, write a summary of the Artist and the Artist's company.

****

Income Sources

3.10
Income Sources

Most Artists have the luxury of multiple income streams. The smart ones are those that capitalize on all, or most of them that have the greatest possibility of success. If a singer-songwriter complains that they cannot make enough income from performing, perhaps they should adjust to their product mix. For Artists, their art is the product. Their performance is their service. The products and services of any Artist can be numerous. In addition to performing, Artists have the potential to make income from licensing songs, recording royalties, publishing, as well as merchandise sales. And, for more established Artists, branding, sponsorships and endorsements are certainly other sources of potential income.

In a recent survey completed by the Future of Music Coalition, it was established that most Artists earn income quantitatively from three sources or more. Here are some of their results:

Multiple "Roles"
More than half of the Artists surveyed earned their income from activity in three roles or more. Some of these Artists are composers and performers and teachers. Others are performers and recording Artists, but also making a bit of money off their brand.

The Future of Music Coalition surveyed the music-related income of 2,794 respondents. More than half of survey respondents said their income was derived from three or more sources. Only 18% said they made 100% of their income last year from only *one* role.

Artists differ in earning money from music relying on several revenue sources. Many Artists wear multiple "hats" including musician, performer, songwriter, recording artist, composer, session player, teacher and/or producer.

Different Types of Artists in the Music Industry

- Performing Artists
- Recording Artists
- Composers and Songwriters
- Salaried Players
- Session Musicians
- Teachers
- Producers

Basic demographics
A "full-time" musician is often defined as someone who derives more than 75% of their income from music, and spends more than 36 hours per week on music. Musicians earn their living in any of eight different and combined ways:

1. Live performance fees earned as a solo performer or as a member of a band or ensemble.
2. Salary as an employee of an ensemble, band or symphony.
3. Session musician earnings, including payment for work in recording studios or for live performances or freelance work.
4. Teaching individual students as well as in classroom settings.
5. Money earned from songwriting and composing including publisher advances, mechanical royalties, performing rights royalties, commissions, composing jingles and soundtracks, synch licensing, ringtone licensing and sheet music sales.
6. Money earned from sound recordings including sales of physical or digital recordings, record company royalties,

payments from interactive streaming services, Internet radio, SoundExchange royalties and master use licensing for synchs or ringtones.
7. Merchandise sales such as t-shirts, hats, mugs, etc.
8. Other

With self-distribution and worldwide access to marketing, the Artist can now be: the songwriter, the performer, the publisher and the record label. While wearing all of these "four hats" at once, Artists are now uniquely positioned to profit from the best possible contractual distribution terms and highest revenue generation via the sale, use, or streaming of their music and recordings. The challenge is that many Artists don't know what these rights are, or how to collect the money they've earned from these revenue streams. A comprehensive, streamlined, and completely inclusive infrastructure does not yet exist that enables every Artist who is owed money to easily collect it. However, there are solutions available such as Performing Rights Organizations and SoundExchange.

Eight Income Sources for Musical Artists

1. Live performances 28%
2. Salaried Player 19%
3. Session Musician 10%
4. Teaching 22%
5. Songwriting 6%
6. Sound Recordings 6%
7. Merchandise 2%
8. Other 7%

Income from Music Performances

For musicians, there are a few areas of potential income dealing with playing of an instrument or voice. The most common is that of a musician who performs live in front of an audience. There are two types of musicians who perform live: one being a solo Artist or a part of an Artist's band, and the other is a salaried player within an orchestra or ensemble. Many musicians do both.

Another income area for a musician is studio work. This again has two types of income for a musician. They may be hired as a session player and paid as a "work for hire" only receiving income for their time and talent, or they may be recording in hopes of receiving ongoing income of royalties from the owner of the recording such as a record company for download sales or hard-copy sales.

Four Income Sources for Performing Musicians

1. Live (solo or in a band)
2. Salaried Player
3. Recording as Session Player
4. Recording as Artist

Income from Teaching

In addition to performing as a musician, teaching is another important income source for Artists with an average share of 22% of total income. Many Artists provide music lessons to students. Some of these Artists teach private lessons and some teach at a school. Some do both.

Income from Songwriting

As another potential income source for Artists, songwriting can also be the trickiest. For starters, the songs have got to be really good, if not great. Anyone can write a song. That doesn't mean they are going to get paid for it. Creating content as a songwriter can be a huge income source. Even average songwriters have a chance at some income in this area.

First of all, copyright law mostly benefits the high earners. When looking at the brackets of Artists, the top bracket, earning an average $330,000 a year, earns by far the most from compositions, which make up 28 percent of their music-related revenue. The lowest income bracket makes most revenue from live performances; more than 40%.

Keep in mind, that Artists who focus their activity on composing rely on composition revenue and are much more vulnerable to possible harm from copyright infringement. The same goes for recording Artists who rely on sales of sound recordings. Free downloads may hurt both songwriters and recording artists.

Here are a few samples of income for a songwriter:

1. Unless the songwriter agrees not to be paid, every single time a song is streamed legally for free on the Internet; money is owed to the songwriter.
2. Every single time a song is played on the radio in the United States (either via the Internet or broadcast from an AM/FM transmitter tower) the songwriter is owed money.
3. If you are a U.S.-based songwriter and distribute the Artist's music into another country thru a company such as iTunes Japan, each time the Artist's music sells in Japan, iTunes pays the Japanese Performing Rights Organization (PRO) money for the "reproduction" of the Artist's song. This money is in addition to the money iTunes pays for the sale of the song. (JASRAC is the Japanese Society for Rights of Authors, Composers and Publishers.)
4. Every time a song is recorded and then duplicated or replicated on a recording via compact disc or Internet download, the songwriter should receive income.

Three Types of Licenses for Streaming

1. **Words and Music**
2. **Recordings of Words and Music**
3. **Storage of Recordings of Music**

Income from Publishing

Many times a songwriter is their own publisher. Other times a songwriter collaborates with a professional music publisher to do the work for them. Either way, publishing can be a major income source for Artists who are songwriters.

A songwriter owns their songs via copyright or until they license those songs to a music publisher. A song's copyright owners holds several important rights, including the right to copy the song, distribute copies of the song, prepare derivative works from the song and perform the song publicly. A song generates revenue for its owner when the owner issues permits (or "licenses"), to others to use these rights, for a fee or royalty. These licenses are offered via Performing Rights Organizations.

In the beginning, the composer of a song is the song's copyright holder. In order to get the song to generate revenue, it may be necessary to self-publish or affiliate with a quality music publisher. A music publisher acquires songs, (and the copyrights), from songwriters and then exploits the songs commercially. There are many shapes and sizes of music publishers. Songwriters will want to affiliate with a publisher that will be able to find uses for their song, issue licenses to the users, collect the revenue, and then share the money with the songwriter.

A song earns money for its copyright owner in many different ways. However there are seven main sources: mechanical royalties, public performance royalties, synchronization royalties, and print royalties as well as grand royalties, foreign royalties and digital royalties. The way publishers get the money, and how much of it they get, depends on its source.

The Entire Music Industry Is Built On Six Legal Copyrights

1. Reproduction
2. Derivatives & Samples
3. Public Display
4. Public Performance
5. Distribution
6. Digital Transmission

---

1. Mechanical Royalties

Mechanical royalties are the main source of income for publishers. Mechanical royalties are monies paid by a record company to a song's copyright owner for the right to use the song in "devices serving to reproduce the composition mechanically," i.e., vinyl, compact discs, MP3 S, etc.

The current statutory rate for mechanical royalties is 9.1 cents per song per record for recordings of up to 5 minutes in length. For recordings over 5 minutes in length, the rate increases depending on the songs total length.

2. Public Performance Royalties

Public performance income is another large source of income to a song's copyright owner. Almost every time any version of a song is performed publicly, whether live or on record, in concert or over radio or television, the copyright owner is entitled to public performance royalties. There are a few narrow exceptions, (for example, educational use in a classroom setting). Songwriters and publishers affiliate with a Performing Rights Organization (PRO) to keep track of air play and other public performances of their songs, and to collect and distribute the resulting license revenue. ASCAP, BMI, and SESAC are the major performing rights organizations in the United States.

3. Synchronization Royalties

A synchronization license is a permit issued by the publisher to use a song in connection with video or film such as a movie, television show or commercial. The producer must obtain a "synch license" from the copyright holder, usually for a one-time fee. This license is negotiated between the copyright owner and the music supervisor of the video or film project. The first broadcast of a "live" show which includes the song does not require a synch license, but re-runs would. The live broadcast would require the public performance license described above.

4. Print Royalties

Print revenues come from sales of sheet music. The relative importance of print revenue has decreased over the years as consumers have come to prefer recordings to sheet music. However, it is still a source of serious money and many industry watchers predict an increase in its importance with the growing popularity of detailed transcriptions (or "tabs") of heavy metal guitar licks, synthesizer programming, and the renewed popularity of acoustic music.

5. Grand Royalties

These royalties are generated when a songwriter's composition is used in connection with a theatrical play or performance. This dramatic performance right (or "grand right") is another "intellectual property right." Built into each and every performance license is specific language which governs how the copyrighted work must be presented and prohibiting changes to the music.

6. Foreign Royalties

If the Artist is from the United States, foreign publishing involves two basic types of publishing: sub-publishing and co-publishing, into one or more territories outside the U.S. borders. Sub-publishing, itself, is one of two forms: sub-publishers who merely license out the original work or those which make and sell the products which are the subject of the license, such as print books and records (with local artists performing the work).

7. Digital Royalties

Digital Performance Right in Sound Recordings Act (DPRA), which became effective in 1996. This Act grants owners of sound recordings the exclusive license to perform the copyrighted work publicly by means of digital audio transmissions but it exempted non-subscription services (and some other services). To recap, under the law three types of licenses are required for streaming of musical recordings:

(a) a performance license applicable for underlying words(lyrics) and music (score)
(b) a performance license applicable to the streaming the sound recording
(c) a storage license for the passage of a sound recording through a file server.

Other Publishing Income

In addition to the sources of income already covered, there are many other royalty-generating areas, many of which can - depending on the composition - generate substantial writer and publisher royalties for Artists. These include:

- Lyric reprints in books
- CD-ROM / Multimedia
- Audiovisual configurations
- Karaoke
- Musical greeting cards
- Singing toys
- Music boxes
- Video games
- Ringtones
- Sampling
- Jukeboxes
- Podcasting

> The income source for Artists focuses specifically on the money that sound recordings can earn when they are sold, licensed or performed. This includes:
>
> 1. Income from physical retail sales (brick and mortar, mail-order)
>
> 2. Income from digital sales (iTunes, Amazon MP3, Bandcamp)
>
> 3. Income from sales of recorded music at shows via the merch table
>
> 4. Interactive streaming services (Spotify, Rhapsody, and Slacker)
>
> 5. Digital performance royalties (Pandora, Sirius XM, via SoundExchange)
>
> 6. Master use license for synchronization with video, ringtones, etc.

Income from Sound Recordings

For the major music record labels, the sales of recorded music represent the majority of their revenue, but a different picture emerges when looking at the income of individual musicians. A new survey among 5,000 U.S. musicians of different genres shows that on average only six percent of all revenue comes from recorded music.

However, more and more Artists are releasing their own recordings on their own record label. In doing so, a few things need to be identified regarding sound recordings.

It's important to remember that a recorded piece of music embodies two copyrights: there's the copyright for the composition (the words and music), and a separate copyright for the sound recording (what gets captured in the studio). There are separate revenue streams earned by these two copyrights; the composition earns mechanical royalties for the songwriter / publisher when it is licensed for reproduction. The composition also earns public performance royalties when it's performed publicly or played on the radio. The recording of the song earns income for the owner of the recording when it is sold via digital downloads or compact discs but also if the recording is licensed for use in a movie or video game. Many times musicians who perform on the recording receive recording royalties from the owner of the recording.

The important thing to know is, who owns the recording? Is it the record label, the Artist, the producer or perhaps a member of the band?

Artists who are songwriters and musicians may reap income from both C-Circle copyrights and P-Circle copyrights.

Whether on vinyl, compact disc or via digital download, income from the sale, license or performance of sound recordings has been a core part of many musicians' income streams for decades. But there's no doubt that income from sound recordings — perhaps more than any other — has experienced significant challenges and undergone serious changes over the past 10 to 15 years.

There's good news and bad news. While the existing music marketplace was fundamentally disrupted by peer to peer files-sharing, we have also seen the decline of brick and mortar stores, and the development of legitimate download stores like iTunes and Amazon, and licensed subscription services like Rhapsody and Spotify. We've also seen the rapid growth in a new revenue stream for sound recordings — the digital performance royalties that are generated when sound recordings are streamed on any non-interactive webcast service like Pandora or played on satellite radio.

Income from Merchandise

There are two areas of income when it comes to merchandise: Sales and Licenses. When an Artist typically thinks about income from merch sales, they are referring to items for sale at their gigs. This is usually done in the lobby of a venue or a side table at a nightclub. Items typically found on an Artist's merch table may include compact discs, t-shirts, stickers, coffee mugs, posters and knick-knacks with the Artists name, photo or logo on them.

The other type of income from merchandise is primarily reserved for the established Artist. These Artists sign a licensing contract with a third-party merchandising company who pay the Artist a fee for the right to manufacture items in the likeness and name of the Artist. This is another good reason for Artists to own and control the trademark of their name and logo.

Income from the Internet

In addition to receiving income from downloads, streaming or online sales of merchandise, another possible income source for Artists is through collaborating with affiliate marketing companies. Some Artists utilize programs like Linkshare, Commission Junction or Amazon by providing links to a variety of possible products from the Artist's website. For example, an Artist may use a particular instrument for their art. The Artist can post on their website that they use that particular instrument. They also post a hyperlink to that instrument's website so that a fan may be able to purchase the instrument right through the Artist's website. If and when this happens, the Artist makes a commission from the affiliate for making the sales referral.

Income from Other Sources

Essentially, this is income tied to an Artist's' creative self, but ancillary to what they earn based on their sound recordings, compositions or performances.

- **YouTube partnership program**: revenue-sharing program that allows creators and producers of original content to earn money from the Artist's videos on YouTube
- **Ad revenue:** or other miscellaneous income from the Artist's website properties (Google AdSense, commissions on Amazon sales, etc.)
- **Fan funding**: Money directly from fans to support an upcoming recording project or tour (Kickstarter, Pledge Music)
- **Fan club:** Money directly from fans who are subscribing to an Artist's fan club

- **Persona licensing:** payments from a brand that is licensing an Artist's name or likeness (video games, comic books, etc.)
- **Product endorsements:** payments from a brand for an Artist endorsing or using their product
- **Acting:** in television, movies, commercials
- **Sponsorship:** corporate support for a tour, or for band/ensemble
- **Grants:** from foundations, state or federal agencies

****

3.10 Task

Write a paragraph or two about the Income Sources for the Artist.

****

Keys to Success

3.11 Keys to Success

The business world for Artists is full of twists and turns. Artist-entrepreneurs are constantly making decisions that affect their business in the short and long terms. While there are always individual procedures they should follow that are specific to their business and industry, there are a few keys for Artist to make their business a success. These keys to success apply to any of an Artist's projects or ventures. When Artist's know the basics of owning and running a successful business, they then have the foundation they need to move their business forward.

There are several keys to success when starting as an Artist and then running the Artist's company. A few major examples can set the stage for Artists to find success in their new business. These major keys will provide a framework to their success.

Keys to Success

1. Focus
2. Have a Plan
3. Customers
4. Record Keeping
5. Follow Interests
6. Networking
7. Look to Save
8. Profitability
9. Customer Service
10. Protection

Focus
Artists cannot be everything to everyone, so Artists need to focus on the key features that they provide. There is a concept called the "unattainable triangle" or the "good, fast, cheap rule." This says that individuals or companies can provide two of the three benefits, but the third will inevitably slip.

For example, when an Artist's records a new song, they may find a studio that is good and fast but not cheap; where another studio may be cheap and fast but not good. The same holds true for the services that an Artist may provide. Is the Artist going to focus on quality products? If so, it likely would be difficult to produce them quickly. So, if the Artist is selling quality recordings, they might choose to focus on quality and price and not try to be the fastest.

Since many Artists provide both products, such as recordings, as well as services, such as performances, the smart idea is identify separate "keys to success" for each one. Then, for each one, pick two of the "unattainable triangle" to focus on.

Have a Plan
Artists sometimes need to make quick decisions on important issues about their business, and the basis for those decisions should always be related to their overall plan. Smart Artists work out a detailed business plan and then follow that plan as their guide to success. Artists should also work their plans for individual things such as meetings, presentations and music industry conferences. Artists should have a well-thought-out plan to work from and then… stick to the plan. Yes, plan the work and work the plan.

Customers
For Artists, the customer is the key to success for their business. Without customers, Artist's won't have a business. For that reason, Artist should spend a considerable amount of time, effort and expenses focused on creating and keeping fans and customers in some way. Since many Artists have two types of customers, fan-customers as well as music industry customers, one way to measure the customer focus of their business is to survey customer satisfaction. If an Artist adds value to their customer's life by actually delivering what they focused on, customer satisfaction will be high and they will return to buy over and over again. Obtaining new customers may be a major expense for Artists, but by retaining satisfied customers their expenses are lower in the long run.

Record Keeping
Another key to running a successful business is good record keeping. Without it, Artists won't know if they are profitable or not, or whether their customers are satisfied. Without good record keeping, Artists may also be in big trouble with the IRS when tax time comes. The key is to track everything from customer and vendor contracts to payroll and other expenses. If the Artist doesn't have expertise in the area of record keeping, it pays to hire someone to help. It can be either a full-time employee, another member of the band, or an outside bookkeeping service or accountant. By hiring a professional, Artists may also gain access to additional advice that may help their business become a success.

Follow Interests

Artists should only get involved in projects that appeals to them. Artists will work harder and strive for better results when involved in a musical project they have a passion for. For example, if the early-touring Artist doesn't like to sleep in small motels or floors provided by fans they may not want to attempt a performance tour. Perhaps the Artist would be better staying in the recording studio. If the Artist finds something that truly appeals to their personal interests, then they will be able to develop ways to make it successful.

Always Be Networking

This business is all about networking and relationships. When an Artist owns their own business, there is no such thing as time off. Vacations can be scheduled, but Artists should keep a regular schedule that best fits their business life from their personal life. However, Artists should always keep their ears and eyes open for a chance to network with people that can help them. Customers and potential business partners can appear at any time from any place, so always be ready to talk business.

Look to Save

Artist should keep their mind open to new ideas that may help them reduce overhead or production costs. Artists should always be looking for new ways to save money on the way they do business. By doing so, this allows Artists to apply more revenue to their company's bottom line as well as prepare budgets for upcoming projects.

Profitability

The bottom line: when it comes to business, it all boils down to profitability. One key to success for an Artist's business is profit margins. Is the Artist making enough profit on each individual product or service and selling enough quantity to cover both their fixed expenses (like rent, property taxes, insurance and interest) and their variable expenses (like labor, supplies, product, etc.)? Does the Artist's income exceed their expenses by enough to provide a good return on both their time and their money?

For example, it may not be feasible for an Artist to tour the country if they are receiving no buzz in the marketplace. Many beginning Artists make the mistake of thinking "If we build it, they will come" attitude. The fact is, most Artists, in their early stages of touring, lose money because they didn't establish a well thought-out plan of what they're doing. Yes, back to planning.

Focus on Customer Service

A business owner should never be too busy to maintain good relationships with their best customers. Artists should make it part of their daily schedule to stay in touch with their top revenue-producing customers such as talent buyers, night club owners and concert promoters. Artists should find out what they can do to be proactive and retain their business for the foreseeable future.

Protection

Artists add stress to their business if they don't have protection in place for their personal assets. Artists should incorporate their business to make sure they don't lose their house, car or copyrights if someone sues the company. Artists should always have liability insurance in place, and discuss any changes in their business with their accountant and lawyer to make sure they make all the right moves.

****

3.11 Task

In this section of the Artist Business Plan, write down the Keys to Success for the Artist.

****

Milestones

3.12 Milestones

While an Artist's business certainly needs a business plan, that plan is useless without some concrete steps to make it happen. To watch the success, Artists must develop milestones. Milestones are measurable achievements that tell Artists whether their business is progressing in the way they planned for it to. Without milestones, Artists may get sidetracked, loose focus and lack a sense of achievement.

Five Steps to Setting Milestones

1. **Identify crucial business-plan goals**
2. **Set start and end dates for each project**
3. **Assign a budget for each project**
4. **Designate who is responsible for the milestone**
5. **Review the success of the milestone program**

Milestones are the events that occur for an Artist on their way toward achieving the desired end results of their business goals. Business milestones are like checkpoints for entrepreneurs. It signals that an Artist's business venture is thriving and growing. Milestones can be short-term or long-term goals and can be easily achievable or challenging. Developing milestones for an Artist's business requires some time and effort, but it is an invaluable exercise, especially if the business is new or has not yet been launched.

Artists need to set short-term goals as well as long-term goals for their business. Goals may focus on profits, marketing, brand recognition or new recordings or gigs. For example, if the Artist is selling mp3 downloads through an online music distributor, the short-term goals may include redesigning their website and reduce their shipping costs; long-term goals may include selling compact discs. To establish milestones, Artists should begin brainstorming about their desires and write down anything that comes to mind related to their business. Writing it down is the exercise. Once written, the milestone becomes more concrete.

Steps to Set Milestones
1. Dream Goals
2. Write them down
3. Eliminate ones not feasible
4. Set Objectives

The next step for Artists is to revise their list of goals by eliminating or changing those that are not feasible. For instance, if the list has the goal of the Artist gaining 50 new performance venues within a year, they are likely find that this goal, though not necessarily impossible, may be very difficult to achieve. Artists might want to revise that goal to gaining 20 new performance venues within a year. Remove unrealistic goals from the list, as they cannot have any effective milestones. The point of a milestone is for Artists to focus on reaching their goals -- not to discourage them by being unreasonable.

Write down the objectives that must be achieved before the Artist can reach their goal; these are their milestones. For example, if an Artist wants their booking agent to reach the goal of making a monthly profit of $10,000, milestones would be making monthly profits of $2,500, then $5,500, then $8,000.

Goals and milestones should be organized in chronological order: short-term, medium-term and long-term. A well-organized list allows for easy modification and alteration as needed. Milestones and goals should only be altered if the Artist's business significantly changes. For example, assume that an Artist's business experiences an 18-percent loss in profits after the first quarter of the year. That is the time they should add new goals and milestones relating to gaining new customers or lowering operating costs, rather than continuing with the items on their initial list. Striving for old goals and milestones may not be possible until their business recovers a bit.

Artists should refer to their list of milestones at least every six months to ensure that they are on track. As milestones are reached, Artists should cross them off their list, highlight them or signify in some way that they have completed a step toward meeting their goals. Some people post their milestones in a prominent location in their office. This can serve as a daily source of motivation.

For this section of the Artist Business Plan, write down a list of milestones and then set objectives of how to meet them.

****

3.12 Task

Write a paragraph or two about some of the Milestones for the artist's company.

****

Contingency Planning

3.13 Contingency Planning

Contingency planning is anticipating unexpected events or situations that may affect the financial health, professional image, or market share of an Artist and the Artist's company. It is usually the planning for a negative event, but can also be plans for an unexpected windfall such as a huge hit song. Anything that unexpectedly disrupts a company's expected operation can harm the company even if the disruption is because of a windfall. This is why an Artist needs to create contingency plans for many possible situations that their company may encounter. Many times company managers pre-research a plan of action before they take the action. Some threats usually covered in contingency plans for Artists are continuity plans, such as a member of the band quits, crisis management, and asset security.

Continuity Plan

Business continuity plans for Artists cover a range of situations, including the death or quitting of a key member of the band or manager. In this case, the crisis threatens to shut down business operations for an extended period of time. This, in turn, may threaten to destroy or injure the company. Continuity plans may involve insurance policies that provide for the cost of keeping the company in operation, and the cost of hiring of consultants to help the Artist through this tough time.

Crisis Management

There are many types of crises that may affect the well-being of an Artist's company including natural disasters, fire in the rehearsal studio, on the job injuries or even angry customers. Plans to deal with crises generally include looking at the Artist's SWOT Analysis (strengths, weaknesses, opportunities, threats) that attempt to identify vulnerabilities and potential challenges.

Asset Security

Theft or destruction of intellectual property, gear and equipment or any other valuable assets that an Artist's needs for its operations are generally covered by a security plan. This also includes the security of the company's internal computer network and confidential files. A security plan attempts to block any negative contingencies that might occur. Legal strategies are also included in a contingency plan for the purpose of helping to mitigate any damage created.

Mismanagement

Fraud, theft, operational errors, mismanagement and personal scandal are all crises that require special public relations strategies as well as various types of insurance for any Artist. The handling of these crises involves careful attention to legal considerations and if not handled immediately with efficiency and confidence, they can ruin the Artist's professional image and ability to do business. For this reason, companies create a system of checks and balances to prevent such problems.

Reorganization

After the worst has happened, the Artist's contingency plan also covers how the company will re-establish normal operations and reorganize to limit any future problems. Reorganization to meet new challenges is important whether the Artist is dealing with negative events or the unexpected pressure of having to a rapidly expanding operation.

Every business has the possibility of a

situation that adversely impacts how they do business. If the Artist's response to the situation is poor, it might have a dramatic impact on the future of their business. They may lose customers (both fans and music industry professionals), data, and even lose the business.

What Kinds of Contingency Planning Should Be Addressed?

A good contingency plan should include any event that might disrupt operations. Here are some specific areas to include:

- Natural Disasters - such as snowstorms or fires.
- Crises - such as threatening band members, on-the-job injuries, and accidents
- Personnel - such as death or quitting of a member of the band
- Data Loss - such as loss due to computer crashes, bank breaches, or an attack on the Artist's web site
- Mismanagement - such as theft or neglect of critical responsibilities
- Product Issues - such as a huge demand from a current hit song that may require additional bookings or a reallocation of resources

---

Developing a Contingency Plan

1. Analyze Risks
2. Determine the Likelihood
3. Develop a Process
4. Identify Alternatives

---

1. Analyze Risks

To begin, Artists should list all the possible events that could disrupt operations. Artists should consider every possible event that could affect their business. For example, a member of the band who is a smoker may accidently set the rehearsal studio on fire, or a snowstorm may cause a cancellation of a gig.

2. Determine the Likelihood and Impact of Risks

Some of the events will be so unlikely that it may not be reasonable to include them in the plan. Here's how to focus in on the most critical events:

A. List all possible events that could disrupt operations

B. Give each one a ranking from 1 to 10 based on its impact on operations. For example, a snowstorm on the day of a gig might be a 10, while a slow delivery of a website might be a 3.

C. Give each one a ranking based on an estimate of the likelihood of occurrence. It might be useful to make a chart for this, with a 1 = might happen once in 100 years, while a 10 = might happen once a month.

D. Multiply the impact ranking by the likelihood of occurrence ranking to get a total score for each possible event.

E. Use the scores to rank the events. Begin working on the highest scores first in the contingency planning, and work down the list. Artists may have a cutoff, so that they don't spend time planning for scores below a specific value. These may have a lower impact and, hence, a lower chance of occurrence. They might not be worth the time to address. Artists might also look at the low score items address any items that occur that aren't specifically addressed in the plan.

3. Develop a Process for Risks

For each item on the "Risk List,"

develop a process that reduces the risk. This way, all anticipated risks can be overcome quickly and the Artist can get back to creating and producing content.

4. Identify Alternatives
Once the risks have been identified, consider a list of alternatives for each. Sometimes a risk may need one alternative and later the same risk may need a different alternative. It's better to know them in advance.

****
3.13 Task
For this section of the Artist Business Plan, begin identifying and list potential risks and the contingency plan of action should the problem occur.

****

Short-Term Plan

3.99
Short Term Plan

In every business, management establishes short-, medium- and long-term objectives. Long-term objectives are addressed in the Artist Business Plan and define the Artist's vision, mission and objectives. Operations management sets the goals and strategies to be used in achieving an Artist's milestones and objectives. As described in the milestones section of the Artist Business Plan, milestones provide a measurement to ensure that an Artist's strategies are effectively moving toward achieving their objectives. The planning process begins with defining the vision of the Artist's company, setting forth the mission, identifying objectives and then designing a tactical strategy to achieve the mission.

Short-term Operational Planning
Within every long-term strategic plan there is a short-term operational plan. The purpose of operations is to generate or create value for the Artist's company. Operations management is responsible for creating value by achieving the various objectives set forth in the Artist's strategic plan. These are the day-to-day business operations that set short-term goals or milestones for the next 12 months.

Benefits of Short-term Planning
In some instances, Artists are very good at articulating or designing a strategic plan but may fail to execute a short-term operational plan. A short-term operation plan is a toolkit to help achieve the goals of the strategic plan. Having short-term plans without having a long-term strategy usually results in an Artist's lack of direction or focus. By combining these two planning components, an Artist is able to set a general path based on their values, goals and objectives.

Successful Business Management
Both long-term strategic and short-term operational planning are important to the future success of any Artist's organization. Strategic plans must account for the operational factors necessary in the short term to achieve the objectives of the company in the long term. Without a tactical short-term plan,

operations management is unable to identify the milestones that are important to achieving the overall strategy set forth in the Artist Business Plan. Therefore, it is necessary to coordinate operational short-term plans to ensure that they are effective in achieving the basic mission of the Artist's company.

Short-term plans start at the current time and reach anywhere from a month to a year into the future. However, many Artists engage in short term planning that might typically cover time frames of less than one year in order to assist their company in moving gradually toward its longer term goals.

An Artist's small business may not have a marketing department to take care of extensive marketing plans. If the Artist is a solo-performer, the responsibility of marketing the business may lie solely with the Artist. A short-term plan could be to implement different marketing strategies, such as printing flyers and postcards, creating a monthly newsletter or making cold calls to talent buyers. Another example of marketing includes using social media, such as Facebook, Instagram or Twitter, to promote an Artist's products or services. Artist should choose the marketing strategies that complement the type of business they own and the musical niche that they are targeting.

Getting Music Industry Customers
While marketing will not guarantee customers or clients, finding and securing new bookings can be a short-term plan for an Artist. For example, an Artist wants to have over 10 talent buyer customers within the first three months or secure three new gigs within the first month of being active in the business. Since having a regular list of talent buyer customers is one way that Artist and their business stay profitable, they should create as many short-term goals as possible.

Increasing Income
With fans and customers come sales and income. An Artist's short-term plan can be to increase their income as a business owner or increase the prices of their performances. This should not be done during the first month of starting operations. Artist will want to establish their business first. When the business starts generating revenue and seeing an increase in sales over a couple of months, then the Artist may consider increasing the overall income of their bookings.

****

3.99 Task

For this section of the Artist Business Plan, consider and write down the short-term plan for the Artist. Be specific.

****

Notes

_____

_____

Chapter 4
Business Plan for Artists
Management & Personnel

The management and personnel of an Artist's company are essential to the success of any Artist. An experienced manager is certainly going to help the company more than a novice., However, in the early stages of an Artist's career, the Artist may have no choice but to manage their own affairs. Most, if not all, Artists do this.

In this section of the Management Plan, Artists begin to understand all those external professional advisors that the Artist's business will use, such as accountants, agents, bankers, lawyers, IT consultants, publishers, business consultants, and/or business coaches. These professionals provide a "web" of advice and support outside the Artist's internal management team that can be invaluable for any Artist.

Another issue an Artist needs to address in the Management Plan section of their business plan is the business' human resources needs.

The trick to writing about an Artist's human resources needs is to be able to describe the human resources needs that an Artist may need specifically.

To write something such as, "We'll need more people once we get up and running" will impress no one.

How many employees will the Artist's business need and what will it cost for each one? This is what will be of most interest to the people reading the business plan.

---
3 Types of Personnel for an Artist

Artist Membership
Management
Administrative Staff

---

3 Types of Personnel for an Artist
1. **Artist Membership** – This includes all members (musicians and singers) involved with the Artist.
2. **Management** – This may include personal managers, agents, producers and publishers. Many times, these individuals do not own a piece of the Artist's company but serve to manage certain aspects of the Artist's career.
3. **Administrative Staff** – This type of personnel may include individuals who assist the Artist as a personal assistant or secretary.

In the entertainment business, everything is project based. Therefore, most individuals working within the Industry are self-employed. However, many times the Artist's company has employees on staff such as musicians, singers, songwriters, managers, as well as agents, publicist and publishers. Some may also be members of the band. Employment is defined as a relationship between two parties, usually based on a contract, one being the employer and the other being the employee.

If introducing the individual players within a band, give very brief bios and then refer the reader to a more detailed bio of each player in the appendix. If individual bios of band members are left out, reference to it in the Business Plan and just put those in the appendix (basically, leave out the "mini bios" in the actual document.

When introducing the other band members, include the functions that each of these people carry out in additional to the actual Artistic endeavor. For example, if the bass player also books all of the shows, then that should be indicated. This allows the reader to get a better understanding of who is going to carry out all of the other activities that makes the Artist successful.

There is also the option of indicating in the respective areas below who will carry out the actual duties. For example, if the plan indicates that the bass player books all of the shows under the Performance Plan section, then reduce the amount of information in this section.

Employee
An employee contributes labor and/or expertise to an endeavor or project of an employer and is usually hired to perform specific duties which are packaged into a job. An employee is a person who is hired to provide services to a company on a regular basis in exchange for compensation and who does not provide these services as part of an independent business. For Artists, typically employees may be members of the band or administrative staff to assist with logistics and organization.

Finding Employees
The entertainment business is all about relationships. The main ways for Artists (employers) to find workers and for people to find employers are via referrals and networking. Entertainment job listings in newspapers and online job boards may assist an Artist with finding the right person for a job but usually Artists find people to work with through their connections and their relationships.

Ending employment
Usually, either an employee or employer may end the relationship at any time. This is referred to as at-will employment. The contract between the two parties specifies the responsibilities of each when ending the relationship and may include requirements such as notice periods, severance pay, and security measures.

****

Management & Personnel Overview

4.01
Management & Personnel

Overview

There are multiple facets in the Personnel Section of an Artist Business Plan.

4.01   Personnel – Overview
4.02   Personnel – Management Team
4.03   Personnel – Musicians
4.04   Personnel – Singers
4.05   Personnel – Songwriters
4.06   Personnel – Producers
4.07   Personnel – Audio Engineers
4.08   Personnel – Agents
4.09   Personnel – Publicists
4.10   Personnel – Publishers
4.98   Personnel – Administrative
4.99   Personnel – Sourcing

****

4.01 Task

For this section of the Artist Business Plan, write about overview of the management and personnel of the Artist's company.

****

Management Team

4.02 Management Team

In this section of the Artist Business Plan, the team is identified. First of all, is there a leader? Who's in charge? Does everyone agree that the "leader of the band" is the same as other member's idea of who is "leader of the band?"

When writing the business plan, the Management Plan section describes the Artist's management team and staff. People reading the business plan will be looking to see not only who's on the management team but how the skills of the management and staff will contribute to the bottom line of the Artist and the Artist's company.

Management Plan Sections

Internal Management Team
External Management Resources
Human Resources Needs

The Internal Management Team

The Internal Management Team section will describe the main business management categories relevant to the Artist's business, such as identify who's going to have responsibility for what category, and then profiling that person's skills. This manager is also described in the Artist Development Plan.

Typically, the manager provides administration and consulting functions as well as, assisting the Artist find qualified individuals to handle bookings, recording, merchandising, producing, promotion, publishing, etc.

It's not necessary for an Artist to have a different person in charge of each business management category they decide to use for their company. Some key management people may fill more than one role; especially early in an

Artist's career. The important thing here is to identify the key management people in the Artist's business and explain what function each team member will fill.

At the beginning of any Artist's career, they may do self-management but one person should be in charge of the whole project.

The management plan will include complete resumes of each member of the Artist's management team (including the Artist), and an explanation of how these person's skills will contribute to the business' success.

Follow this with an explanation of how the management team will be compensated. What salary and benefits will management team members have? Describe any profit-sharing plans that may apply.

If there are any contracts that relate directly to the Artist's management team members, include them in an appendix of the business plan.

The External Management Team
But what about external management? Besides an Artist's internal management team, those reading the business plan will be extremely interested in knowing how the Artist plans to use external management resources.

Think of external management resources as an Artist's internal management team's backup. They give the business management plan credibility and an additional pool of expertise.

The external management resources may include sales and marketing managers, as well as those that have administration functions as well as production managers. Production managers may assist the Artist with a recording (Producer) or a tour (Tour Manager). Artists may find that their company needs additional management categories such as publishing managers and/or distribution managers.

> **Who's running the ship?**

First, consider how the business' human resources needs can best be met. Will it be best for the Artist's business to have employees such as side musicians or should the Artist operate with contract workers or freelancers? Does the Artist need full-time or part-time staff? If the Artist is a band, can members of the band perform with other bands or do they work exclusively with the Artist? Who's running the merchandise table? Who's deciding the set-list? Who is planning the next recording session? Since this business is project based, many of an Artist's staff will be temporary or work-for-hire.

> **How is the Artist going to find the staff for their administrative needs?**

****
4.02 Task

In this section of the Artist Business Plan, outline the staffing requirements and include a description of the specific skills that the people working for the Artist will have to have.

Also describe how the Artist is going to find the staff for their business needs, and how they're going to train them.

Even if the plan for the Artist's business is to start as a solo act, include this section on human resources needs in the business plan to demonstrate that the Artist has thought about the staffing that their business may require as it grows. Also, by putting it in the plan, the Artist's business has (or will have) human resources policies in place. Business plans are about the future, and how the Artist's business is going to succeed.

****

Musicians

4.03
Personnel - Musicians

In addition to the management of the Artist's business, the business plan of the Artist identifies the musicians and participants in the business.

The concept of whether members of the band are also owners of the company should be addressed in the ownership section of the Artist Business Plan but listed here as personnel as well.

In this section, identify the musicians involved with the Artist's business. A brief biography of each musician should be included. In addition, and perhaps better yet, for this portion of the Artist's Business Plan, write the specialties that these musicians bring to the business that will reflect in the Artist's success.

Keep in mind that each project of the Artist may involve other personnel and these individuals may be considered independent contractors and not necessarily an "employee" of the business or member of the band.

Work-For-Hire or Employee?

For example, when the Artist is planning to tour, they may hire independent contractors to perform with the Artist but not work for the Artist. There is a difference. If the Artist is planning on entering the studio to record their next big hit, perhaps the Artist might hire session musicians or background vocalists to complement the production. These individuals do not work for the Artist but with the Artist.

****

4.03 Task

For this section of the Artist Business Plan, write about the musicians involved with the business. Include names and their roles in the description.

****

Singers

4.04
Personnel - Singers

In addition to the musicians involved with the Artist's business, the Artist should identify the singers who are a part of the Artist's business.

The concept of whether these singers are members of the band and also owners of the company should be addressed in the ownership section of the Artist Business Plan but listed here as personnel as well.

In this section, identify the singers involved with the Artist's business. A brief biography of each singer should be included. In addition, and perhaps better yet for this portion of the Artist's Business Plan, write the specialties that these singers bring to the business that will reflect in the Artist's success.

For example, when the Artist is planning to tour, they may hire independent contractors to perform with the Artist but not work for the Artist. Once again, there is a difference. If the Artist is planning on entering the studio to record their next big hit, perhaps the Artist might hire lead singers or background vocalists to complement the production. These individuals do not work for the Artist but with the Artist.

4.04 Task

For this section of the Artist Business Plan, write about the singers involved with the business. Include names and their roles in the description.

****

Songwriters

4.05
Personnel - Songwriters

In addition to the musicians and singers that the Artist works with, the Artist's Business Plan also identifies the songwriters involved with the Artist's business. Sometimes the musicians and/or singers involved with the Artist's company are also songwriters.

Perhaps, the Artist co-writes with other songwriters. These songwriters may, or may not, work for the Artist's company. They may even have a company of their own.

As with musicians and singers, the concept of whether songwriters associated with the Artist are also owners of the company should be addressed in the ownership section of the Artist Business Plan but listed here as personnel as well.

In this section, identify the songwriters involved with the Artist's business. A brief biography of each songwriter should be included. If the songwriter has additional skills that will reflect in the Artist's success, it should be mentioned here as well.

****

4.05 Task

For this section of the Artist Business Plan, write about the songwriters involved with the business. Include names and their roles in the description.

****

Producers

4.06
Professional Services
Producers

A record producer is an individual working within the music industry, whose job is to oversee and manage the recording (i.e. "production") of an Artist's music. Many times an Artist produces their own recordings. The producer "hat," which may or may not be worn by the Artist, may have many roles which include, but are not limited to, gathering ideas for the project, selecting songs and/or musicians, coaching the musicians in the studio, controlling the recording sessions, and supervising the entire process all the way through mixing and mastering. Producers also often take on a wider entrepreneurial role, with responsibility for the budget, schedules, and negotiations.

Artists who include Producing as one of their services, may add another income source to their bottom line.

There are two kinds of producers in the music industry: executive producers and music producers. They each have different roles. An executive producer oversees a project's finances, whereas a music producer oversees the creation of the recording.

A music producer is the person who creatively guides or directs the process of making a record, like a director would a movie. The engineer would be more the cameraman of the movie. The music producer's job is to create, shape, and mold a piece of music on to a recording. The scope of responsibility may be one or two songs or an Artist's entire album – in which case the producer will typically develop an overall vision for the album and how the various songs may interrelate.

With today's relatively easy access to technology, an alternative to the record producer just mentioned, is the so-called 'bedroom producer'. With today's technological advances, it is very easy for a producer to achieve high quality tracks without the use of a single instrument; that happens in modern music such as hip-hop or dance. Many established Artists take this approach.

In most cases the music producer is also a competent arranger, composer, musician or songwriter who can bring fresh ideas to a project. As well as making any songwriting and arrangement adjustments, the producer often selects and/or gives suggestions to the mixing engineer. That engineer takes the raw recorded tracks and edits and modifies them with hardware and software tools and creates a stereo and/or surround sound "mix" of all the individual voices sounds and instruments. The recording will then be given further adjustment by a mastering engineer. The producer will also coordinate activities with the recording engineer who concentrates on the technical aspects of recording. Whereas the executive producer keeps an eye on the overall project's marketability.

Simply put, a producer is the person or persons who achieve an Artist's musical vision during the recording process. A producer might write songs, arrange songs, engineer, and play instruments on the tracks. Or a producer might simply sit between the speakers saying "again" a hundred times until the desired result occurs.

The Artist Business Plan identifies the producers who participate with the Artist in the recording studio.

Again, the concept of whether the producer of the Artist's recordings is also an owner of the company should be addressed in the ownership section of the Artist Business Plan, but listed here as personnel as well.

****

4.06 Task

In this section, identify the producer(s) involved with the Artist's business. A brief biography of each producer should be included. In addition, and perhaps better yet, for this portion of the Artist's Business Plan, write the specialties that these producers bring to the business that will reflect in the Artist's success.

****

Audio Engineers

4.07
Professional Services – Audio Engineers

An audio engineer is an important part of an Artist's musical works as they are the individuals responsible for the recording, manipulation, mixing, reproduction, and reinforcement of sound, both live and in the studio. Audio engineers work on the technical aspect of sound manipulation: the placing of microphones, the turning of pre-amp faders and knobs, as well as the setting of levels.

In the recording studio, Audio Engineers report to the Producer and is the one responsible for ensuring proper sound levels for the recording project. Many times, when an Artist records, the Audio

Engineer does not work for the Artist but for the record studio.

Audio engineers also set up and operate sound reinforcement systems for concert, corporate, theatre, sporting and other events. Depending on the Artist, some Artists have an Audio Engineer as a part of their staff as these engineers know the Artist's live performance better than an in-house engineer. Other times, Audio engineers work for the venue or the production team hired by the concert promoter.

****

4.07 Task

For this section of the Artist Business Plan, write about the audio engineers involved with the business. Include names and their roles in the description.

****

Agents

4.08
Professional Services – Agents

An agent in the entertainment industry is often described as a talent agent or booking agent. There is also a press agent, but that's a different role all together. Typically an agent's job is to find jobs for actors, authors, broadcast journalists, film directors, musicians, models, producers, professional athletes, singers, writers, and other people in various entertainment or broadcast businesses. In addition to finding gigs (jobs) for an Artist, an agent supports and promotes the Artist in various ways. A good booking agent must be totally familiar with their clients and know what kind of work the client can and cannot do in order help them get various jobs. Agencies, where agents work, may specialize in a particular field such as modeling, literary, sports, music, touring and more.

Largest Booking Agencies

- **Creative Artists Agency**
- **William Morris Endeavor**
- **United Talent Agency**
- **Paradigm Talent Agency**
- **The Gersh Agency**
- **ICM Partners**
- **Agency for the Performing Arts**

An Artist may book their own shows and having an agent is not required. It does, however, help the Artist as this business is all about networking and relationships. All top agents have built relationships with a multitude of individuals and companies and may be able to easily secure performances for their clients. Artists who do their own booking may not have such a network.

An Artist typically pays an agent a percentage of the earnings (typically 10%) for any and all gigs that the Agent secures.

In some states, there are regulations that govern different types of agents. Some of these regulations are established by Artist's unions such as the Musicians Union. There are also professional organizations that license talent agencies such as The Association of Talent Agencies (ATA).

There are numerous talent agencies in the United States. The four largest talent agencies are: William Morris Endeavor (WME), Creative Artists Agency (CAA), International Creative Management (ICM), and United Talent Agency (UTA). Many of the major booking agencies will not represent clients who are not already signed to a major record company nor have national distribution of their recordings. Because of this, Artists who have no recordings or Artists on independent record labels often seek booking representation with an independent talent and booking agency.

The cost factor for an Artist of having a booking agent has to be weighed against what they can do. Some agents represent several different types of Artists, while others represent Artists in one main area or genre such as cover bands, touring acts or independent all-original Artists.

****

4.08 Task

For this section of the Artist Business Plan, write down the plan for hiring or collaborating with booking agents.

****

Publicists

4.09
Professional Services
Publicists

Artists of all calibers are reliant on publicity to attract fans and customers. Sometimes the Artist does all the publicity him/herself. Other times, someone in the band does the publicity. Either way, it's is an important part of an Artist's career.

As another potential part of professional services, a publicist works for the Artist while performing public relations duties. Their main role is to be a liaison between the Artist and the media. The publicist creates public relation campaigns that promotes the Artist and attempts to make the Artist more viable within their chosen market. Every industry has publicists. From the healthcare industry to the entertainment industry, a publicist plays a vital role in growing an Artist's business and strengthening its valuation.

> ## Music Publicists
>
> - Ariel Publicity
> - Buzzplant
> - Evolution Promotion
> - Foley Entertainment
> - Moxie Star

A publicist typically must know how to write press releases, network and deal with the media, as well as have strong communication and people skills. Often, a publicist will oversee the public image of the Artist and manages all of the media relations. They also typically coordinate publicity events. Publicists may also generate their own publicity by pitching story ideas to magazines, radio shows and newspapers about the Artist. If the Artist does something that can be perceived negatively, it is up to the publicist to conduct damage control.

> ### Publicist = Brand Manager

Publicists create a buzz for the Artist and help them further build their brand. This can be with new product releases, new performances or new markets for the Artist. Regional, national, and international publications, television, and bloggers are all crucial outlets that a publicist utilizes in order to get the word out about the Artist. A publicist generates positive media attention for the Artist while also addressing any negative attention.

Publicists are essentially brand managers who help the Artist increase their visibility and value. The main question a publicist regularly addresses is, "what makes the Artist or Artist's project worthy of media attention? This is the foundation of a public relations campaign. The Artist's publicist must constantly communicate with and attract new audiences for the Artist. Cultivating relationships with the media is a crucial skill that publicists master in order to gain integrity and produce results for the Artist.

> ### A Publicist Knows How To:
>
> **Write press releases**
>
> **Network and deal with media**
>
> **Have strong communication and people skills**

Five Key Qualities of a Good Publicist

1. **Invisibility** – Their role is to generate a buzz for the Artist behind the scenes.

2. **Involvement** – The publicist maintains a close relationship with the Artist in order to maintain constant communication and flow of ideas.

3. **Ideas** – Exceeds the industry standard by using unconventional methods of generating press.

4. **Individuality** – Each PR campaign should be specifically tailored to the Artist's projects in order to ensure that the Artist is being promoted to their target audiences.

5. **Integrated** – A publicist is constantly cultivating new relationships with the media while maintaining already established relationships.

****

4.09 Task

In this section of an Artist's Business Plan, identify who will complete the role of publicist for the Artist and their company. In the beginning of an Artist's career, this person may be one of the members of the band, a friend of the Artist or perhaps a seasoned professional.

After identifying the person to fill the role of publicist for the Artist, next write a few items that the publicist will focus on first. Does the Artist have a new product about to be released? Is there a tour being scheduled? Be specific and write it down.

****

Publishers

4.10 Professional Services Publishers

If any owners of the Artist's company are songwriters, chances are they are performing the duties as a publisher. In addition to live performances, one of the main sources of income for Artists in the music industry is that of publishing. Setting up self-publishing is also found in the Artist Development Plan.

Publishing is finding a commercial use of a song. Publishers try to convince others to use the song for such things as performances and recordings. This includes the songwriter asking the band to consider the songwriter's next big hit. Publishing is the pitching of the song. That's a different hat to wear than that of a songwriter. It's also a different hat that that of a performer or musician. As soon as the songwriter takes that song to someone to perform it… maybe it's the

Artist's band, or maybe it's the songwriter themselves, that songwriter is now wearing the publisher's hat. A publisher has to make a sale and find a commercial use for the song that songwriters write and publishers pitch.

The pot of gold at the end of the music business rainbow is the income received from the use of those songs. Content is King. Remember this.

Content is King

Smart Artists recognize the importance of securing a long-term income source and nothing does that better than owning original content that can be licensed for many years beyond the death of the author. Publishing involves intellectual property. Intellectual property includes copyrights. Currently, copyrights last for 70 years beyond the death of the author or songwriter.

In this section of an Artist's Business Plan, the management of this important intellectual property must be addressed. Is the Songwriter planning to establish a separate company which deals with the publishing of the songs? Keep in mind that this is a different business than that of the Artist. This may mean a separate business plan for the Artist's publishing company. If there are more than one songwriter who is an owner of the Artist's business, that songwriter may also desire to establish a separate publishing company. The two (or more) publishing companies may choose to collaborate when the two (or more) songwriters co-write.

The copyrights owned and administered by publishing companies are one of the most important forms of intellectual property in the music industry. (The other is the copyright on a master recording which is typically owned by an Artist or an Artist's record company.) Publishing companies play a central role in managing this vital asset of music and lyrics.

A word of warning: Not every songwriter should attempt to be a music publisher. If the songwriter(s) is planning on running their own publishing company, they must be prepared to spend some time actually do the publishing work. Music publishing requires expertise and extra amounts of patience, legwork, and follow-ups: essentially to start a whole new business. Music publishing can be a great way to make a lot of money... after a while. If the Artist is not willing to do this extra work, they would do much better collaborating with an established, reputable music publisher who will work to promote the songwriters' copyrights.

Whether you are a writer, a record company, a publisher - or all three - you should be aware of music publishing basics, and exactly how music publishing generates income. A dedicated songwriter should focus on the love of one's craft, but there is no denying the income potential from publishing and songwriting is one of the highest in the music industry. This is especially true for songwriters with hit songs

****

4.10 Task

For this section of the Artist Business Plan, describe the publisher within the Artist's company or music publishers with whom the Artist is collaborating.

****

Administrative Personnel

4.98
Personnel – Administrative

Who does what in an Artist's business? What is their background and why is the Artist bringing them into the business as collaborators, band members or employees? What are they responsible for? These may seem like unnecessary questions to answer in a one- or two-person organization, but the people reading an Artist's Business Plan want to know who's in charge. So tell them. Give a detailed description of each division or department and its function.

Arts administration is the field that concerns business operations around an arts organization. Arts administrators are responsible for facilitating the day-to-day operations of the organization and fulfilling its mission. Until an Artist can hire an administrator, they will most likely perform their own administrative duties.

The duties of an arts administrator can include staff management, marketing, budget management, public relations, fulfilling online sales, fundraising, program development and evaluation, as well as band relations. An arts administrator in a small organization may also do marketing, event booking, and handle financial issues, public relations, marketing, and writing reports.

Many arts administrators advise the Artist or other project managers on strategic planning and management decisions. An effective arts administrator must also be knowledgeable in local, state and federal public policy as it relates to human resources, health insurance, labor laws and volunteer risk management.

A personnel administrative specialist provides support to the staff of the Artist's personnel department by ensuring the department accomplishes assigned responsibilities on a daily basis. This can include coordinating events, arranging meetings and travel plans, creating presentations, preparing reports, answering phones and taking messages for other department staff when they are unavailable.

Picking a quality administrator may be a bit tricky for Artists. Initially in an Artists career, the administration of operations may fall on the Artist or one of the members of the band. However, as Artists become busier with their career, the need for a qualified administrator is imperative. Friends and family are certainly a possible choice and they may be eager to participate, but working with friends or family can add stress to that relationship. It may be wiser for an Artist to hire someone with experience and business savvy. In addition, hiring someone who is not a friend or family member makes it easier for an Artist to give direction without hurting feelings.

****

4.98 Task

As a start, name at least one reason why an administrator for the Artist may be needed. Write it down and put it into this section of the Artists Business Plan.

****

Sourcing Professional Services

4.99 Professional Services Personnel – Sourcing

Instead of hiring a new person to work for the Artist's company, perhaps the best choice might be to complete certain employee functions through employment sourcing. This option may reduce the costs of hiring a full-time employee which has additional costs such as unemployment tax, social security and medical benefits.

Two Types of Outsourcing
Let's start by pointing out a distinction between two kinds of outsourcing:

1. Managed services is the delivery and use of specific marketing tools and applications that may be owned and hosted by the Artist's company. A vendor that either hosts or uses an Artist's marketing system to execute outbound campaigns provides a managed service. A good example is the Artist's street team. They may not work for the Artist but the Artist provides the flyers to distribute as well as the locations to post them.
2. Business process outsourcing means the management of a specific marketing function, such as radio promotion, public relations, database management, leads generation, or telemarketing, using either internal or outsourced technology. For example, a call center company that handles telemarketing for the Artist is a business process outsourcer. The distinction is useful, and, of note, some vendors provide both services.

One of the biggest areas for Artists to outsource is for marketing. In today's digital market, the cost of recording has dropped significantly. However, getting the word out about an Artist's great new song or recording takes time and money. Perhaps the best solution is to outsource the marketing job(s) to one or more individuals.

10 Reasons to Outsource Marketing
The decision to outsource a marketing function for an Artist or an Artist's new tour or recording can be both strategic and tactical. Many Artists and their companies have a philosophy of outsourcing any activity that is not core to their business. For example, writing a news release may be central to the company; developing a positioning strategy may not be. At the tactical level, Artists often find themselves strapped for marketing resources to respond to a rapid

or unexpected change in the business or perhaps an increased volume of marketing campaigns due to multiple projects for the Artist. What's right for the organization? Following are 10 general guidelines to help Artists determine whether to farm out a complete marketing function or specific project, or to keep it close to the Artist's team.

1. **Lack of Specific Expertise**
Effective marketing organizations require a wide range of expertise. A typical group may include strategists, analysts, technologists, creatives, product specialists, communications professionals, brand managers, event organizers, e-commerce experts, advertising specialists, telemarketers, copywriters, alliance managers, as well as the occasional Webmaster.

Let's face it: There are times when some of those professionals are unavailable or an area is inadequately staffed. Marketing analytics, database marketing, and data hygiene are three common areas of weakness in many Artists' companies. Understanding fans and customers, their demographics, preferences, and buying criteria is the life's blood of any Artist. However, most Artist companies are product-driven and do not have enough people with the requisite skill sets to complete the marketing task at hand.

2. **Lack of Specific Technology**
Artists are notoriously technology-deprived when it comes to marketing. Even in high-technology companies, they're bogged down by a hodgepodge of incompatible technologies. While this situation is being somewhat remedied by the proliferation of marketing automation tools, the marketing of an Artist's products is, many times, overlooked until the last minute.

Getting access to an integrated, technology-rich set of marketing applications can be an expensive exercise for any Artist. A better solution is often to outsource specific marketing functions to specialists who use leading-edge technology. In the long run, this works most effectively when the marketing staff has direct access to the technology so they can develop their skills accordingly. When the staff is sufficiently experienced, deploying new applications internally or subscribing to them on demand can become a simple financial decision.

3. **Manage More Costs as Variable Expenses**
Fixed costs in people, systems, and facilities often account for the largest portion of an Artist's marketing budget. Artists need to quickly adapt to sudden changes in the route of a promotion tour, customer demographics and markets, as well as to take advantage of immediate opportunities. As such, those functions or projects that can be outsourced create a greater overall level of flexibility for the Artist's company and Artist's cash flow.

While the specific costs of outsourcing might appear to be higher than if an Artist does it themselves, there are hidden costs in maintaining internal fixed marketing assets. These include absorbing delays caused by changing priorities, attrition, lack of support when it is needed, etc. Also, the costs of expansion and contraction of marketing functions, even on a monthly basis, can be very expensive when done internally. This is particularly true if an Artist does not stay to the plan or does not release regular products (recordings and songs).

4. **Benchmark Operations Against Best Practices**

Whether an Artist is outsourcing a function like public relations, a channel like telemarketing, a capability like marketing operations, or a technology like data mining, they are almost certainly entrusting it to a company that has done it before. The experience gained by utilizing these outsourced companies may be key to deriving best practices.

Many outsourcers package their understanding of best practices not only in the form of their employees, but in data models, process flows, or partnerships. Artist who build this understanding from scratch in-house may be possible for an Artist, but it takes time. Engaging an expert provides immediate access to expert people and institutional knowledge that can be transferred immediately.

5. **Focus on Insight, not Operations**

Artists should think about the mix of skills in their marketing operations. An Artist's agent, for example, may have the primary responsibility to understand, position, price, and promote performance dates for the Artist. Some may be focused on understanding demographics, segments, and buying patterns. Others may manage relationships with specific promoters or talent buyers or venues, or they focus on consolidating and understanding data about transactions, margins, and other metrics to improve operations. This is the same for producers, managers, publishers and promoters. Bottom line: These people handle the core functions of the marketing organization for an Artist. They are the brain trust.

6. **Grow More Rapidly**

During a high growth phase of an Artist's career, it is usually faster--and often cheaper--to outsource newly required staff or processes. Getting to market quickly with a new product, offer, or distribution channel is very difficult if all the key functions must be identified, hired, and trained before execution. Does the Artist want to wear the Artist hat or take time to learn a new skill?

7. **Experiences a Boom / Bust Investment Cycle**

When revenue or profit falls, most Artists cut costs immediately. Marketing investments are often the first to go; they are a "discretionary" expense. Six months later, whether the pipeline has improved, there are usually a new round of investments to "fuel the engine."

Switching between investment and retrenchment modes is expensive for any Artist. In the short-term, canceling marketing activities will incur costs. In the intermediate-term, the costs associated with attrition, staffing, and the associated erosion of the knowledge base can be more expensive. That's one more reason why it's important for an Artist to stay focused.

Outsourcing functions offers a greater degree of flexibility for an Artist, and can improve the boom/bust cycle. Some outsourcers bill on a project basis, and these can be scaled up or down with a minimal notice period. When an Artist puts a retainer agreement in place, there is a lower degree of flexibility in law, but a significant level in practice.

---

10 Reasons to Outsource

1. **Lack of Specific Expertise**
2. **Lack of Specific Technology**
3. **Manage More Costs as Variable Expenses**
4. **Benchmark Operations Against Best Practices**
5. **Focus on Insight, not Operations**
6. **Grow More Rapidly**
7. **Experiences a Boom / Bust Investment Cycle**
8. **Need to Mitigate Legal Risks**
9. **New Band Member**
10. **New Market or Customer Channel**

---

8. **Need to Mitigate Legal Risks**

Life is changing for marketers around the world. Privacy legislation in the European Union has been adopted by most countries which includes an explicit opt-in policy that spans all communications channels. The approach to privacy in the U.S. (National Do Not Call List, CAN-SPAM, California SB 1386, etc.) has led to an inconsistent set of regulations depending on industry, use, jurisdiction, and channel. Other laws, such as the USA-Patriot Act, specify what information must be provided to the U.S. government and when.

Artists should be aware of legal compliances for all marketing efforts. Most Artists do not have an adequate understanding of the relevant laws or processes in place to ensure compliance. A well-crafted outsourcing agreement that covers fan and customer data privacy and security not only helps Artists to understand these issues, but can also offload at least some legal risk when there is a customer complaint or government audit.

9. **New Band Member**

Acquiring a new member for the Artist has been a fact of life for many years and may continue to be so. While these combinations of talent create new marketing opportunities, they also result in the merging of incompatible systems, databases, relationships, and processes. For example, the new member may have a list of thousands of fans. Shouldn't these fans be notified about the new member's status with the Artist?

Merging data to create a consistent marketing database are core competencies of many Artists and outsourcers. Others specialize in redesigning and automating marketing processes. Some Artists focus on enterprise-wide marketing solutions that can respond rapidly to changes. Finding these resources and performing these operations are an important step for Artists.

Four Tips for Employee Sourcing
Define the Job, Not the Person
Have a Strong Basic Pitch
Write Compelling Advertising
Network

---

10. New Market

Developing a new customer channel or geography is in some ways analogous to managing through an acquisition process. Each new city that the Artist adds to their performance possibilities creates new opportunities and pitfalls for an Artist. There is a heavy cultural element to most marketing campaigns. The more geographies and channels they include, the greater the opportunity to make a cultural or financial mistake.

Multitouch campaigns toward fans that span merchandising at the gigs, advertising, PR, direct mail, e-mail, and the Internet require particular care for an Artist. Cultural differences exist not just in different languages and geographies, but also in communications channels. Effective direct mail techniques do not necessarily translate well to an e-mail campaign. Artists may need an integrated television and radio advertising campaign, but the media have quite different dynamics.

Implementing a new marketing channel for an Artist requires a level of expertise that many, perhaps most, Artist simply do not have. Outsourcing them or using outside resources to supplement internal resources is generally a good idea.

****

Four Tips for Employee Sourcing

Artists can find great candidates on the Internet, but it's still going to take work. Here's what great employee sourcing is all about:

1. Define the Job, Not the Person

Sourcing the best candidates must start with a compelling vision of what the job entails. Artists shouldn't rely on a traditional job description to source candidates. Determine what the person needs to do in the job to be successful, and describe at least three or four major projects that the Artist is planning. The best candidates will only explore a job if it offers growth opportunities.

2. Have a Strong Basic Pitch

"Would you be open to exploring a situation that's clearly superior to what you're doing today?" Ninety-nine percent of candidates will say, "Yes." Artists should use this approach every time they first talk to a top candidate on the phone. Artist should also capture this idea in their advertising.

3. Write Compelling Advertising

When writing the job description, avoid the traditional or boring. Ads need creative titles and copy that describes what the person will be doing, learning and becoming. Don't list skills and years. This filters out -- rather than opts-in -- the best people. Describe the skill in the context of how it's used. For example, "Use the Artist's promotion background to help us build a bigger fan base." If the ad title says, "Promotion Wizard Required," Artists will attract some top people to the candidate pool.

4. Network
Every wise person will tell you that a good recruiting strategy is all about networking; same goes for looking for the best candidates. Artists should ask everyone they talk with if they know someone appropriate for the job. It's a great way to find top candidates. If the job is not compelling though, they'll only provide names of people looking for work. To get a name of a top passive candidate, Artists need to describe a compelling job.

****

4.99 Task
For this section of the Artist Business Plan, write about the potential sourcing of personnel for the Artist's business. Include names and their roles in the description.

****

Notes

_____

_____

_____

_____

_____

_____

_____

Chapter 5
Business Plan for Artists
Products & Services Overview

In this section of the Artist's Business Plan, Artists should identify what product or services they provide. It may be a great live show. It may be exceptional songs. It may be well produced recordings. It may be all of the above.

Products and Services Overview

5.01 Product and Services Overview

- 5.01 Products & Services Overview
- 5.02 Product Development
- 5.03 Product Strategy
- 5.04 Product Mix
- 5.05 Live Performances
- 5.06 Producing
- 5.07 Recorded Audio
- 5.08 Mixing & Editing Audio
- 5.09 Mastering Audio
- 5.10 Recorded Video
- 5.11 Manufacturing Process
- 5.12 Pressing Vinyl
- 5.13 Packaging Process
- 5.14 Non-Audio Merchandise
- 5.99 Future Products & Services

Many times, Artists plan their products and services based on the anticipated income derived from each. Artists in the music industry usually have multiple income streams and usually cannot rely on just one. There are many possibilities including: Live Performances, Teaching, Salary, Session Player, Merchandise, Sound Recordings, Publishing, etc.

Possible Products and Services
Live Performances
Live performances can be both a product and a service. The product could be the "act" or the "show" that fans may be attracted to and the service could be the musicianship offered to talent buyers for festivals and night clubs.

Recorded Audio
Most likely, Artists are in the business of releasing recorded audio. This may or may not be cooperation with a record label. The service part of recorded audio includes the performance of the musicians and the recording and the product is the actual recording. Artists should always know who owns the recording master.

Recorded Video
Many Artists are actively involved with video including performing as well as providing musicianship as well as

providing the recorded sound for video. Once again, Artists should always know who owns the video when it completed.

Song Licensing
If the Artist is a songwriter, they have another product source. Songs have value for recordings, live performances and video beds.

Merchandising
One product that can be expanded as the Artist career grows is merchandising. Artists may want to release products such as t-shirts, hoodies or thongs.

Affiliate Programs
One ancillary product for Artists is through affiliates online such as banner advertising and/or click-throughs on their website of e-mail correspondences.

Demographic Database
Another ancillary product for Artists is the potential to release fan demographics to marketers. Many corporations purchase this data especially if the target is male age 18-24.

***

5.01 Sample

Artist Business Plan – Product & Services Sample
The primary revenue center for the business will come from the sales of musical recordings to the general public as well as sales of musical performances to entertainment promoters. The One-Great-Artist (OGA) will perform a variety of original and cover material. We will advertise both to the general public while concurrently developing relationships with local promoters, talent buyers and night club bookers.

The first type of revenue will be generated by sales of recordings of single songs as well as albums.

The second revenue center for the business will come from the sale of music performances to promoters, talent buyers and night club bookers. This is an extremely important revenue center for the business as the contribution margins generated from providing these services is extremely high.

The third type of product or service of the Artist is their songwriting ability. The songs can be used for television, film and commercials.

***

5.01 Task

Describe the products and services of the Artist. The description should be written as if the customers are the readers. Remember, there are two customers for each Artist: the fan customer and the entertainment industry customer. In the description, include the specific groups of customers served by the product/service, nature of the method(s) in the product/service, outcomes for customers and any other benefits to them, and where they should go next if they are interested in using the product/service. Be careful to describe the product/service in terms of benefits to customers, not to the Artist. For example, address pricing, convenience, location, quality, service, atmosphere, etc.

***

Product Development

5.02 Product Development

Part of the business plan of the Artist involves the ways and means of developing new products. Many Artists have a variety of potential products such as songs, personal appearances, performances, recordings and merchandise.

This section of the Artist Business Plan identifies the products that are being planned by the Artist. Once these planned products are released to the public, or published, they are no longer in "development" and move to the category of products. What are the Artist's planned projects? Perhaps the Artist would like to write a song a week or release a new recording of a song every two weeks. Does the Artist have plans to release an album or a t-shirt, or do they have plans to go on tour?

The planning of the products depends on the overall goals of the Artist.

Product Development focuses on all the business arrangements after the Artist Development details have been completed. Product Development is all about recording, marketing and selling products especially, involved with selling musical downloads, CDs, tapes and vinyl recordings. Once the Artist Development Plan has been completed, product development is implemented. This includes the recording and performing of the songs / persona.

****

5.02 Task

For this section of the Artist Business Plan, write about the development of new products and services for the Artist's company,

****

Product Strategy

5.03 Product Strategy

Promotion Preparation
Before moving into Product Development, smart Artists know to prepare for the promotion of the project first. This preparation makes it easier when the time comes to release the product. While the product is being developed, the promotional aspects can start coming alive. Artists should envision how the music will be promoted and sold by the time the act enters the recording studio.

Producing Recordings

The choices of what studio to record in and what producer or engineer will be hired to make the record are needed to be considered. Experienced Artists are aware that if a certain sound, for a certain music genre, isn't recorded properly, the chances of radio airplay could be hampered. If so, there may be no significant sales of the record. Thus, the production choices, as a part of the Product Development equation, are very important when deciding how to market the recordings of a new Artist or band.

Recording Audio

Researching the right recording studio, right producer and engineer is another key issue in Product Development. Where will the record be recorded? Who will record it? Both of these questions must be considered quite seriously before making a final decision. We're not talking about making a demo at a friend's house but a master product.

Mastering Recordings

Up next is mastering. Mastering is not something to be passed over lightly. The mastering engineer can enhance or hurt the recording. Choose a mastering engineer who understands the genre of music. This is a must.

Discography and Content Management

Recording the project is just the beginning. A good content management system is needed to maximize the use of those recordings. Be prepared by having many different final file formats for the recordings such as WAV, Mp3, etc.

Film & Video

One main investment an Artist should make for their career is that of a quality video camera. With the increasing use of the Internet, video is playing a more important promotional role than ever before.

Packaging

When planning the promotion of the product, remember that the packaging plays an important role. This hold true whether the release is online or offline. The graphics used should be consistent with the Artist's and the products image.

Manufacturing

Who will manufacture the record? Who will design the artwork for the release? These are two more essential questions for product development. Finances will most likely determine this, as they probably determined production decisions. Take the time to make a record that sounds and looks like something you would want to buy yourself. Album cover artwork, packaging material design, and printing issues are important because you are creating a product that will be competing for the attention of music fans that have an abundance of music releases to choose from. Is there something about the album cover that will attract a fan or customer to the record?

Distribution

Luckily for the independent recording Artist, the Internet has made the distribution of music much, much easier. Consignment at area stores is a difficult chore and hooking up with a regional distributor can be costly. The budget for distribution must take in account charge backs, defective products, promotion items and shipping.

Brick & Mortar Distribution: Getting product to the retail stores has always been an issue with record labels, much less Artists releasing their own recordings. Many distributors are looking for a promotional commitment before they'll accept the product for distribution.

Online Distribution: There are numerous outlets on the World Wide Web that offer opportunities to Artists and labels to expose their music while making sales at the same time. Rates vary depending on the Online Music Distributor with whom the Artist or label affiliates with.

Promotion
What has or has not been accomplished in the areas of Artist Development and Product Development will make or break the chances of success with the Artist's music. The Artist or record label will promote and publicize the music and Artist to maximize the prospect of sales and ultimately, income. Promotion should involve offline as well as online exposure.

Publicity
Publicity is the deliberate attempt to manage the public's perception of a product. The subjects of publicity include people (for example, politicians and performing Artists), goods and services, organizations of all kinds, and works of art or entertainment.

Branding
A brand is a name, logo, slogan, and/or design scheme associated with a product or service. Branding is the process of creating a relationship or a connection between a company's product and emotional perception of the customer for the purpose of generation segregation among competition and building loyalty among customers and fans.

Sales:
One a record has been manufactured and is ready to be sold to the public, Product Development turns its attention to sales and income generated through sales. Many young labels and developing Artists forget this in their rush to record their music. If the Artist is going to spend thousands of dollars recording the music, wouldn't it be a good idea to find a way to sell it? That's how professional record labels think. They make sure a system is in place to distribute and sell their records to the Artist's fans. Many young Artists make the mistake of trying to get some radio airplay, or other media attention, before they've found a way for the public to buy their recordings. Make no such mistake. (Section 11)

Live Performances
Another critical part of an Artist's business model involves live performances. This may be accomplished by one of two ways: 1.) Establishing a branch of the Artist's company to act as a booking agency. 2.) Have the Artist work with an established agent. There are advantages and disadvantages to either. In either case, the Artist has a vested interest in their live performances.

Merchandising
In the broadest sense, merchandising is any practice which contributes to the sale of products to a retail consumer. At a retail in-store level, merchandising refers to the variety of products available for sale and the display of those products in such a way that it stimulates interest and entices fans and customers to make a purchase.

Web
The use of the World Wide Web in product development includes promotion and marketing as well as distribution and sales. A quality web presence is essential to the success of any product.

Working the Product

The importance of knowing the various parts of Product Development will be reflected in the success of a release of a sound recording for public sales. It may seem obvious, but all of the items that make up Product Development should be considered in a broad sense. For example, Artists should consider distribution when planning the recording of the songs. There is no sense in having product gather dust in the garage while the Artist scurries to find a way to get it into the marketplace.

The product strategy continues by engaging the fan-customer. This may be accomplished best through the Artist's live performances. Artist's should evaluate and pick the best event where they can meet their target market. After thorough market research, an Artist should already have enough information to develop a segment for their target market based on their geographic, demographic, and psychographic classifications. From this target segment, Artist should then find and utilize the best event that their fan and customer segment is most likely to attend.

Artists need to choose and design the perfect promotional items to fit their market, event, and brand. Again, based on the segment they are targeting, they should then choose the appropriate promotional product that their target market will appreciate. Design also plays a big factor in the success of the Artist's marketing campaign. Examples of design issues to focus on are clearness of logo to t-shirt colors and the clarity of message on printed items.

****

5.03 Task

For this section of the Artist Business Plan, write about the strategy for new products and services of for the Artist's company,

****

Product Mix

5.04
Product Mix

Every Artist has a variety of potential products and services that they may offer potential customers. Remember, Artists typically have two types of customers; fans and music industry professionals. The product mix for the Artist is the array of products or services for sale. Sometimes Artists offer different variations of the same product (such as a live performance of a song or an audio recording of the same song.) In addition, Artists may sell various products such as compact discs, music downloads, t-shirts, or services such as live performances or songwriting for movies.

Artist business owners use the concept of product mix for a variety of reasons, including expanding sales opportunities, targeting different customers and reducing their dependency on only one product or service. If the Artist sells only one product or offers only one service, take a look at their options for expanding what they offer and strengthening their business. One good example is an Artist who may perform all-original material for some gigs and then, using a different name, perform cover-songs for other gigs.

Variations to the Product Mix

One way to expand an Artist's product mix is to vary what is sold. If an Artist can perform live, then perhaps they are selling "fun" to a talent buyer. The talent buyer may be interested in hiring an Artist who can create a fun atmosphere for his or her customers. However, perhaps the Artist also performs "serious" music. There are talent buyers who regularly hire these types of performances. For the fan customer, an Artist may sell a recording of an acoustic version of a song as well as an electric version. Another example of varying a product is offering recordings of songs as singles or as a part of an album to satisfy fans and customers with different needs.

Expansion of Product Mix

Another way to change an Artist's product mix is to add new products or services that are related to the Artist's core business. For example, an Artist might add non-vocal versions of their recordings. This expanding of the product mix might serve a whole new market for the Artist of film producers needing songs or recordings that may be used as instrumentals or song-beds for films and videos.

Both of these methods of expanding the product mix require a more significant investment than simply varying what the Artist is already selling, but the risk might be worth it.

Diversification of Product Mix

Varying and expanding what an Artist sells are examples of vertical market segmentation, because the product lines fit into their business's existing marketplace. A third way for an Artist to expand the product mix is to expand horizontally, or sell products or services not directly related to the Artist's core business. A simple example of horizontal product mix expansion would be an Artist who sells folk or acoustic music and then expands to offer blues and hip hop music, thus entering two new marketplaces. Another example is the Artist who provides a service of performing in a live situation and then expanding their service to perform as a session musician.

Consideration for Product Mix

When an Artist considers changing their product mix, they should examine not only the dollar costs to do so but also the impact on their business's administration. The Artist and the Artist's team will have to split its time among more products and may have to work with unfamiliar products or services. If the Artist produces variations of the same product, such as providing different formats of sound recordings, the production economies of scale will change. Expanding an Artist's repertoire of songs will require the Artist to add more rehearsal time. If the Artist decides to diversify into a completely new area of business, they will need to keep their brands separate to protect each one. One way to change the product mix is to stop items that aren't selling well and gamble more on fewer items or services.

****

5.04 Task

For this section of the Artist Business Plan, consider and write down the current product mix of the Artist. Include all products and services of the Artist.

****

Live Performances

5.05
Live Performances

In addition to the products that an Artist offers to fans and customers, such as sound recordings and merchandise, Artists must also address the services that they offer. One of the best services that an Artist may offer, and the largest income source for the beginning Artist, is that of performing live, on stage, in front of an audience. Concert promoters and talent buyers are always looking for quality talent to fill their stages.

Each time tickets are sold and a performance takes place it is a true miracle. In today's world, live performances are separating farther away from society and recorded performances are becoming more and more prevalent. In many instances, the DJ has replaced the Musician-Artist and their live performance.

Live performances provide a special opportunity for the performer and the audience, whereas recorded performances may not. Live performances may be spontaneous and a spur of the moment experience. This spontaneity creates a more natural performance. As a performer performs live, the audience helps create a positive atmosphere for the performance. This energy can only occur between a live performer and an audience. Since it is difficult to fully understand the energy taking place while watching or listening to a recorded performance, the viewer/listener will not have the same experience as an audience member that watched that exact same performance in a live setting. In addition to the energy, the visual elements of a live performance impacts the audience's experience. Also the body language of the performer often has a deep visual impact on the message as well as the experience of the performance. A performance is not about how the act performed necessarily, but the experience the audience receives during the performance.

Another important aspect to an Artist's live performances is that of another potential income source. If the Artist records their performance on audio and/or video, they have a potential new product. The quality of the performance as well as the quality of the recording of the performance will determine the establishment of this new product. Once again, if the Artist is not 100% positive about their product, they should not release it to the public. Music videos and audio recordings of songs in live performances, as well as variations of songs, are just as important in current music markets as a studio recording from a specific album.

Along with radio promotion, the synchronization of live public appearances is another important factor of exposure for any Artist. Ultimately this process creates a buzz for the Artist's brand. Many times, record labels time their radio campaigns simultaneously with their Artist's live performances within a station's region. They can then focus on plugging that station for spins as the DJ may be more likely to play the record. So the more public appearances that an Artist has, then the more chance they have of building a fan base and generating awareness for themselves as well as getting that all important radio play.

Before the recording of music, all music was heard live. There were special concert halls and band stands designed to create the best acoustics. Once music could be recorded and sold, recording albums became a way of promoting Artists and their live shows. Now, however, Artists go on tour to promote their new album. This shift from importance of live music to the importance of recorded music, created music that was a commodity rather than a work of art. Although a complete shift back to the old form of live performances is impossible, Artists still need to find a way to validate their performance to gain authenticity.

People listen to certain music because it creates meaning for them. Many times a listener connects to the Artist, because the Artist is making them feel like the Artist is singing for the listener. The importance of the live performance is that the audience really sees the Artist playing for them, unlike listening to their music elsewhere. When the music is live, the music seems to be truly played for them. It is important for Artists to reinforce this connection by playing authentic live shows. The audience's connection to the performer is what makes the live show authentic, and this in turn, makes their music more authentic.

It is important for Artists to maintain their authenticity. This is what ultimately drives the fan to become a customer. No customer wants to buy a fake product. Without authenticity the music industry would collapse. The development of new music helps music keep it authentic by keeping the music fresh. Artists have a challenge of keeping the balance between making money and staying authentic as well as to stay true to their ideologies. This is not only shown by an Artist within the recording studio but in their live performances as well.

As an Artist works on their Artist Development Plan, they should pay close attention to the section on Lessons & Coaching. For an Artist to develop a quality live performance, most also need to be proficient playing their instrument. In addition, Artists need to know what works on stage. The coaching an Artist receives regarding their live performances may address stage presence, scripts between songs, set-lists, and interaction with the audience as well as other Artist Development issues such as image, gear, instruments and equipment.

In addition to merging an Artist Development Plan to the Artist Business Plan, this section should be well reflected in their sales plan, marketing plan and short-term plan.

****
5.05 Task

For this section of the Artist Business Plan, write down the plan for live performances for the Artist. Include current plans as well as short term plans.

****

Producing Audio

5.06
Producing Audio

Producing quality recordings is dependent on the personal relationship between the producer and the Artist. A good match of the two can produce amazing results, and bad matches usually end up with time and money wasted.

If an Artist has significant studio experience, either as a player or an engineer, self-production is certainly an option. Many Artists are capable of producing their recordings.

A producer should be involved at the earliest stages of planning a recording. Not the earliest stages of recording, but of planning itself. The biggest aspect of production is pre-production, and this is most effective when pursued outside of the studio. Once all the tracks are recorded, the production is pretty much complete. It's then a matter of mixing or remixing. Production experience is needed most when recording tracks and then deciding on arrangements. If this is done well, a track will mix itself. If done poorly, it's best to leave the poor engineer alone with "production" comments and let him try to salvage the track.

Remember, the "vibe" is decided during the tracking, not mixing, and it's always about the song and its vibe first.

One last tip: Democracy in the studio is the absolute worst method of production. Only one person should be in charge: the producer.

****
5.06 Task

For this section of the Artist Business Plan, write a segment about whether the Artist is planning to add music producing as a part of their products and services.

****

Recorded Audio

5.07
Recorded Audio

This section of an Artist's Business Plan

is similar to the Artist Development Plan – Preparing to Record. From the business perspective, let's examine the plan.

Typically, an Artist who records and releases their own product is running a separate business: that of a Vanity Record Label - an Artist's own record company. So, if the Artist is planning to record and release their own recordings, they should seriously consider the business aspect of what is actually happening. Running a record label is a whole lot different than being an Artist or running an Artist's business: similar but different. A record labels needs a separate Business Plan of its own.

On the other hand, many Artists collaborate with other record companies such as independent labels or major record companies. In this instance, the Artist will follow the direction of the record label executive in the actual process of recording.

Either way, is the Artist ready to record? How will the project start? How long will it take? How much will it cost? These are some of the many questions that the Artist will need to consider.

Planning and executing the steps for recording is no different than any other project, whether it be building a fan base or planning a tour. Artists will be spending some time and money on something that will be part of their experiences for the rest of their existence. Artists should approach it seriously.

Below are some tips for making sure the process stays on time and on budget.

1. Set a Goal for Completing the Recording

Without a goal, the recording project could lag on for years. Set a "target" date to have the recordings completed. Artists can use that not just for planning and scheduling, but as a motivator to keep focused. However, do not call this the "Release Date" and absolutely do not start scheduling CD release parties! It is far too soon in the process, and unexpected delays will surely cause the target date to change. However, set a target date in mind to help with the planning.

2. Determine Cost and Time Budgets

Artists will need to determine up front what the budget for the entire project will be, from recording through manufacturing and then in to promotion and distribution. This is true for vanity labels as well as majors and independents. This will require that the Artist do a lot of research. Balance the results against what can be afforded and how much time will be spent on the project.

- **Recording Budget**
  If the Artist is doing the recording in their own studio, great, but if not, talk with various studios to get a budget estimate. Studios generally charge by the hour or for a block of time. For example, a studio may say their hourly rate is $50, but an entire day is $300, and an entire week is $1,200. Artists should think about how many songs they want to record, and think about how long it will take to track those songs. If the Artist has worked in a recording studio before, they'll have some experience to help determine this. If they haven't, the Artist may rely on the input of the studio staff to provide some realistic numbers. If the studio's estimates for how long the recording process will take are

questionable, then the Artist should use their own estimates, but triple them. Recording always takes longer than anticipated.

- **Mixing Budget**
Once the songs have been recorded, the Artists will need to have them mixed. Most studios will also mix the music. However, some Artists may know someone that they want to specifically mix their songs. Some studios charge an hourly rate for mixing. Some will charge per song, or base their rates on the number of tracks used in each song.

Generally Artists should plan on at least a day per song to complete the mixing process. Also consider the time it takes to transfer recorded tracks from one studio to another if hiring a separate mixing engineer. Don't forget about the time it takes to review the songs and wait for mix changes.

- **Mastering Budget**
Once all songs are mixed, the Artists will get them mastered. Mastering involves leveling the volume and equalization between songs, as well as putting the songs in order on the CD and adjusting spacing between songs and adding fadeouts if necessary.

Typically an Artist will want to have their album mastered by someone other than the person who mixed the songs. This will add a fresh set of ears to the project, and many times mastering engineers have specialized equipment dedicated to the mastering process. Mastering costs can range from $25/song to $100/song for most independent projects. Some manufacturing facilities like DiscMakers offer a mastering service for a flat rate of around $500 for a typical album.

Plan on about a week for the mastering process to be completed, depending on who is chosen to complete the mastering.

3. Putting It All Together
Once an Artist has a budget and schedule planned out, they can get started. Track the progress to make sure the schedule and budget are being followed. Project management techniques work great for this step. Consider using computer spreadsheet software to help track the project. Be sure to track when payments are going to be required for the various project phases so that funds are available, and make sure the payments are made on time.

Remember that delays will happen. Don't panic. Just be diligent about tracking the project's progress and make adjustments as necessary. Don't make the mistake of scheduling and promoting a CD release party. Ideally, Artists should never schedule the CD release until they have the completed CDs in their hands.

****

5.07 Task

For this section of the Artist Business Plan, write down the plan for recording audio for the Artist.

****

Mixing and Editing Audio

5.08
Mixing & Editing Audio

Audio mixing is usually completed by a mixing engineer who is an audio specialist that processes multiple sounds by combining them into one or more channels. In the process, sound levels are manipulated and effects such as reverb may be added. This creative treatment is done in order to produce a mix that is more appealing to listeners.

Before the introduction of multi-track recording, all the sounds and effects that were to be part of a recording were mixed together at one time during a live performance. If the mix wasn't satisfactory, or if one musician made a mistake, the selection had to be performed over until the desired balance and performance was obtained. However, with the introduction of multi-track recording, the production phase of a modern recording has radically changed into one that generally involves three stages: recording (tracking and overdubbing, mixing and mastering.

Audio mixing is done in studios as part of creating an album or single. The mixing stage often follows a multi-track recording. The process is generally carried out by a mixing engineer, though sometimes it is the musical producer, or even the Artist, who mixes the recorded material. After mixing, a mastering engineer prepares the final product for reproduction on a CD, for radio, or otherwise.

Audio for Film & Television

Audio mixing for film and television is a process during the post-production stage of a moving image program by which a multitude of recorded sounds are combined into one or more channels. In the process, the source signals' level, frequency content, dynamics and panoramic position are commonly manipulated and effects such as reverberation might be added.

Audio for Live Sound

Live sound mixing is the process of electrically blending together multiple sound sources at a live event using a mixing console. Sounds used include those from instruments, voices, and pre-recorded material. Individual sources may be equalized and routed to effect processors to ultimately be amplified and reproduced via loudspeakers. The live sound engineer balances the various audio sources in a way that best suits the needs of the event.

Mixing Equipment

A mixer, or mixing console, or mixing desk, or mixing board, or software mixer is the operational heart of the mixing process. Mixers offer a multitude of inputs, each is fed by a track from a multi-track recorder; mixers would normally have 2 main outputs (in the case of two-channel stereo mixing) or 8 (in the case of surround).

Three Functions of Audio Mixing:
1. Mixing – summing signals

together, which is normally done by a dedicated summing amplifier or in the case of digital by a simple algorithm.
2. Routing – allows the routing of source signals to internal buses or external processing units and effects.
3. Processing – many mixers also offer on-board processors, like equalizers and compressors.

Two Function of Outboard Gear and Plug-Ins
Outboard gear (analog) and software plug-ins (digital) can be inserted to the signal path in order to extend processing possibilities. Outboard gear and plug-ins fall into two main categories:
1. Processors – these devices are normally connected in series to the signal path, so the input signal is replaced with the processed signal (e.g. equalizers).
2. Effects – while an effect can be considered as any unit that affects the signal, the term is mostly used to describe units that are connected in parallel to the signal path and therefore they add to the existing sounds, but do not replace them. Examples would include reverb and delay.

****

5.08 Task

In an Artist's Business Plan, the section on Mixing and Editing is just that: The plan. How is the Artist planning on completing the mixing and editing of upcoming recording projects?

****

Mastering Audio

5.09 Mastering Audio

The final stage in the recording process is that of Mastering. Mastering is a form of audio post-production work. It is the process of preparing and transferring recorded audio from a source such as audio tracks, containing the final mix, to a data storage device (the master). The Master becomes the source from which all copies will be produced from methods such as pressing, duplication or replication.

Mastering requires critical listening. Results depend upon the accuracy of speaker monitors and the listening environment. Mastering engineers may also need to apply corrective equalization and dynamic enhancement in order to optimize the sound heard on all playback systems. It is standard practice to make a copy of a master recording, known as a safety copy, in case the master is lost, damaged or stolen.

Mastering Process
The recorded audio material is the source for the mastering project. Ideally the source is the original resolution of the sound. The source is then transformed using equalization, compression, limiting, noise reduction and other processes.

More tasks, such as editing, pre-gapping, leveling, fading in and out, noise reduction and other signal restoration and enhancement processes can be applied as part of the mastering stage. This step prepares the recordings for either digital or analog replication. During mastering, the source material is also put in the proper order. This is commonly referred to as assembly (or 'track') sequencing.

The process of audio mastering varies depending on the specific needs of the audio to be processed. Mastering engineers need to examine the types of input media, the expectations of the source producer or recipient, the limitations of the end medium and process the subject accordingly. General rules of thumb can rarely be applied.

Typical Mastering Steps
1. Transferring the recorded audio tracks into a Digital Audio Workstation.
2. Sequence the separate tracks as they will appear on the final release.
3. Adjust the length of the silence between songs
4. Process or "sweeten" audio to maximize the sound quality
5. Transfer the audio to the final master format

To finish mastering a recording with multiple songs, track markers must be inserted along with International Standard Recording Code (ISRC) and other information necessary to replicate a compact disc. This is referred to as the meta-data that listeners will notice when the recording is played back on digital machines. Vinyl records have their own pre-duplication requirements for a finished master.

****
5.09 Task

For this section of the Artist Business Plan, write about the plan for mastering recordings for the Artist's company,

****

Recorded Video

5.10
Recorded Video

Part of an Artist's Business Plan is a section about video as a product and not just a great promotion tool. Let's face it, video has made a star out of thousands of people. Selfies are the new norm. With the explosion of services like YouTube, Hulu and Netflix, and the cost of video production at an all-time low, the time has never been better for Artists to get into the mix. Artists who don't utilize video are at a great disadvantage when competing for branding, fans and ultimately, sales.

Production
This section will not get into the detail of producing a great music video as that is a whole topic on its own. However, a brief introduction to the planning is important.

> **Video Production Ingredients**
>
> 1. Story-boarding
> 2. Location
> 3. Props
> 4. Equipment
> 5. Wardrobe and Makeup
> 6. Script

1. Story-boarding

Artists may have a brilliant idea for a video in their head but they really need to plan it out on paper. Story-boarding is planning the camera shots ahead of time. It's not good enough to just shoot one shot of the Artist talking to a camera. Artists should break up the video into individual shots. For example instead of the Artist just talking to camera they might try something like this.

- Shot 1. – The Artist talking to camera
- Shot 2. – The Artist writing lyrics
- Shot 3. – The Artist with their instrument
- Shot 4. – The Artist tying their running shoes
- Shot 5. – The Artist running out the door with their instrument

All five shots tell a story. The Artist may be saying the same thing but they are illustrating it by showing viewers that they write lyrics, play an instrument and that they are running late.

Of course the camera shots should complement the content of the video. If the Artist isn't talking about the music or what they like to do when they're not always running late, the shot of the Artist running out the door would be irrelevant.

Tip – Ideally plan one shot for every 10 seconds of the video.

Artists may also need to decide the size of shot that they want to use. For example:

- Shot 1 – a MS (mid shot) – head to waist of the Artist talking to the camera
- Shot 2 – a WS (wide shot) – head to toe of the Artist sitting at a desk writing
- Shot 3 – a CU (close up shot) – The Artist's hands on their instrument
- Shot 4 – a CU of the Artist tying their running shoes
- Shot 5 – a WS of the Artist running out the door towards the camera.

2. Location, Location, Location

Where is the Artist going to shoot the video? Consider these few things about the location:

1. Is it lit well with natural light? If there are a lot of windows that allow natural light in, it means that additional lighting might not be needed. This is not only a cost saver, but a time saver.
2. Is it quiet? Shooting in a noisy location may be a nightmare. It is assumed that the vocals are going to be synching to the screen shots, but a noisy atmosphere creates confusion for the production team. Quiet is better.
3. Is the camera person able to get the shots needed without too much clutter in the background? A very tidy or empty room is a good choice. Artists need to think about what will be in the background of their shot and move the room

around accordingly. Is there something sitting on a shelf behind the Artist that may distract the viewer's attention?
4. Is the location available for the full duration of the shoot plus a couple more hours? It always takes longer than expected.

3. Props
This is very important. Make a list of the props the Artist will need for the shoot. Prepare as many of these as possible before hand and allocate an area within the shooting space for them. This ensures that they may be grabbed quickly when required. Props could be as simple as a guitar, a fancy ink pen, running shoes, or a pop up banner with the Artist's name and logo on it.

4. Equipment
Make a list and check off all the items to ensure everything is ready that may be needed for the video shoot. The basics would be:
- Camera
- Tripod
- Sound recording device
- Microphone
- Lights
- Bounce board (for lighting)

5. Wardrobe and makeup
Artists should take some time to think about what they are going to wear in the video. As a rule of thumb don't wear anything too black, too white or with an intricate pattern. Also avoid logos of other companies.

Men, as well as women, should consider wearing makeup for the video. Video cameras can be very unforgiving and may discover every blemish and shiny patch on an Artist. Even a bit of powder will mean that viewers won't be distracted by the shine from the end of the Artist's nose.

6. Script
A video shoot will run much smoother if a script of what an Artist is going to say is used. In many cases, it won't matter if the Artist doesn't learn it word for word, but if they have the script and rehearses it, they are far less likely to fluff their lines on the day of the video shoot. This saves time and money.

Video Formats
Ever wonder why a video that will play on one device, won't play on another? Well that all comes down to video formats and which video format works with which players. Trying to figure out which video format is needed for an Artist can be very confusing. After all, most of us just want to play a video with ease on whatever device we choose. Knowing a little bit about video formats can help make that process a whole lot easier.

While there isn't one "best video format," there are best video formats for particular jobs. Here are some things to be aware of when choosing a video format.

1. Will fans and customers be watching the Artist's video streaming over the Internet?

2. Do they have a fast connection?

3. Do they have a DVD player or Blu-ray player?

4. What is the longevity of the format and how widespread is it?

****

****

5.10 Task

For this section of the Artist Business Plan, write about the plan for recording video for the Artist's company,

****

Manufacturing Process

5.11
Manufacturing Process

Duplication versus Replication for CD and DVD: What's the Difference?

Understanding the differences is important in determining which process is best for the Artist's project. A duplicated CD/DVD is not only created using a different process than a replicated CD/DVD, but the actual final product is also different.

There are two ways to make a copy of a CD or DVD. Information can be burned on to a blank CD/DVD-R; this method is called duplication. Information about the Artist or recorded tracks can also added during the CD/DVD manufacturing process; this method is referred to as replication.

After the duplication process is complete, the final product is a CD-R or a DVD-R. Replication stampers for CDs produce CD-ROMs. (ROM means Read Only Memory).

The Processes
CD duplication is similar to burning a CD/DVD on the Artist's personal computer. A CD/DVD duplicator extracts data from the master disc and writes it to a blank disc. The difference between burning multiple CD/DVD-Rs at a duplication facility and burning one on the Artist's computer desktop is that the duplication facility burns hundreds at a time on towers that are linked together. Each tower contains several CD/DVD trays so that many copies can be created simultaneously. After all the data has been written unto the blank CD/DVD-R, the information is verified with the master, and the process is complete.

CD/DVD replication, on the other hand, is created during the manufacturing process. In other words, media like a CD/DVD-R does not exist before the process starts. Before the replication process gets underway, the client master is evaluated for possible data corruption. Then, a glass master containing data is created. The glass master is used to develop a stamper. The stamper, in turn, is loaded into an injection molding machine that creates CD/DVD replicates. The quality of CD replication hinges upon the quality of the glass master's data.

The client supplied master for CD-R and DVD-R duplication is the same, a CD/DVD-R. CD-ROM replication also requires a CD-R master. While a DVD-R is acceptable for DVD replication, most facilities prefer to work from a client supplied DLT or Digital Linear Tape.

Advantages of CD/DVD Duplication
- The standard turn-time is 2-3 business days, even for runs up to 5,000 units.
- Digital full color printing is available with no prepress charges.

Disadvantages of CD/DVD Duplication
- The cost per unit for duplication is higher than replication.
- DVDs can have up to 2 layers of information on each side of the media. DVD-R duplicates can have 1 layer of information on the entire DVD.
- Most duplication facilities are small and are commonly limited to hand assembly of the media into packaging as a result of their low volume runs

Advantages of CD/DVD Replication
- The unit costs are lower than duplicated discs.
- Both offset printing and screen printing is available for replicated discs.
- Replicated DVDs can contain 1 layer (DVD-5) of information, 2 layers on one side (DVD-9), 1 layer on each side (DVD-10) or 2 layers on each side (DVD-18). Many replication facilities are not yet set up for DVD-18 replication.
- Most replication facilities, as a result of their high volume run capability, can auto assemble discs into jewel cases, paper/Tyvek sleeves, Amaray cases, or cardboard sleeves.

Disadvantages of CD/DVD Replication
- The standard turn-time is 7-10 business days, longer for runs exceeding 100,000 units. Standard duplication turn times are 2-3 business days.

Most facilities have a minimum order requirement of 1,000 units. Both CD duplication and CD replication extract data from the original in the same way. In terms of manufacturing, however, this is where the similarities end. The finished product of either process performs in the same manner, although there will be difference to the eye depending upon the whether the discs are digitally, screened, or offset printed.

Producing the Artist's own CD with relatively little software and professional help is possible, and there are a collection of companies who offer attractive deals on small production runs. Nevertheless, for a successful and relatively stress-free time, it pays to be well organized, leaving enough time to sort out the inevitable production troubles, and to check things thoroughly at every stage.

****

5.11 Task

For this section of the Artist Business Plan, write about the plan for manufacturing the products of the Artist's company,

****

Pressing Vinyl

5.12
Pressing Vinyl

Vinyl records are a fantastic physical product for Artists and bands to offer to their fan base. Having vinyl records produced may be easier than you think. While there are a lot of great pressing plants still operating around the world, Gotta Groove Records in Cleveland specifically caters to assisting indie musicians in pressing their music on wax. You can get a hold of them and/or place the Artist's vinyl orders online at www.gottagrooverecords.com.

Vinyl does take a bit longer to manufacture than compact discs or DVDs, so please take this into account. The general rule of thumb is to plan for approximately 3 weeks from when you submit the Artist's order to when you will get test pressings; and then three weeks from when you approve test pressings to when the Artist's order is ready to ship. Usually, things move much faster than this. But, if you plan this timeline into the Artist's schedule, you will never be disappointed. Of course, there are things that you can do to move things along – the most important pointers are described below.

The vinyl company will want the Artist's songs in the highest quality possible, so pretty much a WAV or uncompressed AIFF file. Export them as the highest available quality the Artist's software will allow. Obviously, make sure you listen to the Artist's files before transfer to ensure there are no errors.

Vinyl production required special mastering before it can be pressed to vinyl. Most companies do it for you as it's generally included in the Artist's costs as an essential part of the pressing process.

The main cost involved is the cutting of the record (mastering for vinyl will generally be included as part of this process), so make sure all of the Artist's files are free of errors before you submit them, or you'll have to pay for this process again. After that the Artist's cost is determined by the number of records, color or thickness, inner labels and so on.

Test pressings are highly recommended. You don't want to press 300 copies of a record only to find that you forgot to mix one of the tracks properly or that an error has found its way onto one of the Artist's audio files.

Most companies will have a minimum number you can press – 300 copies seems to be a fairly common amount.

Vinyl Masters Preparation: If you know you are going to do a vinyl release, pay special attention during mix and mastering to the high and low end content of the material. Examples of high frequency issues include cymbals and sibilance in vocals (ssss sounds). Try not to make the cymbals too bright and be sure to use a "de-esser" on vocals as needed. Make sure that frequencies below 40 Hz are cut as needed. Use high pass filters on tracks when mixing to keep these frequencies under control.

Watch The Record's Side Lengths: – the length of one side on a record will dramatically affect the final sound. While somewhat flexible depending upon the type of music involved, some general limitations are:

- 7" @ 33 1/3 RPM: ideal limit is 6 minutes per side

- 7" @ 45 RPM: ideal limit is 4.5 minutes per side.

- 12" @ 33 1/3 RPM: 18 minutes per side is ideal, 20 minutes per side is still good, and 22 minutes per side is generally the max.

- 12" @ 45 RPM: 12 minutes per side is ideal, 14 minutes is ok, and 15 minutes per side is generally the max.

Finally, it is actually always ideal to have 7" records cut at 45rpm, if side length permits.

****

5.12 Task

For this section of the Artist Business Plan, write about the plan for pressing vinyl for new products of the Artist's company,

****

Packaging Process

5.13 Packaging Process

As Artists start to develop products such as compact discs or t-shirts, one important consideration is that of packaging. Packaging is the technology of enclosing or protecting these products for distribution, storage, sale, and use. In addition, packaging also refers to the process of design, evaluation, and production of packages.

When an Artist considers the various needs of packaging for their goods, they need to look at the possibilities where the package may be important for either the end-user, the middleman or the transportation of the product.

If an Artist is planning to sell merch at their gigs, they will need to package their compact discs in some sort of wrapper. If the Artist is selling t-shirts at their gigs, how do they plan to transport them to their performance?

If the Artist sends their merch via the postal service, perhaps they need a package to withstand the stresses of many hands, boxes, tossing, and weight of other packages.

And finally, if an Artist is working with a distributor, they may need to send their merch in big bulk boxes to ensure the distributor has enough to sell.

Packaging and Package Labels

1. **Physical Protection** – The objects enclosed in the package may require protection from, among other things, scratching, temperature, water, and theft.

2. **Barrier Protection** – A barrier from oxygen, water vapor, dust, etc., is often required.

3. **Marketing** – The packaging and labels can be used by marketers to encourage potential buyers to purchase the product. Marketing communications and graphic design are applied to the surface of the package and (in many cases) the point of sale display. Most packaging is designed to reflect the brand's message and identity.

4. **Security** – Packaging can play an important role in reducing the security risks of shipment. Packages can be made with improved tamper resistance to deter tampering and also can have tamper-evident features to help indicate tampering. Blister Packs are a perfect example of this. Packages can be engineered to help reduce the risks of package pilferage or the theft and resale of products:

5. **Convenience** – Packages can have features that add convenience in distribution, handling, stacking, display, sale, opening, and ease of disposal

Package Appearance

If the Artist has more than one product such as multiple CDs, T-shirts, etc., their brand and image should be consistent across each one. To be consistent, Artists should review the Image section of their Artist Development Plan. This image will help the Artist command more attention from their fans and customers. More than one product creates an attention grabbing visual area and therefore, more attention equals more sales.

Bag or Box - Plastic or Paper

Shrink Wrap, Baggies, Eco-Pack? Blister Packs? What type of package to put the product into is the question. Many times, the answer is driven by price. It's a balance to package the product to its best advantage without adding too much to the cost. Many times, CD replicators will have packaging available for an additional fee. As far as t-shirts are concerned, many Artists fold them and place them in a one-gallon baggie for their merch table.

Consider Customers Experience

How will the fan or customer interact with the Artist's product? Can they touch it? Is the product completely sealed? Is a retail store willing or encouraged to display one of the Artist's products out of the package?

Package as a Shelf Billboard

Artist should make sure they have enough room on their package to show its benefits. If the product is small, including an area like a header may provide additional room to add selling copy and/or photos.

Make It POP!

Although discussed when an Artist is considering their graphic designs, Artists should consider a color that will help their product get noticed. Some Artists dominate a color such as Stryper with their black and yellow to help them stand out and create their brand. Take a look next time you are in the music store. What color matches the branding? Does the package match the product? That command of color takes time, but planning for it is the key.

It's All About Perception
Typically, Artists only have 4 seconds to catch the shopper's attention and convey the benefits of their product over the competition. In that short time, a shopper makes a decision about the product based on perception derived from what is presented.

Know The Artist's Budget
Packaging in low quantities can be expensive as far as per-piece price goes. Low quantity packaging is possible, but don't expect to get the lowest per-piece price when considering packaging only 1000 pieces.

Barcodes
If the Artist is planning to distribute their CD or t-shirts via brick and mortar stores, barcodes will be necessary. Barcodes are needed for the stock systems of the retailer and distributor as well as for record sales information. If a barcode isn't printed within certain tolerances it's likely to be unreadable, so it should not be resized or stretched in any way.

CD Packaging Options
Four main packaging types are commonly available for compact disc releases: the standard jewel case with booklet, the slimline maxi case, the humble cardboard wallet, and the all-in-one Digipak. Keep in mind, that radio stations prefer the jewel box as their shelves are designed to hold these cases where the spine is easily read.

****

5.13 Task

For this section of the Artist Business Plan, write about the plan for packaging of new products and services of the Artist's company,

****

Merchandising

5.14 Non-Audio Merchandise

In the broadest sense, merchandising is any practice which contributes to the sale of products to a retail consumer. At a retail in-store level, merchandising refers to the variety of products available for sale and the display of those products in such a way that it stimulates interest and entices customers to make a purchase. For Artists, this includes the appearance of their merch table as well as any promotional materials they supply to retailers, both online and offline.

In marketing, a product is anything that can be offered to a market that might satisfy a want or need. In retailing, products are called merchandise and for Artists, that may mean compact discs, t-shirts or even a music download online.

A product can be classified as tangible or intangible. A tangible product is a physical object that can be perceived by touch such as a compact disc, where an intangible product is a product that can only be perceived indirectly such as a recording of a song.

When an Artist contemplates retail commerce, visual displays mean more sales. Merchandising includes product design, product selection, packaging, pricing, and display that stimulate fans and customers to spend more. This includes disciplines and discounting, physical presentation of products and displays, and the decisions about which products should be presented to which customers at what time. Too many items on a merch table, for example, may mean too many decisions by a customer and confusion leads to a lack of sales.

```
┌─────────────────────────────────┐
│                                 │
│   Merchandise Possibilities     │
│                                 │
│            Buttons              │
│             Mugs                │
│             Hats                │
│           T-Shirts              │
│            Thongs               │
│           Hoodies               │
│          Sweatshirts            │
│                                 │
└─────────────────────────────────┘
```

Services
A third type in this is services. Artist services can be broadly classified under intangible products which are usually notes as performances. The main factor about services as a type of product is that it will not be uniform and will vary according to who is performing, where it is performed and on whom/what it is being performed.

Intangible products can further be classified into Virtual Digital Goods ("VDG") that are virtually located on a computer and accessible to users as conventional file types, such as JPG and MP3 files.

****

5.14 Task

For this section of the Artist Business Plan, write about the plan for merchandising new products and services of the Artist's company,

****

```
┌─────────────────────────────────┐
│                                 │
│   Future Products & Services    │
│                                 │
└─────────────────────────────────┘
```

5.99
Future Products and Services

In addition to what an Artist has in their repertoire of songs or recordings, every Artist contemplates releasing new items for their fans and customers. This may include a new t-shirt, compact disc or special event.

As a part of the strategic planning as defined in the Artist Business Plan, many Artists look at the short-term plan as well as the long-term plan. The long-term plan may identify future products and services of the Artists where the short-term plans assists with getting to the long-term goals. The short-term plan is identified in Section 3.99 of the Artist Business Plan. The long-term plan is identified in the Artist's Mission Statement.

For example:
Artists may determine that within the next five years, they will add 3 new compact discs to their product mix. They might want to release these as download or steaming only files or perhaps as physical products in a brick-and-mortar store.

Another example may include the Artist targeting Music Supervisors for possible placement of songs in movies or television programs. In order to do this, the Artist may start compiling a catalog of songs and recordings suitable for this kind of market.

****

5.99 Task

In this section of the Artist Business Plan, write down all possibilities for new products and services of the Artist. Not all of them may actually turn into reality, but without possibilities, there is no reality.

****

Notes

_____

_____

_____

_____

_____

_____

_____

_____

Notes

Chapter 6
Business Plan for Artists
Marketing Plan

An Artist marketing plan may be part of their an overall business plan but it's also a separate plan upon itself. Having a solid marketing strategy is the foundation of a well-written marketing plan. While a marketing plan contains a list of actions, a marketing plan without a sound strategic foundation is of little use. In addition to sales, the importance of marketing may be one of the most important aspects of an Artist's Business Plan.

Marketing Overview

6.01 Marketing Plan Overview
6.02 Marketing Plan
6.03 Marketing Goals & Object
6.04 Market Analysis
6.05 Market Potential
6.06 Market Segmentation
6.07 SWOT Analysis
6.08 Marketing Mix
6.09 Branding Strategy
6.10 Credibility
6.11 Product Testing
6.12 Target Market Strategy
6.13 Pricing Policy
6.14 Packaging Strategy
6.15 Online Marketing
6.16 Social Media Plan
6.17 Monitoring & Evaluation

6.01 Marketing Plan Overview

The Marketing Planning Process
An Artist's marketing plan is a comprehensive blueprint which outlines the businesses overall marketing efforts. The marketing plan can function from two points: strategy and tactics. For most Artists, "strategic planning" is an annual process, typically covering just the year ahead. Many times, Artists look at a practical plan may stretch three or more years ahead. Every Artist is different and every plan is different.

Ingredients of a Marketing Plan

Marketing Strategies
Marketing strategies can be seen as the means, or "game plan," by which marketing objectives will be achieved.

The 8 P's of Marketing

1. **Price** — The amount of money needed to buy the Artist's products, i.e. tickets, download, t-shirts, performances.
2. **Product** — The actual product: i.e.: performances, recording, merch.
3. **Promotion & Advertising** - Getting the product known.

4. **Placement** — Where the product is sold.
5. **People** — Artist members as well as those representing the Artist.
6. **Physical Environment** — The ambiance, mood, or tone of the environment. For example, some venues are a better place to perform than other venues.
7. **Process** — The highlights that differentiate the product from the competition such as better songs, higher quality performances or exclusivity.
8. **Packaging** — How the product will look when presented.

No matter what marketing strategy that an Artist chooses for their company, from the simple distribution of promotional items to a nationwide tri-media campaign, there are tools that can help their business reach their goals. Keep in mind that because this is a business of art, there is no true road to success without quality of content or quality of performance.

The target market of the Artist's business is listed in their business plan. The Artist's business should do an extensive research on their target market. Doing a thorough market research is something that should be present not just in the promotional items strategy, but in ALL marketing strategy. This step is the very foundation of a product strategy campaign, and failing to do this effectively will always lead to disastrous results.

****
6.01 Sample

One-Great-Artist (OGA) goals is to design and provide creative and effective marketing for its name, brand and products. As music is being produced in studio, promotion and marketing strategies will be formulated. It is crucial that the marketing plan for each new release or performance is in motion several weeks before the product is completed in studio.

One-Great-Artist will employ multifaceted promotional strategies for its product releases and performances including: hiring regional independent record promoters and creating radio promotions, Internet sites, broadcast videos, dance club promotions, in-store/co-op promotions and promotions to the general public through print, video and television mediums.

To support the sales of pre-recorded music, One-Great-Artist will produce and release music videos for each album released by the company. Existing affiliations in the video sector of the industry allow the company to produce top quality video productions while minimizing budgets. At this stage, music videos will be created for 3-4 songs on the album which will be released as "singles," as a prelude to the full album release. The team will contract with independent record promoters to interface with radio station program directors and music video network directors. Public relations firms will be hired to publicize and promote.

****
6.01 Task

For this section of the Artist Business Plan, write down the overall plan for marketing of the Artists products and services.

****

Marketing Plan

6.02
Marketing Plan

A marketing plan is a part of an Artist's Business Plan and outlines an Artist's overall marketing efforts. A marketing process can be realized by the marketing mix.

A marketing plan includes everything from understanding the Artist's target market and their competitive position in that market as well as how the Artist intends to reach that market and differentiate from the competition in order to make a sale.

The marketing plan can function from two points: strategy and tactics. In most organizations, "strategic planning" is an annual process, typically covering just the year ahead. Occasionally, a few Artist's may look at a practical plan which stretches three or more years ahead.

MARKETING AND PROMOTION

Public Relations Plan
Media Relations Plan

Public Relations Plan
Portrays the unique role of the Artist's organization and how it fills that role. The statement depicts how Artists want others to view their organization. This statement is the essence of how the Artist want the media, and others, to recognize their organization. The statement is the basis for wording used in ads and other methods of promotion.

Script for Representing the Organization to External Stakeholders
Portrays key points to make when representing the organization to external groups. The script is referenced by key personnel to represent the organization to external stakeholders, for example, funders / investors, reporters, etc.

Stakeholders, Messages and Methods (Media Plan and Calendar)
Consider the major stakeholders for the Artist's organization, for example, band members, funders/investors, reporters, collaborators, associations, etc. Consider what stakeholder may think of the Artist's organization. What media do they read and listen to and when? What media is most practical for the Artist to use in terms of access and affordability?

****

Media Relations Plan
Preferred Media and Contacts
The following media and contacts are preferred when promoting the Artist. These media (newspapers, television, radio, etc.) and contacts may have been used in the past, they may understand the Artist's organization and their marketplace, etc.

als.

****

Description of Product / Service

The overall goals of the Artist's organization very much determine what will be done with each of the Artist's products (recordings) and services (performances). For example, strategic goals might be to expand the number of current customers, expand the number of current products, etc.

Markets, Messages and Methods (Media Plan and Calendar)

What does the Artist want its target market to think about their service? What media do they read and listen to and when? What media is most practical for the Artist to use in terms of access and affordability?

What does the Artist need to do to make the above happen? What resources are needed to accomplish the methods? Who is responsible to implement the methods?

Actions in this area should be worded as specific goals and organized into the section "Goals, Responsibilities ..." later in this plan. That section includes goals, responsibilities, dates for completion and the budgeted amount to achieve the goals.

****

6.02 Task

For this section of the Artist Business Plan, write about the marketing plan for the Artist's company.

****

Marketing Goals & Objectives

6.03
Marketing Goals and Objectives

Behind the actual goals of the Artists and the Artist's business objectives, which in themselves offer the main context for the marketing plan, will lie the "corporate mission." This mission in turn provides the context for these business objectives. This "corporate mission" can be thought of as a definition of who the Artist is and what the Artist does.

The marketing objectives must usually be based, above all, on the organization's financial objectives; converting these financial measurements into the related marketing measurements.

Within every plan, there are goals and objectives. Otherwise, there would be no reason for the plan. In addition to the goals and objectives of an Artist's Business Plan, their marketing plan also has goals and objectives.

Here are a few ideas of some marketing goals and objectives for Artists.
- Begin branding the Artist name in one new market per month
- Ensure that each recording project achieves and sustains a "Top Ten" position on industry music charts
- Release and promote two singles

and accompany music videos per month
- Create revenue streams for each album project
- Utilize a three phase marketing & promotion plan
- Hire independent record promoters in each of four separate regions of the U.S.
- Utilize teams of publicists to coordinate print advertisements, and the Artists' public appearances
- Dedicate advertisement space for non-profits organizations on all products
- Design and implement music education programs for community youth

There is a difference between marketing objectives and marketing goals. Goals and objectives are often defined and used differently within different companies or different parts of a business, but it is clear that solid goals and objectives provide a vehicle for achieving success through the process of measurement.

One of the most important parts of setting goals and objectives for an Artist is the process of reviewing and improving performance. This is done when the quantitative targets are set, tracked and then reviewed and evaluated.

Marketing Goals

Marketing goals are top-level broad goals to show how the Artist's business can benefit through various digital and analog channels. So, goals are the broad aims used to shape the marketing strategy. They describe how the Artist's marketing efforts will be effective in key areas of growing sales as well as communicating with customers.

Marketing Objectives

Marketing objectives provide a clear direction to achieve the goals. Objectives can be used to track performance against each of the Artist's targets.

Marketing Key Performance Indicators (KPI)

Key performance indicators (KPIs) are used to ensure that the objectives are being worked and the goals are being met. KPIs help business stay on track.

Set Business Marketing Plan Goals and Objectives

As part of an Artist's Business Plan, the section on Marketing Goals and Objectives is imperative.

First of all, Artists should review their business goals. Some goals deal with operational, employee, management, and business-development issues. Others deal with marketing issues, including goals such as "increase brand awareness" or "develop new markets for products and services." These business goals become goals of the marketing plan.

When Artists adopt business goals as marketing goals, they will want to add clearly defined targets and timelines. For example, Artists may expand "develop new markets for products and services" to "develop new markets to increase sales of performances by 10 percent over the upcoming one-year period."

Next, Artists need to set objectives defining how they'll achieve those marketing goals.

Each objective should specify an action and a desired outcome.

Goal/Objective	Action	Timeline	Desired Outcome
Goal	To develop new markets	Over the next one-year period	To increase sales of performances by 10 percent
Objective	Establish new media relationships.	During the first quarter	To develop relationships for potential news articles while breaking new markets.
Objective	Place ads in geographically targeted entertainment publications	In early spring	To develop summer sales to regionally targeted outdoor festivals and special events
Objective	Enhance a web presence and expand social networking	Over the first quarter	To develop customer relationships in nearby and targeted distant market areas

****

6.03 Task

For this section of the Artist Business Plan, write about the marketing goals and objectives of the Artist's company.

****

Market Analysis

6.04

Market Analysis

In this section of an Artist's Business Plan, the task is simple. Research the market before launching a new product or service. Researching a business' market has never been more important for companies, especially those related to the arts. Before an Artist starts their business or launches a new product or service, they should test the market to make sure there will be demand for what they're offering. At the beginning, perhaps the Artist will perform for family and friends to build encouragement to continue and then to eventually try to make a living in the entertainment business by performing outside their circle of friends and family.

Artists may start evaluating their potential market by doing some qualitative market research. This may be accomplished through just a few people. Artists should select a few potential customers from the

Artist's target market. They should not choose people that they know. This qualitative research has to be done in an objective and neutral way. This research consists in asking and listening to details about the Artist's idea or project.

Based on the results of the research, Artists should create a way to ask, confirm or invalidate what they have learned. There are many different types of questions but Artists have to think analyze them after the administration of the questions. This step gives Artists figures and stats about their target market.

Then the Artist needs to find the respondents. They need to survey a larger number of people from their market depending on their profile. There is no perfect number of respondents to have but the wider the target market, the more people will be needed to survey. If the target market represents only a tiny percentage of the population then the Artist doesn't need to ask many people. Finding this data (the respondents) could be quite hard because the Artist has to go beyond his or her normal channel of friends and family. It's an essential stage in the business start-up process but many entrepreneurs don't do it - not least because of the supposed time and cost.

****

6.04 Task

For this section of the Artist Business Plan, write about the market analysis of the Artist's company.

****

Market Potential

6.05
Market Potential

The principles of determining market share and market potential are the same for all geographic areas.

First determine a customer profile (who) and the geographic size of the market (how many). This is the general market potential. There are two types of customers for Artists: fans and music business professionals. Usually at the beginning of an Artist's career, fans are friends and family. The customers who are music business professionals are usually the ones who may hire the Artist for a performance. As the Artist builds their career and fans, more and more music business professionals will become more attracted to collaborating with the Artist.

Market Size
The market size is defined through the market volume and the market potential of the Artist's targeted niche. The market volume is the totality of all realized sales volume of a special market. The volume is therefore dependent on the quantity of fans and potential consumers and their ordinary demand of music, recordings and tickets to shows, etc. Furthermore, the market volume is either measured in

quantities or qualities. The quantities can be given in the number of bookings available from talent buyers and/ or promoters, or the number of music downloads or sales of physical compact discs from fans. Qualitative measuring mostly uses the sales turnover as an indicator. That means that the market price and the quantity are taken into account. This is true from sales to music industry professionals as well as sales to fans. Besides the market volume, the market potential is of equal importance. It defines the upper limit of the total demand of the Artist's products and services and takes potential venues and talent buyers as well as fans into consideration. Although the market potential is rather fictitious, it offers good values of orientation. The relation of market volume to market potential provides information about the chances of market growth for any Artist.

Knowing the number and strength of the competition (and then estimating the share of business the Artist will take from them) will provide the market potential specific to their business enterprise. For the beginning Artist, it may be easy to determine the total number of venues within their chosen market. If they do the math, they may also be able to determine the total possible performance opportunities within a given month.

The facts are sobering: the majority of Artist's businesses fail within five years of starting up. There are many reasons why Artist's businesses fail which may have nothing to do with the Artist's business or artistic skills. Although an Artist may love the art, that does not mean fans and customers will love it too. It's also possible that many of those same businesses collapsed simply because they couldn't get enough customers to buy their product or service. If an Artist cannot sell their service of providing a quality performance to talent buyers, they will attract no fans. In other words, if the Artist founded their business on a strategy of "build it and they will come" where, unfortunately, the customers never came. In fact, many Artist start-ups failed because they focused more on their product than on their potential customers.

By estimating the market share or potential, Artists will be able to determine if their markets will support their businesses by covering their costs and paying them a salary. The importance of proper promotion will help ensure the financial success of any Artist.

Generally, the market potential is the highest estimated net revenue that an Artist may realize from their enterprise. When an Artist estimates their market potential and the use the price they calculated, they will see if they will cover their costs. Also, Artists may use their market potential analysis to change their assumptions and then see if they can still cover their costs. They can either lower their expectations of the number of people who will buy from them, or they can raise their prices. Writing down the assumptions to estimate their market potential and the changes they make to those assumptions is essential. The market potential is the number of potential buyers, an average selling price and an estimate of usage for a specific period of time.

Define the market segment
Once an Artist has identified their target market of their customers, they will know who are most likely to buy from them. The target market is generally described using

demographic variables: gender, age, education and income. The market is also described using psychographic variables: lifestyle, interests and belief system variables.

Artists need to define the geographic boundaries of their market. Artists may have defined their market areas by geography, ring analysis or radius, trade area or drive-time. Most likely, Artists use geography, the simplest form of defining a market area. It defines the market area by using landmarks or some jurisdictional boundary, such as:
- Neighborhoods (based on U.S. Census block data)
- Zip codes
- City or county boundaries
- Metropolitan Statistical Areas (MSA) state (multi-state) borders

Determine Average Consumption

Next, Artists need to determine how often their target market segment may use and purchase their product or service. This figure will have a significant impact on the estimated market potential. For instance, is the Artist's product purchased frequently, occasionally or infrequently? Obviously, the more frequently the product is purchased, the larger the market potential.

The good news is that there are a variety of ways an Artist, as an entrepreneur, can conduct some market research to assess the potential demand for their product or service without spending a lot of money or hiring an expensive market research team. An Artist's product is usually a recording and an Artist's service is their ability to perform in front of a live audience.

Collaborator and Partner Analysis

Name of potential collaborator's organization
_____

Name of their product/service
_____

Common markets served
_____

Similarities between products/services
_____

Potential areas of collaboration
_____

Advantages of collaboration
_____

Disadvantages of collaboration
_____

What can the Artist do next to initiate consideration of collaboration with other organizations? What needs to happen next? Who needs to be involved? What resources are needed?

Ask the Right Questions

As a first step to determining the potential market for an Artist's new product or service, they will want to focus on asking a couple of questions, such as:
- Is this product or service going to satisfy a market need?
- Who are the potential customers, and where may they be found?
- What competition is out there? Is it direct or indirect, local, national, or international?
- How distinct is the Artist's recording or performance from what is being offered by the competition?

- Can the product stand the test of changing trends or take advantage of it before it dies out?
- At what prices are fans and/or music business professionals prepared to buy the Artist's product and/or service?
- How long before the Artist makes a profit?

Collect Feedback

Getting direct feedback via surveys or interviews can be another very effective way to gauge interest in an Artist's product or service. The easiest way to test a new business idea is by crowdsourcing the idea first. Getting the perspective of a large group that the Artist may already know may be capable of providing truthful and helpful advice. Crowdsourcing is quick, easy, and an Artist will get an array of positive and negative criticism.

Artists may also consider creating a video of their art, upload to YouTube and see the response in the comments. If there is no response, perhaps the Artist should start over.

If the Artist has written a new song, perhaps they should try to get the opinion of a music publisher before they record a demo. If the Artist is starting to perform, they should get an honest appraisal of their art by a talent buyer. If the Artist has recorded a demo and is preparing for a master release, perhaps they may want to test market the recording in certain sections of the country. There are test marketing companies who specialize in music recordings, which, for a modest application fee, evaluates the idea based on the potential market for it.

What an Artist doesn't want to do, however, is to base their decision on the opinions of their friends and family. It's a mistake to ask people they already know because they cannot be objective. Of course they're going to tell the Artist that it's a good idea.

Sell Something, Anything

While spending time conducting research and gathering information can be helpful in ascertaining the potential of an Artist's product or service, the truth is that the most valuable feedback an Artist can get is whether someone, regardless of what they say, will actually hand over money for it. It is amazing how many people will spend years and hundreds of thousands of dollars on concepts that people 'really like' without ever asking them if they would buy it. Good is not good enough in the entertainment business.

Just Do It

The truth is, in the end, research can take an Artist only so far. There is no sure way to gauge the success of a service type concept except for biting the bullet and start doing it. Many times an Artist can spend just as much trying to research something (and still not know for sure) as it would cost them to just start doing it.

****

6.05 Task

For this section of the Artist Business Plan, write about the market potential for the products and services of the Artist's company.

****

Market Segmentation

> **Market Segments**
>
> Geography
> Demographics
> Psychographics
> Lifestyle
> Life Stage

6.06
Marketing Segmentation

One of the best ways for an Artist to go out of business is to attempt to be all things to all people. Not everyone can or will be the Artist's customer. We're on a planet with more than 6 billion people on it. Many of them may enjoy the Artist's art. Many of them won't.

Identify which consumers will best fit the Artist's business by following these steps to segment a market. (The Disney Store, for example, caters to pleasing children, rather than trying to please every age.)

Evaluate which market or markets to pursue. Decide which methods will define the Artist's segments and which definitions best fit the Artist's business model. For example, a performing Artist who is based in Boston may not include Seattle as a part of their market. Another example might be the Artist who performs heavy-metal may not consider a dance club as their market. The best thing to do, at this point, is to look at the niche. What's the niche of the market? What's the niche of the Artist?

Market segments may be characterized by any of the following categories:

1. **Geography** – This pertains either to the Artist's location or the location of the Artist's target customers. This is where the product or service will be used.
2. **Demographics** – This notes the statistical characteristics of the Artist's target market, such as age, gender, style of music listened to, or income level.
3. **Psychographics** – This characterizes consumers by psychological or emotional traits, based on belief systems or personality types such as early adopters versus those that follow trends, or risk-takers versus those that are risk-averse.
4. **Lifestyle** – This is a behaviorally-based criterion, focusing on the activities and style of venue frequently visited, or the type of friends this customer may have.
5. **Life Stage** – This segment combines some of the demographic and psychographic characteristics that groups may have in common to delineate where or when the Artist's targets are in their life cycle: college and career, young families, etc.

Artists should qualify their chosen market or markets. Once they've evaluated criteria that define the market and selected possible markets to pursue, Artists need to assess the markets based on their potential for profitability to their business. When doing this, Artists should answer the following questions:

1. How large is the current market segment now?
2. Is the current market large enough to support the Artist's business?
3. How easy or difficult will it be for the Artist to reach this segment of customers?
4. How likely is it that competitors will target this segment as well?
5. Will the customer segment expand in the future?
6. Does this segment really fit with the Artist's business model? Is there easier fruit to pick?
7. Can the Artist immediately meet the needs of their customers, or will it take a significant change in direction to meet demand?
8. How difficult will it be to get the data needed to fully understand this segment, to answer these questions?

After Artists have asked these questions, they then need to gather and analyze data on their selected market. As time and budget allow, Artists may use primary and secondary research sources to build a clear picture of their target market.

****

6.06 Task

For this section of the Artist Business Plan, write about the market segmentation of the Artist's company.

****

SWOT Analysis

6.07
SWOT Analysis
*Strengths * Weaknesses * Opportunities * Threats*

A SWOT analysis is a review of an Artist's business's strengths, weaknesses, opportunities and threats all of which are related to an Artist's product (songs or recordings or merchandise) and/or services (performances or entertainment) and its related market. Many Artist managers often use SWOT to help them understand business issues of the Artist and then navigate the challenges of the business to the Artist's target markets. Many times, a SWOT analysis can uncover new and unexplored product and marketing options for the Artist within the entertainment industry.

Strengths
General strengths uncovered in a SWOT analysis could include the Artist's ability to create new songs, produce new recordings as well as the quality of their productions. In addition, marketing capability, touring logistics, working capital, management and proper use of online and offline technology can all be strengths of the Artist's company. Other strengths include the income generated

from tours, merchandising and downloads.

Weaknesses
Attitude, experience, low-quality productions, lack of capital and poor promotions could all be weaknesses for Artists and their companies. Artists who perform too much in any given target market may end up with thin crowds at each show. In addition, Artists who release their recordings only on compact disc may be overlooking the fact that many fan-customers purchase music online. Finally, some Artists are happy with the fan base they have and they don't strive to reach new followers. These are all potential weaknesses of the Artist's company.

Opportunities
Opportunities for Artists are abundant and deciding which opportunity to accept may become an issue. Artists should evaluate the growth of niche markets, new customer demographics, social networks and new technology that may benefit their career. Artists are always looking for ways to increase their income stream: royalties, bookings, merchandise and downloads. Another potential opportunity may be established through networking and building relationships within the entertainment industry.

Threats
Threats are anything that may interfere with an Artist's business strategy. Threats can be risks, and risk analysis is an ongoing process for any business. Risks that increase the need for an Artist's time or money may reduce expected business gains. One big risk in the music industry is online music piracy. There are some that think that piracy is the most destructive threat to Artists.

****
6.07 Task

For this section of the Artist Business Plan, write about the 4 sections of the SWOT analysis of the Artist's company.

****

Marketing Mix

6.08
Marketing Mix

There are four marketing mix variables and they include product, distribution, promotion and price. These 4 strategies will determine the success of the Artist's product in the marketplace. The Artist needs quality product, available to customers who have found out about the Artist via promotion where the price makes sense for them to purchase.

Marketing Mix Variables

Product
Distribution
Promotion
Price

Many marketers define the marketing mix as: putting the right product in the right place, at the right price, at the right time.

Artists need to create a product or service that fans or music industry professionals want, put it on sale at a place that those same people visit regularly, and price it at a level which matches the value they feel they get out of it; and do all that at a time they want to buy. Easy!

This idea has a lot of truth in it, however, it's a lot of hard work to find what customers want, and identifying where they do their shopping. Then to figure out how to produce the item at a price that represents value to these customers, and get it all to come together at the critical time. For Artist attracting talent buyers, this may be easy but for Artists identifying fans wants is a whole different thought. One wrong element could spell disaster. Artists could be left promoting a new performance at the end of the festival season; or publishing a new "summer" song in September, or selling an item at a price that's too high – or too low – to attract the customer's they're targeting.

The marketing mix is a good place to start when an Artist is thinking through their plans for a product or service, and it helps them avoid these kinds of mistakes.

The Four P's of Marketing

Product / Service
Place
Price
Promotion

The marketing mix and the 4Ps of marketing are often used as synonyms for each other. In fact, they are not necessarily the same thing.

A good way to understand the 4Ps is by the questions that an Artist needs to ask to define their marketing mix. Here are some questions that will help an Artist understand and define each of the four elements:

Product/Service
- What does the customer want from the Artist's product/service?
- What features does the Artist's product or service have to meet these needs?
- How and where will the customer use it?
- What does it look like? How will customers experience it?
- What is it to be called?
- How is it branded?
- How is it differentiated versus the Artist's competitors?
- What is the most it can cost to provide, and still be sold sufficiently profitably?

Place
- Where do buyers look for the Artist's product or service?
- If they look in a store, what kind? Online? Direct? Via a catalog?
- How can the Artist access the right distribution channels?
- Does the Artist need to use a sales force? Or attend trade shows? Or make online submissions? Or send samples to publishers or distributors?
- What do the Artist's competitors do, and how can the Artist learn from that and/or be different?

Price
- What is the value of the product or service to the buyer?
- Are there established price points for products or services in this area?

- Is the customer price sensitive? Will a small decrease in price gain extra market share? Or will a small increase be indiscernible, and so gain an extra profit margin?
- What discounts should be offered to trade customers, or to other specific segments of the Artist's market?
- How will the Artist's price compare with their competitors?

Promotion
- Where and when can the Artist get across their marketing messages to their target market?
- Will the Artist reach their audience by advertising in the press, or on TV, or radio, or on billboards or simply word-of-mouth? By using direct marketing? Through Public Relations? On the Internet?
- When is the best time to promote? Is there seasonality in the market? Are there any wider environmental issues that suggest or dictate the timing of the Artist's market launch, or the timing of subsequent promotions?
- How do the Artist's competitors do their promotions? And how does that influence the Artist's choice of promotional activity?

Using the 4Ps of Marketing
The model can be used to help an Artist decide how to take a new offer to market. It can also be used to test an Artist's existing marketing strategy. Whether the Artist is considering a new or existing offer, they should follow the steps below help define and improve their marketing mix.
1. Start by identifying the product or service that needs to be analyzed.
2. Now answer the 4Ps questions – as defined in detail above.
3. Try asking "why" and "what if" questions too, to challenge the offer. For example, ask why your target audience needs a particular feature. What if you drop your price by 5%? What if you offer more songs? Why sell through wholesalers rather than direct channels? What if you improve PR rather than rely on TV advertising?
4. Once a well-defined marketing mix is established, try "testing" the overall offer from the customer's perspective

****

6.08 Task

For this section of the Artist Business Plan, write about the marketing mix for the products and services of the Artist's company.

****

Branding Strategy

6.09
Branding Strategy

Many businesses have to decide when creating their brand, whether they want to brand their name or their company name, or both. This is not so hard for an Artist. Every Artist should be branding themselves. However, many times, a particular song gets its own branding. Many times an album or an Artist's tour will have its own branding as well.

Even if an Artist plans to brand their company, their art or their product, no one knows what it is until the marketing starts. Customers and fans aren't going to be any more likely to be searching for the Artist's company name as they would be searching for the Artist them self. This is why it's important for the Artist to build their brand into something customers and fans will be searching for.

For an Artist, there are distinct advantages to branding their name instead of the name of their company, art, or product. The biggest one is that Artists constantly come up with brilliant ideas. If they lock themselves into a company name then decide later to change their musical direction, they may have to rebrand and start from square one. On the other hand, if the Artist brands their name, they can build credibility (while co-branding the art or product) and then take that credibility with them as they grow on their entrepreneurial journey.

An Artist's brand is an asset. If they handle it right, it will support them through all of their future endeavors and projects.

The bottom line is, the Artist's focus and keywords may change, but their name never will. Many times an individual in a band will also start branding their name. This idea may help the Artist as each brand contributes to the success of the other.

The varied methods that are used for the promotion of an Artist's brand will have a direct impact on the sales of their products, such as recordings, as well as sales of their services, such as their performances. Since that is the case, an understanding of the varied brand promotion strategies is necessary for the Artist to succeed with their business.

An Artist may have the best product in the market, but without people being aware of that product, there are going to be no sales. That is why, having a product that is of the highest quality is not the only important factor, but the ways in which an Artist promotes the product is also just as important. Along with the regular factors that are used in the promotion of an Artist's product or service, one very crucial factor is that of brand promotion as a means of product promotion. The brand forms the identity of a product or service. It is classified as having a distinct name, symbol, logo and a catch phrase (ideally). For example, The Beatles are a brand, whereas the recordings, performances and merchandise are the products that fall under this brand. When most people see The Beatles brand, they see quality: quality in the songs, quality in the performance of the songs and quality in the recordings of those songs.

Brand Promotion Objectives
It is not merely with an objective of increasing sales that strategies for brand promotion are brought into play for an Artist. There are other variables and objectives that drive the brand as well. Brand promotion leads to awareness about the varied products of the Artist that fall under that brand as well as ensuring customer and fan loyalty.

It has been observed that a promotion of the brand leads to a direct promotion of the varied products as well. In that way, Artists and their companies, do not necessarily have to advertise and promote each individual product, but an overall promotion of the Artist's brand will lead to a promotion of the products automatically. This is why it is seen that famous Artist brands are more popular and ensure more sales than lesser known brands. It has also been observed that fans and customers who become loyal to a particular brand or Artist will generally opt to buy the same brand and the products that fall under it. If a fan discovers that their favorite Artist has a new product available, the fan may purchase it without hearing it first. In this case, the fan trusts the brand as being the type of quality that they have previously experienced from the Artist and their brand and purchase the product based on that trust and credibility.

Branding Promotion Objectives

- To dispel information about the Artist's brands
- To making the public aware of the factors that differentiates the brand
- To strategize a way to increase the demand of the brand
- To establish brand equity (The power that the brand adds to the product / service)
- To stabilize sales and survive market fluctuations
- To overcome competitive companies' marketing strategies
- To build a good image in the market

Brand Promotion Methods
Artists are probably aware of traditional marketing and advertising such as advertising on TV, radio, newspapers, or through flyers and posters. Most of these advertising methods, Artists are already familiar with. But there are some methods that make use of an indirect way of advertising and brand promotion: that being the usage of certain brand promotion activities and techniques. Here are a few:

1. **Sponsoring Events**: Sponsoring social events is a great way to promote an Artist's brand. Many Artists contribute their talent to a good cause. Equating brands with a good cause, automatically lends a positive vibe to the Artist's brand. When an Artist performs at a benefit concert, the Artist is, in actuality, sponsoring the event. Event promoters call this a trade-sponsor: someone who trades their product or service for promotion. Many times an Artist may perform for free in the hopes of attracting and promoting their brand, and hence, create new fans who become customers, who then purchase the products and services of the Artist.

2. **Offers, Discounts and More**: Offering discounts and free downloads associated under an Artist's music and brand is a great way of ensuring not only an increase in sales, but also in harboring a positive image in the eyes of the fan-customer. Many times an Artist has a page on their website offering a sample of their latest recording and then promotes it during their live performances. Other times an Artist may provide a web page with a free download of a recent recording available on it.

3. **Public Relations Events**: Public relations is a branch of promotion that

employs another indirect way of advertising. For example, let's say the Artist's brand is holding a re-mix competition. Fans have an opportunity for direct involvement with the Artist. This strategy might seem unrelated, but the brand has been able to offer direct involvement and begin the growth of viral marketing as these fans may be inclined to have their friends and family listen to their re-mix. Hence, the Artist may gain new fans and customers by promoting the Artist's brand.

4. **High Quality Products**: One of the best ways that an Artist can ensure brand promotion is to release only high-quality products as a part of their brand. High quality products ensure that there is word-of-mouth publicity. This form of publicity makes a maximum impact to the general public. Artists should release only quality products. If the Artist is not 100% proud of their product or service, they should not release it.

A review of these brand promotion strategies provides the Artist with the kind of factors that are required in ensuring that their brand becomes popular and thereby helps in promoting the Artist's products and services.

****

6.09 Task

In this part of the Artist's Business Plan, write down the various methods that the Artist will utilize to enhance their brand. Include advertising and promotion ideas into the plan.

****

Credibility

6.10
Credibility

How credible is the Artist? Put another way, how much do the Artist's fans and collaborators trust them as an Artist. Do they trust the music as being fresh and original? Do the fans trust what the Artist advocates, and even what they say? Do the fans trust that the artist will deliver a grand performance if they buy a ticket to the Artist's show? Fans who believe that their Artists are credible are more likely to take their music seriously.

Credibility may be difficult for some Artists because it takes work to establish. It requires self-knowledge, boldness, and persistence in demonstrating behaviors that earn the trust of fans and customers. The good news is the results are well worth it. Credibility correlates with perceived stature of an Artist and affords that Artist more leverage. In addition, these benefits spill over into other areas of the Artist's career.

So how does an Artist know how much credibility they have, and more importantly, how they may build more of it?

There are five basic rules for Artists to boost credibility with their fans and collaborators:

1. **Know Oneself** - Most Artists with credibility problems are unaware of them because they have been blinded by their own good intentions. An honest self-assessment of an Artist's actions (and how well they reflect their intentions) can help establish consistency between what they say and what they do. For extra insight, ask others to provide input on the Artist as a performer, songwriter, or recording Artist. This kind of feedback can be a powerful first step in building credibility, and in overcoming fears about dealing with certain issues head-on.

2. **Be Bold** – Credible Artists practice observable behaviors that demonstrate their commitment to their art. This often means making decisions that go against the status quo. Artists need to show a willingness to admit their mistakes to others as well as give honest information about their art and/or performance. Even if it is not well received, Artists should ask for ideas on how to improve their performances and their recordings.

3. **Set for Success** – Even the best Artists struggle with setting performance expectations in today's "more with less" environment. Too often, priorities perceived as having higher value or more urgency can cause good team members to inadvertently push their activities aside. To make the Artist's expectations credible, Artists need to set targets with a sufficient understanding of all the demands placed on their team. Without it, collaborators who already have full workloads may perceive the Artist's goals and objectives as unrealistic. Artists should work at developing a clear appreciation of where quality performances fits into strategic objectives, gather information on the state of their organization, and deal realistically and actively with competing priorities. The more information an Artist has, the better they can adjust the way they allocate resources and respond to fan and team member needs.

4. **Be Curious** – There's no substitute for knowing what you're talking about. However, knowledge comes through experience. Many otherwise credible Artists get into trouble by thinking that they have to be experts, especially the more successful they become. The reality is that Artists do not need to have all the answers. As a business owner, one of the jobs is to establish optimum conditions for meeting the company targets and goals.

5. **Don't Lose It** – Artist should be vigilant about maintaining the credibility they earn. Many fans and business environments are unforgiving, and credibility that was difficult to foster can be lost very quickly. Fans can be finicky. This is true with fans as well as team members. Vigilance in showing the Artist's credibility gives them leverage; as they gain trust, they earn more benefit of the doubt from those around them.

Not having to be concerned about one's credibility frees up an enormous amount of energy. Being in integrity also causes one to use the freed up energy with greater directness and effectiveness.

An Artist who enjoys the benefit of the doubt as a result of earning credibility makes everything else easier. They don't have to be perfect. Artists should demonstrate integrity in all dealings with others. Integrity is essential to credibility.

> **Steps in Building Credibility**
> 1. Know yourself
> 2. Be Bold
> 3. Set Up for Success
> 4. Be curious
> 5. Don't lose it

The Cost of Not Being, Credible
It should be obvious that if an Artist is not actually credible, it'll be discovered at some point. The Artist may then be considered less reliable, less attractive, and less "cool." If an Artist doesn't have integrity or if they lose it may cost them, big time! Fakes are short-lived in the entertainment business. No one likes a fake.

But the cost of not looking credible pales in comparison to the cost of losing credibility within the Artist them self. The cost of self-doubt and not being positive will show in the music, the recordings and the live performances. In terms of self-respect and in terms of increased anxiety, stress, and the damage to one's health, being credible is one more "high priority" item for any Artist.

Fake personalities and actions always tend to show at some time. Acting consistent with integrity and being credible is a tremendous benefit to the Artist via the fans and the sales generated from tickets and recordings. If an Artist keeps on practicing being credible, they can free up some energy and, therefore, generate other benefits such as being fearless. This will immensely change the quality of the Artist's life.

****

6.10 Task

For this section of the Artist Business Plan, write about the creditability for the products and services of the Artist's company.

****

> **Product Testing**

6.11
Product Testing

How does an Artist know if their new song, video or audio recording is commercially viable? How does an Artist know if their new live show will attract any talent buyers? Remember, this is the music BUSINESS. If the Artist's content is not commercially viable, the Artist will starve and therefore, no more art will be produced. Product testing is the way for an Artist to evaluate their art. Many Artists do this by performing a new song at a gig and asking for audience responses. Others don't care and do whatever they want. Which of the two do you think is more successful for an Artist?

Also called consumer testing or comparative testing, this is a process of measuring the extent to which an Artist's product fulfills the needs of the fan, often in comparison to other Artist's products which may be similar. The theory is that since the advent of mass production, Artists produce branded products which they promote and advertise within some Artistic and technical standard. A market researcher usually hired by the Artist or record label tests the recordings in various markets to see how listeners respond and to determine the potential for the product to sell. If and when the testing shows a positive result, then the Artist may choose to continue marketing the content.

Product testing is all about risk reduction. It shows an Artist the potential problems before they occur. Yes, there are costs involved, but the costs could be much higher if the product is not tested. What if thousands of products are manufactured and consumers don't like the product.

Product testing seeks to ensure that fans and potential consumers are aware of an Artist's products, but more importantly, if the quality is enough for a fan to ultimately purchase the product. Yes, there are plenty of quality songs, recordings and merch which customers have a choice to purchase. They understand the value of an Artist's art and which ones to spend their money on. If a fan thinks an Artist's product is inferior, they may abandon the Artist. They may buy another Artist's music, or attend a performance of another Artist's show.

Term
Product testing is any process by means of which a researcher measures a product's performance, quality, safety and compliance with established standards within a customer's mind.

Industry Roles
The most common industry role in the music business is to provide products (songs, recordings, live performances and merch) according to industry standards. As in any industry, some standards will be voluntary such as the subjective opinion of certain radio station music directors. Everyone is the entertainment industry wants to know how the Artist or how the Artist's music will make them money. A music director at commercial radio station, for example, wants to know if the song is strong enough for listeners to stay tuned to the station. If it is not, the recording of the song will not be played.

Product Life Cycle Stages

The product life cycle has 4 very clearly defined stages, each with its own characteristics that mean different things for Artists. Smart Artists know this and anticipate the life cycle of their particular products and performances. That is why Artists have different tours, new song releases and updated t-shirts, for example.

1. **Introduction Stage** – This stage of the cycle could be the most expensive for an Artist launching a new product. The size of the market for the product may be small, which means sales may be low, although they may increase depending on the promotion and especially the quality of the product. On the other hand, the cost of things like researching a new market to perform, which media outlets might be receptive, consumer testing, and the marketing needed to launch the product can be very high. This is especially true if the market is flooded

with similar Artists or songs.

2. **Growth Stage** – The growth stage is typically characterized by a strong growth in sales and profits, and because the Artist can start to benefit from economies of scale in production. The Artist's profit margins, as well as the overall amount of profit, will increase. This makes it possible for the Artist's businesses to invest more money in the promotional activity to maximize the potential of this growth stage.

3. **Maturity Stage** – During the maturity stage, the Artist's product is established and the aim is now to maintain the market share they have built up. This is probably the most competitive time for most Artists. They will need to invest wisely in any marketing they undertake. They also need to consider any product modifications or improvements to the production process which might give them a competitive advantage.

4. **Decline Stage** – Eventually, the market for an Artist's product will start to shrink, and this is what's known as the decline stage. Although, the life of a song may be decades, the life of a particular product will decline. This shrinkage could be due to the market becoming saturated (i.e. all the customers who will buy the product have already purchased it), or because the fans are switching to a different type of product or Artist. While this decline may be inevitable, it may still be possible for Artists to make some profit on that particular product by switching to less-expensive production methods and/or cheaper markets.

What Products are to be Tested?
- Radio listeners reaction to a new recording
- Performance of a new song
- Design of a new t-shirt
- Response to promotional efforts

Test Markets
A test market, in the field of business and marketing for any Artist, is a geographic region or demographic group used to gauge the viability of a product or service in the mass market prior to a wide scale roll-out. The criteria used to judge the acceptability of a test market region or group includes:

1. A population that is demographically similar to the proposed target market.
2. Relative isolation from densely populated media markets so that advertising to the test audience can be efficient and economical.

Record labels do this as a regular course of business. Successful Artists should do the same.

The test market ideally aims to duplicate "everything" - promotion and distribution as well as "product" - on a smaller scale. The technique replicates, typically in one area, what is planned to occur in a national launch. The results should be carefully monitored, so that they can be extrapolated to projected national results. The area may be any one of the following:
- Radio and Television area
- Internet online test
- New market for performances

Test Market Decisions:
- Which test market?
- What is to be tested?
- How long a test?
- What are the success criteria?

Test markets can be used by Artists to test specific elements of a new product's marketing mix; possibly the version of the product itself, the promotional message and media budget, the distribution channels and the price. In this case, several "matched' test markets (usually small ones) may be used, each testing different marketing mixes. For example, an Artist may test promote the same product in two markets in two completely different ways to determine the better strategy to use for future marketing.

Risk Versus Time

Most of the stages of testing, which are the key parts of the new "product" process, are designed to reduce risk; to ensure that the product or service will be a success. However, all of them take time. When to enter a market with a new product should, in any case, be a conscious decision for every Artist.

Why New Products Fail
- Lack of differentiating advantage
- Poor marketing plan
- Poor timing
- Target market too small
- Poor product quality
- No access to market

New Products?
- New song
- New recording
- New album
- New live show
- New coffee mug or t-shirt

Disadvantages to Test Marketing

1. **Duplication** - Even the largest test market is not totally representative of the national market, and the smaller ones may introduce gross distortions. Test market results therefore have to be treated with reservations, in exactly the same way as other market research. Columbus, Ohio and Cleveland, Ohio are two cities in close proximity to each other and each has a similar size population. However, the two cities are drastically different when it comes to marketing. Cleveland is much more blue-collar and ethnic. The people of Columbus are more upwardly mobile and younger.

2. **Effectiveness** - In many cases the major part of the investment has already been made (recording and rehearsing, for example) before the `product' is ready to be test marketed. Therefore, the reduction in risk may be minimal; and not worth the delays involved.

3. **Cost** - Although the main objective of test markets is to reduce the amount of investment put at risk, they may still involve significant costs.

It has to be recognized that the development and launch of almost any new product or service carries a considerable element of risk. Indeed, in view of the on-going dominance of the existing Artist brands, it has to be questioned whether the risk involved in most major launches is justifiable.

> **Product Development Phases**
>
> New Product Strategy
> Development
> Product Screen and Evaluation
> Business Analysis
> Test Marketing
> Commercialization
> Congruency
> Recognizability
> Distinctiveness
> Flexibility
> Likeability
> Own Ability

Product Development Phases

1. New Product Strategy Development

Only a few songs are good enough to reach commercialization. Songs can be generated by chance, or by systematic approach. Artists need a purposeful, focused effort to identify new ways to serve their chosen market.

2. Product Screening and Evaluation

The constraints identified at the beginning of the project are also important screening factors. A product may be dropped for many reasons: it does not meet the Artist's requirements of quality, there is not sufficient money to develop or to produce it, or the initial feedback from fans is negative. The factors used in screening should be as objective as possible, but sometimes Artists must make subjective decisions for effective evaluation.

3. Business Analysis
- Does the new product idea contribute to sales, costs and profits?
- Does the Artist's new product fit into the current product mix?
- What kind of competitive changes can the Artist anticipate?
- How will these changes effect sales, etc.?
- Are the internal resources adequate?
- What is the cost and time line of new promotions, travel, etc.?
- Is financing available?
- Are there any synergies with distribution channels?

4. Test Marketing

There are a few things that test marketing can achieve for any Artist.
- It can observe actual consumer behavior.
- Limited introduction in geographical areas chosen to represent intended market
- It can determine the reaction of probable buyers
- Launch a sample of a new Marketing Mix
- Once results are determined, Artist can modify the product, modify the marketing plan or drop the product

Alternatively, Artist may want to use a simulated test market. For example: Offer free downloads to fans at the Artist's gigs. In order to get the free download, fans may be required to provide an e-mail address. Artists can now get feedback from the fan about the quality of the download or stream.

5. Commercialization

The commercialization of an Artists product or performances corresponds to Introduction Stage of the Product Life

Cycle. The plans for full-scale marketing and manufacturing must be refined and settled. At this point, Artists need to analyze the results of the test market to determine any changes in the marketing mix. In addition, this is where a lot of money can be spent on advertising, personnel etc. So it's a good idea to prepare. Combined with capital expenditures to record the music or rehearse the performance can make commercialization very expensive.

6. Congruency
The congruency of an Artist's product or service is how well does the sound fit the brand?

7. Recognizability
How easily can the Artist, their sound or their logo be recognized?

8. Distinctiveness
How well does the sound cut through the clutter?

9. Flexibility
How much can the songs, sound or live performances be adapted?

10. Likeability
How much do fans like it?

11. Own ability
How much of it is controlled?

****

6.11 Task

For this section of the Artist Business Plan, write about the plan for product testing for the products and services of the Artist's company.

****

Target Marketing Strategy

6.12
Target Marketing Strategy

A target market is a group of fans and customers to whom an Artist has decided to aim its marketing efforts, via its niche, and ultimately its goods, services, performances, and recordings of music. A well-defined target market is the first element that an Artists needs for their marketing strategy.

Target markets are the specific groups of people whom the Artist will want to benefit with their products and services. The target markets are determined the Artist's strategic goals strategies.

Target Markets
It's best to know and understand what the Artist's customer base is and target market for the product or service. If the Artist has a variety of products on the line, it can be beneficial to separate them into categories and target specific demographic groups for each category.

Target markets are groups of individuals that are separated by distinguishable and noticeable aspects. This is similar to market segmentation as defined above. Here are a few ways to determine a target market:
1. **Geographic Segmentations** - addresses (their location – both on

and off-line)
2. **Demographic / Socioeconomic Segmentation** - (gender, age, income, occupation, education, household size, and stage in the family life cycle)
3. **Psychographic Segmentation** - (similar attitudes, values, and lifestyles)
4. **Behavioral Segmentation** - (occasions, degree of loyalty)
5. **Product-related Segmentation** - (relationship to a product)

Strategies for Reaching Target Markets

Marketers have outlined four basic strategies to satisfy target markets:
1. undifferentiated marketing or mass marketing
2. differentiated marketing
3. concentrated marketing
4. direct marketing.

Mass Marketing
This is a market coverage strategy in which an Artist decides to ignore market segment differences and go after the whole market with one offer. This type of marketing offers a product to a wide audience. The idea is to broadcast a message that will reach the largest number of people possible. Traditionally mass marketing has focused on radio, television and newspapers as the medium used to reach this broad audience.

Differentiated Marketing Strategy
A differentiated marketing strategy is one where an Artist decides to provide separate offerings to different market segment that it targets. It is also called multi-segment marketing and is clearly seen that it tries to appeal to multiple segments in the market. Each segment is targeted uniquely as the Artist provides unique benefits to different segments. It increases the total sales but at the expense of increase in the cost of investing in the business. For example, an Artist may charge one price for a performance in a local venue and a different price to a concert promoter offering a series of gigs.

Concentrated Marketing
A strategy which targets very defined and specific segments of the consumer population is considered concentrated marketing. It is particularly effective for Artists with limited resources as the Artist may not have the funds for mass marketing, mass distribution and mass advertising. There may be no increase in the total profits of the sales as the Artist targets just one segment of the market.

Direct Marketing
For Artists and their sales teams, one way to reach out to target markets is through direct marketing. This is done by utilizing an Artist's database based on the defined segmentation profiles. Their database is updated at every gig as new fans and customers add their name to the Artist's fan club or contact sheet. The database can be filtered to specific target customers such as names, e-mail, phone and geographic market or venue where the information was gathered.

Whether an Artist is selling recorded music or live performances, Artists need to understand their customer if they want to maximize their sales. Who is the Artist selling to? Why should these customers purchase the Artist's product? What does the customer stand to gain? (Customers are further defined in their own section of the Artist Business Plan.)

Questions to Ask before Determining an Artist's Target Market

The better an Artist understands their customer, the faster their business will grow. New Artists often struggle to define their target market and set their sights too broadly.

Who would pay for the Artist's product or service? Is there a reason why an Artist feels that fan-customers may purchase their recordings or tickets to their shows? What about music industry customers who may purchase the services of an Artist for bookings and performances?

Who has already bought from the Artist? To refine both the Artist's target marketing and their pricing strategy, review who has already bought the Artist's product or service in the past. Artists can gain valuable insights by releasing the product in a test phase and letting potential consumers speak with their wallets.

Is the Artist overestimating their reach? It's easy for an Artist to assume that most people will want their goods and services. After all, the Artist believes in their art and why shouldn't everyone else? Rather than making assumptions, reach out to groups of potential customers to get a more realistic picture of the Artist's audience and narrow the marketing efforts. Artists can conduct surveys or do man-on-the-street type interviews in clubs. Sometimes Artists get so passionate about their brand and how good it is that they overestimate the market size.

****

6.12 Task

The more the Artist knows about its customers, the better they will be at serving them. At this point, write down a customer profile, or description of each of the groups of customers (or target markets). Consider, for example, their major needs, how they prefer to have their needs met, where they are and where they prefer to have their needs met and demographics information (their age ranges, family arrangement, education levels, income levels, typical occupations, major interested, etc.).

****

Pricing Policy

6.13
Pricing Policy

As a part of marketing, pricing is the process of determining what an Artist will receive in exchange for its product or service. Since an Artist has two types of customers, fans and entertainment industry professionals, the prices of its good and services may vary. In addition, Artists have both goods and services. The goods are the songs, the recordings, the CDs. The service is their live performance.

Pricing Analysis

What's the current fee for the Artist's product / service?
How much is it costing the Artist to provide this product / service?

Are is the Artist recovering costs to produce and provide the product / service? Is the current price affordable to customers?

> **Factors that Determine Price**
>
> 1. Industry standards such as downloads via I-tunes or mechanical royalties
>
> 2. Promotional consideration such as performing for free at a major festival
>
> 3. Manufacturing cost such as CDs and T-shirts
>
> 4. Competition in the performance market, the songwriting market as well as the recording market
>
> 5. Market condition such as consumer tastes in music or the issues with pirated recordings
>
> 6. Brands with bigger names may be able to charge a higher price
>
> 7. Quality of products and service

Is the Artist's pricing competitive? What should be the pricing structure that used for this product/service (for example, performance deposits, deferred payments from distributors, etc.)?

What does the Artist need to do to make that happen? What major steps must occur? What must be developed? Who should be contacted? What resources might the Artist need?

Pricing is a fundamental aspect of financial modeling and is one of the four Ps of the marketing mix. (The other three aspects are product, promotion, and place.) Price is the only revenue generating element amongst the four Ps, the rest being cost centers. However, the other Ps of marketing enables price increases to further drive greater revenue and profits for the Artist.

One of the most difficult, yet important, issues an Artist must decide as an entrepreneur is how much to charge for their performances, their recordings and their talent. While there is no single right way to determine the pricing of an Artist's good and services, there are guidelines that may help with determining the right strategy.

> **A well-chosen price should do three things:**
>
> 1. Achieve the financial goals of the Artist's company (i.e. profitability)
>
> 2. Fit the realities of the marketplace (Will customers buy at that price?)
>
> 3. Support a product's positioning and be consistent with the marketing mix

Positioning

How is the Artist planning to position their product or service in the market? Is pricing going to be a key part in that positioning? If the Artist is a new act and has very few fans, then setting their price too high may dissuade potential talent buyers to hire them for an upcoming performance. If the Artist is a more established act and set their price too low, then they may be losing potential income.

Demand Curve

How will pricing affect demand? If an Artist charges too much for a performance, many talent buyers will look for other acts. If an Artist charges too much for a compact disc or t-shirt, they may not achieve any sales.

In this business, if the quality is not apparent, sometimes an Artist cannot give away their product or service. Remember, good is not good enough. Even if an Artist lets fans download their music for free, that in itself, does not guarantee they will purchase a ticket to attend the Artist's show. On the other hand, if the Artist is the hottest band in the land and every concert promoter wants to book them, there are only so many days in the year. The Artist's performance price may be determined by the demand of their availability.

> **Types of Pricing**
>
> Fixed Pricing
> Cost-Plus Pricing
> Demand Based pricing
> Value Based Pricing
> Competitor Indexing
> Dynamic Pricing

Types of Pricing
- **Fixed Pricing** – Artists can sell music downloads for one flat fee. They may also book their performance for one set fee.
- **Cost-Plus Pricing** – Artists may charge a performance fee for a certain amount plus expenses such as travel and lodging
- **Demand Based Pricing** – How much is the customer will to pay? That's the price.
- **Value-Based Pricing** – Many Artists will lower their performance fee if multiple dates are booked
- **Competitor Indexing** – Artists that want to price competitively will monitor their competitors' prices

and adjust accordingly.
- **Dynamic Pricing** – Artists may set highly flexible prices for products or services based on current market demands, such as the date of the performance and who else is on the bill.

Elements of Pricing
How much can an Artist charge for their product or service? This question is a typical starting point for discussions about pricing. However, a better question for an Artist to ask is: How much do fans and customers value the products, services, and other intangibles that the Artist may have available for sale?

Pricing Questions
- What are the pricing objectives?
- Should there be a single price or multiple pricing?
- Should prices change in various geographical areas?
- Should there be quantity discounts?
- What prices are competitors charging?
- What image does the price to convey?
- What are customer price sensitivity and elasticity issues?
- How flexible can the Artist be in pricing?

Price Is Determined By What Someone Is Willing To Pay For It

Price vs. Promotion
Many times an Artist must consider whether to perform for free in return for promotion. Sometimes this is a good strategic plan and other times it's an excuse for promoters to not have to pay an Artist for their performance services. Artists are regularly asked to perform for free for events sponsored by non-profit companies or for select causes.

In addition, consider a major performer asking an Artist to perform as an opening act on their entire tour. It may cost the Artist time and money but, in return, they may get thousands of new fans and customers.

From the marketer's point of view, an efficient price is a price that is very close to the maximum that customers are prepared to pay. A good pricing strategy would be the one which could balance between the price floor (the price below which the Artist ends up with losses) and the price ceiling (the price be which the Artist experiences a no-demand situation.) If the price is too low, the Artist may lose money. If the price is too high, the Artist may also lose because no one will purchase the Artist's products or services.

****

6.13 Task

In this section of the Artist Business Plan, consider and write down the pricing structure for the Artist. Include prices for performances as well as prices for recordings. Be realistic.

****

Packaging Strategy

6.14 Packaging Strategy

Product packaging plays an important role in the marketing mix and smart Artists know this. As a part of an Artist's Business Plan and Marketing Plan, the design and presentation of packaging plays an important role as a medium in the marketing mix.

> **Criterion Affecting a Packaging Strategy**
> - **in promotion campaigns**
> - **as a pricing criterion**
> - **in defining the character of new products**
> - **as a setter of trends**
> - **as an instrument to create brand identity**

A central conviction held by the packaging industry is that the shopper wants to receive stimulation for the buying decision he or she is making when standing in front of the Artist's merch table. Many times fans and customers often prefer this to other forms of communication and branding.

There's an old saying: "You can lead a horse to water but you can't make it drink." This is a perfect packaging metaphor, because the fundamental truth is that the final purchasing decision is made at the actual point of sale: whether online or in person.

Many Artists make the mistake of thinking that advertising and sales promotion is what drives the customer's decision-making process and, as a result, this is the area that usually commands the greatest amount of deliberation and debate. The truth is, no matter how much time and money an Artist spends on promoting their recording and/or performances or how much effort their sales team puts into getting bookings for their gigs, if the package fails to deliver at point of sale because it doesn't look good then all that investment spent elsewhere may be largely wasted.

So how does an Artist make the most of all that advertising and promotional work? How do they get people reaching out for their product on the stores shelves or merch table? How do they get talent buyers and concert promoters to pick up the phone and book the band?

Packaging Strategy Tips
1. Make the product stand out
First of all, Artists have to recognize that their products such as compact discs, downloads or t-shirts are competing for a few short seconds of attention. In any one moment, there are thousands of other Artist's products and services available to music listeners worldwide. The first and most important rule, therefore, is to get the Artist's product noticed. It must stand out rather than blend in.

2. Break with Convention
I once received a promo kit from an Artist

that was enclosed in a plastic champagne bottle. This was completely different from the hundreds that come in the mail each day with the standard brown envelope packaging. Shape is the first thing the human eye recognizes, so unique packaging shapes are a great way to help an Artists product stand out.

3. Products with Purpose
Many people have a growing desire to support real brands with real beliefs and values. What this means is that brands, both large and small, need to have a clear purpose beyond price. For example, a talent buyer for an ecology-friendly concert might be interested in hiring a musician who's "green." If an Artist has a purpose, their recordings and performances might get special attention.

4. Add Personality
Part of the image of an Artist is building on the idea of leveraging authenticity. Part of the packaging plan must reflect the image of an Artist. The personality of the packaging shows an image of the Artist. An example is seen by Artists who fall into the niche of heavy metal who use images of fire in their promotions. Similarly, Artists who have a flowery sound, many times will use light watercolor artwork in their packaging.

5. Feel-Good Factor
Anything an Artist can do to make their designs resonate with their anticipated customer will give them an advantage. Packaging that provides a way for fans and customers to feel the image that the Artist is trying to portray, makes the job of selling much easier.

6. Keep it simple
With so much to say about an Artist's product or service, cut back on the amount of packaging. The key is to keep things simple. Going back to the principle of 'standout', Artists should make sure they don't compromise legibility by overcomplicating their presentation with too many messages. In a one-second world, less is definitely more.

In this section of the Artist Business Plan, consider and write down the packaging strategy for the Artist.

****

6.14 Task

In this section of the Artist Business Plan, consider and write down the packaging strategy for the Artist.

****

Online Marketing Plan

6.15
Online Marketing Plan
There are many Artists who are still not using basic online tools to market themselves. Many online marketing tools are free and Artists who avoid this in their marketing strategy are foolish.

However, sending out friend's requests on social networks is not without merit, but is it realistically a wise use of an Artist's time? Perhaps not. If an Artist insists on using this strategy, they should hire an unpaid intern or enlist a friend/sibling in high school to do it for them. On the other hand, there are numerous ways to productively market an Artist online.

A planned, organized Internet marketing campaign is not hard to coordinate, does not need to cost a great deal of money and can generate traffic and sales for the Artist. It takes a bit of research and a solid knowledge of the target customer, but Artists can plan and implement a simple online marketing campaign in the space of a dedicated day.

Website

Websites have become a crucial part of Artist promotion and marketing, and anyone that is serious about their endeavor into the music business should have one. It is the best and easiest way for labels, publishers plus current and potential fans to find an Artist. Websites are also an excellent outlet for selling merchandise and music. Many Artists implement flash, dynamic menus, their performance calendar, guest books, CD sales as well as setting up a personal merchandise shop.

Search Engines

Search engine optimization (SEO) is designing, writing, and coding (in HTML) an Artist's complete website so that there is a great possibility that their web pages will appear at the leading pages of search engine queries for their chosen key phrases. Target the search engines that will give the Artist's website the most targeted traffic. Google is currently the most popular search engine. Wouldn't it be great if a link to the Artist's website showed up on the first page of an customer's inquiry.

Popular Online Search Engines and Directories

AltaVista
AOL Search
Bing
Fast Search
Google
HotBot
Inktomi
LookSmart
Lycos
MSN Search
Netscape Search
Overture
Yahoo

Artists should have a website capable to get indexed nicely by Google, Inktomi, and Yahoo. The two search engines and 1 directory differ in the way they index web sites. Google does not use meta-tag content for relevancy. Inktomi at the moment utilizes meta-tags. And Yahoo is a directory.

Search engine optimization and other marketing approaches (banner advertising, internet copywriting, becoming listed in Yahoo, posting to discussion groups, and so on) are not substitutes for a website with strong content and fantastic layout.

Search engine optimization is a means of helping fans and customers find and uncover the Artist's internet site. It is a highly specialized advertising and marketing tool.

Blogs
Start A Blog – Artists might consider to once or twice a week write a paragraph or two about what they have been doing, what they're thinking, what they like, what they don't like, what they want to do, what influences them, share some performance stories, ask questions, answer questions, post videos of their band or them self, share unreleased material, and engage with fans. Artists should link their blog to their website and a place where their music can be purchased.

Artists may build fans by establishing relationships with other bloggers. Comment on their blogs and link back. To do this, pick 10 or 20 music blogs that the Artist enjoys and which write about music similar to the type that the Artist produces. Comment about something they post. These comments should be genuine and relevant to the post. To avoid problems, Artists should make sure they leave the URL for their website but should not self-promote them self of or their music at all. These comments are about the blog, not about the Artist. Their purpose is to make these bloggers aware that the Artist exists and that they are an interesting person / band.

E-Mail
E-mail is one of the earliest forms of online marketing since the invention of the World Wide Web. According to the experts, if an Artist wants to improve their e-mail marketing results, they must increase the relevance of their messages. Here are some tips.

1. Be relevant
The greatest capability of e-mail marketing technology is segmentation and personalization. Making e-mails as relevant as possible to each recipient is the most critical "must do." Marketing e-mail messages are competing for attention with an increasing number of messages in the subscriber's inbox. Those that resonate most, through personalized subject lines, offers, articles, product showcases, and follow-up e-mails based on recipient activity, will be the clear winners.

2. Minimize Presentation Issues
With a wealth of spam filtering systems and e-mail client software in the marketplace, Artists need to send pre-campaign test messages to discover any potential delivery problems before sending the actual message to real recipients. This also helps the Artist to monitor results after each message. In addition, this will also help identify ISP blocking, filtering and blacklisting problems.

3. Consider Blocked Images and Preview Pane Usage
E-mail messages need to be designed to deliver maximum information in the top 2 to 4 inches of screen space. This will increase their creative use of HTML fonts and colors while relying less on the use of images that ISPs may be blocking.

4. Optimize Early the E-mail Relationship
When a new fan or customer is acquired, Artists should engage their new subscribers immediately. Include a welcome message upon confirmation, followed by the current newsletter or promotion. E-mail an offering of an exclusive music download just for newcomers. It is also important to manage subscribers'

expectations from the start by adequately explaining the e-mail program's value proposition, frequency, type of content, and privacy policy.

5. Get Permission
Artists should review permission practices across their web site and at all customer contact points. Permission-based e-mail is becoming the acknowledged best practice throughout the industry.

6. Double Opt-In
Double opt-in means that once a subscriber opts in to join an Artist's e-mail list, they must confirm that they want to receive messages. This prevents the Artists from buying e-mail lists or adding anyone to their list without permission. It also prevents pranksters from adding others to the Artist's list, which would open the Artist up to accusations of spamming. (Yes, weirdly, this does happen.) Double opt-in is also sometimes called confirmed opt-in.

Auto-Responder
Many Artists set-up an auto-responder on their e-mail account. When a fan or customer e-mails an Artist, they receive an automatic response to their communication from the Artist. Artists should make it personal and friendly, but not try to trick anyone that the Artist is individually sending to the e-mail inquiry. The purpose is to create a sense of friendly connection and also promote the fan to join the Artist's e-mail list as well as providing a link to the Artist's website. In the response, always provide a link to the artist's website.

****

6.15 Task

****

Social Media Plan

6.16 Social Media Plan

Another important aspect of the Marketing Plan of an Artist Business Plan is the prospect of utilizing social media to enhance an Artist's branding via the World Wide Web. Artists are fully aware of the benefits of the Internet for music downloads and sales, but the promotional aspects should not be overlooked.

Many Artists don't have the capacity to use multiple social media outlets for their business. If that is the case, it's important to focus on using only one or two and learning to use them well.

Artists should concentrate on the social media sites that their target market is using. Different social media appeals to different audiences. LinkedIn, for instance, is the biggest network of business professionals; Google+ (so far) is mostly used by young male students and geeks; Pinterest users are mainly women. Both Facebook and Twitter have a much more equally divided gender base of users, although Twitter has a much higher percentage of college users.

> **Artist need to make five decisions about their social media plan and then follow through on them.**
>
> 1. What social media is the best fit with the Artist and their business?
>
> 2. What are the Artist's social media goals?
>
> 3. How will the Artist measure the success of their social media plan?
>
> 4. What is the budget for the Artist's social media plan?
>
> 5. Who is going to implement and maintain the social media plan?

So all an artist needs to do is to pick the "right" social media for their business by exploring which ones their target market is using. This may be accomplished when an Artist starts to define their customers.

One way to find out which social media that an Artist's fans and customers are using is to ask them. It's easy enough to create a little survey that an Artist can use on their website. If the Artist's website gets some traffic, they can set one up online. SurveyMonkey is one tool that may web designers use to create web-based surveys. Entice people to participate with a prize drawing or other tangible benefit.

Another is to use mail plug-ins to find out what social media the Artist's customers use. If the Artist is using Gmail, Rapportive lets them see just what their contacts are doing on their social networks right in their Inbox. If the Artist is using Microsoft Outlook, Microsoft Outlook Connector is a similar program. Xobni offers plugins and phone apps for Gmail, Outlook, Android, BlackBerry, and iPhone that let Artists get updates from LinkedIn, Facebook and Twitter among other things.

If using social media is new to the Artist, perhaps they should set aside time to play around with them and get to know them before doing anything further.

Social Media Goals
After deciding which social media the Artist is planning to use, they need to decide what their purpose is for them. Social media can be used for the same purposes as any other marketing channel; it's how the goal is pursued that's different; not the goal itself. Artists can use social media to:
- build word-of-mouth
- increase product sales
- drive traffic to the Artist's website or blog
- develop new products or services
- provide customer service

In other words, Artists can use social media to pursue and achieve any traditional business goal they can think of.

The trick is to make sure that the Artist has chosen a goal that they can measure.

Social Media Goal Setting Tips
An Artist's social media goals have to have a demonstrable relationship to their business strategy. Artists should write down their social media goals. Make them as specific as possible. Not "Polka-dot pants will get new customers" but "Polka-dots pants will increase sales from new fans customers by 30% over the next three months."

Measure the Social Media Success
Generally, social media success has to be measured by the same yardstick as any other marketing effort; cost and return-on-investment (ROI). That's why it's so critical that an Artist chooses social media goals that they can measure.

To make measuring social media ROI easier, Artists should have a website where they can then use Google Analytics. This is a free tool that lets website owners track and analyze various data. Using the goals feature in Google Analytics makes it simple to see if and how the Artist's site engagement goals are being met.

Budget for the Social Media Plan
There are no freebies when it comes to social media for Artists and their business. If an Artist is going to develop a social media presence for their small business, there are costs. Even if social media outlets such as Twitter, Facebook or Pinterest are free, remember that time is worth money, too.

Social Media Tools

Bitly
FeedBlitz
Foursquare for Business
HootSuite
Social Mention
StepRep
Storefront Social
TweetDeck

---

8 Social Media Tools for Artists
These social media tools for Artists will help do everything from turning an Artist's Facebook and Twitter page into an ecommerce site through converting their blog into a newsletter.

1. Bitly
This shortens a URL and lets Artists send their links and commentary directly to their Facebook and/or Twitter accounts. When working with a 140 character limit, a shortened URL is a necessity and this one is easy to use and has very attractive analytics.

2. FeedBlitz
Artists can convert their blog or website's RSS feeds into automated emails, tweets and Instant Messages with this email and social media subscription service. Use it, for instance, to turn an Artist's blog into an email newsletter and send it to their customers/clients. The cost depends on the number of subscribers.

3. Foursquare for Business
This is a phone app that people use to

share their location and their opinions with their social networks. Artists can use it to promote their business and attract fans and customers.

4. HootSuite
This is a social media dashboard that lets teams "collaboratively schedule updates to Twitter, Facebook, LinkedIn, WordPress and other social networks via web, desktop or mobile platforms plus track campaign results and industry trends to rapidly adjust tactics" according to the HootSuite website.

5. Social Mention
This is a super-easy way to track who's saying what about what. Use this real-time search platform to monitor whatever topic an Artist may choose and it will email them a summary of the latest social media mentions about it. Some Artists use this for songwriting ideas.

6. StepRep
Like other reputation monitoring social media tools, StepRep monitors websites, blogs, social media and local review sites to see what people are saying about the Artist. There is a subscription to this service.

7. Storefront Social
This Facebook application turns an Artist's Facebook page into an ecommerce site. It's easy to use and quite customizable. This also has a subscription fee.

8. TweetDeck
This is a social media tool that lets Artists access Twitter, Facebook, LinkedIn and other social media all from one place. The ability to set up columns, groups and saved searches makes it easy to organize an Artists use of social media.

****

6.16 Task

****

Monitoring & Evaluation

6.17 Monitoring and Evaluating the Plan

The following questions should be modified to suit the nature and needs of the Artist's organization.

Monitoring and evaluation activities will consider the following questions:
1. Are goals and objectives being achieved or not? If they are, then acknowledge, reward and communicate the progress. If not, then consider the following questions.
2. Will the goals be achieved according to the timelines specified in the plan? If not, then why?
3. Should the deadlines for completion be changed (be careful about making these changes -- know why efforts are behind schedule before times and dates are changed)?

4. Do personnel have adequate resources (money, equipment, facilities, training, etc.) to achieve the goals?
5. Are the goals and objectives still realistic?
6. Should priorities be changed to put more focus on achieving the goals?
7. Should the goals be changed (be careful about making these changes -- know why efforts are not achieving the goals before changing the goals)?
8. What can be learned from our monitoring and evaluation in order to improve future planning activities and also to improve future monitoring and evaluation efforts?

Reporting Status of Implementation
Results of monitoring and evaluation will be in writing, and will include:

1. Answers to the "Key Questions While Monitoring Implementation of the Plan"
2. Trends regarding the progress (or lack thereof) toward goals, including which goals and objectives
3. Recommendations about the status
4. Any actions needed by management

Procedure for Changing the Marketing Plan
Regarding any changes to the plan, write down answers to the questions:

1. What is causing changes to be made?
2. Why the changes should be made (the "why" is often different than "what is causing" the changes).
3. What specific changes should be made, including goals, objectives, responsibilities and timelines?

Manage the various versions of the plan (including by putting a new date on each new version of the plan).

Always keep old copies of the plan.

Goals, Responsibilities, Timelines and Budgets

As much as possible, goals should be specified to be "SMARTER," that is, specific, measurable, acceptable to those people working to achieve the goal, realistic, timely, extending the capabilities of those working to achieve the goals and rewarding to them, as well.

****

6.17 Sample

****

6.17 Task

In this section of the Artist Business Plan, consider and write down the plan for monitoring and evaluating whether the Marketing Plan is working.

****

Notes

Chapter 7
Business Plan for Artists
Customers

There are two main customers for Artists: Fans and Music Industry Professionals. The fans purchase tickets, CDs and merchandise of the Artist. The Music Industry professionals purchase performances of the Artist as well as licensing of the Artists songs and recordings.

Question: Who are the customers?

The Artist's audience isn't everyone. Artists should be tracking who comes to the Artist's shows. What is the gender breakdown, age, income levels (optional)? What other Artists do they listen to? How do they purchase music and recordings of music? From where? How big is the Artist's audience? Don't just guess – use statistics

What other events do they attend? Where else do they shop and could you work with those retail outlets to promote the Artist? Are they internet savvy? Etc.

What is their geographical location?

In today's industry, a fan base is considered the most important element to the success of an Artist and the interest that the general industry will take.

Do you have an e-mail list or mailing list to keep in contact with the Artist's fans?

Do you have a database that allows you to target by region?

How do you get news out to them about the Artist's career?

What services do you offer on the Artist's web site? I.e. message boards, a daily Artist journal, contests/promotions, updated news section

Is there an e-mail address or some kind of customer service measure so that fans can get their questions addressed?

Have you been able to make use of key fans to head of street teams in certain areas? Street teams do a great job of posturing, promoting the show word-of-mouth, etc.

Do you offer a newsletter or discounts on merchandise or a fan party?

Caution on all of these things: You should not offer everything! You need to offer what is going to work best for the Artist's fan base.

Are you able to conduct online surveys or in-venue surveys? What have you learned from those surveys (just a synopsis, not details – save that for an appendix).

Basically, how do you get the Artist's fans to feel as though they have enough of a connection to you to buy the Artist's CDs and go to the Artist's shows?

Once an Artist starts concentrating on product development, there are two types of customers for every Artist. There are customers who may purchase items directly related to the Artist, such as tickets to their show, recorded music or downloads. Typically this type of customer is called a Fan.

The other type of customer of the Artist is the entertainment industry's business executives such as agents, promoters, producers, publicists, publishers and record company executives.

Always remember, there are 2 types of customers for every Artist.

The Perfect Customer
What is the Artist's perfect customer really like?
- Is the perfect customer male or female?
- Does the perfect customer work out of the home or in the home?
- What is the job profile of the perfect customer - an executive, manager, worker, entrepreneur, stay-at-home parent, etc.?
- What is the net household income of the perfect customer?
- What level of education does the perfect customer have?
- Does the perfect customer have room in their spending budget for the Artist's product or service? Is their potential buying habit on a one time, occasional or constant basis?
- How does the perfect customer use the Artist's product/service - do they buy it for themselves or as a gift?
- Does the perfect customer spend a lot, some or minimal time on the Internet?
- Where does the perfect customer typically look for the Artist's product/service? Both online and in physical locations?

Next, determine the value proposition. This defines how the Artist differentiates itself to attract, retain and deepen relationships with the targeted customers. There are basically 3 value propositions or disciplines that an Artist can choose from:

1. Cost leadership – In this discipline, an Artist chooses to provide the best price with the least inconvenience to their customers.
2. Product leadership – In this discipline, Artists offer products that push the performance boundary (i.e. newer and better than competitors).
3. Best total solution in this discipline – Artists deliver what the customer wants, cultivate relationships and satisfy unique needs. In this case, Artists may not be the cheapest or the newest, but the total package they deliver to the customer cannot be matched.

In order to help an Artist determine which of these value propositions to use, they may want to work through a value chain:
1. Determine the customer priorities
2. Determine the channels needed to satisfy those priorities
3. Determine the products or services that are best suited to flow through those channels
4. Determine the materials and or

knowledge required to create the product
5. Determine the assets or core competencies essential to the inputs. Artist should ask them self, in order to satisfy their customer, at which processes must they excel? For example, fan development may be the best way to attract a talent buyer customer of the Artist.

After the Artist has started gathering info about their potential customers, they will need to create a system to organize it all. This step is often overlooked since most believe that the success of the promotional item campaign is only measured by the success of the event itself. But in truth, this step will separate the weak from the strong marketing strategy. A solid system in organizing an Artist's gathered information will often determine their return on investment for their efforts.

7.01   Customers Overview
7.02   Fans - Customers
7.03   Music Industry Customers
7.04   Customer Niches
7.05   Customer Profiles
7.06   Customer Demographics

Fan Customers

One obvious source of income is from fans that purchase the products of the Artist. This includes ticket buyers, download purchasers, merchandise collectors

---

Customer Niches
Artists have niches and many times their customers are in the same niche. A musical style is often a life-style for certain customers.

Music Industry Customers

In addition to customers who are fans, there are also customers in the music industry. These customers are just as important and any other customer. These customers purchase the talent of the Artist for live performances or recorded products

---

Customer Profiles
Who is a typical customer of the Artist? The fan may be one who enjoys a good live show and another may be a listener of a particular style of music. Someone in the music industry may not necessarily be a fan but one who is in business to make money selling tickets or recordings or licenses for songs.

Customer Demographics
Who is a typical customer? What is their age? Their ethnicity? Their income level? The more an Artist knows about their customer, the better they can market to them.

Customer Service
How does an Artist know if their customer is satisfied? Are there any suggestions that fans and customers have made that

may help the Artist? Does the Artist pay attention? Does the Artist even care as their art is more important?

****

7.01 Task

For this section of the Artist Business Plan, write about the overview of customers for the products and services of the Artist's company.

****

Fans - Customers

7.02
Fans - Customers

A fan is a person who is enthusiastically devoted to something such as a band or Artist, genre of music. Collectively, fans of an Artist constitute a "fan base." Many music industry people ask about fan base. What they really want to know is, who is a typical fan of the Artist and how many are there?

Early in an Artist's career, their first fans may be parents, siblings and/or friends. These individuals are super-important to an Artist for a few reasons. They are the first in line to encourage the Artist to continue making art. They may provide important feedback to the Artist. They may also be the first to purchase a ticket to the Artist's performance or recording.

Artists should keep in mind that these family and friend fans may come to the Artist's performance the first time an Artist plays a gig. They may even be there for a second gig. After that, their support will still be there, in spirit, but they may stop attending every performance of an Artist unless there's a special reason such as a CD release party, special event or a group of new songs.

For this reason, it is extremely important that the Artist is ready for the stage and can attract new fans as well as provide a reason for friends and family to continue attending their gigs.

In addition to fan customers who may attend an Artist's performance, there are those who may purchase a recording or merchandise from the Artist via a CD or MP3 download. These potential fans and customers may come from anywhere in the world through the use of the World Wide Web or may purchase items of the Artist at the Artist's performances.

Smart Artists know to collect names and text numbers from the people who are attending their performances. They know that fans are obtained one at a time. They stay in touch with these fans with e-mails, online postings, and postcards.

Fan Clubs

Fan Clubs are a collection of fans who enthusiastically support an Artist by participating with fanzines, newsletters, blogs, and fan mail. They often promote the Artist to others who are not yet fans.

****

7.02 Sample Fan Customer Profile

"Most of our customers are 18 to 35 years old and are single or recently married. They live in urban areas, especially on the east and west coasts. They're active online music listeners, and they tend to be affluent and sophisticated. They discover our music on our website primarily through online searches and ads placed in music related magazines and on selected social network websites."

"When making buying decisions, our customers value quality — determined by the unique melodies and chord progressions used in our songs, as well as our explosive live performances — more than price. The bottom line: Our products and services make our customers feel good. By delivering on this promise, we can develop a loyal clientele of repeat fans and buyers."

****

7.02 Task

In this section of the Artist Business Plan, consider and write down the perfect fan-customer of the Artist.

****

Music Industry Customers

7.03 Music Industry Customers

As previously mentioned, Artists in the entertainment industry have two types of customers: Customers who are fans and customers of the entertainment industry who hire or collaborate with the Artist.

Entertainment Industry Customers are a whole different kind of customer. Some of them are also fan-customers, but the Artist needs to know the difference.

For an Artist, customers who are members of the entertainment industry include talent buyers, concert promoters, publishers, record labels, agents, as well as online music distributors and even others Artists. In some cases, these types of customers have to be sold on the idea of working and collaborating with the Artist.

Customer segmentation is a successful marketing tool when implemented correctly. There are many segments to choose from, but only a few that are the Artists specific customers. For this reason, selecting segments and placing the Artist's customers must be done with precision. This segment of the Artist Business Plan deals with customers, who may become collaborators. They are usually music business professionals within the entertainment industry that an Artist may come in contact with.

For steps on how to segment customers of Artists, review the following list of suggestions.

First of all, Artists should organize their current list of entertainment industry customers so the Artist knows what options they are working with. Ideally the

Artist should have their customers set up in an electronic format such as a database. Artists should invest in technological software that allows the Artist to segment their customer base. Since there are many potential entertainment industry customers, Artists are advised to organize their customers in order of descending profit margin. In other words, does the entertainment industry customer purchase services of the Artist for a performance on a regular basis or just once in a while?

Proceed to the customer segmentation process by identifying the basic characteristics of each potential and currents customer. For example, classify each contact by location, venue size, contacts they may have, regular attendees, reputation, distribution scope, promotion power, etc.

Divide the current and potential customers into demographic groups. Entertainment industry consumers primarily purchase the services of an Artist based on either the quality of the Artist's performance or on how many potential fan-customers of the Artist will attend the performance and purchase a ticket or recording. These industry-customers may need and want these fan-customers that are related to where they live, how old they are, their gender and their level of income.

Separate clients based on location, whether it's a small neighborhood or a whole country. Marketing client segments is influenced by factors such as population density and climate.

Segment each customer contact by identifying their purchasing histories. Divide them into groups depending on which products or services they use as well as how often and how they use each of the Artist's products or services. Are these customers repeating or just one time buyers?

Consider dividing customers into benefit groups. A talent buyer may benefit in a totally different way than an Online Music Distributor, for example. This segment considers the ways in which the Artist's products or services are beneficial to the customer.

****

7.03 Sample Music Industry Customer Profile

"Most of our customers are nightclub owners and talent buyers. They are typically 30 to 50 years old and are married with children. They live in urban areas, and commute to their venue Thursdays through Sundays. They pay attention to the local music scene through word-of-mouth and the regional entertainment magazines. They are in the entertainment business because they love the music. They discover our music on our website primarily through promotion from our booking agent who promotes us to them."

> "When making buying decisions, our music industry customers value quality in our stage performance as well in the material that we play. These promoters keep buying our service because we make them money."

****

7.03 Task

In this section of the Artist Business Plan, consider and write down the types of entertainment industry customers that the Artist is planning to target. Look at the proposed projects for the Artist and identify the potential customer for each.

****

Customer Niches

7.04
Customer Niches

For an Artist, a niche market is the subset of the market on which specific products or services of the Artist are focusing. Both the fan-customer and the music industry-customer respond to the niche of which the Artist has chosen. The market niche defines the product features aimed at satisfying specific market needs, as well as the price range, the quality of the art and the demographics that it's intended to impact. It is also a small market segment. For example, online music distributors like CD Baby, Tunecore, Reverb Nation, and Broadjam target a niche of music fans and enthusiasts while Pollstar targets concert and event promoters.

Every product can be defined by its market niche. The niche market is highly specialized, aiming to survive among the competition from numerous possibilities of other performers or large recording companies such as Warner Brothers, Universal or SONY. Even established Artists create products for different niches, for example, Brett Michaels of the band Poison, has crossed-over to the country market. Music of country Artists such as Taylor Swift is now being played on pop radio stations as well as country radio stations.

Fan Customer Niche
Technology and many traditional marketing practices changed with the post-network era and the introduction of the Internet. There is a new drive for niche audiences because audiences are now in much greater control of what they hear and watch. It is very rare to have a substantial audience hear multiple Artists at one time. Still, online music distributors as well as booking agents do target particular demographics. For example, the Warped Tour targets fans of post-hardcore music and the Newport Jazz Festival targets jazz enthusiasts. Talent buyers for these events book Artists with niches that fit their intended audience. The amount of tickets they sell is directly related to the type of fan-customer that the Artist has.

In this context of greater audience control, Artists as well as production companies are trying to discover ways to profit through new scheduling, new shows, and new events. This practice is similar to that of "narrowcasting" which allows advertisers and sponsors to target a more direct audience for their messages. When an Artist is planning their bookings, they need to pay special attention to this concept. Artists should not waste a concert promoters time if the Artist's niche does not fit the intended audience of the promoter's event.

Music Industry Customer Niche
As previously described, the second type

of customer for the Artist is companies and individuals within the music industry. These are music industry customers. Collaborators for any Artist have to be convinced to put time, money and effort into the Artist. So, in effect, they are customers of the Artist. These industry types fall into specific niches. For example, there are radio stations and they are not all the same. They have their own niche market. An Artist who writes, records and releases blues music may find no music industry customers at classical formatted radio stations. The same is true with nightclub owners, record label executives and publishers.

As the Artist begins to focus on their potential customers, they will realize the importance of targeting their niche; whether it's the fan or the music industry customer. We all know that we cannot be everything to everybody, so defining the niche will save many hours of time and frustration.

****

7.04 Task

In this section of the Artist Business Plan, consider and write down the niche(s) that the Artist's perfect customer fits. What other types of people identify with that niche? These are potential fans and customers of the Artist.

****

Customer Profiles

7.05
Customer Profiles

Now that the Artist has identified their niche and the customers who are attracted to that niche, it is time to profile these customers. By completing this step in the Artist Business Plan, an Artist will be better prepared to market to their specific new customers. If an Artist know who their potential customers are, they will save time and money. When planning and directing an Artist's business activities, customer knowledge equals business power. Knowing who the customers are and what they want is just another way to success of any Artist.

Some of the questions that an Artist should ask themselves about their business are:
- How is the customer likely to find the Artist's music in the first place?
- Why would customers choose to buy from this Artist rather than another?
- What motivates the fan to buy — price, quality, availability or special inventory?
- Is the customer likely to be a repeat buyer?
- What convinces the fan customer as well as the music industry customer to come back and purchase the products and/or services of the Artist?

Many times an Artist's description of a customer includes geographic and demographic characteristics — where customers live, their ages, and lifestyle information —plus information about what drives their buying decisions.

Four Types of Customer Profiles

1. Geographic
2. Demographic
3. Psychographic
4. Behavioral Pattern

Four Types of Customer Profiles

1. **Geographic**: This term describes *where* an Artist's customers and their potential customers — or prospects — reside. This can be offline customers or online customers. When an Artist knows this information, they can target their marketing efforts into specific regions, counties, states, countries, or zip codes.
2. **Demographic**: This term describes *who* an Artist's prospects are in factual terms, such as age, gender, ethnicity, education level, marital status, sexual orientation, income level, and household size.
3. **Psychographic**: This term describes *lifestyle characteristics* of a customer including attitudes, beliefs, and opinions that affect customer-purchasing patterns.
4. **Behavioral pattern**: This term describes *how* customers buy, including when, why, how much, and how often they buy as well as their level of loyalty, their purchase occasions and timing, and whether they make buying decisions based on price or quality, on impulse or after careful consideration, based on personal decisions or on the recommendation of others, and other such behavioral patterns.

Based on the Artist's customer description, the Artist is now able to hone a sharp marketing strategy.

Businesses that aim to serve everyone face a budget-breaking proposition. By defining customers by location, descriptive facts, lifestyle characteristics, and purchase behaviors, Artists can compile the information necessary of whom to target their business efforts to and only to the precise audience for their products and services.

In addition, the Artist's customer snapshot reveals that their sales success relies on optimizing their search rankings and then developing loyal buyers who may keep coming back on their own, and referring their friends, as well.

Knowing the customers is an essential part of business planning for every Artist. The more an Artist knows about their customers, the more they know about where to find others just like them, how to reach them with media or other marketing communications, and what kinds of songs, messages, and stage antics move them toward buying.

****

7.05 Task

In this section of the Artist Business Plan, consider and write down the profile of the perfect customer of the Artist. Be specific.

****

Customer Demographics

7.06
Customer Demographics

An Artist needs to know their customers. Demographics is a section of the population that share common characteristics, such as age, sex, income, class, education, etc. Once again, who is the Artist's perfect customer?

A clear definition of an Artist's customer type(s) must be known in order for the Artist to effectively design many aspects of their business, from their products, their services, their marketing campaigns and promotional designs to the strategies they will use to combat competitors. The more that an Artist knows about the people that will listen to their music, the more effective the efforts will be to attract and retain repeat business.

Artists need to ask them self: who are the customers for this business? Better yet, who is the perfect customer? What qualities in the Artist's perfect customer can be identified? What is known about this perfect customer? Are there other customers just like the perfect customer whom has not yet been recognized? Where are they? What is their background? Are they on their way to or from work, or school or an event when they might hear or discover the music of the Artist? How old are they and what are their tastes in style, food and music? What particular social issues are of concern to these people? These questions all deal with the demographics of an Artist's customers: both fan-customers and music industry customers.

A new Artist who tailors their business model to the most likely sources of local and regional business is a smart approach. Consider the venue where the Artist performs. Is there a crowd that regularly attends and patronizes that venue? Understanding the approximate demographics, patterns and interests of these people will allow the Artist to creatively apply ideas to their business (perhaps, preparing a special song for them) and products (such as, passing out cards identifying the Artist's website for a free song download) that will help to engrain the Artist's name and brand as part of the regular-crowd culture. This approach would be similar, with entirely different results, in a location that is, for example, directly across from a high school, college, festival or special event.

A targeted understanding of the intended consumer fan will also help the Artist to effectively market their business in those places and using the methods of communication that will be most effective. For example, direct mail to a surrounding residential community may not be an effective technique as it is always more cost effective to take a finely targeted approach to reach the Artist's individual market segments (no matter how many there may be) rather than the "shotgun" approach of throwing out a broader and weaker message to a wide audience. Knowing the customer demographics will help the Artist target only those who may be interested in the Artist.

****

7.06 Task

In this section of the Artist Business Plan, consider and write down the demographics of the perfect customer of the Artist. Be specific.

****

Customer Service Plan

7.07
Customer Service Plan

When Artists are dealing with customers, their customer service is an important factor in developing a wide and loyal customer and fan base. A customer service plan examines customers' perceptions and expectations of an Artist, and guides them through the process of bringing their customer service activities in line with customers' needs. Creating a customer service plan helps an Artist to continually offer a highly competitive customer experience.

When considering how Artists will ensure strong services to customers, consider: Are customers very satisfied with the services? How does the Artist know? If not, what can the Artist do to improve customer service? How can the Artist do that? What policies and procedures are needed to ensure strong customer service? Include training in considerations and include skills to develop in interpersonal relations, such as questioning, listening, handling difficult people, handling interpersonal conflicts, negotiating.

Are customers highly satisfied with the product/service and how does the Artist know?

What should the Artist be doing to ensure that its customers are highly satisfied? Consider policies and procedures, staff training, scheduled evaluations, basic forms of market research, etc.

What does the Artist need to do to make the above happen? What major steps must occur? What must be developed? Who should be contacted? What resources might the Artist need?

Step 1
Artists should talk with their customers: both fan-customers and music industry customers. This will help the Artist gain a deep understanding of the experiences these customers had with the Artist as well as the competitors. Artists should ask customers to describe their expectations for their type of music or art, and try to discover any unmet needs. Artists should use a variety of survey methods, including in-person interviews and online surveys. Artists should ask customers how they enjoyed their show or the likeability of a new song or the design of a new t-shirt. Keep in mind that these "interviews" should be informal. Artists should ask questions such as "How did you enjoy the performance?" or "What do you think of the new song?"

Step 2
Artists should create a thorough analysis

of their current operations and focus on the customer service element. Artists will need to write a process narrative describing an average customer experience at the gigs or while listening to the musicianship or recording.

Ask other members of the Artist team to assist; these people may have heard from customers about their experience.

Step 3
Create a table that lists the most important customer service factors discovered in the interviews, and rate how the Artist is focusing in each area. Use this chart to identify which areas of customer service that the Artist already excels at, and which areas may need improvement.

Step 4
Generate a list of possible strategies to bring the Artist's operations into line with customers' expectations and unmet needs. Tackle one or two issues at a time, focusing on the identified weaknesses first. Possible strategies for customer service improvement include remixing, adjusting sound levels, redesigning t-shirts, the live show, quickness of website, etc.

Again, Artists should consult with their team again at this step. They are likely to know exactly what they need to accomplish their jobs more effectively, whether it be adding something new, redesigning something, or eliminating something from their daily routine.

Step 5
Now Artists need to implement your their strategies, and conduct more interviews to measure the outcome and gain new insight to customer expectations. Allow some time to pass, depending on the scope of the changes, before surveying customers again. Interview the same groups and individuals in addition to seeking out new voices. Artists may consider surveying their employees at this stage as well, to determine how the changes affect the staff.

****

7.07 Task

In this section of the Artist Business Plan, consider and write down the customer service plan for the Artist.

****

Chapter 8
Business Plan for Artists
Promotion Plan

The Promotion Plan shows how the Artist will promote their product and services.

Within the Artist Business Plan is the Promotion Plan. The Promotion Plan has various segments that all contribute to the success of the Artist. Part of the plan may be to write and issue news releases, requesting songs on the radio or by branding thru a free performance for a needy cause. In addition, part of an Artist's Promotion Plan includes use of items such as television or online social media.

Does the Artist understand the radio stations that they are targeting? Caution: Do not just include a list of radio stations…if the Artist still wants to do that, then it should be referenced to in an appendix. More importantly, does the Artist understand the play formats and needs of those radio stations?

Promotion Plan Overview

8.01
Promotion Plan Overview

What are the Artist's press release and promotional plans for radio? Do they have a database? Are there contests or promotional giveaways for the radio DJs or their audiences?

Are there any special events that the Artist can team up with a radio station on?

Have the Artist received any support already for the single or know that there are radio stations who are interested in promoting a single once they are done? Those letters of intent/e-mails should be included in an appendix.

Is the Artist able to secure an on-air interview for the promotion of the single or any tour dates that they may have in that area?

Does the Artist have a radio tracker? How will the Artist keep track of their success? What has been the Artist's past successes with radio, if any?

What is the Artist's plans for any television media? Are they doing a video? Are there interviews/live performances that the Artist has lined up? Again, get those letters of intent or interest in there! Does the Artist have an understanding of which TV programs are supporting local live performances and have they started conversations with them? Why did the Artist choose the programs that they chose? This is important for lesser-known programs because the Artist needs to show the benefit.

What is the Artist's plans for print media? Who are the newspapers, periodicals and interviewers that the Artist is targeting? Are there any interesting stories or promotional ideas that the Artist is using for the print media? Has the Artist received any confirmed support letters and are there significant relationships from the past, which will serve to benefit them? Why did the Artist choose the newspapers, periodicals or magazines that they chose? This is important if the Artist is dealing with lesser-known publications and need to spell out the benefits for their reader.

Is the Artist making use of any of the online media? For example, MP3.com. Artists should make sure they show the benefit of working with this company.

The object of business is to earn a profit. To earn a profit, Artists and their companies must first make prospective customers aware of their products and their services. They then must convince those customers to buy their products and services and continue buying them. As the customer base grows, so does the reputation of the brand. Obviously, the larger customer base an Artist can build through its reputation, the larger its profits will be.

To make prospective customers aware of an Artists recordings and performances (their products and services), an Artist must market and promote them. Promotion is done through radio, television and print advertisements, social media outlets and community presence. The more awareness an Artist creates, the more likely it is to draw fans and customers. Therefore, promotion is typically a very large part of an Artist's annual budget. Although some Artists are very successful through word-of-mouth promotion, it is very unusual for an Artist to do well without spending a large amount of time and money on promotions. Obtaining customers, however, is not enough to sustain a profitable business. Artists must also convince customers the products and services they offer are needed and worth repeat purchases.

These are goals that the Artist sets to build a customer base while promoting awareness of their brand. The overall goal of promotion is to create awareness for the Artist's products or services. Promotional objectives are specific goals to be achieved through a range of marketing activities, including promotional items, sales events, advertising, fan club membership programs, press releases, media events, coupons for free music downloads, community involvement, on-line marketing and music industry trade shows.

Types of Promotion and Advertising
Promotion is generally divided in two parts:
- Above the line promotion: Promotion in the media.
- Below the line promotion: All other promotion. Much of this is intended to be subtle enough that both the fan consumer as well as the music industry professional customer is unaware that promotion is taking place. This happens all the time with sponsorships, product placement, endorsements, sales promotion, merchandising, direct mail, personal selling, public relations, trade shows and more.

> **Promotion Plan**
>
> - Promotion Analysis
> - Promotion Objectives
> - Promotion Potential
> - Promotion Strategies
> - Communication Strategies
> - Co-Op Promotion Strategies
> - Radio Promotion Strategies
> - Video Promotion Strategies
> - Performance Promotion
> - Indie Record Promoters

Promotion Analysis
This is a detailed review of the prospects for an Artist and an Artist's products and services within a potential market. For example, an Artist may perform a promotion analysis for a particular new market where the Artist wishes to start performing. This helps the Artists forecast whether market demand conditions will support launching a promotional effort into that market

Promotion Objectives
Promotional objectives are goals Artists set to build a customer base of fans and music industry professionals while promoting awareness of their brand. Common marketing campaigns include flyers, posters, radio spots, television advertisements, billboard placements and social media updates.

Promotion Potential
In a perfect world, the Artist may consider numerous ways to promote their brand. In doing so, they must look at the true potential for the promotion that they are planning. Artists must first evaluate the reach and cost to accomplish their promotional objectives.

Promotion Strategies
In order for the Artist to achieve the goals and objectives set forth in the promotion plan, they will need to build a strategy. This is the "how" part. How does the Artist plan to achieve their promotions?

Communication Strategies
In addition to targeting media outlets, Artists are also going to need a strategy for the ways to communicate their message to them, and ultimately to their fans and customers.

Cross Promotion Strategies
There are many cases where promotion can be shared with other companies, Artists and brands. This is called cross or cooperative promotions.

Radio Promotion Strategies
Using radio to help expose an Artist's songs and recordings is still the number one way that potential fans discover a new Artist. What's the plan? What radio stations will be most receptive to the Artist?

Video Promotion Strategies
In today's world, eyes are turning video in a bigger and better way. With the plethora of video outlets on the Internet, cable stations, local stations as well as the BIG 4 television networks, Artists now have more outlets than ever to promote their brand.

Performance Promotion Strategies
There are many promotion strategies for all Artists and one of the most important, especially for new Artists, is their plan to promote their upcoming performances. Fans are acquired one at a time and live performances is one great way for Artists

to accomplish fan acquisition.

Independent Record Promoters
Most of the time, but not always, Artists and their record labels team up to promote their recordings through the use of Independent Record Promoters. To complete their promotion objectives, Artists need a strategy. What's the plan?

The following sections provide more detail about each of the foregoing strategies.

****

8.01 Task

For this section of the Artist Business Plan, write about the overview of the planned promotion for the products and services of the Artist's company.

****

Promotion Analysis

8.02
Promotion Analysis
In the Promotional Plan of the Artist Business Plan is a section on Promotion Analysis.

As mentioned previously in the Artist Business Plan, there are four components of the "marketing mix," also called the Four Ps: the product, its price, the place of sale and the tactics used to promote it. Artist brand and sales promotions are elements of the promotion component, and takes place at the point of sale.

Sales promotion tactics intend to arouse consumer interest in an Artist's products or services. As previously described, there are two types of customers of Artists: fan customers and music industry customers. Promotional tactics may include customer discounts, gifts and free samples. Such initiatives prompt the customers to purchase items as well as the services of an Artist.

When an Artist expands into new markets, it uses sales promotion schemes to comprehend the acceptability of their product. The Artist's sales and profits increase as more customers are lured into purchasing its products. Customers may benefit because they are able to try the product before they make their final purchase. This is especially true with websites that offer snippets of the Artist's music before a fan-customer makes a purchase.

Types of Sales Promotions

Customer Sales Based
Sales-Force Based
Retail Sales Based

Types of Sales Promotions
Sales promotions fall into three main types. Customer-based sales promotions inform consumers that a product exists. Artists sometimes spend a lot of time,

money and effort on these strategies. This type of sales promotion may include flyers and posters.

Sales-force based promotions for an Artist may include the promo kits that their agent gives to talent buyers. Retail sales promotion tactics offer commissions to consignment retailers who sell and promote an Artist's CD products or the person who sells the Artist's merchandise at their gigs.

****

8.02 Task

In this section of the Artist Business Plan, consider and analyze the promotion potential for the Artist. Be specific.

****

Promotion Objectives

8.03 Promotion Objectives

Any promotion that an Artist undertakes must be clearly defined with objectives and goals, especially when dealing with the entertainment industry. Since there is a plethora of entertainment activities and products for customers to consider to purchase, promotion is a major part of this business.

For an Artist's business and brand, marketing and promotions are essential both to grow and to retain customers. These customers may be fans as well as music industry professionals. As with any goal or objective, a promotion objective should specifically focus on one aspect of the promotional strategy. By having a collection of promotion objectives, an Artist is more likely to meet its goals.

Purpose

The purpose of promotion objectives is to give an Artist clearly defined goals to meet through promotional activities. A promotional objective should be set with the intent to attract new customers, increase frequency of sales, increase average customers expenditures and build larger attendances of fans to the Artist's live performances.

Features

A promotional objective ideally expresses a goal in terms of numbers and within a flexible time frame. For example, a promotion should not have the goal of increasing ticket sales; it should have the goal of increasing ticket sales by 10 percent each time an Artist performs at a venue. This gives the Artist a solid idea of what must be accomplished. Objectives should always be realistic and meeting those goals will encourage Artists to set higher goals next time.

Types

Promotion objectives focus on a variety of goal types. One is to build awareness of the Artist, its products, services and/or the Artist's brand in general. This should, in turn, generate more interest in the Artist. Objectives also help stimulate demand by encouraging customers to take advantage of a "buy advance tickets offer" and inform the customer so that they might buy at a time when they might not have otherwise. Another type of promotion objective is to reinforce the Artist's brand and strengthen the relationship between them and their customers.

Expert Insight
Smart Artists us a "promotional mix" when planning their promotional goals. This means targeting goals with a wide variety of strategies, including personal selling, sales promotion, radio airplay, public relations, direct mail, trade fairs, advertising and sponsorship in order to reach different types of audiences and receive feedback.

****

8.03 Task

In this section of the Artist Business Plan, consider and write down the promotion objectives of the Artist. Be realistic and specific.

****

Promotion Potential

8.04
Promotion Potential

To grow the business of an Artist, a market analysis studies the attractiveness and the dynamics of a special market within a special industry such as entertainment, and more specifically, music. It is part of the industry analysis to know the promotion potential. As mentioned in a previous section of the Artist Business Plan, with the help of a SWOT analysis, business strategies of an Artist's company can be defined. The market analysis is used to inform an Artist and their company of project planning activities such as new recordings or gigs, purchases of gear and equipment, new market expansion, and many other aspects of their company.

Market Trends
Market trends are the upward or downward movement of a market, during a period of time. For example, the amount of possible performances in December may be higher than February due to the holidays and relatively warmer weather. The market size is more difficult to estimate if one is starting with something completely new. In this case, Artists will have to derive the figures from the number of potential customers, or segments.

Another important market trend in the music industry is the issue of fans downloading recordings of music for free.

Market Growth Rate
A simple means of forecasting the market growth rate for an Artist is to extrapolate historical data into the future. New Artists may not have historical data yet, but as their business plan continues to evolve, this data may easily become identifiable.

Ultimately, many markets mature and decline. For example, when a city has a few venues providing live music, it is natural that others will want to get into the game. However, once too many new venues start offering live music, the number cannot maintain the level of total customers that attend live performances and the total number of venues will decline.

Promotion Potential

Once an Artist determines the price they want for their product (recordings) or services (performances), they need to access the geographic location of their market, their possible customers (both music industry professionals as well as fans), and who and where their competition is. Next, they must calculate the portion of the market they can reasonably expect to capture. Market potential is an estimate of the amount of money an Artist can expect to make from the product or service they plan to market. Their estimate will only be as good as the information they use and the assumptions they make.

Seven Steps to Estimating Market Potential

1. Define the market segment (target market)
2. Define the geographic boundaries of the market
3. Define the competition
4. Define the market size
5. Estimate market share
6. Determine the average annual consumption
7. Estimate an average selling price

****

8.04 Task

For this section of the Artist Business Plan, write about the promotion potential for the products and services of the Artist's company.

****

Promotion Strategy

8.05 Promotion Strategy

A quality product will have a hard time failing, especially if the promotion strategy is to execute a well thought-out plan. No matter how wonderful an Artist's music, recordings, merchandise or performances are, the world is unlikely to beat a path to their door unless they know the product or service is available to purchase. Artists cannot sit in their garage waiting for the phone to ring. Sales don't happen by them self. Artists need to carry out promotional activities to attract the right sort of business, in the right quantity, and at the right time. Artists need to distinguish themselves from the competition; and there's plenty of that out there.

Promotion is not just about exposing the Artist's art, nor is it just about selling. It's about pulling together a range of techniques, in the most cost-effective way possible, to initiate, increase and maintain awareness of what the Artist offers to their fans / customers. It is imperative that Artists move their customers from total lack of awareness to the point at where they actually buy… and then buy again and again.

Parts of a Promotional Mix

1. Public Relations
2. Advertising
3. Promotion
4. Packaging

There is an onslaught of new recordings released in the music / video market each month (1,200 new releases) worldwide. For an Artist's success, it is crucial to ensure the visibility of each project. If the promotion budget is high enough, financial success of a quality album can almost be guaranteed. However, without the dollars necessary "to win" success is often just a chance that enough people will find the music. With properly established budgets, the Artist may generate large streams of profits from each of its projects including downloads, merchandise and performances.

Three Phases of an Artist's Promotion Campaign

Phase 1 – When an Artist is preparing to release an album, they should be thinking long-term. No one knows that album is being release except the Artist. No one really cares either (that is until the Artists starts gaining some traction.) The Artists should consider the first 3 songs to be released (as singles) and then create a music video for each of them. Once these videos have been shot and edited, the first "single" and its video counterpart should be released to the public. The Artist may want to hire independent promoters to canvas radio stations, video networks and dance clubs (depending on the genre of the release) to ensure proper air play. Within the next four to six weeks, a second "single" release should be promoted in the same way to the public. This strategy will enable the Artist to achieve two important outcomes-- increasing the number of "singles" that are sold online and/or offline in retail outlets. It also builds anticipation for the release of the Artist's full-length album.

Phase 2 – Many times, phase 2 is planned and executed at the same time as Phase 1. This phase is worked by the Artist's publicist who will generate media exposure and print advertisements. These media targets will hear and learn more about the Artist through news releases and follow-up by the publicist. This should generate articles in trade and non-trade magazines, as well as radio, television and Internet interviews. Furthermore, the publicist will also be able to create valuable exposure for the charity/non-profit organization that the Artist may have chosen to assist and promote.

Phase 3 – The planning for phase 3 begins early although the execution of the plan begins with the release of the full-length album. Depending on the promotion budget, phase 3 may be accompanied by intense in-store and retailer co-op advertising. Retailer programs may be designed to secure valuable listening posts, end-cap displays, window/wall posters, point of sale advertisements and co-op advertising in mailers and store circulars. Additionally, the third and fourth "singles" will be released during this phase. Artists need to show a consistent flow of material to show their fans and customers that they are "here to stay." The systematic release of "singles" will sustain the Artist's popularity while increasing and prolonging sales of the full length album. So, when the album is finally released, the fans may say, "Wow, this album has all these great songs on it. I have to buy it." Furthermore, during Phase 3, the Artists will make promotional appearances at clubs, retailers, radio stations and charity events in conjunction with scheduled concerts.

****

8.05 Task

In this section of the Artist Business Plan, consider and write down the promotion strategy for the Artist. Be specific.

****

Communication Strategy

8.06 Communication Strategy

Writing an integrated communications plan involves bringing all the different parts of an Artist's promotion plan together into a document that can be used as a guide during the implementation of the plan. As a key part of brand building, an integrated communications plan encompasses all parts of a promotional campaign for an Artist, from the Artist's background and description of the target market to print advertising and online promotions. A communications strategy should offer a well-researched and effective method to get the Artist's message about their product or service to their target market at the most effective time and place.

Here's a good way to write an integrated communications plan for an Artist.

Artists should collect all necessary information about their company, their product(s) and service(s), their competition and their target market. Whether the Artist has the information in print reports or on computer files, it needs to be accessed easily while an integrated communications plan is written.

An outline of the integrated communications plan from beginning to end is a good start. Then the Artist should write all of the detailed parts of their plan. Make sure grammar and spelling is correct, and check the facts and figures for mistakes.

Integrated Communications Plan
1. **Artist Background**
   The background part briefly describes the Artist's company's history and gives a description of the Artists product(s) and service(s) that will be marketed. Include features, structure, and other components of the product or service that are important to the promotion plan.

2. **Target Market**
Describe the Artists target market. Include the market's demographics as well as the product or service's benefits to the target market. Also, state how the target market currently perceives the Artist and their company. Be thorough and clear. The more an Artist knows about their market, the more effectively they can tailor their marketing campaign to it.

3. **Positioning**
Discuss positioning within the market. This part of the plan describes attributes of the Artist's product or service, its benefits, and how it compares to the competition. If possible, describe the Artist's competitive advantage, which means something unique about the Artist's product or service, or their brand. What sets them apart from and above the competition?

4. **SWOT Use**
Use the Artist's SWOT analysis (section 6.07) that pinpoints the strengths, weaknesses, opportunities, and threats associated with marketing the Artist's product(s) and service(s). This can include aspects such as price, availability, and competition.

5. **Competition**
Examine the Artist's local, national, and international competition. This is one of the most important aspects of the promotion plan as it allows business owners to see exactly what media and messaging they use in their own marketing and promotion campaigns. In addition, it informs an Artist how they reach their market and generate business. Artists should also examine their target market to make sure it's the same as their plan. If not, discuss how it's different and analyze whether there's an opportunity to enlarge the Artist's own target market.

6. **Objectives**
Determine the objective of the Artist's integrated communications plan. Identify the goals, and indicate how progress will be measured.

7. **Market Specifics**
Specify what marketing tools and strategies that will be used to get the message to the Artist's market. Determine if print, media, Internet, appearances, or all of the aforementioned will be utilized.

8. **Budget**
Allocate a budget for each aspect of the promotion strategy. Determine which department in the company will take care of each aspect, or whether the Artist will outsource part, or all, of their promotion plan.

When complete, Artists should review their integrated communications plan. If there's anything that may need more research or additional information, do the extra work.

Periodically review the results of the plan, and adapt any aspects needed to in order to achieve better results.

****

8.06 Task

For this section of the Artist Business Plan, write about the communication strategy for the Artist's company.

Co-Op Promotions

8.07
Co-Op Promotions

Co-promotion is a marketing practice where a company uses another company's sales force, in addition to its own, to promote the same brand or range of brands. The term is frequently confused with Co-marketing.

Cross-promotion is a form of marketing promotion where customers of one product or service are targeted with promotion of a related product, whether within the same company or in conjunction with other companies. This happens all the time at events where the event is being promoted but so are the sponsors of the event. Another typical example of cross-media marketing of a brand, for example Oprah Winfrey's promotion on her television show, of her books, magazines and website. Cross-promotion may involve two or more companies working together in promoting a service or product, in a way that benefits both. For example, a mobile phone network may work together with a popular music Artist and package some of their songs as exclusive ringtones - promoting these ringtones can benefit both the network and the Artist.

Advantages of Cross Promotions

1. Cost of promotion is less. If two promote one, it's cheaper for each of the two

2. Win-win situation for both parties

3. Cross-promotion marketing is the easiest and often one of the most successful marketing strategies

4. Both businesses can promote themselves simultaneously

So, even the busiest entrepreneur can attract more customers with less effort through the right cross-promotions. If an Artist's plan is doing cross-promotion then they will be teaming-up with other credible businesses. These businesses also reach out to the same market of the Artist. Through cross-promotion, Artists can get in touch with their fans and customers with more efficiency, and their business will look more credible to people. This happens when an Artist has a gig with other Artists at a venue that promotes using radio, for example. In this case, each Artist is promoting the venue as well as the other Artist on the bill. Sometimes these Artists will even help promote the radio station as a sponsor of the event. On the other hand, the venue promotes each Artist and so does the radio station.

Huge marketing pay-off is highly possible in a cross-promotion strategy. Through cross-promotion, the Artist, as the partner, has the ability to successfully expand using the other businesses customer base and vice-versa. Cross-promotion gives businesses the chance to introduce their business the inexpensive way, and it is also more effective than with the traditional "solo" methods of networking, advertising, or public relations.

Benefits of Cross-Promotion:

1. **It builds the Artist's business' credibility.**
   When Artists decide to go with cross-promotion they team up with another business and this business is basically backing-up the products and services that the Artist is trying to offer when they advertise the Artist on their website or their marketing.

   As their partner of course, the Artist will do the same thing for them: back-up whatever products and services they sell. Because they are respected and valued by their customer base, the Artist's offering will garner added interest and consideration, too. It's important for an Artist to know and, believe in, the product or business that they are endorsing.

2. **This venture lets the Artist save money.**
   In cross-promotion ventures, the Artist saves money because the expense and resource is split in two or more ways. The Artist and their partner split the costs of a common "offer." This can be promotional cards, free gifts, etc. When an Artist partners with another company for cross-promotion, the Artist is combining their marketing efforts and budgets to reach the same market.

   So, basically with cross-promotion, the Artist may spend half the amount for double the impact.

3. **It expands the current database.**
   Another good thing about cross-promotion is that an Artist can make use of their own database and at the same they can also make use the other company's database. Whenever an Artist decides to start a cross-promotion strategy, they should remember that they have the opportunity to reach out to more customers compared to when they were doing it alone.

   Cross-promotion gives an Artist the ability to target customers, including those they have not considered in the first place. This means that Artists are able to increase their chances of gaining more customers who might be interested in their performances or recordings; hence, they will also be able to broaden their market reach.

4. **It saves time and resources.**
   By using cross-promotion, Artists get in contact with their target market at a much quicker phase because it is not only the Artist that is working but all the other members in their team as well. In this case, the Artist's team

includes the other Artists or companies they are doing cross promotion with.

The Artist's task is to not only promote their own products and services but also the other company's products and services too. The workload is equally shared and fairly distributed; therefore Artist's get to finish tasks faster.

5. **Provides better exposure.**
By using cross-promotion, Artists are able to promote their products and services well because there are many people working on the same goal. Hence, Artists get better advertising exposure.

6. **It builds trust.**
Cross-promotion is a marketing strategy that helps an Artist's fans and customers to see that other businesses trust them. Other businesses trust the Artist enough to get them to market the Artist's products and services.

This particular move may help make an Artist look good depending on the trust a fan has in the collaborator.

7. **This type of strategy stands-out.**
Cross promotions stand out. Why? Because this type of advertisement is more eye-catching and this not like any other advertisements people see. People will be more interested to know the benefits of both businesses and of course they will be curious as to who are the businesses involved.

****

8.07 Task

For this section of the Artist Business Plan, write about the plan for co-op promotions for the products and services of the Artist's company.

****

Radio Promotions

8.08
Radio Promotions

Getting radio play is a delicate balance of targeting the right stations with the right information at the right time. This is true for Artists as well as their record label.

To get an Artist's song played on the radio, either the Artist, the Artist's team, or the Artist's radio promotion company approaches music directors and/or program directors at radio stations, promotes the recording to them and then using a combination of press releases, one sheets, e-mails, phone calls and faxes, convinces them to play the song on the airwaves. Some may play it, others may not. Not so tough. Wrong!

Radio promotion is hard work. It is incredibly competitive to get a song on the radio. Getting airplay on large commercial radio stations in major radio markets is almost impossible. If an Artist is an independent and not signed to a major record label it could be very difficult. However, radio airplay is not out of reach though.

What musician doesn't want to hear their song played on the radio? Music Directors at radio stations are always on the hunt for new music that they think their listeners will love. The trick to having a successful radio promotion campaign is taking the time to understand how radio works and what makes a song radio friendly.

If an Artist does not have a big budget or power players on their side, they need to understand a few basic things about the world of radio.

First of all, there are two kinds of radio: non-commercial radio and commercial radio. Non-commercial radio encompasses college radio and community radio stations. Commercial radio is everything else (in other words, the stations with lots of commercials.

Although it might not be obvious to the casual listener taking a spin through the radio dial, not all radio stations are created the same. Sure, different stations play different kinds of music, but it's more than that. In reality, across that radio dial, there are two distinct kinds of radio stations: commercial radio and non-commercial radio. From the perspective of a musician trying to get their songs played on the radio or a radio promotion company pitching the recordings, the difference in these stations comes down to a lot more than formatting.

8.08.01 - Commercial vs Non-Commercial Radio Stations
- Funding
- Listener Type
- Genre
- Competition

Non-Commercial Radio
Non-commercial radio includes college radio and community based radio stations, including local NPR affiliates. Though these stations may carry advertising, it is widely spaced, unobtrusive and not the main source of station funding. It's usually called "underwriting" instead of advertising for non-commercial radio stations. Commercial radio, on the other hand, is just the opposite. The commercials are frequent and commercial breaks between songs may be quite long. Advertising is the source of funding for this type of radio station.

Non-commercial radio wants to introduce people to the Artist's music. In most cases, they're quite familiar with trying to make things happen on a shoestring budget, as many up-and-coming musicians find themselves doing. The financial barriers to entry on non-comm radio are much smaller than commercial radio.

For anyone doing a radio promotion campaign, these distinctions are significant. Why? Because non-commercial radio tends to have a lot more flexibility in their playlists. They tend to be much more willing to play music from up-and-coming Artists and non-mainstream Artists than commercial radio. Many times airplay on non-commercial radio stations is the doorway through which up and coming musicians break into radio. In fact, it may be the only sector of radio on which some genres of music get played regularly. This is especially true for indie musicians and musicians operating in niche genres.

Non-commercial radio stations' flexibility comes from the fact that their funding isn't reliant solely (or at all) on advertising dollars. Although they certainly need listener numbers to keep their independent sources of funding, wherever they come from, they don't have to secure the kinds of ratings commercial radio stations need to show to advertisers to convince them to spend money with the station. That means that they can afford to take a chance on a new Artist that listeners may not have heard of before. The scenario is a little bit chicken or egg – of all radio audiences, non-comm radio listeners tend to be the most open to new music. In fact, by playing new Artists, non-comm radio stations are usually giving their audiences exactly what they want. However, because they don't need as large an audience as a commercial radio station does, they can afford to lose the listeners who want to hear music by established Artists they also encounter in national magazines, television, newspapers and tours. It's a self-reinforcing cycle that works in favor of indie music.

Non-commercial radio stations may also focus on niche genres of music. This is especially true of community radio stations, which may, for instance, only play jazz or folk music. This genre specific approach means that they have to delve deeper into a genre to fill up their playlist. This is good news for up and coming musicians in that genre looking for exposure. For some genres, non-comm radio may be their only outlet - and that's fine, because these are the stations fans of those genres turn to when they want radio.

In addition to playlist flexibility, non-comm radio is a great entry point for many musicians because there is less competition. Major labels tend to ignore non-comm entirely, which means radio promoters have an easier time getting the attention the radio staff and getting them to check out new recordings.

Non-commercial radio is the most likely starting place for an up and coming independent Artist. College radio is VERY friendly to such Artists, and community radio stations often are as well. Any radio is good radio for Artists. Don't feel like getting plays on this kind of radio is somehow "less" than getting played on a commercial station. Some non-comm stations are hugely popular. Further, succeeding in the non-comm arena can lead commercial radio stations to take notice.

There are also benefits for songwriters when they receive their performance royalty statements from their Performing Rights Organization or SoundExchange.

Commercial Radio
After non-commercial radio, independent Artists often turn to small commercial radio stations. In this way, getting songs played on radio is a bit like building blocks. Artists develop a foundation of plays on non-comm radio, which they use to build up to small commercial stations, which may in turn lead to play at medium stations and so on and so forth. However, it is important to note that there is more to the process of moving up the radio ladder than just getting plays at smaller stations. Radio stations want to see an Artist's entire music career progressing along

with their radio plays. If the Artist isn't touring, picking up more and bigger pieces of press and selling an increasing amount of music, then larger stations aren't going to play their song. Why? They judge an Artist's songs on their ability to increase their ratings by playing the Artist's music, not on the song quality itself. Showing music directors at bigger stations that the Artist's whole career is growing, shows them that the Artist is a good rating risk, since the Artist is probably on their audience's radar.

The world of commercial radio is completely different. Commercial radio operates on the basis of ratings. They need to show big listener numbers, and they need those numbers to be consistent, or indeed to be growing. These ratings are used by the station to demonstrate to potential advertisers that buying commercial advertising on the station will reach a significant number of people and is a worthwhile investment. These numbers are also used to price advertising. The more listeners a station has, the more they can charge for ad spots - and the more money they will have in their operating budget. If a commercial radio station could only run advertisements, and no music, then they would. They use music to attract listeners, which in turn, attracts advertisers.

Because these stations need ratings so badly, they need to play music by musicians that can bring them those listeners. They therefore look for musicians with enough clout and budget to be reaching their listeners outside of radio. They want to play musicians that are getting major press - both nationally and in that radio station's market. They want musicians that are selling well in local record shops and nationally. They want to play music by musicians who are playing shows in that station's market. They want to play musicians and Artists who are advertising.

Many up and coming musicians simply don't have the budget or the reach yet to meet the demands of commercial radio stations, so they are don't get played there as often as established Artists do.

8.08.02 - College Radio
College radio is a non-commercial type radio station and can be an indie musician's best friend. These stations have playlist flexibility and a dedication to new music that just has no equal in the commercial radio world. Plus, making it big on college radio often attracts the attention of larger commercial radio stations, not to mention booking agents, bigger record labels, publishers and more.

8.08.03 - Radio Markets
Radio station markets are one of the first things an Artists needs to know about radio before they go about trying to place their songs there. Choosing the right markets for the Artist's music will increase their odds of getting plays - and when an Artist is getting started at radio, only targeting stations likely to give them the time of day will save you time and valuable resources.

If an Artist is planning to promote their music to radio - whether they are going to try to do promotion in-house or they plan to hire a radio promotion company – they're bound to hear lots of talk about radio markets. What are these markets, and what do they mean to the Artist?

The term "radio market" simply refers to the broadcast area of a radio station. Radio stations broadcasting in Cleveland, Ohio, are in the Cleveland market, and so on and so forth.

In that sense, radio markets are pretty straight forward. However, there is more to the Artist's radio promotion campaign than simply geographical distinctions. Why? Because radio markets are also broken into types and sizes. There are major radio markets, medium markets, small markets, and non-rated stations. In addition, there are radio stations that only play hit songs, others that only play oldies, or only jazz or blues.

These markets are segmented on the basis of the population of their broadcast area - the biggest 30 cities or so are major markets, the next 31 - 100 or so are medium radio markets, 101 to 300ish are small markets, and radio stations in all other smaller cities and towns are non-rated stations. These divisions are important for radio promoters to know because it helps them decide which stations to target - for both the biggest impact AND the realistic ability of the Artist being promoted to get airplay in that certain market.

Which, of course, is why even non-major label Artists covet those stations? In fact, many Artists - no matter how far along they are in their careers - want to approach those major markets by any and all means necessary, no matter what the cost. This plan is a bad one for up and coming Artists. First of all, "no matter the cost" really isn't a realistic idea in this realm - major market radio campaigns can costs six - or even seven - figures. The real reason trying to target the major markets on a radio campaign is a bad play, however, is that it simply won't work. The Artist simply won't get played. Period. Doesn't matter how good the Artist's song is. It's just not an accessible world for an independent Artist without a big budget behind them. There are reasons.

It is far more realistic for an Artist to plan and tailor the markets they target based on the level they're at with their career. If the Artist is new to radio, especially commercial radio, then non-rated stations are their best bet for getting plays. In these markets, Artist will have less competition from better funded, better known musicians, so the stations are going to be more responsive to the Artist's calls and therefore, their music. If the Artist has conquered non-rated radio, it may be time to target small markets. Artists should be able to come in to that station with a track record of plays and listener reactions to the Artist's music to help convince them that THEIR listeners will be interested in hearing the Artist's tracks too. Being successful with small markets can mean it is time to transition to medium markets, provided the Artist has the budget required to book the tour dates and pay for the advertising these stations will want to see to convince them the Artist has a serious campaign. For some Artists, major market radio never happens - and there is nothing wrong with that. For others, it comes when there is a solid promotional budget, a record of national press and large market tour dates on the Artist's agenda.

In a nutshell, radio markets describe both geography and size - which in turn, indicates accessibility to an Artist. Before an Artist embarks on a radio promotion campaign, they should make sure they understand which market is the best fit for what they're trying to achieve.

> **Some of the main formats are:**
>
> A3
> Adult Alternative
> Adult Contemporary
> Americana
> College
> Country
> Gospel
> Latin
> New Age
> R&B
> Rap
> Rock
> Smooth Jazz
> Urban
> World Music

8.08.04 - Playlists

The term playlist can be used in a few different ways. First, a playlist is a list of songs that a radio station plays on a regular basis. The same term is used by MTV, VH1 and other music television channels for videos they play regularly. Radio stations that work with playlists usually have a tiered listing system - songs that are on the A list get played X number of times a day, the B list slightly fewer times, and the C list fewer again. In most cases, DJs are bound by the playlist and obligated to meet the requirements of the list before they can select music themselves to play, if at all. In fact, many radio shows are determined entirely by the playlist. Some Disk Jockeys may get as a few as one or two "free plays" that they can use to play songs they think are great. If a song is in "heavy rotation," it means that it is high on the playlist.

These kinds of playlists are typically determined in playlist meetings, during which individuals known as Record Pluggers meet with reps from the radio station, play the songs they are promoting and try to convince the music director or program director at the radio station to put the songs into rotation. Radio is controversial these days because a lot of playlist decisions are seemingly made based on the budget of the record label. The Sony BMG payola case is one of many recent examples of how big budgets can sway playlists. More about Payola later.

Playlist can also mean a list of songs played by a DJ during their show. This includes songs on the official station playlist and songs the DJ selects. If an Artist or their record label hires a record promotions company, and if they get a station to play the Artist's song, they will send a copy of the playlist that features the song. Keep in mind, that just because an Artist is on the playlist for one show for one certain day, it does not mean that they are on the official station playlist, or that their recording will be in rotation to play on a regular basis.

****

8.08.05 - Radio Promotions

Despite the fact that radio no longer possesses the sole influence on record sales, sharing the spotlight now with video resources, it is still a heavyweight medium for record promotion. It is still the number one way that consumers become aware of new music.

There are two methods of radio promotions to consider-- hiring a radio promotion company or doing radio promotion on the Artist's own. Here is a set of criteria to help you decide which works best for the Artist.

Major record labels utilize both in-house and independent promoters to assist in the effort to maximize the airplay of a new recording or album. An in-house radio promotion staff makes financial sense assuming the company maintains a steady and consistent release schedule to a specific genre or radio format. Gaining personal relationships with radio station's music directors is the name of the game in this arena. Bombarded by new recordings of songs and album releases each month, music directors and program directors are inclined to assist those with who they are familiar and friendly. Remember, this business is all about relationships and networking. This is true with radio as well.

Radio promotion is charged with placing recordings on the radio. They maintain relationships with music / program directors at radio stations and attempt to persuade them to play singles. This, in turn, promotes the sale of recordings, such as CDs, sold by the record company. They may also pay a fee to a third party, known as an independent radio promoter, who has an ongoing relationship with the radio station or its parent company. If an independent Artist releases their own recordings, then they are acting as their own record company and may have to complete the same steps as an independent or major record label.

****

8.08.06 - Self-Managed Radio Promotion

Many Artists cannot afford to hire independent radio promoters for their recordings and often try to self-manage their own promotion to radio stations. There are few Pros and Cons of doing it yourself.

The Pros of Working as a Radio Plugger

Although it's hard work, working as the Artist's own record plugger has its upsides:
1. You get to work closely with the media.
2. You are in control of the Artist's own career. Make it or break it.
3. It's a great feeling to hear a track you've been working being played on the radio.
4. It's a new learning opportunity
5. It helps build relationships
6. It's much cheaper

The Cons of Working as a Radio Plugger

Of course, there are some downsides as well:
1. It can be depressing when a track you really believe in fails to get any exposure.
2. No income. In the United States, owners of recordings being played

on the radio receive no compensation. Songwriters and publishers of the song do, but not the owner of the recording.
3. It can be repetitive sending CDs to, and phoning, the same people over and over again. Radio pluggers have to become accustomed to being ignored again and again and again.

Radio Promotion Tips

If an Artist wants to self-manage their own radio promotion, here are a few tips.

1. Consider the geographic locations of where the Artist performs and what the size of their tour is. If an Artist tours within a specific region or remains close to the Artist's home base, it may prove more cost effective for them to manage their own radio promotion. Although some independent promotion companies concentrate on a select regions of the country, most conduct national promotions campaigns. If the Artist has no intention of touring outside their region, or plan to move more slowly, region by region, the expense for a national campaign may be prohibitive and unnecessary. The money the Artist spends on the regions that they do not intend to tour will be wasted. When touring is restricted to one area, it is easier for Artists to select tour cities and research the appropriate radio stations, city by city, as needed. The Artist's costs are then spread out over an extended period, as are the necessary promo CDs. The Artist is able to concentrate on each city they intend to tour. The main concern for the Artist is scheduling time to send the promo CDs, make initial calls to the station to check on the CD arrival and then, at least once a week, make a follow-up call to check on the airplay the CD is receiving. This is no small task and it is time consuming.

2. Use radio promotions to identify hot markets for performing and touring.

Artists should be prepared to tour in the markets where they are receiving the greatest airplay. The best use of a radio campaign is to track the cities and radio stations that have added the recording. The Artist should plan performances and tour dates in those cities no later than four to six weeks after the campaign has been completed. Once the radio stations become familiar with the Artist's music, those stations become key points of contact to help promote a tour date. Notify the station of the upcoming tour as they are likely to extend airplay, promote the date, do phone or live interviews and possibly even work with the promoter or venue as a co-sponsor. The radio station may even be able to recommend specific venues and promoters in the area at the start of the Artist's booking process.

Use the radio promotion's campaign to leverage better dates. As the agent or the Artist contacts the various venues in the markets of greatest airplay, mention the radio campaign, the station playing the recording and what degree of airplay the recording is receiving. Knowing that radio is supporting the act can often be the persuasive factor necessary to land a date. Talent buyers and concert promoters need to know this information.

3. Hire a friend or fan part time or assign someone from the band to do the work. The solution to the time consuming nature of this project might be to hire someone for a few weeks at an hourly rate, the total being much lower than a professional record promotion company. If they are organized and have a pleasant phone manner, they can accomplish much the same result as a professional company. The difference will be that the professional company has an established relationship and reputation and music directors at the various stations will take their calls. The Artist's employee will have to spend some time establishing a relationship first. Then again, the Artist's campaign doesn't necessarily have to be completed within a specific time frame. Target the cities of greatest importance as you decide to set tour dates in those markets.

4. When making the recording budget, include money for promoting the recording. Set aside dollars for shipping costs, phone calls, promotional CDs and packaging materials. Research the number of stations likely to be targeted and make sure to include that number in the Artist's initial count for manufacturing. Most Artists' recording budgets omit any additional money for promotion. Make booking gigs and building an audience easier designating funds to market the new recording. This, in turn, will help leverage the Artist's bookings with targeted talent buyers and concert promoters in desired performance markets.

The goal of any radio promotion campaign, large or small, is to create audience awareness of the Artist and their new recording. National promotions companies use charts to mark progress. For Artists who do their own regional campaign, their benchmark will be the number of stations that begin playing the CD. (This step should be identified in other sections of an Artist's Business Plan such as the Financial Plan, Products and Services Plan, and Marketing Plan sections.) If those stations report to a specific chart, it is not unheard of for an independently, self-promoted Artist's recording to achieve chart notoriety. Many Artists conduct their own campaigns with great success and chart. They spent many hours of each day calling and then recalling. Their efforts were rewarded.

Ultimately, the Artist's goal is to use the radio airplay to boost awareness of the Artist which should translate to an increase performance bookings and an increase in sales of recordings and merch. Radio recognition helps both causes. Include some aspects of radio campaigning in the Artist's marketing program.

The average American company devotes 40% of their budget to promotion and marketing. But unfortunately, musical Artists become so busy putting energy, time, and money into the songwriting, recording, and performing that sometimes they forget that having a great new collection of songs can be fruitless without a plan to get that music out to the general public.

Radio Promotion in a Nutshell…

For Artists to actually run a decent radio campaign they need at least four weeks in advance of their add date, and a few extra weeks may be needed if the Artist is new to the game. During the start of the Artist's radio promotion push, Artists should mail out promo CDs to music directors of the stations being targeted. Then spend a week or two confirming that the Artist's promo packages were received, solicit initial feedback and re-send any promos that may have been misplaced or lost.

The next few weeks will be spent soliciting feedback about the single while trying to get commitments from stations saying that they will be adding the single - or, indeed, that they won't be. All the while, update the program director with news about the musicians relevant to that market - shows, sales and so on. At this stage, place ads in radio trade publications announcing the single and that the Artist is going for ads - especially when going for plays in larger markets.

During the last week of the campaign, Artists should do a final push for ads and then wait for the results to come in. That's a short rendition of the process, but that's it in a nutshell. It's the same process used to promote to non-comm radio right up to the top major station in large market.

The bottom line? The best way to get the Artist's song on the radio is to approach the radio stations that are appropriate for the Artist's stage of career. If the Artist is just trying to break into radio, focus on the non-comms and take it from there. Some Artists never get airplay anywhere but college radio and thrive in their music careers. Build a realistic, easily managed radio campaign, and start to see success on the airwaves.

8.08.07 - What to Submit to Radio

There are a few things an Artist can do to increase their chances of getting airplay listed at the radio stations they approach. Some radio stations require compact discs and other MP3 S. There are still a few that want vinyl.

A CD for non-comm radio doesn't have to be a professionally-pressed, full-art completed version. A simple promo - even without artwork - will do, as long as you provide the information they need to add music to their playlists is provided. However, as previously mentioned, Artists should release only quality. If you act like a professional, you will be treated as a professional.

Some stations are just the opposite - some prefer to get their submissions via e-mail. That means the cost to the Artist is virtually zero. Research the targeted stations and follow their submission policies.

Commercial radio is much different. Most commercial radio stations - especially the big ones - want a CD. They don't want any old CD, either. They want a professionally-pressed CD complete with all the trimming. Don't try to pass off the Artist's self-burned CD with the Artist's handmade artwork. It won't work.

Commercial radio stations really want a finished product because they want proof that the Artist is for real and that they have a plan and the financial ability to pull it off - things like distribution, national touring, and so on. Remember, commercial radio is in the business of selling ads. If they play music their listeners want to hear and know about, they can charge more money for their ads. Their listeners will want to hear the Artist's music and know about them if they have a complete promo campaign, local shows, a presence in the stores, and ideally some national presence. Completed CDs are considered an important tool of the trade by commercial radio, so that's why they want to see them.

> **As you package up the Artist's CDs, keep the following in mind:**
>
> • Yes, send promo CDs. You'd be surprised how many radio stations still operate by pulling the CD off the shelf and playing it.
>
> • Put a sticker on the front of the CD with the Artist's band name, album name, two sentences about the Artist and three or so suggested tracks. They won't have time to listen to the Artist's whole album, so direct them to the stand out songs.
>
> • Sending promos is fine, but put them in a jewel case. Even if there is no artwork, write the name of the Artist's band and the album title on the spine of the jewel using a marker. If you do have artwork and this info is not easily readable on the spine, write it in. This helps DJs find the Artist's album on the big station shelves.
>
> • Start with the Artist's local stations. Write on the envelope that you are a local band - it may help get the Artist's CD listened to first.

Of course, some commercial radio stations want MP3 S, and that will probably and eventually become a norm - but for now, Artists and record label have to play by the stations' rules to have any hope of getting airplay.

8.08.08 - Record Pluggers

For Artists not choosing to run their own radio promotion campaign, there are other solutions.

Many Artists use the services of a record promotion company to help boost airplay and build new audiences on radio stations. Record promotion companies plug recordings, and hence, are called record pluggers or radio pluggers. This should not be confused with song pluggers, who work for publishing companies, pitching songs to Artists, Producers, record label personnel, music supervisors and advertising companies.

Most Artists believe they ought to launch into a full-blown campaign as soon as they have their hot-off-the-press CD. Some Artists should do just that, others should not, depending on their career goals, budget and team.

Record pluggers are the people who try to get a recording played on the radio. For Artist who run their own radio campaigns, they take off the "hat" of Artist and put on the "hat" of Record Plugger: 2 different jobs, 2 different hats. Getting a good plugger can make the difference between a single becoming a hit or a flop and between an Artist having a successful career or disappearing into obscurity. These record pluggers are the link between Artist and/or record labels and radio station managers, music directors, show producers and disk jockeys.

Record pluggers specialize in promoting music to radio stations. They are hired by record labels and Artists to take new recordings (usually singles, but in certain cases, full albums) to music directors, radio show producers and DJs to try and secure radio plays. Record pluggers try to get the releases they are representing put on playlists, but if they can't get them on a regular rotation playlist, they try to at least score a few plays. Record pluggers may also try to set up radio sessions (during which an Artist either plays live or pre-records a live performance for use on a radio show) or interviews with the Artist.

Most record pluggers work on a campaign basis - that is, they work on a specific release for a pre-determined period of time. Further, some pluggers have a more specific focus, such as specializing in college radio.

What is a Record Plugger's Job?

Basically, the job of a record plugger is to get the recordings they're representing exposure on the radio. The different kinds of exposure they might try to get include:

Radio plays for the Artist's music. Depending on the recording, this could mean inclusion on the stations' playlists, spot plays or plays on specialist music shows.

Live performance sessions and interviews for the Artist on radio.

Organizing competitions on radio that give away the Artist's CDs, T-shirts, posters, gig tickets, etc., as prizes.

Getting the Artist's releases and upcoming live shows mentioned on air.

The Crucial Ingredient - Contacts:
A record plugger is essentially being paid for their contacts in radio and the relationships they have built up with those contacts. A good record plugger will have a range of contacts across different radio stations, covering music and program directors, DJs and producers as well as music and playlist programmers. A good record plugger will have a database filled with contact info, as well as the type of music the contact's into, the format they

like releases in (do they prefer MP3 S, CDs or vinyl) and the results they've had from them in the past.

8.08.09 - Hiring Record Pluggers

Records Pluggers will often only take on acts that they believe in and like and that they think their radio contacts will play. Collaborating with a record promotion company or record plugger is like getting any other music industry professional to work with the Artist. Research and approach pluggers that work with acts in a similar genre as the Artist. There's no point trying to get a plugger who works predominately with rock to take on the hip hop act. Pluggers will be more likely to work with an act that has shown they're prepared to work hard.

If the Artist or the Artist's record label is planning to hire a promoter to push their recording to radio, here are a few things to consider which may help for the greatest chance of success. The big concern with this process is, if the wrong person is chosen to promote the recording, and end up with bad results, the promotion can't just go back and start over again. That's it for that recording at those stations. That recording is now "an old project," and Artists can't go back to those stations until they have a new release.

Smart Artists create a network of independent promoters who interface with radio stations. Specifically, these Artists create and design goal oriented and incentive based contracts. Measurable criteria includes peak chart position obtained as well as the number of weeks on the charts.

Independent promoters focus their efforts and attention on reporting stations. A reporting station is one that trade papers/magazines and tip sheet publishers use each week to learn which recordings were and are planned to be programmed. This information is gathered and tabulated from all around the world. It is presented to the public in the form of a chart which shows such information as current chart position, previous chart position, Artist, record label, etc.

Using a Friend: Non-experienced friends sometimes offer to help Artists get on the radio for free or "for a few dollars." This is fine as long as the Artist uses them for the right tasks, such as helping with the mailing, etc. If an Artist is promoting to college radio, maybe 20-30 stations, then friends could help the Artist with some phone calls too. But if they try to call any more stations than this, or if they try to call commercial radio, they will probably stumble after just a couple of weeks. Artists should not expect friends to complete reports or trade charts. Usually this does not work well for the Artist.

Someone From The Majors: Staff promoters at major labels sometimes offer to "help Artist out on the side" for a fee. On their days off, or on the weekend, they say they will "make some calls for the Artist." What happens is that their company finds out and disallows it, or, the person gets tied up on their days off and can't do it. The Artist is then stuck. Either way, it is a conflict of interest for them. This approach usually does not work well for the Artist.

PR People: Public Relations (or "publicity") people sometimes offer to work an Artist to radio for airplay. However Artists should not confuse PR with airplay. A real radio campaign has nothing to do with publicity. They are two separate techniques, with different contacts, different lead times, different terminologies, call frequencies, and so on. A person who is good at one is usually terrible at the other. This is why they are always separate departments at labels. Once again, this approach usually does not work well for an Artist.

Station People: Station employees are sometimes recruited to help an Artist with promotion. This sounds convincing, but in reality, taking the calls (which they do/did at the station), and making the calls, are very different jobs. Until station people are trained (at a label or indie), they usually make poor promoters.

Own Chart: When an Artist hires a real promoter, they should make sure he/she is not affiliated with the chart that they say they are going to promote to. Some promoters actually publish their own chart, and they can put an Artist on it wherever they want to. And they can take the Artist off just as quick.

Big Clients: When an Artist is considering hiring an independent promoter who says they've worked with big-name Artists, they should ask them what they mean by "worked." Were they solely responsible for charting that Artist? More than likely, the promoter probably partnered with a label or another promoter, or was just an assistant or sidekick.

What to Expect of Radio Promoters

Reports: Reports are a requirement that well-organized promoters provide to an Artist or a record label. There is no other way to understand what is going on with airplay each week. Reports also let others such as stores, papers, clubs know what is going on.

Office: If the promoter does not have an office (even a small one), then the Artist will be competing with things like the promoter's sleep, TV, neighbors, dinner, etc.

Assistants: If a promoter handles more than one genre of music at the same time, or if the promoter does college radio at all, then assistants are mandatory. The phone calls have to be made, and no one person can call more than 150 stations a week AND do reports AND do faxes AND do e-mails AND talk to the Artist when they call. Impossible.

College Radio: College radio should be considered for every campaign, even if the Artist is doing high-level commercial radio. College radio is relatively inexpensive, and will make some good-looking charts and reports to show retail, press and clubs.

References: Any promoter worth consideration will have a list of clients or past clients.

When interviewing companies to work with, they will review the recording before taking on the project. They are just as anxious to have a successful campaign as the Artist is. They have a reputation to maintain with the various radio stations. Their credibility is at stake with every project they pitch. Once again, the quality of the Artist's work is imperative.

- Discuss fees upfront. Some companies charge per project. Some charge per time commitment. Additionally some companies charge for expenses like shipping, phone

and photocopies.
- Press enough promo copies of the CD. Each promotions company will tell you how many stations they service.
- Select a company that is well established in promoting to the Artist's genre of music and radio format.
- Know which format the Artist's recording fits. If you intend to use radio promotions as a tool to push the act to the next level, you should research formats and listen to the stations playing those formats prior to making the recording.
- Ensure that the recording will be available in the markets where the campaign is concentrating. This can include signing with a distributor who will stock the local stores, or it can mean the recording is available through any of the online retailers. If the recording begins to receive airplay, radio stations may want to make purchase information available to callers.

Record Promotion Fees

A record promotion company and/or record plugger will charge a fee for their services. Costs range from $400-$600 per week for an eight to twelve week campaign. Artists should be prepared to spend at least $2400 for an eight-week campaign. If all goes well, consider adding an additional two to four-weeks. These costs are just for the company. It's up to a record plugger to agree a fee with the client. This is best done before the campaign starts, to avoid any dispute later on. Some clients will pay by results - the record plugger will get a certain fee when a certain level of exposure is reached. The problem with this model is that a record plugger can put in a lot of work, yet the track could get very little (if any) exposure. Conversely, a track may get a huge amount of exposure even though the plugger has done hardly anything. A good compromise is that the plugger gets a basic fee, with bonuses for achieving certain results. On top of any fee, the Artist or record label will be expected to pay the costs of the campaign - postage, phone calls etc. What is included in the costs and what isn't should be agreed before the campaign starts. Sometimes, the Artist or label will put a cap on these approved costs as well. For instance, postage may be an approved cost, but if the total cost of postage surpasses X amount of dollars, the Artist must clear the expense.

Many new record pluggers will do a campaign for free, or for a greatly reduced rate, allowing them to get experience. Even established record pluggers will do jobs for cost, or cheaply, if they really believe in an Artist. They may work for free if they think the Artist is going to go on and become successful, so that they get work from that Artist later.

Timing - Radio Add Date

A radio add date is the date you want a radio station to add the Artist's music to their playlist. It can be the Artist's single release date, but it doesn't have to be - in fact, you may have good reason for the add date differing from the Artist's release date, whether you're trying to build a buzz a week or so before the actual release or you're releasing the Artist's single to commercial radio long after the Artist's actual release date because it did so well on college and non-commercial stations.

A Few Record Promotion Companies

Flanagan Promotions
http://www.flanaganpromotions.com

Howard Rosen Promotion
http://howiewood.com

Jerry Duncan Promotions
http://www.duncanpromo.com

M:M Music
http://www.mmmusicsite.com/

Notorious Radio
http://www.notoriousradio.com

Parlatone
http://parlatone.com/

Planetary Group
http://www.planetarygroup.com/

Powderfinger Promotions

Radio Airplay Pros
http://www.radioairplaypros.com/

Radiodirectx
http://www.radiodirectx.com/

Team Clermont
http://www.teamclermont.com/

Tinderbox
http://www.tinderboxmusic.com/

Here's how it works: After deciding on a date that you want radio stations to start playing the Artist's recording, put that date - clearly labeled "add date" - on all of the promotional communications used to get the station interested in the Artist's song. That add date will also set the schedule for the Artist's campaign. Then start reaching out to stations and convincing them to add the Artist's single or album around four to six weeks prior to that add date. Put this date on the Artist's backdate promotion calendar.

Up to the add date, you've got time to get music / program directors at radio stations to agree to add the Artist's recording to their station on that date. It's hard work that they'll be adding the Artist's song, in advance of that date, so you know who is on board and who isn't. You probably won't get a commitment one way or the other from absolutely everyone, but you've got up to that date to win over as many stations as possible.

The problem comes once the add date passes. After that date has come and gone, any station that did not add the Artist's single isn't going to add it. You can't go back and ask them to reconsider that decision and add it at a future date. The Artist's add date is also a deadline, and once it is has passed, so have the Artist's add chances with those stations for that recording.

That sounds scary, right? Why would you put that kind of pressure on the Artist? Why not skip the add date and let the stations get around to the Artist's stuff whenever they want?

Well, although there may be some flexibility with add dates in promotion to some college and small non-commercial radio stations, using an add date is absolutely crucial in almost every radio promotional campaign. You should certainly never approach a commercial radio station without an add date. Add dates communicate seriousness about the Artist's radio promotion and overall plans for the Artist's music that stations want to see before they put the Artist's recordings on the air.

When choosing an add date, the most important thing to consider is selecting a date that gives ample time to work the Artist's single to the stations.

Many people, when planning the date that their radio campaign will start, think that starting the campaign at a certain time of the year will make a huge difference in the outcome of the project. It won't. There are many other factors which are far more important, and these factors will determine what happens with the Artist's release, such as sequentially pushing a second and third release from the same Artist; not abandoning a campaign until awareness has been built; providing the proper packaging; and properly choosing "album vs. single."

January Through April:
Many Artists know that this is the best time for indie releases. Advertising on commercial radio certainly is cheapest, and most major labels are taking a short break before starting heavy promotion again (but you won't be able to tell this by listening to the radio… you'll just hear the same number of songs. What you don't hear is how many releases are being PUSHED to radio.) Advertising in most trades is also cheapest at this time. So commercial regular rotation, or commercial specialty/mixshow, is a favorite at this time.

For college radio, obviously, most stations are in session during this period. Don't worry about spring break; there is no national "one week" that every school is closed. Instead, spring break varies from school to school, with some doing it in mid-February, and others doing it as late as mid-May.

May Through August: For both commercial and college radio, this is a good time to use the Artist's radio campaign to help Artists set up a tour.

For college radio, this is the easiest time to chart, since college stations are getting the fewest number of releases. Many Artists may think they can't work a record to college during the summer… not true. Yes, about 150 stations during the summer are off the air, but about 650 of them remain.

Also with college, when the students go home for summer, they still want to hear non-commercial radio; so they simply tune into the college station that is in their hometown.

The biggest advantage of summer college radio is that the CMJ charting is easiest here, due to the lower amount of competition from real labels.

September Through December: For commercial radio, this is the time to work radio in order to sell lots of records. (That is, provided you are set-up and experienced enough, and have enough of a sales staff, to sell twenty or thirty thousand records.) This is the technique used by larger labels to sell most of their product.

For college, they are of course back in session, so for many Artists that is all that needs to be said… college it's going to be! Even though college radio receives many times more CDs in the fall than it does during the summer, many Radio

Promoters are going to push here nevertheless.

The period between Thanksgiving and Christmas is actually a great time to start the Artist's college project, because the bulk of CDs have already arrived and passed, and for about three weeks there is very little competition again. Radio Promoters simply carry the Artist's project through the holiday, and start back up after the New Year.

Bottom line: You can find something good about any time of the year to start the Artist's project.

8.08.10 - Payola

Payola, in the American music industry, is the illegal practice of payment or other inducement by record companies for the broadcast of recordings on music radio in which the song is presented as being part of the normal day's broadcast. Under U.S. law, 47 U.S.C. § 317, a radio station can play a specific song in exchange for money, but this must be disclosed on the air as being sponsored airtime, and that play of the song should not be counted as a "regular airplay."

The term has come to refer to any secret payment made to cast a product in a favorable light (such as obtaining positive reviews).

Some radio stations report spins of the newest and most popular songs to industry publications. The number of times the songs are played can influence the perceived popularity of a song. This skews the charts used by Performing Rights Organizations, and can therefore, change the amount a songwriter and publisher earn on performance royalties.

Pros to Payola
Are there any pros to payola? Unless you are the Artist whose career gets a boost or the label that sees increased sales, there are no benefits. Unfortunately, since exposure is 99% of the battle in the business, payola CAN pay off for these people. That's why they do it!

Cons to Payola
- The public does not get to hear Artists who can't afford to pay off the DJ, or whose label refuses to engage in the practice.
- Artists whose albums come out at the same time as another Artist whose label is engaging in payola may see dismal sales because of a lack of exposure - leading to tour cancellations and being dropped by their label. It is especially damaging to independent Artists and small labels.
- It hurts the integrity of the music business and everyone involved in it.
- It pushes up the cost of music, since labels involved in payola need the money in their budget to pay the DJs
- It's bad for radio, because it makes radio homogenous. People turn off when the same old song is on every station. It also hurts the radio stations that refuse to accept bribes for plays, as the other stations get cash injections from the labels.

****

8.09 Task

For this section of the Artist Business Plan, write about the plan for radio promotions for the products and services of the Artist's company.

Video Promotion

8.09
Video Promotions

Just as Video Promoters follow the same rules are Radio Promoters, one of the various parts of a Promotion Plan is that of video promotion. Rivaling radio in terms of the most powerful promotional tool for pre-recorded music sales, broadcast music videos are a crucial instrument to ensuring successful product launches for every Artist. In today's digital world, Artists should produce a music video for each new recording. Videos should be created to appeal to the target audience of the particular song; a niche video for a niche song.

There are many ways to promote an Artist and video is becoming a primary vehicle to do so. As with audio promotion, it's a good idea to anticipate the promotion of the video in advance. Artists should review their business plan to ensure that their proposed video matches their image, budget, and niche. A great video is only great when people watch it. If they don't know it's available, the video will not be useful. Here are a few tips to promote an Artist through the use of video.

#1: Start now
Practice makes perfect. Start now. Mistakes will be made. Improving techniques will be developed over time. Most Artists wish they started earlier with video. Professional gear is not needed and neither are expert editing skills or software. A fancy script is also not needed. Artists don't even need to be confident in front of the camera. Artists should present a great song, and deliver content that fans and customers can use and enjoy. There is no time like the present. Get started now. However, Artists should remember to release only products that they are proud of.

#2: Start publishing regularly
Video can seem like just another challenge for Artists to overcome, but there may be a major increase in bookings, sales and brand awareness all from the power of video. Fans and customers want to see a consistent flow of content from the Artist; both audio and video. It's important to publish videos on a consistent basis.

#3: Be transparent and authentic
Artists want to be as transparent and authentic as they can be when expressing themselves on video. When preparing a video, Artists should keep in mind their Image as defined in their Artist Development Plan as well as their credibility.

#4: Include Other People
When planning a video script, Artists should include fans in some way. These fans become the videos' best marketers. If a fan is included in an Artist's video, they will let everyone know that they are in it. The word-of-mouth will be tremendous.

#5: Create Compelling Content Collaboratively

Videos are a fantastic opportunity to create compelling content collaboratively. If, for example, an Artist is doing an interview, they can tell a story and create content in a very personalized way. Sharing their experience or thoughts in a conversation with someone else makes it a lot more fun to listen to.

#6: Run a Video Contest
Many Artists take advantage of user-generated content (UGC) and create a social video marketing campaign. One way they do this is to set up and run a video contest. The majority of people who may participate in the Artist's video contest are amateurs, so solid guidelines should be in place to help participants produce a better-quality product. This will certainly help to make the video contest a better success.

#7: Create a Series of Videos
One-off videos are great, but the key to attracting a larger audience is to create series of several videos of different songs or recordings. When an Artist does this, they encourage viewers to watch one video after the next, which means more views and more clicks to the Artist's website.

#8: Use videos to enhance and Artist's e-mail list
To keep the momentum going for an Artist, they need a growing list of people they can regularly reach out to via e-mail. To help grow the e-mail list, Artists should create videos to encourage fans to provide their name and e-mail in exchange for a free download or ticket to an upcoming performance.

#9: Make the videos personal
Shoot impromptu, personal videos to spark deeper engagement on an Artist's social network's fan page. Keep the videos short in length (under 90 seconds) and don't worry about getting it perfect. Artists need to look into the lens of the camera and talk directly to the fans. This creates more intimacy and connection and builds better relationships with fans.

#10: Utilize Interesting Video Topics
These days, when online video is everywhere, it is hard to come up with an interesting and catchy topic and perspective. The song title may provide some ideas on the video content.

#11: Jump Right into the Action
Artists need to grab the attention of viewers by jumping right into the action. Introductions of any kind undermine the purpose of video, which is to communicate a message through action. Captivate the attention of viewers by planning an opening scene as if it were a major motion picture.

#12: Check the Audio Equipment
Artists can make a great-looking video very cheaply and easily but the one thing they do want to spend a few bucks on is the audio equipment. If an Artist is using a camera with a built-in audio microphone, they should make sure they are within about 3 feet of the mic so fans can hear what they have to say. That mic is not recommended but will do in a pinch. Test it, and make any adjustments. Artists can be forgiven for bad lighting, but never for bad sound. If the viewer can't hear the message, they will press the stop button.

#13: Use YouTube Annotations
Artists should use YouTube Annotations to direct traffic to other videos, the Artist's YouTube channel or a call to action for viewers to subscribe to the Artist's channel.

#14: Follow up
For any new tool or strategy, Artists must test it as part of their social media marketing campaign. There is no better way to learn from the experience than through follow-up. Rather than doing all the hard work getting the video made and promoting it, and thinking the journey is over, taking action after posting the video online will give the Artist an idea of the reception it is getting, and whether the venture has been successful.

#15: Improve the Video Marketing
The most underutilized space on YouTube is the description below the video where Artists can describe their sounds and put in their website's URL that can be clicked through. Add a call to action at the end of the video; for example, "If you liked this video, please click through the link below to find more information." This is a great way to increase engagement. Also add the Annotations feature from YouTube to create links in the videos. This is very powerful.

#16: Use Captions and Subtitles
Anchor the Artist's message. Use captions especially at the beginning and end of the video to identify the Artist, the name of song, website, etc. Also search engines cannot read video unless there is some text. Words may be utilized in the video itself, or in the properties of the file. YouTube has an underutilized feature that will allow the video to be translated for multi-languages. Using Google Trends, you can find the non-U.S. areas that have high interest in the song's topic.

#17: Multi-Use
Any video that an Artist uploads to YouTube should also be uploaded to Facebook. The embed code from Facebook should be used in the Artist's blog or website. If the viewer is not a fan of the Artist's Facebook page, he or she can click on video and it drops the user to the Artist's page to "Like" them. This can be a very powerful marketing tool for Artists.

#18: Optimize the Video for Search Engine Optimization (SEO)
When marketing a video, Artists need to make sure that the Internet search engines can find it. The search engines can't crawl a video like they can a text-based web page, so Artists have got to give them a little extra help. Use a couple of keywords in the title of the video and be sure that it matches the title tag of the page.

Also, Artists should make sure to submit a video sitemap just as they would an XML sitemap. This creates an index of the videos on the Artist's site, making it easier for Google to find them. If the Artist is using WordPress for their website, there are a number of plugins that make it easy to create video sitemaps.

#19: SEO the Videos and Make them Shareable
We all know that YouTube is the most popular video site, but did you know that YouTube's search algorithms are different from search engine algorithms like Google? Five quick tips:
- Create the video title to engage users while keeping in mind the SEO aspect.
- Use keywords in the video description, title and keyword tags.
- Include a link in the description of the video back to the Artist's website.
- Share the video on YouTube and post it on the Artist's website.

- Remember to keep the song or video titles SEO- and social media–friendly.
- Include a transcript of all the videos when posting them on the Artist's website. This process can be manual, but in the long term, it helps with SEO.

#20: Create a Podcast feed for Videos
As Artists integrate videos into their marketing plan, they shouldn't make the mistake of thinking YouTube is the only game in town. While it is considered the second-biggest search engine on the web, Artists have many other avenues for getting their videos in front of their target audience.

To extend visibility and tap into millions of potential viewers, Artists should add a video podcast to syndication tactics. ITunes has 160 million users in 23 countries, so adding a video podcast to their directory should be at the top of the Artist's marketing list.

To do this, the Artists must have a web host for their video files and create a podcast feed. Then, submit that feed to the iTunes store for approval and listing in their directory.

Video Channels
It's not as difficult as one might think to submit a music video to popular online and television channels. Some require strange formats, and in those cases it's best to enlist the help of professionals. Some video channels accept a simple QuickTime file on DVD or a .mov file. One of these examples is the hugely popular California Music Channel, which is open to independent Artists of all genres.

Public Access
All hope for national exposure is not lost. Alas: Public Access Cable TV. Most cities now have their own Public Access station whose sole mission is to provide an outlet for noncommercial programming from their community. It is relatively easy to get an Artist's video content aired and it is a great way to get the music heard by a large potential audience.

Blip.TV
Blip.tv focus on original content and their audience is well worth reaching out to. They also offer a distribution service which will promote the Artist's video to YouTube, Flickr, Myspace, and AOL Video among others. They offer both free and pro accounts, but you need a pro account to use their special features.

Metacafe
Metacafe.com is a video sharing website that surpasses 40 million visitors a month. That's some heavy traffic. This community is moderated, and all new videos are checked out by volunteers. They also have a focus on short videos clocking in at less than 10 minutes – perfect for the music video format.

Daily Motion
Dailymotion.com is similar to YouTube in the sense that it's not moderated and as such, allows just about everything.

Vimeo
Vimeo describes itself as "a respectful community of creative people who are passionate about sharing the videos they make. Vimeo has long been a hub for Artists and video directors.

Vimeo's channels and groups are quite easy to search for, and communicating with the users in charge is easy too. On top of this, Vimeo has member forums where you can get involved and cross-promote with others. Basic accounts allow up to 500MB of storage.

Video Outlets

Here are a few websites that accept music video submissions.
- Bug Videos - www.bugvideos.co.uk
- Dead Sink Online - www.deadsinkonline.com
- Indie 360 magazine - www.indie360magazine.com
- Indie Feed - www.indiefeed.com
- IndiMusic - www.indimusictv.com/submitvideo.cm.
- Pitchfork – www.pitchfork.com/tv/
- Roxwel - www.roxwel.com
- Trendy Music Videos - http://trendymusicvideos.com/submit
- Vevo – www.vevo.com

Want a bigger list? Check out: http://www.ovguide.com/browse_sites?c=music&ci=407 for a listing of major and independent music video websites. Do some research to find niche music outlets.

****

8.09 Task

For this section of the Artist Business Plan, write about the plan for video promotion for the products and services of the Artist's company.

****

Performance Promotion

8.10 Performance Promotions

Perhaps one of the most effective marketing tools are concerts and promotional appearances which are instrumental in "breaking" a new act and creating a loyal fan base. Public relations personnel in conjunction with the Artist's management will create and plan these performances which will be directed toward the particular target market. For instance, the Artist may make an appearance at a local record store, provide an interview for a radio station, and perform a concert the same evening.

In addition to the long-term benefit of creating a loyal customer base, Artists may utilize these opportunities to immediately sell copies of the Artist's compact discs at merchandise tables at concerts and performances.

So an Artist may ask: why should I promote my performances? Isn't that the promoter's job? The answer is simple; an Artist is not just an Artist as there are many "hats" that Artists wear every day. In addition to being a songwriter, musician and performer, many Artists understand that to succeed in the entertainment business, they are also promoters, publicists and public relation specialists. Artists that regularly promote themselves to their fans are in greater demand to talent buyers because it makes the talent buyer's job easier. Yes, sometimes Artists are also promoters. With that in mind, let's looks at what makes an Artist (promoter) successful.

A live performance promoter presents music events, festivals, concerts and/or nightclubs. One part of their job is to generate enough publicity and promotion to maximize the attendance to their event.

The promoter's role is critical. An Artist's performance in a particular market will generally generate a minimum level of sales from their core fan base. The promoter will exploit local advertising avenues - from posters and fliers to college and mainstream radio - in order to raise the profile of their event. It is in the best interests of the promoter to ensure the highest possible turnout.

Pre-Promotion as a Part of the Artist Development Plan

As a part of the Artist Development Plan, Artists began thinking about how to make a living in this industry. Before an Artist begins planning their product development such as performing, recording, licensing or merchandising, a good plan of attack should be contemplated. That's what the business plan is all about. The first part of Product Development for an Artist is not booking a gig, or recording a song, it's the promotion of that product that should be addressed. Why? Because the easiest way for an Artist to get a gig or sell a recording is through promotion. An Artist should think about the presentation of their goods and their services for each and every product that they are planning to release.

In addition to an Artist promo kit, an Artist will need to understand how their customer (fan or music industry professional) will be attracted to the Artist in the first place. This is a big part of branding. Yes, Artists are brands and need to recognize this.

An Artist must constantly look at how they can develop their profile and their brand to their customers. To do so, Artists must invest time and energy in their promotional work.

> **No Publicity = No Audience**
> **No Audience = No Money**
> **No Money = No Success**

In addition to the Artist's plan to perform, an Artist must consider their promotion first. This is not the actual implementation of promotion but the vision about the promotion of the planned performance. As an Artist contemplates their upcoming gigs, a plan to promote should be incorporated into their project management tasks.

There are many items to consider for an Artist when planning to promote each and every one of their performances, such as media calendars, flyers, interviews, posters, post cards, press releases, print media, signage, ticket buys, venue co-promotions, video, and web. In addition, don't forget there's print media, radio, and television.

Promo Ammo

Artists should prepare all possible promotional material for their upcoming posters, flyers and other promotions. This promotional ammunition includes logos, photos, recordings, and any other material that may be used to help promote the gig.

Promotion Incentives
Artists need to plan special promotional incentives to their fans such as free downloads, and promotional goods. Invite guests from the music industry (record labels, A & R etc.) and put them on the guest list. Invite journalists to review the gig.

Artists should make every gig "special." Think about the overall atmosphere, lighting, sound and the "buzz" in the venue.

The Artist / Publicist
Until the Artist can afford a publicist, the job of getting press will probably fall on the Artist. Believe it or not, Artists do not have to be well connected to get a music editor to write about them, but they should be well prepared. Reporters and media writers need to report on happening bands, and voila, here comes a happening Artist, coming to their rescue. Remembering that the Artist is doing him or her a service may help take the sting out of those cold calls.

Publicity is mention in the media. Artists usually have little control over the message in the media, at least, not as they do in advertising. Regarding publicity, reporters and writers decide what will be said.

Publicity is the deliberate attempt to manage the public's perception of a subject. The subjects of publicity include people (for example, politicians and performing Artists), goods and services, organizations of all kinds, and works of art or entertainment.

From a marketing perspective, publicity is one component of promotion which is one component of marketing. The other elements of the promotional mix are advertising, sales promotion, direct marketing and personal selling.

The advantages of publicity are low cost, and credibility (particularly if the publicity is aired in between news stories like on evening TV news casts). New technologies such as weblogs, web cameras, web affiliates, and convergence (phone-camera posting of pictures and videos to websites) are changing the cost-structure. The disadvantages are lack of control over how the Artist's releases will be used, and frustration over the low percentage of releases that are reported up by the media.

Though there are many aspects to a publicist's job, their main function is to persuade the press to report about the Artist in the most positive way possible. Publicists are adept at identifying and pulling out "newsworthy" aspects of products and personalities to offer to the press as possible reportage ideas. Publicists offer this information to reporters in the specific format of a magazine, newspaper, TV or radio show, or online outlet. The third aspect of a publicist's job is to shape "stories" at a time that fits within a media outlet's news cycle.

Publicity
It's a shame to arrange a concert, and have minimal attendance because no one knew about it. If an artist is going to promote a concert, PROMOTE IT! Make press releases and send them to everyone who can possibly use the information: television & radio stations, individual DJ's, local and regional

newspapers, newsletters, the area college, local schools, etc.

Posters
Sometimes, a good poster design can draw more people than the performers themselves. There are lots of choices for posters including silk screened posters, hand-made, professionally offset-printed, or the ever-popular local copy center. Computers can make some dynamite posters as well as reasonable costs of color copies. Use the best that you can afford and one that will convey the feeling of the Artist's performance.

Radio
Try to get the Artist's music played on the radio. See if the radio station DJ can interview the Artist. Give a copy of a quality recording to the radio station.

Newspapers
Provide as much promotional material as possible to the Artist's local newspaper and talk to the person who does the "What's Happening" column. Perhaps the Artist might get the cover of the weekend section if they're lucky.

Street Team
Make sure publicity material is distributed well in advance of their gig and to a wide range of sites. (Shops, pubs, colleges, venues etc.)

Television / Cable & Broadcast
Local cable companies may allow public service announcements. Call them.

Word of Mouth
Artist should talk to all their friends about their upcoming gig. Get them involved. At least they'll be going to the event, and they'll probably tell their friends about it too.

Publicity Tips

1. **Plan the Artist's work, and work the Artist's plan.** Music writers are busy. Newspapers and local magazines need to have the Artist's promo kit at least three weeks before the issue hits the street. Magazines need the Artist's info two to three months ahead.

2. **Do the Artist's homework.** Make sure that the publication buys what you're selling. Don't send a rock promo kit to a classical music editor. No matter how good it is, you're wasting his time and the Artist's. If you want to send the Artist's kit to a national or regional paper, find out beforehand if they review unsigned and independent bands.

3. **Keep a Contact Log.** Keep a chart or database with publications, editor names, date contacted, etc. When you're approaching more than one publication, it's difficult to keep the Artist's information straight by using memory alone (or scraps of paper).

4. **What's the Artist's Story?** You're playing a show next month. So are 10,000 other bands. To get a writer to come to a show that's not a CD release party will take some planning. Can you tie in the Artist's show to an unofficial holiday or a charity fundraiser? Are you doing something out of the ordinary in the Artist's performance that a writer should come to the Artist's show instead of another band's? Help them help you.

5. **Patience is a virtue.** You may have to call a few times before an editor will be at his desk, or even take the Artist's call. Keep trying. Call at different times of the day.

6. **Rehearse the Artist's pitch** when talking to a newspaper writers. Be friendly. Be brief. Be considerate of their time. Have an idea of what you're going to say beforehand or you're wasting their time.
7. **Help them to help you**. Do not send handwritten press releases or bios. Make the Artist's materials easy to read. Type it clearly. Send CDs without shrink wrap. If they leave a message for you, return the call ASAP.
8. **Follow up, Follow up, Follow up.** There is a Bermuda Triangle in the press industry. Yes, things get lost. Confirm receipt of the Artist's press release and/or promo kit. If the first one was not received, send it again and keep the Artist's mouth shut.
9. **If he/she turns you down**. There may another band playing that night in the Artist's same genre. The magazine may not cover the Artist's style of music at all. The writer may personally not like the Artist's music. Ask why and make note of the reason in the Artist's log. Thank them, hang up, and move on.
10. Say Thank You. If you get press, send a note, letter, or small gift. Not many people do.

****

8.10 Sample

****

8.10 Task

For this section of the Artist Business Plan, write about the plan for promoting performances of the Artist..

****

****

Notes

_____

_____

_____

_____

_____

Notes

Chapter 9
Business Plan for Artists
Advertising Plan

The Advertising Plan shows how the Artist will advertise their product and services. An Artist's advertising plan is a basic subset of their marketing plan. It helps the Artist to establish smaller goals as part of their larger marketing strategy.

Advertising and Promotions Plan
The plan includes what target markets the Artist may want to reach, what features and benefits the Artist wants to convey to each of them, what methods and media will be used to convey it to them, who is responsible to implement the methods and how much money is budgeted for this effort. The plan often includes plans for a promotional campaign, including an advertising calendar and media plan. The goals of the plans should depend very much on the overall goals and strategies of the organization, and the results of the marketing analysis, including the positioning statement.

When selecting methods, consider what communications methods and media will be most effective in reaching target markets (groups of customers) and when. What are their preferences for media and when do they use them? Consider, for example, radio, newsletters, classifieds, displays/signs, posters, word of mouth, press releases, direct mail, special events, brochures, neighborhood newsletters, etc. What media is most practical for us to use in terms of access and affordability?

There are various types of advertising available for Artists. What is the Artist's strategy for when to purchase certain ads? More importantly, remember the big picture lends itself to specific advertising.

What are the Artist's plans for advertising in magazines and newspapers? Is there a plan to advertise on radio, or television? Do you have a database? Are there contests or promotional giveaways for the radio DJs or their audiences?

What have been the Artist's past successes with the Artist's advertising media outlets, if any?

What is the plan to coordinate the Artist's advertising with the Artist's promotion? Is there a way to leverage them together?

Of all the off-line advertising possibilities, which ones are being targeted? What are the Artist's plans for print media? What are the newspapers and periodicals that are being targeted? Why did you choose newspapers, periodicals or magazines that you chose? What are the Artist's plans for direct mail, if any? This is important if dealing with lesser-known publications and need to spell out the benefits for the Artist's reader.

What are the plans for using any of the online medias? What social networks such as Facebook, MySpace, ReverbNation or Tunecore do you plan to advertise with? Make sure to show the benefit of working with these companies.

Appendix: background information on any lesser known TV, print, or online medias. This way, you don't make this section too large.

For example, an advertising plan may be created for a few months to a year, where an Artist's overall marketing strategy may focus to increase 10 new performance markets in 5 years. The plan includes objectives, reports, market research, media outlets, a budget and both offline and online strategies. When it is completed, an advertising plan helps an Artist stay on track during their advertising campaigns.

Sales vs. Advertising and Promotion
Typically promotions are directly linked with sales while advertising is an assumption that it may lead to sales. For example: Giving a free download on products may attract a fan customer and induce an instant sale while purchasing a general brand advertisement for the Artist in a newspaper may not induce an immediate sale.

Promotions are directly linked to sales and hence for small companies it may be easier to use promotional methods. Advertising may be more expensive for small companies and it may not be feasible for them.

For example: An Artist may give away a free download on its products which may increase sales while the same Artist may find it difficult to advertise this in various media outlets.

The Artist's Business Plan should have an overview of marketing objectives, along with financial, website support and a calendar of company objectives. Review the Artist's broader marketing timeline and goals for the Artist's marketing team.

First of all, Artists need to review their marketing plan. The marketing plan takes into account all modes of business strategy to increase sales of both recordings as well as performances. In addition, the advertising plan should be coordinated with the promotion plan of the Artist.

Next, Artists should review their database to determine their targets. Identify those targets and see how those targets fit the overall strategy of their marketing plan as well as their promotion plan.

Advertising Plan Overview

9.01
Advertising Plan Overview

With this completed, Artists can take the information provided in the subsections of the Advertising plan and put it into the overview.

Advertising Strategy
The strategy for advertising for an Artist depends on their budget as well as their targets. Once an Artist has a plan, then they can devise the strategy to implement that plan.

Advertising Analysis
This is a detailed review of the advertising prospects for an Artist and an Artist's products and services within a potential market. For example, an Artist may perform an advertising analysis for new recordings the Artist wishes to release. This helps the Artists forecast whether market conditions will support launching an advertising effort into that market

Advertising Objectives
These are objectives that the Artist sets to build a customer base while advertising their brand. The overall goal of advertising is to create a need for the Artist's products or services in the consumer's mind. Advertising objectives are achieved through a range of marketing activities, including newspaper and radio advertising, online advertising, as well as printing flyers and posters.

Advertising Potential
Every media outlet wants to sell advertising in inches or airtime. This may be cost prohibitive to an Artist. If this is the case, the Artist must look at the potential for their advertising and their blend of promotion and public relations.

Advertising Budget
All financial decisions should be in complete agreement with the finance plan for any Artist and any business. As the Artist establishes their goals and objectives for their new products and services, they need to analyze the costs and weigh it against potential sales. This budget may be reflected in the Finance Plan.

Advertising Co-Op
There are many cases where advertising for an Artist can be shared with other companies, Artists and brands. Perhaps, the Artist can tag the end of radio spots bought by the promoter or venue where they are performing. Another example is the sharing of a street team with other Artists.

Creative Talent
Who is the creative talent behind the design, layout, and graphics for an Artist's advertising campaign. As a part of the advertising plan, Artists are encouraged to look at the personnel section of the Artist Business Plan to see how the creative talents work in harmony with the Artist's flyers, posters, web banners, web site design, etc.

Advertising Offline Strategy
As a part of the Artist's Advertising Plan is the strategy for both online and offline advertising objectives In this section, Artists should consider flyers, posters, postcards, telephone messages, marquees, as well as street teams and word-of-mouth.

The Online Advertising Strategy for an Artist may consider e-mail, tweets, the Artist's website, social networks, as well as advertising through Online Music Distributors,

****

9.01 Task

In this part of an Artist Business Plan, condense the sections of the advertising plan and put it here in the overview.

****

Advertising Strategy

9.02
Advertising Strategy

Advertising is an almost universal tool for every business and every product. Artists use it to gain the attention of their customers and potential customers as well as create desire for their recordings, music, or tickets to the Artist's performances. More importantly, the advertising strategy is used to prompt customers to buy.

Advertising is defined by the American Marketing Association as: 'Any paid form of non-personal presentation and promotion of ideas, goods or services by an identifiable sponsor'. There are many activities that may be classified as advertising.

Artists have many ways to advertise their art and their business. New opportunities are developed every day. Advertisements of an Artist's gigs and recordings can be placed in local and national press, in magazines, and on the Internet. Artists may also create ads for poster sites, radio spots and television commercials. Advertising can be as simple as dropping leaflets and flyers, placing posters in shop windows, record stores, bulletin boards, etc. The use of direct mail may be used as a direct promotional shot to potential customers, and existing customers.

In many cases, especially with simple advertisements, the newspaper or magazine experts may be able to assist an Artist with the layout of their ads. For more ambitious advertising campaigns, an Artist will probably need the help of an ad agency.

In order for an Artist to create an advertising strategy, they need a clear understanding of a few things:
- The message – this should be simple and consistent throughout the Artist's activities, performances and projects.
- The target audience – Artists should know what products or services they want to send to which market segments. This target market is defined in the Artist's Business Plan.

Artists will then need to decide which type of activity best reaches their target audience, and which will carry the message. Advertising in movie theaters is good for targeting young people, while entertainment industry trade magazines are good for targeting customers who are music industry professionals.

Established Artists have a built-in advantage of repeat customers (provided they keep their quality high.) Artist's businesses often find impact can be significantly improved by repeating campaigns or running the same campaign in different media e.g. posters and flyers.

Word of mouth is excellent small business advertising tactic but it's slow, and may be practically non-existent for new Artists. If the Artist wants to grow their customer base more quickly, they have to advertise.

****

9.02 Task

For this section of the Artist Business Plan, write about the advertising strategy for the products and services of the Artist's company.

****

Advertising Analysis

9.03 Advertising Analysis

The use of media has never been more important for Artists of all genres and styles.

Specific techniques to construct believable stories, hook our attention through psychological devices and technical effects.

Advertising analysis is a specialized form of market research and has become increasingly common as the costs of promotion have escalated. Because any mistake can be costly, analysis is done at every stage of the advertising process: while the Artist's message is developed, when the copy is being prepared, and after the advertisement runs. Smart Artists use a range of techniques to test the effectiveness of advertising approaches.

Developmental Research
Analysis of potential advertising messages is known as developmental research. Its goal is to understand the kinds of promises and solutions sought by the Artist's target audience. One approach, called concept testing, involves asking consumers for feedback on the Artist's suggested message or new product ideas.

Evaluative Research
Evaluative research is used to judge the effectiveness of proposed copy and visuals of the artist's message. One method of analysis is a communication test, where members of the Artist's target audience view the ad and then give their opinions or respond to a questionnaire about it. Two other approaches are recall and recognition tests.

Field Research
After an Artist's ad is launched, the goal of analysis is to evaluate how well it is working. A common approach surveys members of the target audience over time. This allows the Artist to track ongoing changes in the fans and customers attitudes, purchase intent and knowledge of the Artist or the Artist's products. Artists then assess the effectiveness of their advertising based on number of direct responses, like the number of inquiries or sales generated by a particular ad.

Challenges
While no form of marketing research is easy, advertising analysis faces unique challenges. First is the problem of audience distraction. If fans and customers engage in other activities such as eating or talking to friends, a poor recall score may say little about its effectiveness. Similarly, someone who

casually flips through a magazine may be unable to give meaningful feedback about a particular print ad. Another challenge is posed by Internet advertising, which is believed to influence people in different ways than traditional media vehicles.

****
9.03 Task

For this section of the Artist Business Plan, write about the advertising analysis for the products and services of the Artist's company.

****

Advertising Objectives

9.04 Advertising Objectives

Advertising is a one-way communication whose purpose is to inform potential fans and customers about the Artist's products and services: their songs, recordings and upcoming performances. Advertising is also the plan on how to obtain them. It involves disseminating information about an Artist's live show as well as their recorded products. In addition, advertising contributes to Artist branding. Advertising is one form of promotion.

Differences in Timeframe
Promotions are time specific and may be short term while advertising may be generically long term. For example: an Artist's company may start a promotion of giving away music downloads at gigs during the festival season, while advertising about their music may start before the festival season and extend during and beyond the season. Advertising is aimed towards the long term building of the Artist's brand while promotion is aimed at the short term tactical goal of moving ahead in sales.

****

	Advertising	Promotion
Time	Long term	Short term
Price	Expensive in most cases	Not very expensive in most cases.
Suitable for	Medium to large companies	Small to large companies
Sales	Assumption that it will lead to sales	Directly related to sales.
Example	Purchasing an advertisement in the newspaper about the major products of an Artist	Giving free products, sample music downloads, coupons etc.
Definition	Advertising is a one-way communication whose purpose is to inform potential customers about products and services and how to obtain them.	A Promotion usually involves an immediate incentive for a buyer which could be an intermediate distributor or end consumer. It can also involve disseminating information about an Artists product, performances, product line, or brand.
Purpose	Increase sales, brand building.	Increase sales.
Result	Slowly	Very Soon

Advertising Types:
- Media: Commercial advertising media can include wall paintings, billboards, street furniture components, printed flyers and rack cards, radio, cinema and television ads, web banners, mobile telephone screens, shopping carts, web pop-ups, skywriting, bus stop benches etc.
- Covert Advertising: Covert advertising is when a product or brand is embedded in entertainment and media. For example: John Travolta wearing only "Diesel" clothing in a movie.
- Television Commercials: Virtual advertisements may be inserted into regular television programming through computer graphics. It is typically inserted into otherwise blank backdrops.
- Internet Advertising: This is the newest form of advertising wherein web space is used and e-mail advertising is utilized.

****

9.04 Task

For this section of the Artist Business Plan, write about the advertising objectives for the products and services of the Artist's company.

****

Advertising Potential

9.05
Advertising Potential

The promise of media advertising is great. It's an opportunity for an Artist to tell its story directly to the ultimate consumer; whether a fan or a music industry professional. It's an opportunity to build awareness and project a powerful brand image. It's an opportunity to create and build brand equity. It's an opportunity to bypass the trade as well as an opportunity to circumvent competitors. In actual practice, however, the promise of media advertising is seldom realized. In fact, the opposite is true. Media advertising is probably the most inefficient, least productive expenditure in the typical company's marketing budget. Why is media advertising's potential not realized?

First, few Artists do basic strategy research to develop a creative blueprint to guide the development of their advertising. Second, fewer Artists pretest their advertising creative to make sure it has a chance to work. Third, even fewer Artists track their advertising once it's "on air" to measure the effects of the advertising over time. Advertising tends to be created in an informational vacuum and is rarely evaluated in any consistent, systematic way thereafter. In effect, there is no reliable feedback loop, so the advertising muddles along from year to year, never getting any better.

No wonder that many Artists have grown weary of traditional media advertising and have shifted media dollars into sales promotion and direct-response marketing activities—where effects tend to be immediate, easy to see, and to measure.

The strategic potential of media advertising is just as great as ever, perhaps even greater, since so few companies seem to understand how to create and deploy consumer advertising that really works.

****

9.05 Task

For this section of the Artist Business Plan, write about the advertising potential for the products and services of the Artist's company.

****

Advertising Budget

9.06
Advertising Budget

The best approach to advertising is for Artists to think of it in terms of media and which media will be most effective in reaching their target market. Then they can make decisions about how much of their annual advertising budget they're going to spend on each medium.

Consider what percentage of an Artist's annual advertising budget will be invested in each of the following?
- the Internet
- television
- radio
- newspapers
- magazines
- telephone books/directories
- billboards
- bench/bus/subway ads
- direct mail
- cooperative advertising

Artists should include not only the cost of the advertising but their projections about how much business the advertising will bring in as a result of their efforts.

Advertising is probably the toughest part of any business. How much to spend, where to place the ads, how often, what message to send, and to whom? It's not possible to answer all these questions all at once but they should be considered none the less.

How Much To Spend?
The most common answer to this question is, "How much have you got?" Advertising has a way of depleting an Artist's bank account very quickly. If you asked 100 businesses that question, the most common answer would be, "a percentage of gross sales." This not only works for advertising but most other budgets too. Here's how it works.

Percentage of Sales Method
Take the Artists total last year's gross sales or (if you don't have a last year) use average industry standards. Set a specific percentage of that amount which will be allocated for advertising. Depending on the business this amount may be a daily, weekly, monthly or quarterly expense. The percentage amount will also vary depending on the Artist's profit margins, industry, location and market size. Most Artists businesses operate with an advertising budget of 2-5 percent of their previous years gross sales.

One of the main reasons most Artists like this form of budgeting is the safety factor. Rather than having to "predict" the future and adjust, they are always dealing with a "known" amount.

Sales Objectives Method
Using this method, advertising managers will set sales objectives they feel are attainable in the current business climate. Advertising and promotion is then used as needed to help realize the sales goals regardless of what happened in previous years.

The up side is that if the advertising is done correctly it becomes an investment, not an expense and can fuel more advertising at later dates. The Artist grows and expands at a faster rate than it would with the percentage of sales method.

The down side is that advertising based on a bad promotion or incorrect advertising can be very costly. Suddenly future advertising becomes an expense not an investment. Costs like this cannot always be recouped quickly and may start a downhill slide that can destroy an Artist and their company.

How to Budget for an Individual Ad
Now that you know two methods for budgeting your advertising it's time to look at putting them to work. Advertising is like eating an elephant. It's done in small bites not one big one. Artists can run several ads over a period of time rather than one large ad. How much the ad will cost depends on the answers to the following questions.

All advertising must accomplish a specific definable goal. What will this ad do for your business? What is the short-term benefit to the Artist for running this ad? The long-term benefit?

Is this ad financed by the percentage of sales method or a sales objective percentage method? What is the dollar amount allocated to this ad? Are Co-Op funds available? What is the expected revenue this ad will produce?

Are comparable ads being run for competitive products? What size ads do they use? Can you run similar size ads?

What is the specific time period for achieving the advertising goal? What form of evaluation will be used to assure that the ad is working or not working?

****

9.06 Task

For this section of the Artist Business Plan, write about the advertising budget for the products and services of the Artist's company.

****

| **Advertising Mix** |

9.07 Advertising Mix

The advertising mix is the combination of techniques used to advertise and market a brand.

Products and Service
Branding
Price
Place
Promotion
People
Physical Presence
Process
Physical Evidence

Products and Service: what the Artist sells, and the variety or range of products they sell. This includes the quality.

Branding and reputation of the product. For a service, support for the customers after the purchase is important. For example, an Artists logo placed on a receipt of a customer's purchase.

Price: how much the product or service costs.

Place: where the product or service is sold. This means the location of the Artist's products with online or offline, or the accessibility of their service – how easy it is to access.

Promotion: how the Artist tells consumers about their product or service. The promotional mix is a blend of the promotional tools used to communicate about the Artist's products and services – for example, TV advertising or newspaper ads.

People: how the members of the band, staff (or employees), are different from those in a competitor's organization, and how the Artist's customers are different from the competitors.

Physical Presence: how your merch table or website looks.

Process: how the Artist's products are recorded, manufactured, built and delivered, or how the service is sold, delivered and accessed.

Physical Evidence: how the Artist's service becomes tangible. For example, tickets, t-shirts policies and brochures create something the customers can touch and hold.

****

9.07 Task

For this section of the Artist Business Plan, write about the advertising mix for the products and services of the Artist's company.

****

Co-Op Advertising

9.08 Co-Op Advertising

Cooperative advertising is a cost-effective way for Artists and their businesses to reach their target markets. Although co-op advertising policies differ, many Artists pay a portion of the advertising costs and co-op (cooperate) with retailers.

An Artist's contribution to a cooperative advertising campaign can range from a large amount of money to promotional gimmicks and point-of-purchase displays. Using co-op advertising cuts down not only on an Artist's media costs but also on their ad production and creative expenses as well. Artists who want to be smart advertisers should factor co-op advertising, if available, into their budget.

Another example of cooperative advertising is when Artists who are performing at the same stage on the same co-bill may join together and split costs and distribution of flyers and posters of their upcoming gig with other artists on the bill. The venue might want to get involved with the co-op promotion as well. These promotions may also be used to join forces in local newspapers, flyers, radio ads, and so on.

Artists should be careful to coordinate any co-op advertising they do within their overall marketing scheme. Artists should only use co-op advertising if it meets their needs. If the Artist has chosen a different approach in their advertising campaign, they shouldn't switch in midstream just to take advantage of free advertising dollars.

Here are some tips to help Artists get the most out of co-op advertising:

1. Keep careful records of how much is purchased from each collaborator.

2. If you try something unusual, such as a sales video or catalog, get prior approval from each collaborator before proceeding.

3. If you're preparing your own ads, work with an advertising professional to prepare an ad you think will appeal to your the fans and customers.

4. Make sure the Artist's name stands out in the ad. Your goal is not so much to sell the product but to get customers to pay attention. It's branding.

5. If a concert promoter or music retailer has no established co-op program in place, pitch your ad campaign to them anyway.

6. Expect vendors such as nightclubs to help out; after all, you're bringing them business. If your collaborator doesn't offer co-op advertising money, you should look for another who does.

****

9.08 Task

For this section of the Artist Business Plan, write about the plan for co-op advertising for the products and services of the Artist's company.

****

Creative Talent

9.09 Creative Talent

Although individuals who are considered creative talent for advertising may be considered in the personnel section of the Artist Business Plan, it is included here so it will not be forgotten.

An Artist may have a great marketing plan, but now they need to hire the creative talent to implement their plan.

Although many Artists feel they are creative enough to design graphics for advertising, they may not know the standards for newspapers, magazines and printers as far as formatting, graphic registration and layout. It may be better if the Artist communicate with a professional about their creative ideas and let the professional do their job.

Finding the right creative partner to design an Artist's marketing material can be challenging and frustrating. Here are a few tips that may help with the process.

1. Artist should take time to determine what their budget is for their project. This way they know what kind of creative services they should target. If an Artists budget is limited, a small design firm or freelancer may be the best partner for the project.

2. Set up a personal meeting with your creative prospects to get a feel for their working style and view their work. Be prepared to make a decision to choose your creative partner from the quality of the work they have already done. Creative concepts takes time and most creative professionals will not start working for you until you have made a commitment to hire them for the project. A deposit is usually required to start a project.

3. Artists should receive an estimate from their creative prospects for the scope of their project. Make sure it is detailed and both parties understand what will be delivered. Do not start the project until an estimate and an agreement have been finalized by both parties.

4. Artists need to know a deadline and request a timeline for their project. Keep in mind that meeting a timeline is not just the creative partner's responsibility, but the Artists as well. Artists must keep their end of the bargain in order to meet the deadline. If the Artist has agreed to give feedback on the creative design on a certain day and they do not, then that may affect the deadline.

5. Artists should not be afraid to communicate what they like or don't like about a design. Give clear direction so the creative team can meet expectations. Keep an open mind and sit back and let them do what they're being paid to do.

6. Make sure all decision makers are present during creative reviews. This way everyone can provide feedback and agree on the next steps. This will save time and money for the Artist.

7. It is not unusual to review several rounds of revisions before reaching the final design. It is the creative partner's responsibility to know the Artist's consumers and provide the marketing material needed.

****

9.09 Task

For this section of the Artist Business Plan, write about the marketing creative talent for advertising of the products and services of the Artist's company.

****

Offline Advertising

9.10
Offline Advertising

Many Artists jump into doing business online and neglect real-world or offline advertising. There are still many offline opportunities to grow their operations. A good mix of offline ads with online campaigns is a good strategic plan. It helps present the Artist's message and even reinforces it for those fans that have already followed the Artist online.

In addition, Artists can use offline-advertising to draw fans and customers, who have Internet access and email capabilities, to their online presence. Smart Artists know to add their URL or web site address and / or their e-mail address in all of their promotions; online and offline.

To succeed on social media, an Artist needs an offline strategy. In order to run a successful social media campaign, offline activity matters as much as activity online.

While it is relatively easy to set up social media channels, many Artists struggle with the next step; that of attracting fans and followers. This is not only a problem for Artists and their businesses but also the major corporations. Many major brand names have Facebook and Twitter pages but struggle to get their fan and customer numbers beyond double digits.

To understand the difference between Artists who attract fans and those who don't, take a quick look around the next time you go to a major show. Look at the number of the Artist's products that include social media references. Many young Artists forget to integrate social media into their existing offline marketing. The result is that fans and potential customers simply don't know about them.

Before embarking on a social media campaign, Artists need to ensure their offline marketing is an integral part of that campaign.

Offline Tips for Online Ads

- **Keep URLs short - redirect to a much longer address**
- **Keep Facebook usernames and twitter handles short**

Artists should do some offline planning for online advertising. Make sure that all of the Artist's offline marketing efforts reflect online promotions. This ensures the social media presence is ubiquitous. The Artist's printed material, such as business cards, flyers, posters and letterhead, should all include references to the Artist's online presence. The Artist's advertising material, such as pull-up banners, flyers, posters and stands that are used at the merch table or special trade events should have a reference to the Artist's online music and website. Many Artists are now using QR Codes for fans with smart-phone technology that may be able to access the Artist's website with a click of a button. Include it on ALL of the product packaging as well as point of sale material. If the Artist is planning to purchase advertising on TV or radio, make the reference here too.

When adding the Artist' social media sites to the printed material, don't overdo it. Rather than have a listing of every single channel, focus on the one or two that is most relevant to the Artist's target audience. Remember, the simpler the reference, the more impact it has on the customer, fan or music industry professional. The same applies to all other forms of advertising.

Think outside the box. Be creative. Think about all the places where the Artist may interact offline with fans and/or music industry professionals. How can the Artist attract their attention?

Smart Artists use offline promotions for online advertising. Here's a good example: An Artist may consider having a Twitter wall at their live performances. Twitter walls are low cost and low maintenance but another way to publicize an Artist's social media sites. All that is needed is a large screen and a trending Hash Tag around the event. The screen both encourages fans to interact as well as publicizing the Artist's online presence in the process. The interaction will continue long after the event is over.

The Artist's offline marketing channels will help promote the social media activity. The main benefit is that the Artist will make the fans experience more interactive, easier and more fun.

Many Artists struggle at finding effective strategies for marketing their art. Perhaps, the problem is not on the actual "finding" but more the implementation of that strategy. It's back to that old line about waiting for the phone to ring. The problem for many Artists is not just the time needed to think about the marketing but then to actually think about a strategy to implement that marketing.

****

Offline Advertising Tips

1. Magazines & E-Zines – When an Artist places display ads or classified ads targeting their website, some magazines that have a computer related section for the posting. This will help attract fans with Internet access and email.

2. Direct Mail Campaigns – The best place for an Artist to obtain addresses of fans is at their live performances. Artists should have a way for fans to write down their mailing address as well as e-mail address. Some Artists purchase or rent postal mailing lists and set up regular direct mail campaigns. Artists should cross-promote via email to help draw fans to their site.

3. Radio spots – Artists may want to buy commercial spots on local radio. Price ranges vary, and many times ad prices are a bargain in the very early morning. That very early morning could be on a Saturday or Sunday as many potential fans are still awake from the previous evening. It's also a good spot & catch business people who are early risers. Target the ad campaigns around particular shows that may present music or feature Internet use. A good strategy is to use the same spot just before or after a regularly scheduled program to target the same listeners over and over, so that they'll commit the web site to memory.

4. Event Marketing – Artist may want to create a CD-ROM, disk or DVD about the Artist, the Artist's website, as well as their products. If so, they should distribute them at live performances, trade shows, workshops and other special events. Make sure the Artist's contact information and web site on the cover.

5. Free Stuff – Many businesses give away free pens, pencils, mouse pads, note pads, yellow stickers, etc. that carry their website on them and contact information. Some Artists put advertising on guitar picks and give them away at the gigs. Here are some other free stuff that an Artist may consider to give away.
- Print and distribute cards that offer a free download.
- Have the fan e-mail list for a free samples
- Try to obtain information about the fan when they reach out to the Artist, such as an e-mail address, text number or mailing address. When the Artist sends their free sample, send them a card for another free sample for a friend.
- Have the ad offer free shipping and handling.
- Offer a "Buy One Get One Free" Promotion.
- Have them contact the Artist for a free catalog of the Artist's merch or other recordings.

6. Track how the advertisements are working. Some ads are better than others. The plan should reflect how the Artist plans to evaluate why and how some ads just don't work. One way to track an ad is to have the fans email/call/mail their orders to the Artist. Another way is to provide a special code fans will need to use to receive the special download. Use a different code for each campaign.

7. Contests – One strategy used by many performers is to have fans email/call/mail an entry to a free contest. Artists may use a copy of their recordings as the prize. After fans have won the free download, offer an additional discount for a purchase of a CD or t-shirt.

8. Keep Track - Once a fan has contacted the Artist, with some interest in their art, the Artist needs to keep in contact with that fan customer. First of all, reply to them in a timely manner and be sure to thank them for their interest. Offer the fan yet another form of a discount. Ask them if they would like to receive updates about upcoming performances or recordings. Then add them to the mailing list with their permission.

9. Follow-up – After sending the fan their free sample / free download / order / prize be sure to contact them again in a few days. Tell them that you wanted to make sure that they received it and then ask them for any thoughts/questions about it.

Remember:

Artists Build Fans One at a Time

****

Direct Mail

9.10.01
Direct Mail

Definition of Direct Mail: A marketing effort that uses a mail service to deliver a printed piece to the target audience.

Direct mail encompasses a wide variety of marketing materials, including flyers, brochures, catalogs, postcards, newsletters and sales letters. Many Artists as well as major corporations know that direct-mail advertising is one of the most effective and profitable ways to reach out to new and existing fans.

In most forms of advertising, Artists never know for sure just who's getting the message. Direct mail gives the Artist another way (music being the first) to communicate one-on-one with the fan. One great thing about that is now the Artist controls who receives the message, when it's delivered, what's in the envelope and how many people it reaches.

Tip: To learn about direct mail, put the Artist's name on a mailing list of a few entertainment industry companies. Take note of the Artist's reaction to each piece of mail, and save the ones that communicate most effectively, whether they come from large or small companies.

The most effective direct-mail inserts often use key words and colors. Make sure the colors used promote the appropriate image. Neon colors, for example, can attract attention for partiers and youthful festival attendees. On the other hand, ivory and gray are usually the colors of choice for lawyers, financial planners and other business services.

Involve the reader of the direct mail piece in the ordering process. Many mailers enclose "yes" or "no" stickers that are to be stuck onto the order form. Companies such as Publisher's Clearing House take this technique farther by asking recipients to find hidden stickers throughout the mailing and stick them on the sweepstakes entry. It also asks customers to choose their prizes, which gets them even more involved.

There is an association that may assist Artists who want to do more direct mail advertising. The Direct Marketing Association (DMA) is a national trade organization for direct marketers. They offer a free brochure that lists a variety of direct marketing institutes and seminars across the country.

With any type of direct mail, appropriately timed follow-up is very important. Mailings with phone follow-ups are most effective. Artists should follow-up when trying to promote an upcoming performance. In those cities that demand that the Artist sell tickets to their own show, direct mail with telephone follow-up works great. Don't wait too long to contact the fans / customer after doing the Artist's mailing: After several days, call to ask if they've received the mailing, letter or e-mail. If they have, now's the time to make the sales pitch. If they haven't, mail them another ASAP.

Postcards

Postcards are perfect for direct marketing. Unlike their enveloped cousins, postcards arrive already 'opened.' Glossy 4-color printing reproduces photography beautifully. Headlines and short copy are more memorable than letters. They have long shelf lives on refrigerators and cubicle walls. Use them for invitations, announcements, thank you's, couponing, gathering survey data and driving traffic to the Artist's business or website. A postcard's powerful impact combined with reduced postage rates make for a winning return on investment.

Mailing Lists

When it comes to prospecting for new customers, consider using a specialty mailing list. Three great sources are:

1) **Association Membership Rosters**. Many associations rent their mailing lists for industry-related marketing.

2) **Subscribers**. Almost all magazines and newsletters rent their readership files. These lists tend to be highly targeted, up-to-date and very responsive to direct mail.

3) **Tradeshow, conference and seminar attendees**. When matched up to the Artist's industry, these lists always perform.

Personalization Increases Response

Research proves that personalizing Artist's direct mail can lift the response rates by 30-50%*. Personalization can take the form of 'speaking' to the recipient by name, or customizing the imagery and messaging to be as relevant as possible. Plus, the combination of personalized postcards and a personalized web landing page can sometimes double response rates. Use a mail-merge option on your word processor to best handle this.

Call to Action

With direct marketing it's vitally important to invite response with calls to action. Call for action at least three times. Imply it in the wording of the offer (e.g. Enter to Win); follow the Artist's body copy with something like "call" or "click today"; and in the footer or 'PS' remind them to why they don't want to forget to do it today. Make the Call to Action large, bold and bright and use ample exclamation marks! Artists need to give the reader every possible vehicle to respond such as 800 #, local #, fax #, e-mail, reply card, website or personal URL.

Sell with Benefits...Not Features

When developing the postcard copy, it's critically important for Artists to phrase the features of their upcoming performance or upcoming recording as benefits to the fan / reader. Features are benefits; it's just a difference in perspective. To do this, simply ask the Artist "who, what or why a fan would want this feature?" The answer to the question becomes the benefit. Be sure to surround every benefit with the words 'you' and 'yourself' as often as possible. Always think "what's in it for them?" And finally, consider positioning these benefits as 3-5 bullets sandwiched between the opening and closing text.

First Class or Bulk?

The nice thing about sending mail First-Class is that the mail is often delivered in 2-5 days. It also gets forwarded and gets returned if undeliverable. Standard bulk mail, on the other hand, delivers typically in 5-7 days and does not get forward or return privileges. If time allows, selecting

Bulk Mail can save 6%-12% of the mail campaign. Smart Artists use both. Use First-Class postage to maintain and clean the database mailing list a few times a year and Bulk Mail postage at other times.

40/40/20 Rule of Direct Mail Marketing
The success or failure of a direct marketing campaign depends 40% on a targeted mailing list, 40% on a compelling offer and 20% on the mail piece format and design. That's right. It's most important to get the message in front of the right audience with an irresistible offer. Make sure the list is targeted, accurate and current. Make sure a valuable discount is offered, bonus or contest. Pretty pictures and 4-color glossy printing can certainly help generate interest and response, but the list and offer matter four times as much.

****

Newsletters

9.10.02
Newsletters

According to the Nielsen Norman Group's extensive E-mail Newsletter Usability report (based on 270 e-mail newsletters across 6 different countries), readers feel an emotional attachment to their e-mail newsletters.

Newsletters feel personal because they arrive in users' inboxes, and users have an ongoing relationship with them… The positive aspect of this emotional relationship is that newsletters can create much more of a bond between users and a company than a website can." – Nielsen Norman Group

So how do we keep that bond with customers and ensure we remain connected to our fans? Follow these seven steps and you'll be golden:

5. Be informative
Being informative and relevant is the end-all, be-all in the newsletter realm. Telling useful and/or compelling stories is also used to catch up with fans. If the Artist's e-mail looks like a newsletter, but isn't full of valuable, interesting, educational content, then it isn't really a newsletter. But what do people consider valuable content?

According to the Nielsen Norman Group, more than 40% of users said that each of the following aspects make for valuable e-mail newsletters:
    a. Informs of Artist-related news or company actions.
    b. Informs about personal interests/hobbies
    c. Informs about events / deadlines / important dates
    d. Reports prices/sales

Here are some examples of informative content you can include in a newsletter:
    a. Informative content e-mail newsletter
    b. Blog posts
    c. Tips, tactics, how-to's, tutorials
    d. Industry news/third party news
    e. Events & dates to remember, holidays
    f. Interesting facts

g. Reviews
h. Photos
i. Contests/contest winners
j. Resources
k. Artist news – updates, new products and shows, etc.
l. Infographics
m. Webinars and/or videos
n. Testimonials
o. Fan photos

6.   Lose the (sales) hype
People like to be informed of sales, but selling shouldn't be the main focus of an e-mail newsletter. Send the Artist's offers in promo-specific e-mails. Think of the Artist's newsletter as a trusted friend that the Artist's reader has let into their home/inbox. If someone lets you into their home and you instantly transform into a pushy salesman with a pitch, they're going to think twice about opening the door for you (i.e., opening the Artist's newsletter) again. If you want to plug a sale or a product in the Artist's newsletter, do so like a friend would: "Did you know we're having a friends and family sale this Saturday? You can save 50%!" and leave it at that.

7. Keep it brief & aim for a click
Guess how long the average person spends reading a newsletter? 51 seconds! Don't let that get you down though – attention spans are spread thin. Keeping the Artist's content scannable with content blocks, brief blurbs, snapshots, takeaways and/or bullet points and including call-to-action buttons will give the Artist's readers' eyes a scanning sigh of relief. But remember, friendship is give and take, and you deserve something too! Satisfy the Artist's readers with just enough info, but leave them eager to learn more. Lead readers back to the Artist's site/blog/social media network for more info. The point of a newsletter isn't to make a sale, it's to build a relationship with the Artist's audience, to inform/educate, and snag some clicks … which, with any luck, will eventually lead to a sale.get-the-click2

Put clear, strong and specific calls-to-actions after each content block so the Artist's readers know they need to "Learn More," "Read More," "Watch the Video" for more juicy details.

Newsletters need to be smooth and easy: they must be seen to reduce the burdens of modern life. Even if free, the cost in e-mail clutter must be paid for by being helpful and relevant to users – and by communicating these benefits in a few characters in the subject line." – Nielsen Norman Group

8.   Be reliable and consistent
Flaky fans – We have them, love them, but they're unreliable, unpredictable, and the more they flake, the less likely we look to them as customers. The same goes for the Artist's newsletter. If you tell readers to look for the Artist's newsletter each week, you better be there. Pick a frequency, whether it be daily, weekly, monthly, etc. and stick to it. Make sure to tell readers on the Artist's opt-in form just how often they can expect to hear from you – some people don't like surprises, last minute drop ins or no shows.

69% of users said that they look forward to receiving at least one newsletter, and most users said a newsletter had become part of their routine. Very few other promotional efforts can claim this degree of customer buy-in." – Nielsen Norman Group

9. Have a Compelling Opening Line

First impressions are important for establishing any type of relationship, professional or personal. How you introduce the Artist to someone can either pique or fizzle his or her interest in continuing a conversation. The same goes for the Artist's e-mail newsletter's subject line. If the subject line isn't compelling, interesting, intriguing, thought provoking, etc. the Artist's reader may not make it past "Hello." In fact, the Nielson Norman Group even found that "Some users who forwarded e-mail newsletters on to others said they sometimes changed the subject line to make it more interesting."

In the Artist's "From Label," state clearly whom the e-mail newsletter is coming from. Typically, using the Artist's company name (since it's more recognizable than a personal name) is advisable.

When crafting up the Artist's newsletter subject line, avoid using generic lines like: June Newsletter, The Artist's Monthly Newsletter, This Week's Newsletter, and The Insider, etc. and make sure to take advantage of the Artist's pre-header – It's like a secondary subject line (and possibly a second chance!).

The word "newsletter" isn't instructive or informative, and pushes valuable information-about the content-out of view in an e-mail inbox." – Nielsen Norman Group

10. Respond

Nothing's worse than talking to a friend who clearly isn't listening. You ask a question and all you get are crickets. Using a "do not reply" e-mail address when sending out a newsletter indicates to recipients that any responses will not be seen or answered. Allowing customers to reply to the Artist's e-mail newsletter, and responding to those inquiries or comments lets the Artist's readers know the Artist listening on the other end. You'll also receive valuable insight, feedback, and questions that very well may improve the Artist's newsletter for next time.

11. Let them opt-out easily

Break ups are rough, but would you rather someone break up with you calmly, or unknowingly throw you under a bus? A person unsubscribing from the Artist's newsletter is just a fact of life, and it's nothing to take personally. However, the harder you make it for someone to unsubscribe, the easier it allows them to click that seemingly insignificant "spam" button, and under the bus you go. Let the Artist's readers go easily if they so desire (they can always come back!) and make the Artist's unsubscribe link easy to find. Otherwise, sitting in a spam box will only cause the Artist's delivery, open, click through, etc. rates to go down.

Creating a personable, presentable and effective e-mail newsletter takes work, but it creates a good bond with the Artist's customers that most marketing strategies can't.

****

9.10 Task

For this section of the Artist Business Plan, write about the plan for offline advertising for the products and services of the Artist's company.

****

Online Advertising

9.11
Online Advertising

There are many Artists who are still not using basic online tools to advertise themselves. Perhaps, they never put together a plan of action for online advertising. Another important part of an Artist Business Plan is that of planning for advertising online.

A Five Step Internet Advertising Plan
By doing each of the actions, Artist may quickly create an online advertising plan that can be implemented immediately and begin reaping sales successes.

Step 1 - Define the Customer
Defining an Artist's customer is as important as defining their products or naming their company or band. Remember there are two types of customers for every Artist: fan customers and music industry customers. The advertising plan should be specific on who it intends to target.

Once this has been written out, Artists should have a good picture of where to start looking to place their message and how to write the message copy.

Step 2 - Choose the Online Targets
Now, where is a good place to post the ads? A coordinated effort across several sites and venues commonly frequented by an Artist's fans and customers is the most effective marketing campaign. If the Artist's ad is seen in several places, their visibility and retained message is much stronger.

Complementary sites may help cross-promote the Artist to visitors, who will then see the Artist there too. This may provide excellent reinforcement of the Artist's message.

When considering a website or social media network for an Artist's ad, look at factors such as traffic, search engine placement, external linking, quality of current ads and types of messages being presented in current ads.
- Are there many competitors of the Artist using this same online media?
- Is there advertising of a complementary nature to the Artist's business?
- Are the ads completely unrelated to the business and to the intended site?

These are all clues to measure a best fit of the Artist's message to the traffic of the site.

Step 3 - Budget
Artists can better create the budget for their online advertising plan when they have a good idea of the costs involved. This can only be done once the targets have been identified. Based on the Artist's Financial Plan, (Section 14) how much can be spent on Internet advertising?

Don't forget to consider ad swaps and bartering as part of the Artist's payment and marketing budget. Many sites will swap ads or banner ads for similar placement on the Artist's site. It never hurts to ask.

Step 4 - Creating Ad Content

Online advertising works best when it is focused only on one or two things. Artist's may have a variety of products but should pick one or two items that are good sellers and that have a solid appeal to the target market for the advertising campaign.

The most successful ads use words that relate to the fan or customer. Use words like You and Yours and never put the focus on Me, Mine, Our, My or We. Create several emotional words associated with the product - fun, comforting, relaxing, stimulating, and addictive - and use at least one of them in the ad.

Once the text ads have been created, go through the banner inventory. Attach an image. Does every image have an appropriate ALT tag? Is the graphic properly optimized for size (under 20-50kb) and resolution (72dpi)?

Step 5 - Track & Monitor the Ads

Tracking and reacting to the success of an Artist's advertising campaign is are critical in maintaining an effective campaign. From the Artist's website stats to Pay Per Click (PPC) stats, there are many ways to determine what is working and what isn't. By paying attention, Artists may learn volumes about their ads and how to hone them for best results.

Tracking tricks include using specific coupon or sales codes for each ad placement, setting up separate entry pages on the Artist's website for each ad, and utilizing a service that helps track activity. There are advertising management services that help advertisers to track ad performance, such as Google's DFP Small Business. This is a free service that is relatively easy to implement and gives powerful ad tracking management and support. Some venues, such as Facebook ads, provide their own reports.

Having an analytics program such as Google Analytics on the Artist's website is needed to continuously monitor their website performance. There are several important parameters an Artist can monitor. The three key items that support their online display advertising campaign are:
- Where visitors are coming from; called referral websites.
- Average time visitors spend on their website; or bounce rate.
- Conversion of visitors visiting the website taking the action that was intended by the ad. This based on conversion goals that the Artist sets up.

After placing ads, review the results of the various ads on a daily basis for the first 2 weeks. Write them up in a tracking sheet and look for any trends or patterns. Which ads are performing, where and why? If some aren't working, replace them with others that are or try another from the hold list.

4 Steps to Building an Artist's Online Advertising Campaign

1. What products or services are being offered?
2. Where can they buy them? The artist's website?
3. How attractive is the ad and content?

4. Who is the audience the ads are intended to influence?

To start an effective advertising campaign a simple written plan should be put in place outlining the Artist's advertising strategies:
- The Artist's overall expectations for the Artist's online display advertising campaign
- The Artist's market; who are you trying to reach, the Artist's target audience
- Online advertising mediums for reaching the Artist's target audience
- The Artist's sales cycle
- The Artist's marketing and advertising goals
- The Artist's budget

The next steps for preparing an effective online advertising plan are:
1. Define Sale Goals:
   a. Produce immediate responses for building revenue
   b. Long term – support long sales cycles, build relationships.
   c. Recurring Revenue - selling services
2. Define Marketing Goals:
   a. Branding
   b. E-mail list building
   c. Market Awareness
   d. Search Engine Optimization
   e. All of the above

Artists should define their expectation as this will provide them the base information for putting their advertising strategies in place as well as developing the ads. The plan does not have to be extensive. Each topic of the plan should be briefly defined along with forecast numbers for monitoring results against expectations.

****

Social Network Advertising

9.11.01
Social Network Advertising

As a part of the Advertising Plan for any Artist, is the prospects available online; especially with social networks. As with any advertising method, success in social advertising is totally dependent on the likes or dislikes of the fan or customer.

Generally speaking, there is a misconception that social media advertising is ineffective because it is so easily ignored. But any advertising an Artist does is ignored if it doesn't appeal to an audience. It is important for Artists to know as much as possible about the customer or the potential customer.

The advantage of social advertising has always been in the amount of personal data about a user's lifestyle and interests stored by each network. This allows Artists to select smaller, highly targeted audiences and share the most relevant content with those audiences. One great feature of online advertising is the possibility to greatly filter customer who fit a specific demographic.

Moreover, ads being placed in newsfeeds are much more effective at gaining audiences' attention because they look and feel just like standard updates — only with a little extra (paid) boost. In order to give an Artist a simple starting point, let's take a look at two of the most likely social advertising opportunities they will want to take advantage of — Facebook and LinkedIn: Facebook advertising is aimed at fans whereas LinkedIn advertising is aimed at Music Business Professionals.

Advertising to Fans

Facebook isn't the first company to make sponsored updates available to advertisers, but with its deep knowledge of users and massive reach, the social network is a perfect place to promote the Artist's content to fans.

Using Facebook's Promoted Posts ad unit, Artists can take the content they've already shared on their web site and have it appear in mobile and desktop newsfeeds alongside other non-promoted content. Just remember to make advertised content both appealing and relevant. To that end, here are some tips on how you can take advantage of Facebook's promoted posts:
- Don't just promote a link to the Artist's web site. Try promoting an image and putting a tracked link in the text section of the status. This makes the Artist's promoted post stand out on both mobile and desktop platforms.
- Always promote posts via Facebook's ad manager: This allows you to hyper-target the Artist's audience just like a standard Facebook ad unit.
- Promote the Artist's post to three groups: Non-fans, friends of fans, and even the Artist's existing Facebook fans. This combination creates new connections and reinforces old ones.
- Don't over-promote: Facebook post promotion is delicate, and Artists don't want to be considered spammy. So Artists should be selective of what is being promoted, and avoid promoting everything they have for sale.

Advertising to the Music Industry

LinkedIn recently followed in Facebook's footsteps by creating Sponsored Updates, an ad unit that takes a company page's status update and places it in users' newsfeeds. Unlike on Facebook, however, Artists can only promote a link using Sponsored Updates.

This makes it harder to stand out, so make sure the Artist's content is positioned to succeed. Here are a few tips:
- Share content of high value only: These include lengthy blog posts, eBooks, or white papers. LinkedIn audiences generally prefer more substance in their content than a list of top tips blog post.
- Make sure the content that is shared has a great image: Artists can't upload their own image on LinkedIn. Instead, they are limited to choosing one of the images on the page they're sharing. A great image on the shared page is essential to successful promotion.
- Don't forget to target LinkedIn groups: While Artists can target based on location, title to industry, groups on LinkedIn get right to the heart of what people are most interested in, similar to a Facebook page "like."

****

E-Mail Advertising

9.11.02
E-Mail Advertising

E-mail marketing is trackable, affordable and has a high return rate, making it valuable for small and medium-sized Artists. Here's a step-by-step guide on how to advertise via e-mail.

Advertise via E-mail

1. Prepare a list. E-mail lists used for marketing gather the names and e-mail addresses of all people interested in receiving communications from the Artist.

The easiest way to gather these addresses is by adding a field to the Artist's website that allows visitors to submit their names and e-mail addresses.

2. Decide on the frequency of e-mails you will be sending to the Artist's list. Once a week or every 2 weeks is a starting point.

3. Create a message to send to the list. Be brief and deliver a targeted message to the Artist's audience.

4. Write any follow-up messages for the Artist's e-mail campaign. •Follow-up messages provide emphasis on the Artist's product and remind customers of the Artist's recordings, merch or gigs.

Send multiple different e-mails to pique readers' interest if you're trying to launch a specific deal or a new product.

5. Proofread and polish the Artist's messages. Errors in spelling and grammar can be disastrous to the Artist's reputation.

6. Send the first message to the Artist's list. Follow up according to the Artist's schedule.

E-mail marketing works best when it contains a variety of engaging and relevant content. The Artist's messages should alternate between alerts and reminders, educational content and offers targeted at people on the Artist's list who have recently purchased items from you.

There are numerous low-cost or free software programs available to help manage mailing to large lists if you're spending too much time on e-mail marketing or if the Artist's customer base has boomed.

If the Artist's company doesn't have a website, you can solicit e-mail addresses for the Artist's list through customer questionnaires, a printed or e-mailed newsletter or by registering a customer in the Artist's database.

Warnings

Ask every customer if he or she wants to be contacted by the Artist's business. Including a customer that declines contact in the Artist's e-mail campaign is a violation of anti-SPAM law and can result in massive fines.

E-mail is the sweetheart of the current advertising models. Why are e-mail advertisements so successful? Because e-mail advertisements create dialogue, the Artist's customers can respond to you, a real human being, instead of watching a Web page.

E-Mail Tips
Here are some pointers on the best way to do e-mail advertising:

• Ask for e-mail addresses — never send unsolicited e-mail. People don't like to have e-mail forced into their mailbox, piling up without an end in sight. Make sure the e-mail addresses are given voluntarily from customers who really want to hear from you.

• Keep records of all registrations forever. Sometimes, years later, people tell you they never signed up. With great courtesy, show them their original registration and the date you received it.

• Always offer a chance to opt out. In each e-mail, tell people how they can stop receiving the mail (unsubscribe). Make the instructions clear and prominent.

• State the Artist's privacy policy. Tell people that you will never share or sell their e-mail addresses.

• Appoint a real, live person to handle problems and inquiries. You may want to have an automated reply that's sent immediately and lets the person know you received his or her message. Be sure to follow up with a personalized reply as soon as possible.

• Keep the Artist's list secure. Make sure that the recipients can't see each other's e-mail addresses. Make an alias list and put that list in the blind carbon copy (BCC) area when sent.

• Check the e-mail you send out for typos, misspellings, and so on. Always put the Artist's best foot forward.

• Choose the Artist's subject line with care. Make it provocative — and make it sound like something other than an ad.

• Avoid closing down communication. Never close off communication with a customer.

The Internet is no longer a free resource. Access to and a presence on the 'Net comes at a cost to the participants, the service provider, and the recipients of those services made available by the Internet. Due to the rapid growth and "mainstream" acceptance of the 'Net, new opportunities have been found for the distribution of information to the vast and ever-growing community of Internet users. For this very reason the Internet is a very useful medium to access a large audience.

****

9.11 Task

For this section of the Artist Business Plan, write about the plan for online advertising for the products and services of the Artist's company.

Create a spreadsheet or document of all the sites or social networks that are a consideration in the Artist's online advertising campaign.

Go through the list of targets and prioritize the ads in terms of where the Artist may get the most exposure and results that fit within their budget. Move the others into a holding list. Remember, as the ads start to pull in results, Artists can always go back and expand their campaign from that holding list.

Create a text ad for each item in the Internet advertising campaign, making sure to hit at least one to three prime keywords in the text. Text ads typically run 60 characters wide by 3, 5, 7 or 10 lines long.

****

Advertising Ideas

Here is a collection of small business advertising ideas for an Artist to effectively reach the target markets and attract new fans and customers.

1. Newspaper advertising
In addition to box ads and advertising inserts, local newspapers also often offer special advertising features showcasing particular businesses. Don't overlook special interest newspapers as an advertising idea if they exist in the Artist's area. They may be delivered to exactly the audience the Artist wants to reach.

2. Direct mail
Direct mail can be very effective small business advertising tactic and is much more favorably received than other direct marketing media, such as e-mail or telemarketing. Even if an Artist doesn't have a mailing list yet, they can still geographically target their mail based on their fans postal code. Postcards are inexpensive and easy to use with direct mail.

3. Magazine advertising
This advertising idea can be a very effective way of reaching a target market. The trick is to choose the magazines or e-zines that best match the customer market the Artist is targeting.

4. Business cards
Sure, they're advertising. Every time an Artist hands one out to a prospective fan or customer, they're advertising their small business. But why not take this advertising idea further by offering free downloads. This turns an Artist's business card into a marketing tool. Perhaps an Artist may put a QR Code with a link right to their website, or utilize the back of their business card.

5. Joining professional and business organizations
Every professional or business organization offers exclusive advertising opportunities for their members, ranging from free promotion on the organization's website through specialized section newspaper advertising. Being a member can be good advertising tactic in itself. A few good ones for Artists are performing rights organizations, songwriting associations, musician unions and many online groups.

6. Vehicle advertising
The reason there are so many vehicles emblazoned with advertising on their side is that it works. Vehicle advertising is very visible advertising tactic. If an Artist is not ready for custom graphics or a magnet quad sign that sits atop their vehicle, they may use a magnetic sign that they can take off when they want. If the sign is magnetic, Artists shouldn't forget to take it off the vehicle while they are performing.

7. Sending promos with invoices

Little advertising ideas can be powerful, too. If an Artist sends out an invoice, they may want to take the opportunity to include some advertising. To draw new customers, some Artists try promotions such as a "bring-a-friend" campaign. Or, every time a fan purchases a CD online, they may include a promotional piece with the shipment.

8. Cable TV advertising
Most Artists cannot afford to advertise their brand during the Super Bowl. That doesn't mean they have to miss out on the household reach of TV. Cable TV companies offer advertising ideas within the budget of small businesses, from advertising on the TV Guide Listings or M-TV Music channels through running infomercials. Look at what Boxcar Willie did for his career with television advertising.

9. Radio advertising
Another advertising idea that Artists may not have thought of is radio advertising. Running ads on a local radio station can be both effective and relatively inexpensive. If the cost is still out of reach, try purchasing time after midnight on Fridays or Saturdays. The Artist's target audience may be tuning in as they return from a show they just attended.

10. Bench or bus stop advertising
Looking to reach a mass audience? Then transit advertising may be the best advertising idea for an Artist. Contact the local transit company for information on bench, bus and shelter advertising possibilities.

11. Local website advertising
More people are spending more time online than ever before. Artists should cover all their small business advertising bases by ensuring that their business is listed on websites providing business information for the local area. Many municipalities, for instance, offer business listings on their sites.

12. Trade show participation
One of the main reasons to participate in trade shows is to be seen and get known. This is really for the Artist who is trying to attract the attention of music industry professionals. While participating in big trade shows can be quite expensive, there are a lot of smaller opportunities that may work well for the Artist's business, from trade shows put on by music conferences to trade shows focused on particular parts of the entertainment industry such as radio conferences or touring & booking seminars. Remember, an Artist's customer is not only the fan, but the music business professional as well.

13. E-mail advertising
If an Artist already has an in-house mailing list or is able to develop one, e-mail advertising can work. This advertising idea is more of a way to communicate with current customers than to bring in new ones because of the ever-growing hostility to spam.

14. Cross-promotion
Joining forces with other businesses can greatly increase an Artist's advertising power and their marketing reach. Many Artists team up with other Artists to co-promote a show that they are both a part of. While the Artist promotes their show to their fans, these other Artists may promote the show to their fans. This works really well for both Artists.

Will all of these advertising ideas work for an Artist's small business? No! But by choosing several of these advertising ideas and focusing on them, Artists will be able to grow their customer base much more quickly than they would by relying on word-of-mouth alone. Like any kind of marketing an Artist does, of course, their small business advertising will be most effective if they plan ahead. Write it down. Put it in the plan.

Notes

_____

_____

_____

_____

_____

_____

_____

_____

_____

Chapter 10
Business Plan for Artists
Competition

After completing the Industry Analysis, who are the top industry participants. If you are a new Artist, who gets the most gigs in town? How do you compare? Who are the Artist's top 10 main competitors?

Competition Overview

10.01
Competition Overview

This section of the Artist's Business Plan evaluates the potential competitors of the Artist including other performers, other songwriters, competing gigs and ultimately any potential dollar spent somewhere else by fans and customers.

Competitor Analysis
The music industry is a major part of the entertainment industry. Music is used everywhere and in the industry in places like nightclubs, movies, restaurants and recordings. Musicianship is needed for each of these parts.

How does the Artist plan to compete, for example, offer better quality products / services, lower prices, more support, easier access, etc.?

Actions in this area should be worded as specific goals and organized into the section "Goals, Responsibilities ..." later in this plan. That section includes goals, responsibilities, dates for completion and the budgeted amount to achieve the goals.

Tips
• Don't ask too many questions on the Artist's questionnaire as people are losing their concentration after a while - keep it quick and simple to get more qualitative, relevant answers

• Don't ask too many opened question. They give you precise answer but it will be harder and longer to analyze.

Industry Participants
The music industry is full of participants who expose and exploit the creative endeavors of the first industry participant, the Artists. These "second level participants" include record labels, booking agents, concert promoters, and publishers. In addition, there's a third level of industry participants who participate which include radio stations, movie producers and ticket takers.

Competitive Research
Competitor analysis in marketing and strategic management is an assessment

of the strengths and weaknesses of current and potential competitors. This analysis provides both an offensive and defensive strategic context to identify opportunities and threats for artists on all levels of their career. Competitor analysis is an essential component of an Artist's corporate strategy.

Competitive Comparisons
After the Artist has identified their competitors, they are now able to compare why they are more or less successful. This could be attributed to creative ability or to the team that the Artist has assembled.

Main Competitors
An Artist has thousands of potential competitors. Depending on the Artist's level of success and area of dominant influence, an Artist may have local competition and/or regional competition as well as national and international competition. If the Artist can identify their main competitor, they can either learn of their own mistakes and/or stay one step ahead by anticipating their competitor's next move.

Competitive Strategy
How does an Artist stay ahead of the competition? One good way is to have a good team of managers, agents, producers. These key team players are essential to spotting trends as well as staying current with the state of the music / entertainment industry.

****

10.01 Task
For this section of the Artist Business Plan, write about overview of the competition for the products and services of the Artist's company.

Competitor Analysis
(for each main competitor)

Name of competitor's organization
_____

Name of their service
_____

Common markets served
_____

Benefits of their product/service
_____

Comparison of competitors pricing and the Artist's pricing
_____

Strengths and weaknesses of their product/service
_____

How the Artists product/service compares to theirs
_____

****

Competition Industry Analysis

10.02
Competition Industry Analysis
The industry analysis section of the Artist Business Plan should illustrate the music

industry as well as the entertainment business. Artist's industry and market knowledge as well as any of the Artist's research findings and conclusions

The competitive analysis identifies an Artist's competition by product line or service and market segment. Assess the following characteristics of the competitive landscape include:
• Market share
• Strengths and weaknesses
• How important is the Artist's target market to the Artist's competitors?
• Are there any barriers that may hinder the Artist as they enter the market?
• What is the Artist's window of opportunity to enter the market?
• Are there any indirect or secondary competitors who may impact the Artist's success?
• What barriers to market are there (e.g., changing technology, high investment cost, lack of personnel)?

Competitor analysis in marketing and strategic management is an assessment of the strengths and weaknesses of current and potential competitors. Every Artist has competitors. By analyzing the marketplace for an Artist's products and services, competitors can be identified. This analysis provides both an offensive and defensive strategy to identify opportunities and threats. Fans and customers only have a certain amount of money that they are willing to spend on downloads, merchandise and live performances.

Competitor analysis is an essential component of an Artist's business strategy. It is argued that most Artists do not conduct this type of analysis systematically enough. Instead, they evaluate their competitors through informal impressions and intuition and not by actually studying the market. As a result, many Artists risk not getting enough bookings or not selling enough sales of recorded products.

The first step of preparing the competitive analysis is to determine who the competitors are. This isn't the hard part. If an Artist is planning to start performing locally, they can identify their competitors just by looking in the local music magazine. The main question for Artists will be one of range; if the Artist's performance is in the middle of town, how far will fans and customers be willing to drive to attend the show?

Accumulating a solid base of data is the opening step in creating a powerful competitive analysis. Artists then must analyze the report and use it to support their competitive strategy.

Distinguishing characteristics – What are the critical needs of an Artist's potential customers? Are those needs being met? What are the demographics of the group and where are they located? Are there any seasonal purchasing trends that may impact the Artist's business?

Size of the primary target market – In addition to the size of the Artist's market, what data can be included about the annual purchases that customers in an Artist market makes? What is the forecasted market growth for this group?

How much market share can be gained? – What is the market share percentage and number of customers that an Artist expects to obtain in a defined geographic area? Explain the logic behind this calculation.

Pricing and gross margin targets – Define the Artist's pricing structure, gross margin levels, and any discount that they plan to use.

When an Artist includes information about any of the market tests or research studies they have completed, they should be sure to focus only on the results of these tests. Any other details should be included in the appendix of the Artist Business Plan.

****

10.02 Task

Describe the industry, including its current size and historic growth rate as well as other trends and characteristics (e.g., life cycle stage, projected growth rate). Next, list the major customer groups within the industry, especially in the Artist's niche.

****

Industry Participants

10.03
Industry Participants

Whether the Artist is a performer, session player, professional songwriter or recording artist, they must know their role in the entertainment industry inside and out. Knowing entertainment industry participants is a part of networking and building relationships. As previously mentioned, this business is all about networking and relationships. These participants may include local nightclub owners to international touring professionals and the Artist's involvement with any of them will depend on their career stage as well as the project that they are currently working.

Depending on which project that the Artist is working, they need to know who else sells in that market. It's not easy to describe a type of any business without describing the nature of the participants. There is a huge difference, for example, between an entertainment industry segment of film producing, in which there are only a few huge companies, and ones like open-mic coffee shops, in which there are tens of thousands of smaller participants.

This can make a big difference to an Artist's business and their business plan. The local performance market, for example, may be "pulverized," meaning that it, like the independent record labels industry, is made up of many small participants. The mid-level touring market, on the other hand, is composed of a few regional and national bands participating in thousands of branded outlets such as large concert clubs or arena venues.

Economists talk of consolidation in an industry as a time when many small participants tend to disappear and a few large players emerge. In the record industry, for example, there are a few large international firms whose names are well known and tens of thousands of smaller labels. The mega-tour part of the entertainment business is composed of a few national brands participating in thousands of branded arenas. In the professional songwriting part of the business, for example, there are a few large international publishing firms whose names are well known, and thousands of smaller ones who are obviously unknown.

****

10.03 Task

For this section of the artist Business Plan, consider and write down the types of music industry participants that the Artist is, or will be, working with. If known, be specific.

****

Competitive Research

10.04 Competitive Research

Artists should assess the industry and the competition. This basically comes down to assessing a few factors:
1. Understanding who the competition is and factors such as competitor strengths and weaknesses, market position, pricing, new product development, advertising, marketing and branding. Artist should determine how they compare to their competitors.

2. Assessing the threat of new entrants into the industry and any potential reactions from existing Artists. There are basically six barriers to entry an Artist can evaluate: economies of scale, product differentiation, capital requirements, cost disadvantages, access to distribution channels, government policy.

3. Assessing the threat of substitute products or services that can place a ceiling on pricing.

4. Assessing the bargaining power of customers, such as talent buyers, who can force down prices or demand better quality, more services and play the Artist against a competitor.

Assess the Customer. This is a key step. Artists who get it wrong may not be able to recover. In fact, the customer value proposition and how it translates into growth and profitability for the Artist is the foundation of the competitive strategy.
For Artists to achieve their goals and vision, they must determine who are their target customers that will generate growth and a profitable mix of the Artist's products and services? (Section 7.01)

Competitor Profiling
Since Artists have two types of customers, fans and music industry professionals, it's important to note that their competitors may also have some of these same customers. After all, Artists performing in a local market compete for gigs, while Artists releasing recorded material on the World Wide Web may be competing with mega-stars for attention and sales. The strategic rationale of competitor profiling is powerfully simple as knowledge of rivals offers a legitimate source of competitive advantage. The raw material of competitive advantage consists of offering superior customer

value to both fans and music industry professionals. Yes, back to the issue of quality. Customer value is defined relative to rival offerings, making competitor knowledge a key component of an Artist's marketing strategy.

---

3 Ways to Profile a Competitor

1. Profiling competitors can reveal competitors strategic weaknesses

2. Profiling competitors allows the Artist to anticipate the strategic response of their rivals to the Artist's planned strategies, the strategies of other competing firms, and changes in the environment.

3. Profiling competitors gives the Artist strategic agility. Offensive strategy can be implemented more quickly in order to exploit opportunities and capitalize on strengths. Similarly, defensive strategy can be employed more deftly in order to counter the threat of rival acts from exploiting the Artist's own weaknesses.

Clearly, Artists who practice systematic and advanced competitor profiling have a significant advantage. One advantage is that the Artist may discover new fans. If an Artist studies the pattern of booking that their competitors acquires, they may discover new venues and new talent buyers to target.

There are common techniques that Artist's use is to create detailed profiles on each of their major competitors. These profiles give an in-depth description of the competitor's background, finances, products, markets, facilities, personnel, and strategies.

Competitor Considerations
 Location of gigs and venues
 Online presences
 History
 Marketing segments served
 Share of the market
 Customer base
 Growth rate
 Customer loyalty
 Promotional mix
 Promotional budgets
 Advertising themes
 Online promotional strategy
 Distribution channels
 Exclusivity agreements
 Alliances
 Geographical coverage
 Pricing

****

10.04 Task

For this section of the Artist Business Plan, write about the plan for researching the competition for the products and services of the Artist's company.

****

Competitive Comparisons

10.05
Competitive Comparisons

The competitive analysis section can be the most difficult section to compile when writing an Artist's Business Plan. Yes, art does have competition. On any given night, fans decide which live performance to attend. On any given website, fans have to decide which song to listen to. Before an Artist can analyze their competitors, they have to investigate them.

Knowing the industry is important. Knowing the competition and filling a niche is key.

It may be that the Artist will also have non-local competitors. If the Artist is selling tickets to a new performance, they may also have to compete with online gaming, television shows, and other Artist's live performances. Fans only have a limited amount of time and money to spend. Artists want to make sure that they identify all their possible competitors at this stage. By doing so, they'll be able to identify new ways to generate attention as well as dollars from their customers.

Secondly, Artists need to gather the information about their competition that may be needed for the competitive analysis. This can be the hard part. While Artists can always approach their competitors directly, the competition may or may not be willing to part with any of their internal business activity. How did the competition get their booking? How did they sell so many tickets? What relationship do they have with the customer? Where are they performing? ?

Learn from the competition. What markets or market segments do the competitors serve? What benefits does the competition offer? Why do fans / customers buy from them? It's also a good idea for an Artist to know as much as possible about their competitor's products and/or services, pricing, and promotion. Many times an Artist will find a new venue where they can perform just by examining their competitor's performance schedule.

Go see the competition. Yes, gather Information about the competitors. A visit to the competitor's gig is still the most obvious starting point. Also visit their website. Artists can learn a lot about their competitor's products and services, pricing, and even promotion strategies by visiting their competitor's web site, and may even be able to deduce quite a bit about the benefits the competitor offers. Watch how fans are treated. Check out the prices for merch. Investigate their music business relationships.

Artists can also learn a fair bit about their competitors from talking to their fan customers as well as music industry customers. A club owner knows exactly why they hired that particular Artist.

Once the competitor comparison section has been completed, Artists should be prepared to analyze it and determine new avenues for performances, promotions and online sales.

****
10.05 Task

For this section of the Artist Business Plan, write about the plan to compare the Artist's products and services with those of the direct and main competitors.

****

Main Competitors

10.06
Main Competitors

In addition to an Artist's competitive research and competitive comparisons as defined in the Artist Business Plan, this section identifies the Artist's main competitors. Depending on where an Artist is located on their latter to international fame and fortune, competitors may change regularly. In a local performance market there may only be a few venues for Artists to perform, their competition may be defined as any other Artist who gets a booking instead of them.

A huge amount of Artists presume they only need to get a gig and customers will appear; but what those Artists regularly fail to remember is that the overwhelming majority of their fine new customers are another Artists present customers. This includes fan customers as well as music industry customers. An Artist who thinks that these fans and customers will promptly shift and use their business is probably not a good approach. It is extremely imperative to distinguish who an Artist's competitors are.

On a national scale, many Artist look at the Billboard charts to determine direct competitors as one may be a higher ranking on the charts. Every Artist on the charts knows the name of the Artist directly above them; so does their record company.

The key to unveiling the information, around what an Artist's adversaries are up to, is to compile instances of any analysis, store these, and then carefully evaluate them. Does the competitor have a better live show? Do they write better songs? Do they have a well-connected manager or agent? Have they been around longer?

In this section of an Artist Business Plan, write down the direct competitors of the Artist.

****
10.06 Task

For this section of the Artist Business Plan, write about the main competitors for the products and services of the Artist's company.

****

Competitive Strategy

10.07
Competitive Strategy

When an Artists looks at their business, whether it's a new venture or a company with a long history, they should consider the following questions?

- What does the Artist do better than anyone else?
- What unique value does the Artist provide to their customers?
- How will the Artist increase that value in the next year?

Artists that fail to answer these questions, and don't believe they are of paramount importance, relegate themselves to marginal profitability at best and failure at worst. But Artists that can answer these questions are able to raise the value bar for their customers will reap the benefits of success.

> **Artists should focus on what they are good at and do that**

Of course, for an Artist to answer these three simple questions does not ensure success. However, it's an important step in creating a strategic and focused operation which leads to a successful business for any Artist. With today's music business environment being so competitive, Artists need to re-invent the rules on which they compete in order to be successful. Many Artists have figured this out and have redefined competition in their market by delivering a unique value to their selected customer group. By maintaining a focus on quality, Artists make it difficult for other Artists to compete.

Competitive strategy has never been more important for success in today's music business environment. It does not matter what type of musical niche that the Artist is in or whether they are small, big or just starting out. An Artist cannot survive without an adequate and focused strategic plan to maximize sales and trump the competition. Yet many Artists fail to execute a successful competitive strategy and it is these Artists that languish in the zero profit zone.

In simple terms, for an Artist to achieve success, they must first decide where they will stake their focus and their niche in the marketplace and what kind of value it will offer its customers. An Artist needs a clear marketing thrust, a precise knowledge of its customer base, and a product or service with a niche or some competitive advantage to be successful. Unfortunately, many Artists get stuck in the process of defining their competitive strategy. They often have an idea of the art and their products or services, but are not sure how to define their market. Even worse, many Artists assume or guess their target market and often glaze over a competitive strategy. BIG mistake.

The business model for an Artist shows how all the elements and activities of their business work together. This could be viewed as a whole approach by outlining how the business generates revenue, how cash flows through the business and how the product flows through the business. By this time, Artists should understand the revenue capability of their business, how the industry works and their competition, who the customer is, what the Artist is going to offer them and how their products or services are going to be offered. By drawing a flow chart that shows how these activities are linked together, Artists will understand how their business activities flow to generate projected profit. This is also a good step to see if something is missing in the Artist's analysis.

****

10.07 Task

For this section of the Artist Business Plan, write about the competitive strategy for the products and services of the Artist's company.

****

Notes

_____

_____

_____

_____

_____

_____

_____

_____

Chapter 11
Business Plan for Artists
Sales Plan

The Artist's Sales Plan is a part of the Artist Business Plan. Yes, another plan within a plan. The Sales Plan incorporates essential factors for the success of the direction and survival of every Artist in the entertainment industry. The sales goals and projections as well as the marketing approach are a key to every Artist's success. An important point to remember is that the Sales Plan is directly related to the Artist's Marketing Plan, Products and Services Plan and the Finance Plan.

Sales Plan Overview

11.01
Sales Plan Overview

The Sales Plan incorporates essential factors for the success of the direction and survival of an Artist in the entertainment industry. The sales goals and projections as well as the marketing approach is a key to the Artist's success. Refer to the sales plan to make changes according to any economic gains or challenges the Artist experiences as well as the growth and expansion.

Sales Methods
How will the Artist's products and services be sold? Who is going to sell them? The methods used by the Artist will ultimately determine the Artist's success or failure in the entertainment industry.

Sales Goals
Additional thoughts / comments and any resulting actions that the Artist should take.

Consider: What does the Artist need to do to make the sales methods and goals happen? What major steps must occur? What must be developed? Who should be contacted? What resources might the Artist need? Should staff attend sales training?

Actions in this area should be worded as specific goals and organized into the section "Goals, Responsibilities ..." later in this plan. That section includes goals, responsibilities, dates for completion and the budgeted amount to achieve the goals.

Developing the Sales Plan
A typical sales plan has two distinct sections---a sales plan outline and a business sales plan template. The sales plan outline consists of the marketing strategy, sales projections, sales forecasting and pricing structure. The business sales plan template will consist of a specific listing of the financial

information such as capital requirement, balance sheet, break-even analysis, projected income statements and cash flow projections.

Determine the products and quantity needed to sell to reach the sales projections. Include factors such as how the sales team is to approach selling the Artist's products and services. For example, if the Artist offers recorded products, the sales plan can include sending out postcards or posting online downloads. They should develop a competitive pricing structure for the products as downloads or compact discs.

The actual sales will help modify the sales approach, and the profits will reflect whether the sales plan is working. Keep in mind that different sales strategies will require different approaches, such as e-mails, Internet advertising, online music distributors, booking agent relationships, catalogs or retail stores.

Artists should conduct market research and focus groups for the Artist's products and services to help the Artist make educated decisions on the sales approach.

The Artist needs to know their customer base and target market for their product or service. If the Artist has a variety of products, it can be beneficial to separate them into categories and target specific demographic groups for each category.

Artists should set sales goals and projections for specific time periods. The Artist's weekly and monthly sales will determine how the sales plan may be adjusted and will have a significant impact on reaching annual sales projections. Artists need to review the sales goals and cash flow and make any necessary strategy adjustments during each set period.

The cash flow is the Artist's net income. It is important to determine the difference between gross sales and net sales. For example, if the Artist operates an online retail store, the MP3 download gross sales will be reduced by any buying and marketing expenses, which will in turn give the Artist their net income and cash flow for more purchases.

In addition, Artists need to set specific funds within the operating budget for advertising and promotional tools such as allowances for advertising, public relations, marketing sales promotion and lead-generation expenses. These are necessary expenses to promote the Artist's new products as well as existing merchandise. By keeping records of increased sales when using specific marketing strategies and Artists can implement them in other nonperforming sales areas.

Every Artists should develop an annual sales plan goal and budget. If Artists refer to the sales plan and projections weekly, they will operate at peak sales performance levels and stay on track to reach the annual sales goal.

There are many parts of an Artist's Sales Plan. Here are a few:

Sales Management is a business practice for Artists which focuses on use of sales techniques and the management of the Artist's sales operations. For the Artist to survive, this important business function drives the sale of its recordings, licenses and performances.

Sales Objectives are self-defining by the Artist in that they represent projected levels of sales of recordings, content licenses and performances to be sold. Everything that follows in the plan is designed to meet the sales objectives from confirming the size of the target market and establishing realistic marketing objectives, to determining the amount of advertising and promotion dollars to be budgeted for each of the Artist's projects, to the actual hiring or collaborating with marketing and sales personnel, to the number and kinds of distribution channels either online or offline or both, and, very important, to the amount of product produced.

Sales Strategy gives direction to the Artist in identifying and qualifying sales opportunities. It also provides a foundation upon which to develop appropriate sales tactics.

Pricing Strategy is the pursuit of identifying the optimum price for the Artist's performances, merch, song licensing and recordings. The pricing strategy tends to be one of the more critical components of the product mix and is focused on generating revenue and ultimately profit for the Artist.

Profit Sources helps the Artist to focus and refocus its resources on its best opportunities. Artists need to evaluate and maximize each income source: performances, song licensing, royalties, merch and recordings.

Sales Forecasts helps an Artist estimate their future profits. By forecasting sales, Artists can be guided about their expectations of profits or other financial measures, without being too specific.

Growth Strategy is the mean estimate of long-term earnings and growth for the Artist.

Sales Programs include incentives, pricing schedules, and cooperative advertising programs that may be used by an Artist. An Artist, for instance, may be engaged in making a transition from direct sales for its bookings to using Agents instead.

Sales Affiliates is strategy of income from referrals. Artist may consider another income source through affiliating with online retailers
.

Merchandise Sales Strategy is the attempt by the Artist to ensure the display, promotion, inventory and pricing is appealing to the fan or music industry professional.

Online Sales Strategy has become a great significance to an Artist's success. In order to create an efficient online sales strategy, the Artist needs to look at their long-term goal as well as analyze their business sales cycle with new songs and new recordings. An online sales strategy must be specific and detailed.

Recordings Sales Strategy is used when an Artist is determining the next song to record and, more importantly, the reason why that particular song was chosen to record.

Performance Sales Strategy helps an Artist focus on the types of performances to be targeting as well as the scope such as local shows or national tours.

Publishing Sales Strategy is all about targeting music supervisors, producers and others for use of the Artist's songs or about the strategy of attracting quality music publishers to collaborate with.

Distribution of an Artist's goods (recordings) and services (performances) needs to be set into place. This is done both offline through brick and mortar retailers as well as online music distributors. Brick & Mortar Distribution is one strategy that Artists utilize get their physical products into the hands of their fans and customers. Online Distribution is essential to the sales strategy of any Artist wanting to have their digital files shared with fans and customers.

Content Licensing is a sales strategy for Artists who are songwriters and/or Artists who own their audio recordings. The strategy is how to license that content..

Tickets Sales Strategy should be essential to any Artist preparing for a performance. Every Artist wants to perform for as many people as possible. Either directly or indirectly, an Artist needs a strategy to help sell tickets to their performances.

****

11.01 Task

For this section of the Artist Business Plan, write about the sales plan overview for the products and services of the Artist's company.

****

Sales Management

11.02
Sales Management

With good organization, sales management can fulfill expectations.

Having a quality team is an important part of any Artist's business. In the early stages of an Artist's career, the Artist wears many "hats." Many of those "hats" deal with sales. These are sales that an Artist tries to obtain for booking a performance. This hat is that of an agent. When an Artist tries to convince the rest of the members of the band to perform or record his or her new song, then the Artist may be wearing the publisher hat. Another example is when an Artist is trying to collaborate with a record label. They must sell their talents as a reason why a record label may want to collaborate with them in the first place.

To manage all the potential sales for an Artist can be daunting. The person who coordinates all of the sales may be the Artist or the Artist's manager; either way sales management is all about staffing, training, coaching and leading the team. They must also help close the big sales and be a liaison between the sales team and others within the Artist's company, such as the person who designs flyers for a gig that was just contracted. Being organized and following a plan can help the sales manager create order out of chaos.

Foundation
Lay the groundwork. For an Artist or Artist manager to establish a sales plan, the planning process begins with decisions about hiring or collaborating salespeople, writing a compensation plan and laying out territories. When assembling the team, the person managing sales must look at the various products and services of the artist and then decide the type of salespeople needed for the job. For example, an agent sells performances of an Artist for a booking, where a record distributor sells records to retail stores, or a friend sells merch at their gigs.

Establish the pay scales. The compensation plan must be sufficiently rewarding to assure that the team will be well-motivated. Assignments might be geographic or by product line. Commissions are the most common type of compensation. The sales person only gets paid when there is a sale completed. Typically, agents charge 10% commission when they obtain a booking for an Artist, where a brick-and-mortar retailer may charge 50% for carrying an Artist's CDs.

Ground Game
Organize the territory. A major part of sales management is forecasting revenue. The Artist or Artist manager must determine how many prospects there are in the sales territory, how many are likely to become customers, and what the average revenue per sale is likely to be. This will provide a rough guide that can be revised as actual numbers become available.

A good sales person develops a sense of how many prospects will become qualified leads that may convert to customers. It is also important to know how long the sales cycle is. For talent buyers, the cycle may be every 6 weeks for new Artists to every year or two for most established Artists.

A part of the sales management plan is to budget for salaries, commissions and miscellaneous expenses. The sales part of an Artist's organization is typically run as a profit center, so the Artist must plan for cash outflow as well as cash inflow.

Maintenance
Smart Artists know to monitor weekly reports and make necessary adjustments to their sales plan. The weekly report by sales reps is the manager's best tool for monitoring activity. Reports should contain a record of sales completed, prospects, projected revenue, closing probability and time frames. Monitoring weekly reports will reveal who is succeeding and who needs help.

Set aside time for trouble-shooting. Whether it is to help a rep close a sale or to calm a disgruntled customer, the Artist or sales manager must schedule available time for these activities. The manager must also be a liaison with the rest of the Artist's company and collaborators.

****

11.02 Task

For this section of the Artist Business Plan, write about the plan for sales management for the products and services of the Artist's company.

****

Sales Objectives

11.03
Sales Objectives

Obviously, a good sales objective would be for an Artist to sell millions and millions of dollars' worth of downloads, bookings, licenses, and merchandise. This is not a practical sales objective.

Identifying objectives, developing new prospects, reviewing previous annual sales and establishing a new sales forecast are all important for developing new products and assigning new sales teams.

When setting sales objectives, Artists should consider new sales-planning objectives by a sales promotion based on the target market of the Artist. This encourages new consumers and fans to switch to the Artist's brand or for entertainment industry customers to book the Artist's performance, sell recordings of the Artist's music, distribute the Artist's products in retail establishments as well as build new brand loyalty.

By reviewing previous sales performance objectives and goals. Artist will estimate what new sales-planning objectives will be used. They will be based on sales dollars spent on promotions, incentives, rewarding customers and business leads.

Artists should estimate whether their Artist's sales projections will be high enough to yield satisfactory projected income. Consider keeping products that continue to have a life-cycle in sales reporting and discontinue products that decrease in repeated purchases. For example, if an Artist releases a second compact disc and realizes that their first effort is failing in sales; perhaps the Artist should consider not pressing more of the first compact disc.

In addition, Artists should establish sales team quotas by region and/or territory. Keep in mind that if the sales team doesn't meet its quotas, it will fail in meeting the Artist's sales plan objective.

Once sales objectives are implemented, Artists need to prepare an annual marketing plan for the Artist's sales team to outline its individual program for developing new customers and keeping the existing customers. This reporting will also include expenses, new business and lost business.

****

11.03 Task

For this section of the Artist Business Plan, write about the sales objectives for the products and services of the Artist's company.

****

Sales Strategy

11.04
Sales Strategy

Inside the Sales Plan of an Artist's Business Plan is the section about Sales Strategy. Understanding that there are two customer bases, fan-customers and entertainment industry professionals, means there are two separate, but related, sales strategies for every Artist. Keep in mind that if the Artist can generate significant fan customers without the help of others in the music industry, then the second type of customer is much easier to acquire. At that point, the industry will pursue the Artist for possible collaborative projects such as performances and recordings. In other words, if an Artist has thousands of fans, music industry professionals will be much more eager to collaborate with the Artist.

An Artist's sales strategy is a plan that positions the Artist's brand and/or product to gain a competitive advantage. Why do some Artists always of keep their booking calendar filled and others don't? Perhaps their strategy is to book further in advance. Successful strategies help the Artist and the Artist's sales force focus on target market customers and communicate with them in relevant, meaningful ways. Timing is everything.

Plan ahead. Yes, Artists have sales representatives just like any other company. An Artist's sales reps are the agents, distributors, song-pluggers, and merchandisers. All of them need to how the Artist's products and services can solve their customers' needs. This way the sales force spends time targeting the correct customers at the right time.

Long-Term Sales Goal
To begin looking at an Artist's long-term sales goal, Artists should look at their five-year calendar. They should anticipate various strategies. For example, there are seasonal changes. There are holidays that very often present special events. There are other special days to complete on the Artist's calendar and task agenda. Planning and creating an effective sales strategy requires looking at long-term sales goals and analyzing the business sales cycle. After creating the long-term sales strategy based on long-term goals, the Artist should create monthly and weekly sales strategies based on the long-term strategy. With this, Artists will have a good direction for their short-term goals and tasks.

An Artist's successful sales strategy includes promotion, product placement, and testimonials. Brand awareness for the Artist now comes into play.

There are many marketing channels today and product placement and promotion has numerous outlets to create brand awareness. Most social media networks offer a free platform for increasing brand awareness. Artists can utilize these tools effectively by spending time each day to communicate with fans and followers on their social networks. Fan testimonials will help the Artist know what's working and what needs work.

****

11.04 Task

For this section of the Artist Business Plan, write about the sales strategy for the products and services of the Artist's company.

****

| **Pricing Strategy** |

11.05
Pricing Strategy

If a new Artist is about to start a new business, they need to keep in mind that launching a new product (recordings) or service (performances) requires detailed thought and planning. A critical piece of that planning is deciding how they should price their art; their products and their services. The pricing strategy they choose dramatically impacts the profit margins of their business. It also determines the pace at which it can grow. Yes, potentially, every Artist is the next viral hit. But overall (and realistically) every Artist has a building stage. Several pricing strategies should exist for the Artist's products and services, and choosing the best for their business depends greatly upon their overall long-term business goals and objectives.

The entertainment business is full of competition. Every Artist fights to survive, when planning what to charge, new Artists will face competition-based pricing strategies and focus solely on what the competition is charging, which, at the beginning may be pay-to-play situations. As Artists become more established they will still have to play the competition-based pricing issues but will be able to be more selective to the paying dates.

This pricing strategy is a difficult one for new Artists and their small business to maintain, because it provides very narrow profit margins that make it challenging for the business to achieve enough momentum to grow. However, just because an Artist may know how to play an instrument, does not mean they are worth any performance money to a concert promoter or talent buyers.

Since Artists have multiple potential product lines they will need evaluate the market for what is the current norm. For example, if the Artist wants to charge $5 for an I-tunes download, when I-tunes customers are accustomed to paying $.99, it will be very difficult for the Artist to make ANY sales. However, Artists who perform for audiences do charge different amounts for different gigs. Much of this pricing strategy involves the manager and the agent.

There is an old saying, "If it's free it not worth anything." That may be true for some things but many Artists give away their music and hope for a donation. Some Artists request a donation. This is another pricing strategy for an Artist.

Some Artists set a premium price on their product or service while some Artists may be justified for doing this while others are not. Many times Artists without the back-up of a large fan base will attempt to bypass the lowest-price-in-town mentality and strike at a segment of consumers who believe high quality comes at a premium price. Instead of trying to have the lowest price amongst competitors, Artists who use the premium pricing strategy attempt to price their products and services at the highest in their market. The idea is that if it costs more, it must be good. Sometimes this works and sometimes it doesn't.

****

11.05 Task

For this section of the Artist Business Plan, write about the pricing strategy for the products and services of the Artist's company.

****

Eight Sources of Income for Musical Artists

- Live performances   28%
- Salaried Player   19%
- Session Musician   10%
- Teaching   22%
- Songwriting   6%
- Sound Recordings   6%
- Merchandise   2%
- Other   7%

A great business idea isn't good enough to ensure long-term success. Artists must define and develop a workable plan and business model, or a method they use to generate revenue, earn profits, and protect their position within the marketplace.

In the early planning stages, while the Artist is defining their business and describing its purpose, they should think something very basic: "Show me the money." Not literally, of course, but from the very beginning, the Artist needs to be clear about how they expect their business to make money and be profitable.

Way too many art-related businesses start without a clear idea of where the money will come from. Many make general broad-brush assumptions to which they give no second thought or scrutiny. Delusional Artists with the flippant answer that customers will give the money in exchange for the Artist's products or services may be easy. Business models, however, aren't always that straightforward.

Profit Sources

11.06
Profit Sources

For an Artist's business to become successful, they must keep their eyes on the prize. Artists need to identify all profit sources if they are survive in this over-saturated glamour industry. The music business is one of the hardest businesses in the world. For an Artist to survive, they must identify and take advantage of every source of income.

Secondary markets within the entertainment business make money in many ways. With this in mind, why should an Artist only have one source of income?

A first step toward defining the Artist's business is to detail how it will make enough money to stay in business — for the sake of the owners, the investors, the customers, the employees and, of course, the Artist.

Income Sources for Artists

Most Artists have the luxury of multiple income streams. The smart ones are those that capitalize on all, or most, of them that have the greatest possibility of success. If a singer-songwriter complains that they cannot make enough income from performing, perhaps they should adjust their product mix. For Artists, their art is the product. Their performance is their service. The products and services of any Artist can be numerous. In addition to performing, Artists have the potential to make income from licensing songs, recording royalties, publishing, as well as merchandise sales. And, for more established Artists, branding, sponsorships and endorsements are certainly other sources of income.

In a recent survey completed by the Future of Music Coalition, it was established that most Artists earn revenue from three or more income sources. Here are some of their results:

Multiple "Roles"

More than half of the Artists surveyed earned their income from activity in three roles or more. Some of these Artists are composers and performers and teachers. Others are performers and recording Artists, but also making a bit of money off their brand.

Secondary Market Income Sources

- The local live-music nightclub gets revenue from ticket sales, but that's only the beginning. The venue may also make money by selling food & beverages. Some clubs also generate income from projecting billboard-style ads on video screens prior to the concert showings. They may also make money from selling t-shirts.

- Online music distributors make money on monthly subscription fees, but they also generate income from selling their data to marketers. Some record labels may pay them a fee to have their recordings listed near the top of their music list as well as post on the distributor's web site.

- Many event promoters earn revenue from online ticketing agencies, but another source of income for the promoter is the sale of sponsorships as well as the sale of merchandise. Some event and concert promoters also generate income from food and beverage.

- Publishers make money from the use of the songs they license for recording but also earn income from the songs use in a movie or TV show.

They surveyed the music-related income of 2,794 respondents. More than half of survey respondents said their income was derived from three or more sources. Only 18% said they made 100% of their income rom only *one* role.

Musicians differ in earning money from music relying on several revenue sources.

Different Types of Artists in the Music Industry
- **Performing Artists**
- **Recording Artists**
- **Composers and Songwriters**
- **Salaried Players**
- **Session Musicians**
- **Teachers**
- **Producers**

Basic Demographics

A "full-time" musician is often defined as someone who derives more than 75% of their income from music and spends more than 36 hours per week on music.

With self-distribution and access to marketing, the Artist is now: the label, the performer, the publisher and the songwriter. While wearing all of these "four hats" at once, Artists are now uniquely positioned to profit from the best possible contractual distribution terms and highest revenue generation via the sale, use, or streaming of their music and recordings. The challenge is that many Artists don't know what these rights are, or how to collect the money they've earned from these revenue streams.

Musicians earn their living in any of eight different and combined ways:

1. Live performance fees earned as a solo performer or as a band member

2. Salary as an employee of an ensemble, band or symphony

3. Session musician earnings, including payment for work in recording studios or for live performance freelance work

4. Teaching

5. Money from songwriting and composing including publisher advances, mechanical royalties, performing rights royalties, commissions, composing jingles and soundtracks, synchronization licensing, sheet music sales and gaming.

6. Money from sound recordings including sales of physical or digital recordings, payments from interactive streaming services, Internet radio, SoundExchange royalties, master use licensing for synchs or ringtones

7. Merchandise sales

8. Other

A comprehensive, streamlined, and completely inclusive infrastructure does not yet exist that enables every Artist who is owed money to easily collect it. However, there are solutions available.

Income from Music Performances

For musicians there are a few areas of potential income dealing with playing of their instrument or using their voice. The most common is that of a musician who performs live in front of an audience. There are two types of musicians who perform live: one being a solo Artist or a part of an Artist's band, and the other is a salaried player within an orchestra or ensemble. Many musicians do both.

Another income area for a musician is studio work. This again has two types of income for a musician. They may be hired as a session player and receiving a flat-fee for their service or they may be recording in hopes of receiving royalties from the record label for download sales or hard-copy sales.

Four Income Sources for Music Performances

- Live (solo or in a band)
- Salaried Player
- Recording as Session Player
- Recording as Artist

Income from Teaching

In addition to performing as a musician, teaching is another important income source for Artists with a share of 22%. Many Artists provide music lessons to students. Some of these Artists teach private lessons and some teach at a school. Some do both.

Income from Songwriting

As another potential income source for Artists, songwriting can also be the trickiest. For starters, the songs have got to be really good. Anyone can write a song. That doesn't mean they are going to get paid for it. Creating content as a songwriter can be a huge income source for Artists. Even average songwriters may still have a chance at some income in this area.

First of all, copyright law mostly benefits the high earners. When looking at the brackets of Artists, the top bracket, earning an average $330,000 a year, earns by far the most from compositions, which make up 28% of their music-related revenue. (The lowest income bracket makes most revenue from live performances; more than 40%.)

Keep in mind, that Artists who focus their activity on composing rely on composition revenue and are much more vulnerable to possible harm from copyright infringement. The same goes for recording Artists who rely on sales of sound recordings. Free downloads may hurt both songwriters and recording Artists.

Income for Songwriters.

1. Unless the songwriter agrees not to be paid, every single time a song is streamed legally for free on the Internet; money is owed to the songwriter. This money is paid to the songwriter's Performing Rights Organizations (PRO) nor SoundExchange.
2. Every single time a song is played on the radio in the United States (either via the Internet or broadcast from an AM/FM transmitter tower) the songwriter is

owed money. Once again, the money is paid to the songwriter via their affiliation with a Performing Rights Organization.

3. If you are a U.S.-based songwriter and your song is distributed into another country thru a company such as iTunes Japan, each time their music sells in Japan, iTunes pays the Japanese PRO money for the "reproduction" of the Artist-Songwriter's song. This money is in addition to the money iTunes pays for the sale of the song.
4. Every time a song is recorded and then duplicated such as on a recording via compact disc or Internet download, the songwriter gets paid. This is a mechanical royalty.

The Entire Music Industry Is Built On Six Legal Copyrights

1. Reproduction
2. Derivatives & Samples
3. Public Display
4. Public Performance
5. Distribution
6. Digital Transmission

Income from Publishing

Many times a songwriter is their own publisher. Other times a songwriter collaborates with a music publisher to do the publishing work for them. Either way, publishing can be a major income source for Artists who are songwriters. A performing Artist-Songwriter has the biggest opportunity to reap the largest revenues.

A songwriter owns their songs via copyright or until they license those songs to a music publisher. A song's copyright holder owns several important rights, including the right to copy the song, distribute copies of the song, prepare derivative works from the song and perform the song publicly. A song generates revenue for its owner when the owner issues permits, or "licenses," others to use those rights, for a fee or royalty.

In the beginning, the composer of a song is the song's copyright holder. In order to get the song to generate revenue, it may be necessary for the Artist-Songwriter to affiliate with a music publisher. A music publisher acquires songs, (and the copyrights), from songwriters and then exploits the songs commercially. There are many shapes and sizes of music publishers. Songwriters will want to affiliate with a publisher that will be able to find uses for their song, issue licenses to the users, collect the revenue, and then share the money with the songwriter.

Royalties

1. Mechanical Royalties
2. Public Performance Royalties
3. Synchronization Royalties
4. Print Royalties
5. Foreign Royalties
6. Grand Royalties
7. Digital Royalties

A song earns money for its copyright holder in many different ways. However there are a few main sources: mechanical royalties, public performance royalties, synchronization royalties, print royalties, digital royalties, grand royalties and foreign royalties. The way publishers get the money, and how much of it they get, depends on its source.

1. Mechanical Royalties

Mechanical royalties are the main source of income for publishers. Mechanical royalties are moneys paid by a record company to a song's copyright holder for the right to use the song in "devices serving to reproduce the composition mechanically," i.e., vinyl, compact discs, MP3 S, etc.

The current statutory rate for mechanical royalties is 9.1 cents per song per duplication or replication for recordings of up to 5 minutes in length. For recordings over 5 minutes in length, the rate increases depending on its total length.

2. Public Performance Royalties

Public performance income is the second largest source of income to a song's copyright holder. Almost every time any version of a song is performed publicly, whether live or on "record," in concert or over radio or television, the copyright holder is entitled to a public performance royalty. There are a few narrow exceptions, (for example, educational use in a classroom setting). Songwriters and publishers affiliate with a Performing Rights Organization (PRO) to keep track of air play and other public performances of their songs, and to collect and distribute the resulting license revenue. ASCAP, BMI, and SESAC are the major performing rights societies in the United States. The Artist-Songwriter defined their Performing Rights Organization in their Artist Development Plan.

3. Synchronization Royalties

A synchronization license is a permit to use a song in connection with video or film such as a movie or television show. The producer must obtain a "synch license" from the copyright holder, usually for a one-time fee. Every time a song is used in synchronization with video, a synch license is required. The first broadcast of a "live" show which includes the song does not require a synch license, but re-runs would. The live broadcast would require the public performance license described above. In the case of Synchronization Royalties, a video or film producer negotiates a fee with the owner of the song's copyright.

4. Print Royalties

Print revenues come from sales of sheet music. The relative importance of print revenue has decreased over the years as consumers have come to prefer records to sheet music. However, it is still a source of serious money and many industry watchers predict an increase in its importance with the growing popularity of detailed transcriptions (or "tabs") of heavy metal guitar licks, synthesizer programming, and the renewed popularity of acoustic music.

5. Foreign Royalties

Many music publishers either team-up with foreign music publishers or have a branch office in foreign countries.

The royalties generated outside the United States should not be forgotten or overlooked.

6. Grand Royalties

Grand rights refers to the permissions necessary to stage an opera, play with music, or a work of musical theater. Performance rights organizations such as

BMI and ASCAP do not license grand rights in the United States. Grand rights must be negotiated between the producer of a production and the publishers and owners of the copyright of the work.

Other Publishing Income

In addition to the sources of income already covered, there are many other royalty-generating areas, many of which can - depending on the composition - generate substantial writer and publisher royalties for Artist-Songwriters. These include:
- Lyric reprints in books
- CD-ROM/Multimedia audiovisual configurations
- Karaoke
- Musical greeting cards and singing toys
- Music boxes
- Video games
- Ringtones
- Sampling
- Jukeboxes
- Podcasting

Income from Sound Recordings

For the major music labels the sales of recorded music represent the majority of their revenue, but a different picture emerges when looking at the income of individual musicians. A new survey among 5,000 U.S. musicians of different genres shows that on average only six percent of all revenue comes from recorded music.

However, more and more Artists are releasing their own recordings on their own record label. In doing so, a few things need to be identified regarding sound recordings.

It's important to remember that a recorded piece of music embodies two copyrights: there's the copyright for the composition (the lyrics and the music), and a separate copyright for the sound recording (what gets captured in the studio). There are separate revenue streams earned by these two copyrights; the composition earns mechanical royalties when it is licensed for reproduction. The recording of the song earns income when it is sold via digital downloads or compact discs but also if the recording is licensed for use in a movie or video game. This is a master-use license.

The important thing to know is, who owns the recording? Is it the record label, the Artist, the producer or perhaps a member of the band?

Whether on vinyl, compact disc or via digital download, income from the sale, license or performance of sound recordings has been a core part of many musicians' income streams for decades. But there's no doubt that income from sound recordings — perhaps more than any other — has experienced significant challenges and undergone serious changes in the past 10 to 15 years.

There's good news and bad news. While the existing music marketplace was fundamentally disrupted by peer to peer files-sharing, we have also seen the decline of brick and mortar stores, and the development of legitimate download stores like iTunes and Amazon, and licensed subscription services like Rhapsody and Spotify. We've also seen a rapid growth in a new revenue stream for sound recordings: the digital performance royalties that are generated when sound recordings are streamed on any webcast service like Pandora or played on satellite radio.

> **The income source for Artist-Songwriters focuses specifically on the money that sound recordings can earn when they are sold, licensed or performed. This includes:**
>
> 1. Income from physical retail sales (brick and mortar, mail-order)
>
> 2. Income from digital sales (iTunes, Amazon MP3, Bandcamp)
>
> 3. Income from sales of recorded music at shows/merch table
>
> 4. Interactive streaming services (Spotify, Rhapsody, Slacker)
>
> 5. Digital performance royalties (Pandora, Sirius XM, via SoundExchange)
>
> 6. Master use license for synchs, ringtones, etc.

Income from Merchandise

There are two areas of income when it comes to merchandise: Sales and Licenses. When an Artist typically thinks about income from merch sales, they are referring to items for sale at their gigs. This is usually done in the lobby of a venue or a side table at a nightclub. Items typically found on an Artist's merch table may include compact discs, t-shirts, stickers, coffee mugs, posters and other knick-knacks with the Artists name on them.

The other type of income from the sales of merchandise is primarily reserved for the established Artist. These Artists sign a licensing contract with a third-party merchandising company who pay the Artist a fee for the right to manufacture items in the likeness and name of the Artist. This is another good reason for Artists to own their own trademark.

Income from the Internet

In addition to receiving income from downloads, streaming or online sales of merchandise, another possible income source for Artists is through collaborating with affiliate marketing companies. Some Artists utilize programs like Linkshare or Commission Junction or Amazon by providing links to a variety of possible products from the Artist's website. For example, an Artist may use a particular instrument for their art. The Artist can post on their website that they use that particular instrument. They also post a hyperlink to that instrument on a third-party affiliate website so a fan may be able to purchase it. If and when this happens, the Artist makes a commission from the affiliate for making the referral.

Income from Other Sources

Essentially, this is income tied to an Artist's' creative self, but ancillary to what they earn based on their sound recordings, compositions or performances.

- **YouTube partnership program**: revenue-sharing program that

allows creators and producers of original content to earn money from the Artist's videos on YouTube
- **Ad revenue:** or other miscellaneous income from the Artist's website properties (Google AdSense, commissions on Amazon sales, etc.)
- **Fan funding**: Money directly from fans to support an upcoming recording project or tour (Kickstarter, Pledge Music)
- **Fan club:** Money directly from fans who are subscribing to an Artist's fan club
- **Persona licensing:** payments from a brand that is licensing an Artist's name or likeness (video games, comic books, etc.)
- **Product endorsements:** payments from a brand for an Artist endorsing or using their product
- **Acting:** in television, movies, commercials
- **Sponsorship:** corporate support for a tour, or for band/ensemble
- **Grants:** from foundations, state or federal agencies

****

11.06 Task

For this section of the Artist Business Plan, write about the profit sources for the products and services of the Artist's company.

****

Sales Forecasts

11.07 Sales Forecasts

Forecasting sales can be one of the more important tasks an Artist can do before starting their business. Although a precise estimation is impossible to get, this step will give the Artist a sense of the magnitude of sales that may be possible. Even established Artists need to forecast revenues.

Forecast sales before starting a business: any business.

First, identify the market that the Artist is serving. It's important to know the potential of whom and how many people are going to be the Artist's customers. A few questions should be asked by the Artist. Who are the people that are going to buy their product(s) (recordings) and/or service(s) (performances)? How can they be characterized? What do they have in common? By completing these questions, Artists will end up with a series of characteristics that represent their potential clients & customers. Remember, there are two types of customers for every Artist: fans and music business professionals. (This was addressed in greater detail in a previous chapter.)

Estimate how big is the market for the Artist? Now that the Artist has identified their potential types of customers, it is necessary to find out how many of them there are. If a local Artist wants to perform at local venues, how many music industry professional customers are there? Artists should try to be as accurate as possible and not afraid to make big estimations. Although it is not possible to get an exact number, it doesn't mean that Artists shouldn't try as hard as possible to get close to it.

Artists need to estimate their market power. Even if there are a lot of people that could buy the Artist's products or services, there must be something special that that the Artist could offer in order to get customers to choose them over their competitors. It is unrealistic to assume a 100% market power, because there are always things to consider that will reduce the Artist's estimated market. This is the part where Artists should consider the weakness and threats that their business has and materialize them in a reduction of the market. Things like location, availability or even the fact that some part of the market may not be aware of the Artists' existence can lead to a reduction in the size of the market. When considering all the possible things that could drive away potential customers, the number an Artist ends up with will be the real market size and the number of sales that could, be obtained.

Tips for Sales Projections

- Try to get as much information as possible, by surveys or data available
- Be realistic about what product or service that an Artist is offering to the market
- Consider the price charged for the product or the service
- Make sure estimates are realistic. Get comparable scenarios or historical data
- Make a best case and a worst case scenario if the estimation can considerably change the result of forecasts.

Financial projections are critical to planning what the Artist is anticipated to produce in the future during given time periods. These time periods will become "benchmarks" as the plan is implemented and completed. This allows an Artist to review and follow how closely the actual figures are compared to the projections listed in their plan. Most business plans will project forward for a period of five years, projected by months for the first two years and annually for the last three years.

Projections are based on "assumptions" that are carefully prepared by doing research of the Artist's market, competitors and music industry, in general. Much of the research information in preparing the sales projections is identified in other sections of the Artist's Business Plan such as the Marketing Plan, and the Competitive Analysis. If the Artist has not performed this research, they should do so before entering numbers into their projections. "Assumptions" should be based on available facts obtained through that research, and for the Artist's Business Plan to be credible, these assumptions should be backed by information to document where the information came from, and how the figures were arrived at. These documents are usually placed in the Appendix of the completed business plan for reference to those reviewing the plan.

Note: Simply "guessing" at what the Artist's business will do in the future is a recipe for failure. Properly researching the industry, the Artist's customers, and their competition provides a factual framework that allows educated estimates, not "guesswork."

Creating good projections is conceptually easy but takes thought and legwork to get right. Sales projections are an act of faith. They're backed by the Artist's assumptions about sales, channels and markets, but in the end, it comes down to simple faith. Expense estimates are easier to determine as these numbers will be obtained with a little research.

Whether the Artist is setting up a business plan to present to investors or they're just trying to focus their music business attention, sales projections can be a valuable management tool if done right. When an Artist project sales and follow through by comparing actual figures to the forecast, they will more accurately gauge what's going on in their business and more quickly make course corrections as needed.

Method 1 of 4: Review Manageable Sales and Expense Units

1. Start with expenses. Consider fixed and variable expenses, from rents and fixed loans to payroll and utilities, plus capital equipment and inventory, as well as a marketing or advertising budget. Allow for bad debt or returns and a profit margin.

2. Factor in income sources. Any business, whether product or service, will have units to measure. Artists can measure how many gigs they have or can perform as well as how many music downloads they may receive for an upcoming recording.

3. Review past sales figures to determine the cycle the Artist's business operates in: its ebb and flow. For example, if an Artist is based in a geographic location that tends to get heavy snow, their amount of winter bookings may be slow.

4. Divide income by expenses to arrive at a baseline sales price. To manage the Artist business going forward, tie this sales price back to the income units, such as by product type or by seasonality. This way Artists can compare future figures to past sales.

Method 2 of 4: Analyze the Market

1. Compare the average sales per booking as the amount that competitor Artists may receive. Compare these Artists based on similar niche, history and locale.

2. Create a target zone around the business and estimate the total number of consumers using or needing the Artist's product or service within each zone (for example, within a 2 hour drive, 4 hour drive and 6 hour drive to performances.) Determine market share. Which competing Artists do fans and customers patronize instead of the product or service of the Artist? What percentage of bookings does the Artist get compared to their competitors?

3. Use the Artist's unit breakdown and weight the per-unit figure by overall sales. For example: an Artist sells five item categories total. 1 category sells 5 units per day, 2 sell

3 units each, and 2 sell 1 unit each. Multiply the price of each unit by the number sold for a total current revenue figure.

Method 3 of 4: Develop a Marketing Projection
1. Decide how best to promote the Artists products and services, and estimate the number of customers they anticipate reaching.
2. List how the Artist plans to grow their business. Options include selling more current products to existing customers, attracting more customers with current products and introducing new products to current or prospective customers.
3. Review past marketing approaches to see which yielded the best results. How well do these promotions match the Artist's current product and customer mix? Can they replicate the promotions? Do different promotions promote sales to different customer groups, or move different product categories?
4. Match the promotion, product, and customer base to estimate how much the Artist anticipates selling as they move forward.

Method 4 of 4: Do the Math
1. Calculate projected sales with this simple equation: Multiply total number of customers times the average per-unit price.
2. Run this equation several times: by product category, by customer type, by number of bookings and by the anticipated outcome of promotions. The more meticulous the Artist has been in breaking down their business, the more accurately they can project sales.
3. Compare sales figures against industry norms. Ask a business associate or mentor to look over the figures.

****
11.07 Task

For this section of the Artist Business Plan, write about the sales forecast for the products and services of the Artist's company.

****

Growth Strategy

11.08
Growth Strategy

Although writing a business plan is very comparable to a growth plan or growth strategy. It differs in that a business growth strategy concentrates on how an Artist will actually achieve their desired progress. The growth plan aids in keeping the Artist's business on track and in line with preferred efforts towards the advancement of their company.

Artists should study the past successes of their company and use this to create new ideas for future projects. Also, study the competition, the trends of the target market, and economic trends to forecast a quality growth plan. All the plans within the Artist Business Plan are related.

A good way to establish as quality growth plan is to look over the similar growth plans of other Artists and their companies. Artists should use these ideas as motivation to create their own development strategy, unique to their company.

Artists need to determine where their expansion opportunities are. Perhaps they should present or release new products or services, target a new market, or expand their performance locations, both at locally and regionally. Artists need to determine where they want their company to go, and figure out the actions to get it there. What is the strategy for growth?

To do this, Artists need to realistically assess their current efficiency, abilities, talent and adaptability. This will help the Artist realize what they can or cannot do with their current situation. If the Artist needs to hire supplemental staff or members then they will need to know what skills they should attain, and/or what training will be needed for their development strategy as well as how they are to fund those personnel.

Artists should create a thorough proposal on how the Artist will raise excess capital to support the expansion. Begin with looking at the financial stability of the Artist's company as it is in its current state. Get an analysis of the Artist's business' finances and see if funding is possible with internal growth or if outside funding is necessary.

With that Artists can generate a high intensity marketing strategy that will catapult the Artist's new development efforts into the population's conscious. Include this in the growth plan and especially focus on how any marketing efforts will continue. This concentrated marketing will aid the Artist with a new development strategy demonstrating its effectiveness and growth.

Now it's time to write down the Artist's business growth plan. Include the following:
- Explanation of development opportunities
- Financial plans per each quarter as well as yearly
- Marketing strategy to accomplish said growth
- Financial breakdown of internal or external capital and its accessibility throughout the development process
- The company's employee breakdown of what will be needed, cut, and expanded.

****

11.08 Task

For this section of the Artist Business Plan, write about the growth strategy for the products and services of the Artist's company.

****

Sales Programs

11.09
Sales Programs

Details are critical to implementation. Use this topic to list the specific information related to the Artist's sales programs with the specific persons responsible, deadlines, and budgets. How is the Artist planning to implement their strategy? Are there concrete and specific plans? How will implementation be measured?

Business plans are about results, and generating results depends in part on how specific the details are in the plan. For anything related to sales for the Artists include it here and list the person responsible, dates required, and budgets. All of that will make the Artist's Business Plan more real.

Since the Artist's company is sales driven, it is important to plan ahead when creating a sales program. Planning, management, and implementation all need to come together for the sales program to be successful.

Sales Plan Mission Statement

Artists need to write a mission statement for their sales program. This will be different than the mission statement of the Artist's company, but should incorporate the same business values.

This step in strategic planning ensures that the Artist has a compass in place for making decisions about their sales program. Later, when the Artist builds their staff of sales professionals, it will serve as a rallying point, giving the sales team an identity and sense of pride about the sales mission.

Compensation for Sales

How will the sales program will compensate the people actually doing the sales? This includes paying a member of the band who may secure a performance booking or the person selling cd's and t-shirts at the merchandise table. Compensations paid to agents and publishers are identified in their agreements.

Options for compensation are numerous: commission only, base pay plus commission, hourly pay with productivity requirements, salaried or hourly pay, and base pay with bonuses.

Sales Management

The Artist may want to designate someone from their team to run their sales program. This person may be called a sales manager and they are responsible for the productivity of the team. Many times it's the talent manager who also assumes the sales manager role.

Training for Sales Persons

Depending on the target customer, Artists may need to train their sales persons as an integral part of the sales program.

Training should not be done only when initially hiring, nor should it be an afterthought. In successful sales programs, training is an ongoing, continuous, integral part of the sales program. For example, the person who is selling merchandise at the Artist's gig should know the names of the members of the group, the products available for sale and the upcoming gigs for the Artist. They know this information from their training.

Tools for Success
Tools for success include things that the sales manager and staff need to sell. Tools may include flyers, posters, Internet access, presentation slicks, professional receipts, access to product or service information, business cards, laptop computers and any other tools needed.

Revisit the Sales Program
Every year, Artists and their team need to check their sales progress. If necessary, they should revise the plan and discuss with the sales manager what is working.

The review should be an annual exercise, as the economy changes, competition changes, markets emerge, or the dynamics of the sales team changes.

Tips & Warnings
Artist should make a long-term commitment and be patient with the sales program as it is going through its learning curve.

Hold the sales manager or responsible individuals accountable for their goals.

Don't forget to budget for sales contest incentives, bonuses, and an annual office party when creating the Business Plan.

****

11.09 Task

For this section of the Artist Business Plan, write about the plan for sales programs for the products and services of the Artist's company.

Sales Affiliates

11.10
Sales Affiliates

Affiliate marketing is a type of performance-based marketing in which a business rewards one or more affiliates for each visitor or customer brought by the affiliate's own marketing efforts. In other words, this is another income source for Artists as monies derived from referring customers to the products and services of others on the World Wide Web. A good example of this is the Artist who refers a person to a specific instrument on an affiliate's website, and then get paid for the referral when a purchase is completed.

There are four core players in the online affiliate market:
1. the merchant (also known as 'retailer' or 'brand')
2. the network (offers for the affiliates and a way to process payments)
3. the publisher (also known as 'the affiliate') (in this example, it is the Artist)
4. the customer who purchases the product of the merchant of the publisher through the network.

Affiliate marketing for Artists may overlap with other Internet marketing methods that they use, because affiliates often use regular advertising methods to increase income. In addition to organic search engine optimization (SEO), paid search engine marketing (PPC - Pay Per Click), e-mail marketing, and content marketing, many Artists set this income source on their website. On the other hand, some Artist affiliates use less orthodox techniques, such as publishing reviews of products or services offered by a partner.

Affiliate marketing is commonly confused with referral marketing, as both forms of marketing use third parties to drive sales to the retailer. However, both are distinct forms of marketing and the main difference between them is that affiliate marketing relies purely on financial motivations to drive sales while referral marketing relies on trust and personal relationships to drive sales.

Affiliate marketing is frequently overlooked by Artists as an income source but it is another income source none-the-less. While search engines, e-mail, and website syndication capture much of the attention of online retailers, affiliate marketing carries a much lower profile.

Eighty percent of affiliate programs today use revenue sharing or pay per sale (PPS) as a compensation method, nineteen percent use cost per action (CPA), and the remaining programs use other methods such as cost per click (CPC) or cost per mile (CPM, cost per estimated 1000 views).

****

11.10 Task

In this section of an Artist's Business Plan, investigate a plan for an affiliate marketing program though networks such as Commission Junction or Linkshare.

****

Merchandise Sales Strategy

11.11 Merchandise Sales Strategy

Merchandising strategies are a valuable component of any Artist's retail success, but a "one size fits all" approach will not work in today's competitive environment. Strategies should vary by category and sometimes by segment depending on the overall objective for the Artist's brand, category and retailer. Each strategy for an Artist should be carefully crafted to target a specific objective such as increasing downloads, inviting new fans / customers to a show, developing loyal committed customers or increasing sales.

Inventory is typically one of the biggest investments for Artists and retailers, so having a budget that is strategic and flexible is critical. How much is the right amount of merchandise to order? This is for both immediate and future merchandise buys. When an Artist orders too many t-shirts and they don't sell, that's money that the Artist could have used for a different project.

> **Effective merchandising means having the right product, in the right amount, in the right place, at the right price, at the right time, all the time!**

Product Assortment
Developing a compelling assortment is one of the most enjoyable and rewarding aspects of merchandising for an Artist but can also be one of the most challenging. However, too many items on the merch table may not be a good thing. An assortment of merchandise may include the Artist's compact discs, a few shirts, mugs or bumper stickers.

Purchase Order System
A purchase order system can be a big investment so it is critical to choose one that truly fits the merchandise needs of the Artist. Often, cash is the best answer. However, many Artists loose a sale because they don't have the capacity to accept charge cards or debit cards. There are some good purchase systems available for Artists to use at their merch tables.

Merchandise Pricing Strategy
Strategically planning the markup and markdown strategy can make all the difference in the profitability of an Artist's merchandise. Artist should be very attuned to the market and proactively anticipating customer behavior to ensure maximizing product potential. For example, if an Artist sells a T-shirt for $50, there might be zero sales.

Shortage Control
Even in the smallest way, if a fan cannot buy a piece of merchandise because the Artist forgot to get an inventory of what merch is available for sale, the Artist may not make a sale. Part of the plan should include a way for Artists to recognize the lack of inventory and when to re-order.

Strategies include a variety of components: pricing, promotion, product placement, ad support, consumer education, etc. Together, the different components help achieve the goals of the Artist / retailer.

Credit and Debit Cards
Artists will want to make it as easy for fans and customers to buy their merchandise as possible. Artists should be able to take credit and debit cards at their gigs. If someone at a gig wants to buy the Artist's CD or t-shirt and just spent their last $10 bill at the bar and the Artist doesn't have a swipe machine, they've just lost a sale.

> **Six Effective Merchandising Strategies for Artists**
> 1. Traffic Building
> 2. Transaction Building
> 3. Profit Generation
> 4. Cash Generation
> 5. Excitement
> 6. Image Creating

Merchandising Strategies

1. Traffic Building: This strategy focuses on drawing consumer traffic to the merchandise in the first place. Smart Artists always inform their audience where the merch table is located. An announcement from stage is a good starting point.

2. Transaction Building: This strategy focuses on increasing the size of the average transaction. Perhaps after a fan a purchased a t-shirt, ask them if they would like a compact disc too.

3. Profit Generating: Higher gross margin and higher turns. This strategy focuses on the ability of the category of the item to generate profits. Profit margins can be higher in this area due to the value added. Higher quality products may cost more to the fan.

4. Cash Generating: This strategy focuses on the ability of the category to generate incremental cash flow. Some Artists have subscription sales on their website. As the Artist releases new material, loyal fans have the opportunity to hear it (and download it or stream it) first.

5. Excitement: This strategy communicates a sense of urgency or a limited-time sensitive opportunity to the consumer. As Artists release new merchandise, they may get to a point where they are running low on inventory and don't want to do more manufacturing of the same product. Instead, they announce the items are limited. Usually, this helps get rid of any excess inventory.

6. Image Creating: This strategy communicates an image to the fan / consumer in one of the following areas: price, service, quality, specialty items or assortment.

****

11.11 Task

For this part of the Artist Business Plan, write down some strategies for selling merchandise. Include various products such as compact discs, t-shirts, etc. This would come from the Artist Product List.

****

Online Sales Strategy

11.12
Online Sales Strategy

Artists who are online retailers need to be more strategic in the ever increasingly competitive online retail industry. Artists see this all the time. Businesses and entrepreneurs must undertake adequate research and planning prior to launching their online retail ventures to become the most successful. It helps to develop a plan through the strategic steps of establishing objectives, options, methods, implementation, measurement of results and revisions as necessary.

Both online and brick-and-mortar businesses require Internet marketing strategies. An Artist's comprehensive Internet marketing strategy can substantially launch or increase sales. To market online effectively, an Artist should have knowledge of social media, search engine optimization (SEO), blogs, e-mail lists, affiliate marketing and more.

If the Artist is ready to launch their business or a new product, they should research, create and track an online sales strategy.

1. As defined in the Artist Development Plan, Artists need to develop a brand name and image before communicating with their anticipated market. In today's marketing world, a brand name and image is as important as the strategy itself. The Artist's brand makes them recognizable amongst competitors.

2. As defined in the Artist Development Plan, Artist should study their competitors. Study them from their website through their sales process, including their marketing strategies. Identify the past and ongoing marketing strategies of the Artist's largest competitors. This way the Artist will know what works in their given market.

3. Study the market. Most Artists are part of a niche market. They will want to center their strategy on that demographic, instead of all Internet consumers. A part of this is to choose the ideal consumer.

4. Mimic the successful marketing strategies of competitors. The Artist's market research should estimate how many followers the competitors may have on their social media sites, how many people they send their e-mail list to and how many people comment on their blog entries. This means that the demographic responds well, and these campaigns should be the first on the Artist's list for their strategy.

5. Create a multi-faceted Internet marketing strategy. In order to increase the Artist's brand recognition, they should launch several marketing campaigns at once. The following are marketing strategies that should be starting within a few weeks of each other:

a. Create social media accounts and assign someone to launch interesting material every day. In order to attract followers, social media accounts and blogs must be consistently updated. Hootsuite is an online product that may help with this.

b. Create or pay someone to write SEO (Search Engine Optimization) articles. Articles that mention popular keywords related to the Artist or Artist's product, but also offer tips or advice are a great way to introduce people to the Artist. They also help the Artist's website to show up on the first pages of an Internet search.

c. Collect e-mail lists. Artists who have live performances have most likely collected e-mails throughout the years, which can be used for e-mail blasts. Send an initial blast and monthly blasts updating the potential fans and customers about new performances or recordings.

d. Create videos of fans attending the Artist's performances or listening to the Artist's recordings. Encourage fans and customers to tell their friends. This works well for helping an Artist's product to go viral. Artists can launch these videos via their website, You Tube, Hulu, Vimeo, Facebook or other places in order to draw interest to their website.

e. Buy ads on sites that cater to the Artist's market. Communicate the Artist's brand image, videos or other product info on banner ads.

f. Set up tracking capabilities for all of the campaigns. The easiest way to do this is to set up a Google Analytics account through the Artist's main Google account. Create a campaign for each facet of the marketing strategy. Later, the Artist will be able to look back and see which ones had the best return on investment (ROI).

g. Consider buying print ads that cater to the Artist's market that also launches at the same time as the Artist's Internet marketing campaign. Track this ad by buying a similar domain name that redirects to this site. Let a Google Analytics campaign track the success of the print ad, in comparison to the Artist's Internet marketing, through this other domain.

h. Launch the campaign in the same few days and weeks. Be consistent, if the method requires communication with fans and customers. Follow through with all of the orders as quickly as possible, in order to create good reviews on the website and other marketplaces

i. Evaluate the Return on Investment and then repeat any strategies that were successful. Some campaigns are ongoing and Artists can try to slowly or virally increase their following.

In order to ensure the success of any Artist, there are many specific online tactics used to increase sales.

> **There are six distinct, tactical areas for an Artist to consider when planning their online sales strategy.**
>
> 1. Creative design of the Artist's web site
> 2. Ease the purchase process
> 3. Feedback and testimonials
> 4. Pricing strategies
> 5. Time factors
> 6. Additional actions

Design factors to draw in online fans
- Color create different emotional responses
- Use targeted selection of words and descriptions for each product
- Insert video into web pages to sell more

Online Retail Purchase Process:
- One click buying
- Quick loading of pages
- Mobile enabled, as online mobile purchase trends are favorable
- Safe and secure sites, allowing safe data storage for future sales

Reviews, Feedback and Testimonials:
- Endorsements bring sales
- Consumer reviews are powerful
- Ratings and feedback mechanisms result in better sales, better ROI

Online Retail Pricing Strategies:
- Free trial then buy works

- With free shipping, more spent on items
- Revenues add up fast with additional discounted items offered

Time Factor with Online Retail:
- Personalized deal time window is effective
- Adding timing creates urgency to the process
- Time or number limitations initiates more interest

Additional Call to Actions:
- Reminders and ancillary purchase links generate more add-on sales
- Links on additional buys is an effective sales strategy
- Ads centered on certain buys assist in future sales

****
11.12 Task

For this section of the Artist Business Plan, write about the online sales strategy for the products and services of the Artist's company.

****

Recordings Sales Strategy

11.13 Recordings Sales Strategy

Before an Artist embarks on the journey of a recording session, they should know, in advance, the strategy of how they plan to sell copies of their efforts. Sales of recordings can be completed offline or online.

Offline Sales
Compact discs still make up around half of the total music sales and more in some countries; despite recent downturns, it is still a huge market. So how does an Artist make and sell their CD easily and without giving away profits? Here are a few ways:

1. **Sell CDs at the Merch Table**
   Artists should always have CD available for sale at their gigs. Encourage fans to purchase the CDs by announcing their availability from the stage.

2. **Sell CDs in Local Record Shops**
   Artists may try and sell their CDs in local record shops on a sale or return basis. This is also known as "on consignment." To do this, Artists should take a few copies to their local independent record stores. They should inform the store that they are from a small independent record label and offer to leave four or five copies on a sale or return basis. Sale or return, or consignment, means that the Artist gives them a few copies and the retailer will pay when they sell. No commitment from the record shops encourages them to take them for sale. Artist should communicate to them on a professional level.

3. **Sell in National Chain Stores**
   This is for Artists who are guaranteed to ship a large number of copies; meaning thousands. This is usually done through a music distributor.

Artists must have a large fan base and some press coverage for distributors to want to work with them. This route is expensive though, with manufacturing and transport costs as well as the 20-30% commission they will take.

Online Sales
In addition to offline sales of recordings, Artists must also consider online sales. One of the great things about the music business today is that as an indie musician, Artists can easily sell their own CDs from their website and their live performances without a label.

As another important income source, sales of recordings is a must if the Artist is planning on being successful in the music business. In addition to selling recordings from the Artist's website, there are many online music distributors

Sell CDs using PayPal
The simplest and most profitable method of selling CDs of an Artist is through their website. If an Artist has a PayPal account, they can accept credit and debit cards direct from the consumer and send a CD via the US Postal Service. The proper way to do this is to establish a bank account for the Artist and then sign up for a PayPal account. PayPal will deposit funds from sales to that bank account. Artists should retain around 93% of what they sell, after fees and shipping.

CD Baby is easy to sign up for and very fair! In a regular record deal or distribution deal, musicians only make $1-$2 per CD, if they ever get paid by their label. When selling through CD Baby, musicians make $6-$12 per CD, and get paid weekly. They've been in business, and thriving, since March 1998. In fact they are the second-largest seller of independent CDs on the web, second only to Amazon.

Selling Individual Downloadable Songs
Artist might want the ability to sell individual recordings of songs on their web site in downloadable format. Artists also might want more control over selling their CD including the ability to offer discounts, sales and easily follow up with people who buy their music.

One of the great things about the World Wide Web is the popularity for Artists to sell individual recordings in downloadable MP3 format - rather than whole CDs. It is like the rebirth of the "single" or "45." This is a benefit for Artists for several reasons:

• Artists don't have to wait until they have the time or money to record a whole CD. They can write and record a great new song and sell it online the next day.

• Artists can increase their fan base and market by getting people who might not normally buy a whole CD from an Artist they don't know well to buy a few of their songs and slowly get into the Artist's music.

Website
If the Artist does not have a web site, why not? In today's world, it's the front door for Artists and their fans. The website must have the capability of streaming a few songs from the Artist's CD and a link to where fans can buy it. Artists should NOT make their only musical presence on the Internet via their MySpace or Facebook pages. Instead, Facebook should direct customers to the Artist's website.

Digital Downloads
With no physical product to manufacture,

selling digital downloads is one of the easiest ways to set up an Artist's first online store and make a little extra cash. Digital downloads include things like music, software, e-books, photos and videos. The Artist's store should focus on any one, or all, of these items.

1. **Use standard digital file formats**
When selling digital downloads, Artists will want to make sure that all users will be able to download and use their product. Use standard file formats, PDF for e-books, MP3 for audio files, etc. In addition, some Artists compress their digital files into zip files. This helps reduce the size of the file to be downloaded. It's one of the secrets of how to sell digital downloads.

2. **Use the right shopping cart software**
There are plenty of different shopping cart software solutions on the market, but some aren't quite as flexible as the rest. Look for a cart that is rich in features like full FTP access. This will help Artists to easily manage their files. Also, look for the ability to restrict the number of the days the download link will be active. This prevents link sharing with people that haven't paid for the download. The right shopping cart can help Artists learn how to sell digital downloads without too much effort.

3. **Immediate Availability**
The advantage of digital downloads versus physical products is the ability to immediately access these online. No customer wants to wait 24 hours for an Artist to e-mail them an MP3 file. Artists should look for a solution that delivers their electronic products automatically as soon as the payment is confirmed. The Artist's website should display a message letting visitors know when a product is available for immediate download. This could be the deciding factor for fans and customers between purchasing a downloadable product and a physical audio CD.

****

11.13 Task

For this section of the Artist Business Plan, write about the strategy for sales of recordings for the products and services of the Artist's company.

****

Performances Sales Strategy

11.14 Performances Sales Strategy

In the early stages of an Artist's career, performances play an important role in branding, building a fan base and creating income. The income derived from live performances is the number one income source for beginning Artists. (As the Artist becomes more established, the income from songwriting becomes the number one source of income.)

Part of an Artist's Business Plan is a section about the strategy for securing performances. From local open-mic performances to world tours, there is always a plan. Successful Artists plan well in advance. They know their career moves for the next year as well as their goals for the next 5 years.

Local Bookings

Getting an Artist booked in the local club scene can be a challenging task. It's hard enough to get an Artist's e-mail or promo kit noticed by the club booker or talent buyer, but once they get their foot in the door, there are still numerous factors that can dictate whether or not they actually get a gig. Create a strategy to greatly increase the odds of getting the gig while making the club booker and/or talent buyer happy.

Step 1. Get familiar with the venue's calendar – There are many inside tips and secrets that can be earned just from consistently checking out a venues calendar. Most good clubs keep their calendar posted online. Start looking for specific clues. Do they have a standard number of bands on the bill every night? Is there a night where they tend to give new bands a shot? Do they book the same Artist on a regular basis?

Step 2. Look for holes in the schedule – Once the club's booking patterns are identified and the Artist has acknowledged that their music niche fits, they should start finding holes in their schedule where the venue is in need of a band.

Step 3. Now narrow down the potential dates to the shows where the music is a true fit. Remember, in order for this strategy to work, Artists must only pitch to the shows where they fit. Artists should make sure that the date is available with the members of their team before the sales pitch is made.

Step 4. Target that specific show in an e-mail pitch. By now the Artist is prepared to approach the club booker in a way that HELPS THEM. Just put the show name and date in the subject line of the e-mail and politely let them know that the Artist would be a good fit for a performance on the day or that bill. The chances of getting a response to the e-mail and to get the gig just went way up.

Remember: Booking a venue is a tough job, and the talent buyer of the club is always happy to solidify a show and get it off their plate. When an Artist approaches them in a way that helps them out, the Artist will see results. If the Artist constantly spams them wanting to play dates that are already filled on their calendar, then the Artist will never be taken seriously. It can take a long time for a new band to a get a gig at a highly regarded venue / club. That is, if the Artist does what every other band does and expects the club booker to do all the work for them. Instead, stop looking to the venue to solve the booking problems and start thinking about how the Artist can help them out.

Booking a Tour

First of all, Artists shouldn't book a tour until they are successful in their own hometown. If the Artist hasn't figured out how to get big crowds out to their local shows, then they are probably not ready to tour. There are no real "big breaks" anymore. If an Artist is serious about having music as their profession then they need to put in the work and accept that it's a slow game.

- **Pre-Planning a Tour**

Most importantly, Artists planning to tour need plenty of time from beginning the booking process until the first show. For a tour containing mostly cities that an Artist has never been to before, start this process at least five months out. Artists should have nearly all of the shows booked two months in advance of the first show so they have plenty of time to promote the tour. Most likely the Artist is going to spend the first month routing the cities, researching venues and gaining contact info. This is a perfect time for an Artist to put their database to use.

- **Routing**

The routing of the cities will never be perfect. This means that an Artist may have to expect they'll do a little bit of backtracking and have a few off days. It's almost impossible to get every venue's schedule to line up with the Artists'. Obviously, the Artists will want to keep the backtracking and off days to a minimum.

First, plot out the targeted cities on a map. Try to keep drives shorter than six hours on a show day and shorter than 10 hours on a non-show day. When on tour, Artists are going to spend most of their time on the road. Spreading the long drives out will save from burnout. Also plan for about an hour of stops for every four hours of driving.

The more members an Artist has on tour, the easier it is to split up the driving, but it drastically increases the tour expenses.

- **Identifying Venues**

Once the targeted cities have been identified, Artists will have to find the venues that are appropriate for their sound and their potential draw. If the Artist has never been to this city before it's going to be much more difficult for them to convince the talent buyer at the venue to give them a gig, but it's possible.

Decide what kind of rooms that the Artist wants to play. Is the Artist a mellow singer-songwriter? Seek out art galleries, listening rooms, museums, cultural centers, black box theaters and living rooms. Is the Artist a rock band? Seek out rock clubs, basement venues, frat parties, festivals and block parties.

- **The Pitch**

Most talent buyers at venues work over e-mail, but some still work exclusively over the phone. Remember this and don't be afraid of the phone.

The Artist's initial e-mail pitch should be short and to the point. The subject line should be the date and the word "booking." If there are other Artists already on the bill, write their names on the subject line as well. e.g. "Booking for Oct 10 - Yellow Shoes and Tom Peterson." Check the venue's calendar FIRST and make sure that date is open. Don't ask for a night that is clearly marked on the calendar as a weekly '80 S night or something. It won't work. In addition, it may irritate the talent buyer because it shows that the Artist has not done their research and doesn't care about the club. This may hamper the Artist for future bookings as well.

Keep the e-mail under eight sentences and in lower case letters. Include a link to a live video and a link to the Artist's website and/or Facebook account. Talk about the Artist's history in the area (if any) and explain briefly how the Artist is going to promote the show. MOST IMPORTANTLY: say how many people the Artist expects to attend this show. This is what 98% of talent buyers care about. +50 is the magic number for less established Artists.

- **Local Openers**
Many venues may want the Artist to put the bill together, but sometimes they will happily place a proven local act similar to the Artist's style on the bill. It's best, though, if the Artist can take a complete bill to the venue.

The closest online service that can be used for this purpose is ReverbNation. However, not all bands are on this site. Artists may have to do a little bit more digging, but it's a good place to start. Also, Artists may want to consider doing "show trades" in a few cities they've never been to before.

- **Payment**
Most original music clubs will not offer guarantees to new or fairly-established Artists. Most likely, they will offer a cut of the door after expenses, ranging from $50 - $350 for smaller clubs. A typical deal for clubs a 70%-100% cut for 21+ venues, 70-85% for 18+ venues, and around 50-70% cut for all-age venues with higher off-the-top expenses. For these types of venues, there is not much negotiating power, especially if it's the Artists first time in the market and they aren't proven. This means that basically, Artists take what they can get.

If the Artist has a large cover-song repertoire, it's a completely different ballgame. In venues that hire cover-bands, Artists can get guarantees. However, most likely the venue will book their local cover bands first.

****

11.14 Task

For this section of the Artist Business Plan, write about the sales plan strategy for the performances and gigs of the Artist.

****

Publishing Sales Strategy

11.15 Publishing Sales Strategy

As another important income source for Artists, especially, Artist-Songwriters, securing a music publishing contract may be a perfect strategy. Remember, Publishers only wants to represent songs that have a potential to make money.

Many songwriters and composers are unable to gain a music publishing deal due to the fact that their song or instrumental theme has only minor or no commercial value. No amount of promotion or auditioning will make their song succeed. The song or instrumental theme could be unsuitable for many different reasons such as bad structure, weak lyrics on a good melody, good lyrics on a weak melody, poor recording, or quite simply sent to the wrong music publisher. Some songs may be singer/songwriter songs suitable only for recording, gigging and exploitation of the singer-songwriter through any record deal they obtain. It may, therefore, not have any commercial value for a music publisher to sign in respect to promoting and exploiting just the song.

The Guild of International Songwriters & Composers can help its songwriting members in many areas of identifying weakness, lack of commercial value in their songs/compositions and advise on market direction. The Guild of International Songwriters & Composers Song Assessment service is free to all members.

Music publishers are an Artist-Songwriter's promotional vehicle for songs and instrumental themes if they are not retaining and exploiting their own copyrights. In some instances publishers will nurture and develop Artist-Singer-Songwriters to help them gain a record deal. Music publishers promote and exploit songs and instrumental themes which are signed to them under an assignment of rights publishing contract. Music publishers also register the copyrights as assigned to their catalog with a Performing Rights Organization in the countries in which they operate.

Pitching Music Publishers

Songwriters are all looking for recognized success of their talent, publication of their songs and instrumental themes, and to receive money earned as royalties from the exploitation of their songwriting, composing and performances. The main difference is that songwriters and composers seek music publishing deals in order to have recording-Artists record their songs and to see any instrumental themes succeed in television program and advertising. Performing songwriters are not only seeking music publishing deals but also management deals and record deals.

Artists, who are songwriters, need to get their songs and/or instrumental themes to music publishers, record companies, management companies, Artists, producers, etc. Every songwriter, composer, lyricist, performing songwriter, singer, group, musician, etc. needs to know how to contact music publishers, record companies, management companies, music industry personnel, recording Artists etc.

Sales and marketing strategies for publishers are driven by experience, connections and credibility. Artists who does their own publishing or who license their material to a third-party publisher, need to understand this.

Tips about Music Publishers
1. Do not flood a Publisher with songs. Sending a CD or ten-song tape, without suggesting one or two specific tracks will probably result in getting none of the Artist-Songwriters songs heard. Forget sending reviews, pictures, or other promotional materials. Send a professionally mastered compact disc, with a typewritten lyric sheet, and ALL of the Artists contact information on the CD and the lyric

sheet. Send no more than two songs at a time. If a Publisher sees a CD with 8 songs, and a CD with 2 songs, chances are the 2-song CD gets listened to first. (It's off the desk more quickly that way.) The longer the pitch is, the longer it takes to get a publisher to get through the material.

2. TARGET!! The most difficult part of Publishing is finding the perfect place to pitch a song. When a Artist-Songwriter sends a song for publishing consideration, try to name a few acts or Artists whom the song may fit best. Be sure that these Artists do NOT write their own material, and that the song fits musically, subject-wise, stance wise with the latest work by the Artist. Songwriters may be able to write a GREAT song...but if it is not in the style being used today, their chances of a cut are slim. If the Artist is pitching for TV or Film usage, try to remember that 90% of those songs are genre specific. I.E., if it's a country genre song, they usually would like to hear fiddles or steel or both, so there is no doubt about the feel of the scene. In a Biker Bar, they might want songs with heavy guitar leads. When pitching material for publishing, it is the quality of the WRITING more than the flavor or production.

3. Be educated. Artists should make sure they know what they are trying to do. Is the Artist a writer? Is the Artist a singer? Is the Artist a singer who writes? Is the Artist a writer who is also performs live? All these paths are different. This should be defined in the Artist Development Plan. Most publishers work with dedicated writers as a first choice, simply because it is not a publisher's job to find a home for an Artist-Songwriter. Their job is to find a place for the song.

4. Songwriting is like any other skilled profession. There are rules and tools. It's always okay to challenge or break the rules... as long as it is by choice, and not by ignorance. Smart Artists study the craft of songwriting. They use tight rhyming schemes where they can. Artists should be familiar with the work of who it is they are trying to pitch. Why should anyone cut the Artist-Songwriter's song? Perhaps, Artists should listen to the radio for what's happening in their genre NOW. Remember- The competition is not the bad stuff heard on the radio, it is the BEST of the BEST.

Content knows no boundaries

****

11.15 Task

For this section of the Artist Business Plan, write about the publishing sales strategy for the songs of the Artist.

****

Distribution Overview

11.16
Distribution Overview

Artists also need to plan a distribution program for their promotional items during their live events. This may include the following questions: 1) how can an Artist's target market find or get attracted to their merch booth during their events? 2) How can the Artist effectively distribute their promotional items to giveaway? 3) How can the Artist deliver their message (sales pitch) or gather information from their target market (contact details) during the distribution process?

If an Artist is releasing their own recordings, compact discs, t-shirts, etc. they need to prepare a distribution plan. How is a fan going to purchase an Artist's product? The key to selling merch is to find a way for consumers to purchase them. This may be accomplished through brick and mortar retailers as well as those on the World Wide Web, or via the merch table at the Artist's gig. Typically, distribution comes in the form of either major, independent or online distribution. An Artist who releases their own recording for sale is actually running their own record label.

It isn't enough to say an Artist is going to try and get a distribution deal. It's very hard work to get a distribution deal.

As far as retail goes, Artists should be able to identify independent stores that will take product (if they do not have a distributor or distribution deal). It's important to identify those retail outlets that will support the Artist's project and it's even better if the artist has started discussions with them.

Some Artists, who operate their own independent record label form a distribution agreement through major labels and their distribution affiliate. This usually happens only if the independent label has several successful recordings in its catalog (distributors are interested in a steady flow of product). Occasionally, a major label may offer an Artist an agreement to re-release the record under the major label banner.

Distributor's Obligation

1. Warehouse Inventory
2. Solicit Sales from Stores
3. Fill Orders
4. Process Returns
5. Bill / Collect
6. Generate Sales Reports

Distributor Roles

The primary job of a Distributor is to get CD's and records into retail outlets. They do this by working closely with the record labels to promote and market their products. Most distributors regularly publish catalogs listing the labels they carry, and the titles available. They accept product on a negotiable billing schedule of between 60 to 120 days per invoice. They expect to receive a negotiated number of "free goods" to be used as incentives for retailers to carry the product, and also need "promotional copies" to be used in-house, as well as to give away to contacts in the media, and at retail. They can also arrange for "co-op" advertising, wherein the costs of media ads are split between the record label and a retailer.

Independent Distributors

Independent distribution can put records in stores, although to a lesser extent than working with major distributors. Some independent distributors have huge territories, while others are much more regional. Independent distributors generally distribute the product of smaller labels. Occasionally, they will distribute an unsigned Artist's record if they can be convinced that there is potential for substantial airplay and sales first,

---

The record label / distributor relationship at its most basic level is as follows:

1. The Artist records a record

2. Once the record is manufactured, a distributor will sell the record to a store

3. The store will, in turn, sell the record to a record buyer

---

Hence, the distributor's main job is to sell. Ancillary to the function of selling, the distributor will also warehouse the record, ship the record, collect the money from the store, and pay the label.

Occasionally, a distributor will also promote and advertise an Artist whom they believe in.

Major label distribution has some other players that contribute to sales.

One Stops are middlemen who buy records from labels and then make them available to local record stores that prefer the convenience of one stop shopping.

Rack Jobbers are middleman that buy records from labels and then stock them in the racks that they operate within retail stores.

Chain Stores such as K-Mart buy records from labels and then place them in their stores.

Record Clubs buy from labels and then resell to their members at discount prices.

Record Label Roles

Whether an Artist releases recordings on their own label or whether they are collaborating with an independent or major record label, the primary job of a record label is to attract the attention of distributors by having achieved a modicum of success on their own, by selling product on consignment, or at live shows, and through various mail order and direct sales methods. Having gotten their product accepted by a distributor, the job of a record label is to work closely with their distributor(s), providing them with information on successful airplay, print media support, and live performance successes. In addition the record labels create "Distributor One Sheets," or fact sheets that include promotion and marketing plans, and list price information. The record labels also provide the distributor with "P.O.P.'s" (Point of Purchase) items, such as posters, flyers, cardboard stand-ups etc., which can be used for in-store display.

What a Record Distributor Wants to Know about an Artist

1. Has the Artist had any success with established mainstream labels?
2. Does the Artist have a following, if so, how well known are they?
3. If the Artist is unknown, what specific promotion ideas does the label have?
4. Are there any well-known "guest" musicians on the recording?
5. Does the recording and artwork meet the standards of the musical genre?
6. Is there any current airplay on commercial or non-commercial radio?
7. Will there be independent promotion on the release to retail and to radio?
8. Has the Artist hired a publicist, and/or what is the publicity campaign?
9. Will the Artist be touring in support of their release, and is there a schedule?
10. Does the label have the financial resources to provide "co-op" advertising?
11. Does the label have the financial resources to press additional product?
12. Does the label have a salable "back catalog" of proven sellers?
13. How much product from the label is already out in the stores?
14. Does the label have other distributors selling the same product?
15. What are the next releases from the label, and when are they coming out?
16. Does the Artist have a sales track record in the mainstream record trade?
17. If this is a new Artist, what sort of promotion can they expect from the label or the Artist that will help sell records?
18. Is there any current radio activity on this title?
19. Does the label have the resources to press enough product if the demand becomes great?
20. What are the label's upcoming releases, and when can they expect them?
21. Does the label also sell to competing distributors in their territory?
22. Does the quality of the recording, and the artwork measure up to the standards of its genre?

Inventory

Proper management of inventory is one of those necessary functions that all too often is neglected by Artists and their record companies, large and small. Inventory equals dollars -- every CD in inventory represents money that is no longer available for other use. Artists need to know approximately, how many pieces of every catalog number and configuration they own, and what this represents in dollars. They also need to know how much of this is active, saleable stock, representing titles still in demand by fans and distributors. Artists need to keep track of how much is overstock and obsolete, in other words, no longer salable. They need to know how much inventory is sitting idly in their distributor's warehouse and which will eventually come back to them as returns.

What the Record Label Must Supply to a Distributor

A record label wishing to have their product carried by a distributor must have the following:

1. Its own trademarked name

2. Catalog numbers on each release (usually a 3 letter abbreviation followed by the numbers, i.e. UCR415).

3. A Universal Product Code

4. The Barcode on the back of the product. This is required because most retail sales are now tracked through the Soundscan technology that monitors retail sales.

Shipping
The shipping charges are usually the burden of the label, but may be negotiated after a label has established itself as a customer. Most national distributors require an "exclusive" arrangement, making them the sole distributor of a label's product.

Advertising Requirements
Many distributors have monthly newsletters, and/or update sheets, as well as catalogs. They may require labels to advertise in them, with the costs of the ad deducted from a particular invoice.

The Distributor One Sheet

The Distributor One Sheet is one page (8 1/2" x 11") of basic information about the band, and includes:

1. Label's logo and contact information

2. Artist Name/Logo

3. Catalog # and UPC code (Barcode)

4. List price (i.e. $15.98) of each available format

5. Release Date (to Radio)
6. Street Date (for Retailers, if different from Release Date)

7. A brief Artist background description

8. Selling Points (Discounts, Marketing, and Promotion plans)

Promo Copies
All "Promotional" products should have the artwork "punched, clipped, or drilled." This is to make sure that they are not returned to the distributor as "cleans." "Cleans" are the name for regular product sold in stores. Many people who receive "Promos" have friends in retail or at distributors, and can exchange "cleans" for CD's they personally want. This is why they need to be identified as promo copies.

Pricing

Labels sell their CD's and Tapes to distributors for approximately 50% of the list price of the release. For example a $15.98 list CD might be purchased by the distributor for $8. A $9.98 vinyl record would be purchased for $5.

Payment Terms

When an invoice becomes due for payment, the distributor may not necessarily pay that invoice in full. For example, let's say a record label has billed a distributor for a total of $5,000 worth of product. Let's assume that $1,500 of this product is still in their warehouse. This means that $3,500 worth of product is out in the stores, some of which is probably still on the store's shelves, unsold. The distributor is responsible for paying the $3,500 worth of product placed (less a reserve of 15% to 20% for the label's product which may be returned to the distributor by the stores.) The distributor would hopefully send a check to the label for about $2,800 to $3,000.

Co-op Advertising

As previously discussed in the Advertising Plan of the artist Business Plan, Co-Op advertising is also used by record labels and distributors. This is a way for record labels to pay for media ad space with product, and is an effective way to use their inventory to promote sales. For example, when a label wants to promote one of their Artist's recordings, they approach a retailer through their distributor. The label will pay for the cost of the ad, the retailer can deduct their agreed upon "buy-in" of the label's product from their invoice with the distributor, while the distributor then deducts the amount from their account with the label. In return for this, the ad features the Artist's release, with a mention of the recording. The retailer, in addition to carrying the product (the buy-in), also agrees to give it good placement in their store(s), and put the product on sale for a limited time. Basically, this arrangement is a win/win situation for all parties involved.

Returns

It is a standard practice that 100% of any defective and overstocked product can be returned by the record stores to the distributors. They insist that every record label they deal with accept this policy. If a specific title from a label is deleted from their catalog, the label must notify the distributor, and it can take up to one year for the distributor to get deleted product back from the larger chain stores. These larger chains will withhold up to 20% of their payables to distributors as a reserve against returns.

Shipping Instructions

A packing slip must be enclosed with each order sent from a record label to a distributor. This must include details on what was ordered, what has been shipped, the number of cartons in the shipment, and the Purchase Order number from the distributor. All products must be shrink wrapped. In most cases, for CD's, the jewel box is the standard package.

Invoices are sent separately, through the mail. The invoice should include an Invoice Number, invoice date, a detail of what was shipped, a ship date, and unit prices of each title/format sent. The distributors PO number, and the total amount due, should also appear on the invoice. Each shipment must have its own invoice.

Summary
The distributor's job is to make the buyers at retail outlets aware of a label's product. They use their sales tools; promos, one-sheets, airplay, press, and live performance reports to try and convince the buyers that they should stock the product they carry. If a specific title sells, it is the job of the distributor, in cooperation with the record label to provide the retailers with a continuous flow of the product. It is essential that a record label have a consistent, professional, and mutually respectful relationship with their distributors. Selling recorded product is a team effort. Don't forget it.

Distribution - Brick & Mortar

11.16.01
Distribution – Brick & Mortar

In the traditional sense of distribution for an Artist's or record label's recordings, physical retail stores were the norm. Brick and mortar describes the physical presence of a building(s) or other structures. The term brick-and-mortar business is often used to refer to a company that possesses buildings or stores for operations. If an Artist, and/or their record label, is planning to sell compact discs and/or merchandise to physical retail outlets, they should have a plan and a budget to deal with brick-and-mortar retail stores.

Artists want to make sure that they have a reason to put their CD in a store to begin with. Is the music on the CD getting radio airplay in the area? Is the Artist playing lots of gigs in the area? If an Artist isn't promoting their music in that area of the country, then getting their CDs into stores is going to be a waste of time.

It can be very expensive for an Artist to enter the business of physical copies in a digital world. Many businesses, not just entertainment businesses, suffer from the financial strains of manufacturing, inventory, shipping and distribution. In one sense, the Artist is very lucky to have some of their products available online, in a digital format.

However, if an Artist wants to explore every income source, they need to consider physical distribution through brick and mortar retail stores. Artists should keep in mind that a budget analysis should be prepared prior to launching any physical release.

Which Outlets?
An Artist who performs and records in a regional area should pay attention to local outlets that may be interested in carrying the Artist's product(s). The first and most obvious solution is the mom-and-pop record store (if you can still find one.) Other possibilities are game stores, coffee shops and the venue(s) where the Artist may perform a lot.

Consignment?
The cheapest, and often easiest way to get an Artists compact discs into record stores, is to put them on consignment. When this happens, there is no risk for the store owners. Compact discs from regional Artists aren't generally going to

have the same value to a record store owner, as a heavy seller on the Billboard charts. Music store owners need to sell product to make money and only have a limited amount of shelf space. If an Artist's CD is going to be a relatively small-end seller, then it's not going to have the same priority as CDs that are going to sell 30 copies a day.

Since independent CDs don't generally sell in high numbers (at least at first), record store owners would prefer either not to carry them at all, or in very small quantities. Allowing independent Artists and bands to put a few CDs on consignment is a no-risk situation for them. They will usually take about 5-10 copies from the Artist and put it in the store with no up-front payment. If they sell something, then both the Artist (or Artist's label, or both) and the music retailer will profit. The percentage of each sale should be negotiated upfront. If the retailer doesn't sell any of the Artist's CDs, then they simply give them back. No risk for the owner, means that selling on consignment is relatively easy for Artists.

****

11.17 Task

For this section of the Artist Business Plan, write about the plan for distribution of the Artist's products and services.

****

Distribution - Online

11.16.02
Distribution – Online

For any Artist to reach their fans and customers, they need a way to have their art available for those fans and customers to purchase. This is where distribution plays a major role in the success of any Artist.

In addition to the traditional "brick-and-mortar" stores that sell compact discs or vinyl records for Artists and record labels, a cheaper and faster way to distribute music is electronically. Online distribution should be planned, and tracked.

Digital distribution describes the delivery of media content such as audio, video, and video games, without the use of physical media or outlets. Usually digital distribution is completed through online delivery mediums, such as the Internet.

Content distributed online may be streamed or downloaded. Streaming involves downloading and using content "on-demand" as it is needed. Meanwhile, fully downloading the content to a hard drive or other form of storage media allows for quick access.

2 Types of Online Distribution

Streamed
Downloaded

Alternative technologies for content delivery includes peer-to-peer file sharing technologies. Content can only be delivered if it exists on a computer that another user has made available to others.

One of the major attractions for online distribution for Artists is its ease and direct nature to the fan or consumer. By opting for online distribution, an Artist can get their work to the public easily with potentially minimum business overhead. This often leads to cheaper goods for the consumer, increased profits for the Artist, as well as increased Artistic freedom. Online distribution platforms often contain or act as a form of digital rights management.

Online distribution also opens the door to new business models (e.g., the Open Music Model). For instance, an Artist could release one track at a time from an album instead of waiting for them all to be completed. This either gives them a cash boost to help the Artist continue their projects or warns that their work is not financially viable. Hopefully, Artists recognize this before they have spent excessive money and time on a project deemed unviable.

Music Distribution via Artist's Website
Indie Artists are for the first time able to access the same distribution channels as major record labels, with none of the restrictive practices or inflated manufacturing costs. There is a growing collection of 'Internet labels' that offer distribution to unsigned or independent Artists directly to online music stores, and in some cases marketing and promotion services. Further, many Artists are able to bypass this completely, and offer their music for sale via their own independently controlled websites. This gives even further advantage to the Artist, as it completely cuts out a distributor—and their cut of the profits.

The online domain has also given Artists more control over their music in terms of ownership, rights, creative process, pricing, and more. The Internet prevents Artists from incurring any distribution costs even into the international scene since the Internet allows users from all over the world to access the same material. In addition to providing users with easier access to music, it allows users to pick and choose the songs they wish instead of having to purchase an entire album from which there may only be one or two songs that the buyer enjoys. Now more than ever, more and more customers are choosing to purchase select tracks instead of an entire album.

Online Music Distributors
Online music distribution has changed the music industry, but which digital distributors are the best for musicians and labels? Which sites pay the most? Which sites don't pay when they say they will?

Before an Artist signs up with an online music distribution service, they will want to get their music in shape. The first task is to have the Artist's recording mastered, which means a professional mastering engineer has optimized the Artist's digital music file to sound its best. As part of this process, an Artist may make decisions like which music files they really want to make publicly available. Artists can just release a single or an entire album.

Once an Artist knows what they want to upload, they'll need both a UPC (universal price code) and ISRC (international standard recording code). Most of the distribution services will arrange these codes for the Artist if needed; some may bill an additional fee for this.

Pricing models used by the different services vary widely. It can be a monthly subscription with no royalties to the service; flat fee per track or album with an additional royalty percentage going to the service; or a low flat set-up fee with additional per track/album fees and low royalty percentage. Some services will bill a range of flat fees depending on the number of digital music stores where an Artist wants their music.

> **The two most important points to understand about pricing are:**
>
> A. the cost to enter the market through these services is quite low, so there are no barriers anymore to getting the Artist's music out there; and
>
> B. the pricing model that makes sense for the Artist will depend on the volume they want to post.

I-Tunes

ITunes won't deal directly with individual Artists. Not to worry, though -- the digital age has indeed democratized access for individual Artists to the newest distribution channel. Artists may sign up with any one of a number of distribution intermediaries who can get the Artist's music on iTunes, as well as other digital music stores. These intermediaries are called aggregators. They receive a percentage of every recording from their catalog that is sold by iTunes.

> **6 Aggregators for I-Tunes**
>
> 1. Believe Digital
> 2. Catapult
> 3. CD Baby
> 4. In Grooves / Fontana
> 5. The Orchard
> 6. Tunecore

Online Music Distributors
Amazon Music – http://www.amazon.com
Best Buy – http://www.bestbuy.com
Borders – http://www.borders.com
Buy.com - http://www.buy.com
CD Connection www.cdconnection.com
CD Now (Amazon) http://www.cdnow.com
CD Plus – http://www.cd-plus.com
CD Universe – http://cduniverse.com
CD Zone – http://www.cdzone.co.uk
Coalition of Independent Music Stores – http://www.cimsmusic.com
Djangos – http://www.djangos.com
Half.com – http://www.half.com
ITunes – http://www.itunes.com
Music Millennium – http://www.musicmillennium.com
Overstock.com – http://www.overstock.com
Sam Goody – http://www.samgoody.com
Song Search – http://www.songsearch.com
Spun – http://www.spun.com
Target – http://www.target.com
The Music Resource – http://www.themusicresource.com
Tower Records –

http://www.towerrecords.com
Twec – http://www.twec.com
Virgin Megastore – http://www.virginmega.com
Walmart – http://www.walmart.com

Other Online Sales for Artists
Amie Street - http://amiestreet.com/welcome
Fonogenic - http://www.fonogenic.com/
Mindawn - http://www.mindawn.com/
Tuneshout – http://www.tuneshout.com
Absolute Punk – www.absolutepunk.net
Audio Galaxy – www.audiogalaxy.com
Audio Lunch Box – www.audiolunchbox.com
Buy Music – www.buymusic.com
Connect – www.connect.com
E Music – www.emusic.com
Inter Punk – www.interpunk.com
Listen – www.listen.com
Mighty Rhapsody – www.mightyrhapsody.com
Monster Market Place – www.monstermarketplace.com/searchw36.asp?q=pop+music
MP3 – www.mp3.com
MSN – www.music.msn.com
Music Central – www.musiccentral.msn.com
Music Match – www.musicmatch.com
Music Net – www.musicnet.com
Napster – www.napster.com
Oriental Tunes – www.orientaltunes.com
Pure Tracks – www.puretracks.com
R Labels – www.rlabels.com
Real – www.real.com
Real Networks – www.realnetworks.com
Rhapsody - www.rhapsody.com
Smark Punk – www.smartpunk.com
Sound Beat Radio – www.soundbeatradio.com
Stereo Killer – www.stereokiller.com
Top 40 Countdown – www.top40countdown.com
Yahoo – www.music.yahoo.com

****

11.16 Task

For this section of the Artist Business Plan, write about the plan for distribution for the products and services of the Artist's company.

****

Content Licensing

11.17
Content Licensing

Content licensing implies monetizing content in some way. In the music industry, this is especially true for songwriters and owners of sound recordings. Although there are numerous types of Artist's content, the two main types in the music industry are songs and recordings of songs.

The term "content licensing" is an ambiguous one, especially among publishers. Some consider reprints and e-prints to be a full-fledged content licensing operation; while others leasing out logos and awards for third-party use count it as their content licensing service. Still others have moved custom publishing under the umbrella term of "content licensing," with syndication often finding itself in this category as well.

For publishers who choose to monetize their property beyond advertising and subscriptions, servicing appropriate partners, managing the business and monitoring client contracts can equate to a full-time job. For what can seem like an overwhelming task, deciding which content to barter with may be the first step for companies considering a move into the content licensing business.

In order for an Artist to license content to a customer, they must first own or control that content. This is another reason why copyrights are so important. An Artist's copyrights are identified in the Artist Development Plan.

****

11.17 Task

For this section of the Artist Business Plan, write about the plan for content licensing for the products and services of the Artist's company.

****

Tickets Sales Strategy

11.18 Tickets Sales Strategy

In today's live performance world, many young Artists are required to sell tickets as a part of their performance agreement. There are arguments to the validity of this fairly new process in the industry. By requiring Artists to sell tickets, lazy promoters may actually be doing a favor to these Artists. Artists typically are not promoters. That's not their job. However, smart Artists know that when they promote, the crowd at their performance is larger and hence, a re-booking from that talent buyer or promoter becomes a bigger possibility.

In addition to young Artists selling tickets for their show, many super-star Artists have developed a strategy of buying their own tickets and re-selling on sites such as Stub-Hub or the Ticket Network. Yes, super-star Artists also buy and re-sell tickets to their performances. Why? It's another potential income source.

Either way, here are a few ideas for Artists developing their ticket sales strategy:

1. Many Artists can promote the sale of individual performance tickets to fans
2. Advance sales encourage fans to purchase tickets to individual events in advance to eliminate the risk of people changing their minds on the day of the show
3. Premium seats are tickets to an event may feature additional benefits or values
4. Premium seats could include anything from select sections apart of the general crowd or VIP tables near the front of the stage.

Online Sources
A basic premise is that the Artist has built some sort of audience for their online presence. In addition, Artists who collect e-mail addresses and text-numbers from fans are at an advantage. They can easily

notify them of upcoming performances and direct them to their website to complete the transaction.

- Sell Tickets on the Artist's website
- Deliver Fans-Only Early Birds
- Offer Tickets for Remote Attendees
- Use Facebook Ads
- Incentivize Friends Referrals
- Add a Group Buying Twist
- Make The Artist's Tickets Become Gifts

****

11.18 Task

For this section of the Artist Business Plan, write about the plan for selling tickets to the Artist's performances.

****

Notes

_____

_____

_____

_____

_____

Chapter 12
Business Plan for Artists
Intellectual Property

A very important component in the entertainment is intellectual property. Intellectual property refers to creations of the mind for which exclusive rights are recognized by governments across the globe. Under intellectual property law, owners are granted certain exclusive rights to a variety of intangible assets, such as musical, literary, and artistic works; discoveries and inventions; and words, phrases, symbols, and designs.

Intellectual Property Overview

12.01
Intellectual Property Overview

For some Artists, songwriting is a key component of their activities and should be highlighted in the business plan. There are a lot of industry professionals who place a higher value on an Artist that can write their own really good songs.

Artists should know whether the songs they write will be used strictly by them or whether they will be pitching these songs to other Artists.

If the Artist is planning to pitch songs to other Artists, they need to show a well-developed strategy for tackling that. Is the Artist planning to solicit a music publishing company? If so, the Artist should be able to show that they have researched who the Artist is going to target and that they will be making a contact. A letter of interest from a publisher can definitely strengthen an Artist's Business Plan. Again, the reader wants to ensure that the Artist has done their homework. Is the Artist planning to promote their songs directly to other Artists in their community and what is the strategy for doing that?

If the Artist has no publisher, then they should indicate who will be taking care of their publishing and how that will be managed internally.

If the Artist is working with a lesser-known publishing company, then they should provide some background information on the success of this publishing company. The Artist also has the option of giving a quick introduction to the company and providing a longer background.

There are many types of intellectual property and the rights they may be associated. Rights include copyright, trademarks, patents, industrial design rights, and in some jurisdictions, trade secrets.

Copyright
A copyright gives the creator of an original work, exclusive rights to their creation. Usually, copyright is only valid for a limited time. Copyright may apply to a wide range of creative, intellectual, or artistic forms, or "works." Copyright, however, does not cover song titles, band names, ideas and information themselves; only the form or manner in which they are expressed.

Patents
A patent grants an inventor exclusive rights to make, use, sell, and import an invention. Patents, like copyrights, also have a limited time period. Inventors receive this in exchange for the public disclosure of the invention. An invention is a usually solution to a specific technological problem, which may be a product or a process.

Trademarks
A trademark is a recognizable sign, design or expression which distinguishes products or services of a particular trader from the similar products or services of other traders. Artists need a trademark to distinguish themselves from other Artists or businesses. Some Artists trademark their logo and some even trademark their signature.

Discography
Discography is the catalog of published sound recordings of the Artist and/or their record company. The exact information included in the discography catalog varies depending on the type and scope, but typically lists such details as the names of the Artists or musicians or producer involved, the time and place of the recording, the title of the piece performed, release dates, chart positions, and sales figures.

Performing Rights Organizations
A P.R.O. (Performing Rights Organization) helps an Artist-Songwriter collect fees for the use of their songs in public performances, radio broadcasts, etc. Every songwriter should be affiliated with a P.R.O.

Registration of Intellectual Property
To protect the Intellectual Property of every Artist, registration of their claim to copyright, trademark or patent is imperative in case of infringement.

Content Development
In the music industry there are many ways for individuals to be creative. The two most recognized is the songwriter and the producer. Some Artists are one or the other and many times, both. Creating a strategy of content development for the Artist will help focus on the art as well as the business. Remember, the owning or controlling of content is the crux of the entertainment business. What would Disney do without that little mouse?

Content Clearances
As a part of Intellectual Property, a strategy of clearing content licensing should be addressed. How does the Artist-Songwriter license their works to others, as well as, how does the Artist license songs or audio samples from others?

Intellectual Property Plan

12.02 - Copyrights
12.03 - Patents
12.04 - Trademarks
12.05 - Discography
12.06 - Performing Rights Organizations
12.07 - Registration
12.08 - Content Development
12.09 - Content Clearances
12.10 - Digital Rights Management

****

12.01 Task

For this section of the Artist Business Plan, write about the overall plan for intellectual property of the products and services of the Artist's company.

****

Copyrights

12.02 Copyrights

There have been many technological advances in the past few years and the World Wide Web is one of them. For many, the good came with the bad. Messages can now be sent and received in seconds. We no longer have to go to the store and buy a CD. We can purchase recordings online. Better yet, we can download it from many online distribution websites; sometimes for free. We can print sheet music, and have access to movies before they even come out. Doesn't this all seem too good to be true? Well it is. A lot of what people do on the Internet is not legal at all. Surprisingly many people are not sure about the legalities when it comes to music and piracy.

According to the newest copyright law, copyright protection is acquired automatically when a work is "created." The definition of "created" is when a work is fixed in a copy or recording for the first time. A copyright has to be in tangible form to be valid. A copyright is valid as soon as the work is in tangible form. This means that the content creator must write it down or record it to put it into tangible form. However, this does not mean that the work is a registered copyright.

Copyright law gives the owner the right to prevent others from copying, creating derivative works, or publicly performing their works. Copyrights, like patent rights, can be divided in many different ways, including ownership, by geographic or market territories, or by more specific criteria. Each copyright may be the subject of a separate license and royalty arrangement.

The owner of a copyright has five exclusive rights:
1. to make copies of the songs through print or recordings
2. to distribute them to the public for profit
3. to perform the song live or through a broadcast

4. to create a derivative work which may include elements of the original work
5. to "display" it (not very relevant in music business context).

Where the music and the lyric of a composition may be contributions of different persons, each of them is an equal owner of the copyrights.

---

5 Rights to Copyrights

1. To make copies of the songs through print or recordings

2. To distribute them to the public for profit

3. To the perform the song live or through a broadcast

4. To create a derivative work which may include elements of the original work

5. To "display" it (not very relevant in music business context).

Copyright ownership is one thing but proving copyright ownership is completely different. Proof of ownership and copyright is achieved by registration of the copyrighted content such as a song or lyric. This is done by filing Copyright form with a check for the proper fees, and one copy of the unpublished song on a record, tape, CD, or lead sheet to the U.S. Copyright Office. If the song has been published, two copies should be sent. Registration becomes effective upon receipt of the application form, copies of the content, and the fee.

Copyright registration of songs is necessary in order to protect a song from being used without permission, and is necessary to present in a court of law and to sue for copyright infringement. If the work is not a registered copyright, courts generally will delay hearings until copyright registration is completed. Therefore, protection for possible infringement cannot happen until the work is a registered copyright.

Copyright forms can be found in many published books, or may be obtained from the copyright office:

Copyright Office
Library of Congress
Washington, DC 20559
www.copyright.gov for details.

Artist-Songwriters should put a copyright notice on all published copies of the song. A circle with a small 'c' [©] in it is the usual mark, but the word 'copyright' is also acceptable. Follow the mark with the year and the songwriter's names. Note: the year stated is the year the song was first published, not necessarily when the song was written. Unpublished works need no copyright notice, but it is still a good idea to put the mark and use the phrase, for example "unpublished 2016, John Doe."

Please note: Song titles are not copyrightable. However, be aware that using the exact title of a song that has established itself as part of the culture, can open the doors for a lawsuit based on property rights in the title, which belong to the copyright owner of the famous song. One example is "White Christmas" by Irving Berlin.

Expiration of Copyright

The expiration of a copyright is more complex than that of a patent. Historically the United States has specified terms of a number of years following creation; this number has been increased several times. Most other countries specify terms of a number of years following the death of the last surviving creator; this number varies from one country to another (50 years and 70 years are the most common). In the United States, copyright expires 70 years beyond the death of the creator.

A copyrighted work has protection under the law for the life of the content creator(s) (songwriter(s)), plus 70 years after his/her/their death.

Circle and Circle P

A song and a recording of the same song have two different copyrights.

The sound recording copyright is for the protection of the sounds on the recording, and usually belongs to the record company owns the recording. The copyright of the work on the recording usually belongs to the Publisher of the song. The same person may own the copyright to the song as well as the copyright to the recording of the song.

What are these symbols? What do they mean? Most people would think they had an idea of the first one and very few would know of the second. If you are a musician of any kind these symbols should mean a lot, but even that is not the case sometimes.

With the rise of technology the once definite line between legal and illegal has become a bit confusing. When can a person copy a piece of music or sing a song at a local concert? The simple answer is when they own or control the copyright or they have permission via a license to do so.

Many people get these two rights mixed up. Most think that when a singer puts out a song on a CD, it's the singer who would have to be contacted to get permission to use the song. But we have to remember that most of the singers we listen to didn't write the songs they sing. Permission would be granted by songwriter / publisher.

Writing and Producing Music

You see the two symbols above and they represent two types of copyright.

The Circle C is a symbol that represents creation copyright. This copyright basically covers writers and composers. A Artist-Songwriter has the rights to the song that he/she composed, and there may be a publisher who is assigned to 'sell' the song. Until a Artist-Songwriter assigns their rights to copy to a third-party music publisher, they are the publisher.

The Circle P is a symbol that represents a recording performance production copyright which is the right of the record label or producer or the Artists to their specific interpretation of that moment in time of the song / music which is recorded. The owner of the proposed recording will obtain permission, in the form of a license, from the Circle-C copyright owner to record their song, unless it is a piece in public domain. The record label, producer or Artist create an additional copyright of their performance in the recording production – on top of the composer/lyricist creation copyright. That is why those "recording rights" are called, in legal terminology, "Neighboring Rights." The symbol, a circled P, is the copyright symbol used to provide notice of copyright in a sound recording (phonogram). The use of the symbol is described by United States copyright law and internationally by the Convention for the Protection of Producers of Phonograms against Unauthorized Duplication of Their Phonograms.

A sound recording has a separate copyright that is distinct from that of the underlying work (the musical notation and lyrics). It is to the aural copyright that the sound recording copyright notice pertains. In countries respecting the Berne convention, copyright may be asserted over the underlying work beyond that indicated by the sound recording copyright symbol.

A sound recording copyright notice consists of three elements:

1. The circle-p (p) symbol

2. The year of first publication of the sound recording

3. An identification of the owner of the copyright.

****

12.02 Task

For this section of the Artist Business Plan, write about the plan for copyrights for the products of the Artist's company.

****

Patents

12.03 Patents

Patents are a part of Intellectual Property for an Artist. Typically, Artists are more concerned with the Intellectual of Copyrights and Trademarks in the entertainment industry, but occasionally the need for a patent comes into play for an Artist.

Basically patents refer to inventions. As a part of Intellectual Property, which is a legal way to protect all creations of the human mind, Intellectual Property can be divided into two segments: Industrial Property (patents, trademarks and industrial designs) and copyright.

The invention can either be a product or a process that provides a new way of doing something, or offers a new technical solution to a problem. In order to invent, inventors first identify a need or a problem. Then they think of a creative way to solve that problem. Have you ever heard the proverb 'necessity is the mother of invention'?

Advantages to Securing a Patent

1. to secure an exclusive market
2. to license the innovation
3. to find capital and/or partners

There are several reasons why patents are important. Firstly, patents provide incentives to the individuals, who deserve recognition for their creativity and material reward for their inventions. Secondly, the incentives encourage innovation. Thirdly, protection stimulates research, which results in technological development. Fourthly, it enables the inventor (s) to recoup their investment for the money and time spent developing their idea.

In the United States, a patent application must be filed with the Patent & Trademark Office (www.uspto.gov) no later than one year after a description of the invention is published or publicly disclosed or the invention is first put on sale or made available for commercial use. In general, disclosure under a signed confidentiality agreement is not deemed to be "public disclosure."

Obtaining a patent in the United States usually takes 18 to 24 months and can be expensive, depending on how well the inventor does in describing the invention in writing. Plan on budgeting between $10K and $25K for obtaining a patent in the U.S. - maintenance fees and foreign filing fees are extra.

****

12.03 Task

For this section of the Artist Business Plan, write about the plan for patents for the products of the Artist's company.

****

Trademarks

12.04 Trademarks

Another part of Intellectual Property for an Artist is that of protecting their 'mark." This mark could be their logo or their signature. A trademark is a symbol and is generally used to identify a particular product, which indicates its source. A trademark can be a combination of words, phrases, symbols, logos, designs, images, or devices. It is used by an individual, legal entity or business organization to distinguish their products from others. For example, fans and customers may be able to identify the products of many musical Artists from their logo, which may be embossed on their products. Once registered, trademarks are protected legally and the owners can sue persons or businesses for unauthorized use of their trademarks.

Trademarks also prevent counterfeit products through registration with the US Trademark Office. Once registered, an Artist and their business can prevent the import of counterfeit products by registering the mark with the U.S. Customs Department.

Another crucial step in securing Intellectual Property is securing a registered Trademark with the United States Trademark Office. (This is also defined in the Artist Development Plan.) Other than equipment and gear, securing a Trademark is probably the most expensive item that an Artist may have to spend for their artist development. The good news: A Trademark is valid for 10 years before it must be renewed. As explained in the image section of the Artist Development Plan, the name of the Artist is of upmost importance in establishing a brand. When an Artist starts to establish their brand, many times they develop a logo and that logo is protected with a trademark.

In starting the brand of a musical band or Artist, choosing a good name may be a difficult task. The Artist's name will highlight the Artist's unique identity. If the Artist is attempting to make it big in the music industry, by writing songs, making recordings, performing and selling merchandise; it becomes necessary have to trademark of their Artist's name. This is applicable to both solo musicians as well as bands and ensembles.

A trademark is an intellectual property and it can assume the form of a word, a phrase, a logo, or a combination of them all. As described earlier in this section, intellectual property is a creation that has commercial value, and can be protected by patents, copyrights and trademarks.

What is a Trademark?

According to the United States Trademark Office, a trademark can be defined as a distinct name, sign or any type of indicator (logo, slogan, word, symbol, design or a combination of all) that is used by an individual, legal entity or business organization, such as a singer-songwriter or band, to distinguish and identify their goods or services from that of others. In other words, trademarks of the Artist, or the Artist's products, shows their source of origin and helps the fans and customers in identifying them as well as their particular product.

A trademark is used by companies or business organizations in order to associate their name or logo as a unique brand. The existence of a trademark on any product plays an excellent psychological effect on fans and consumers. The trademark basically helps the fan to identify the Artist's product. The logic behind the use of trademark is extremely simple. It's easy for humans to remember graphics and pictures as opposed to plain written language or text. The logos and symbols that are used for the trademark make it easy to identify, and get registered into the minds of fans and potential customers.

Trademarks are another way of branding for an Artist

Trademark Types
There are 3 types of trademarks that are currently in use in the United States.
1. **Non-Registered Trademark**
   The first type of Trademark is the unregistered trademark, represented

by letters TM. Violation of this trademark is not legally enforceable. A non-registered trademark is a logo and name that is not registered in accordance with the trademark office. In case of violation of such a trademark, the case that is filed often remains undecided.

2. **Service Trademark**
This type of mark is represented by letters 'SM', and is commonly used by the service sector brands.

3. **Registered Trademark**
The registered trademark is the most commonly used trademark, and is legally enforceable, and is represented by an 'R', enclosed in a circle ®, also known as a Circle-R. A registered trademark is recorded with the U.S. Trademark Office. Violating a registered trademark is an offense and the accused may have to pay heavy fines and compensations.

Trademark Symbols
Generally, two symbols are used to denote a trademark. One is '™', which represents a non-registered trademark symbol and the other is '®', which is used to denote an application for registered trademark. These symbols are displayed immediately after the trademark, in a superscript style. If the product carries the symbol '™', then the trademark may have never been registered or may be in the process of registration. If the symbol is '®', then, it denotes a trademark that is registered with the United States Trademark Office.

vs.

In the United States, the government authority to issue and validate a Trademark is the U.S. Patent and Trademark Office (USPTO or PTO). The proprietary rights of the trademark can be established with its first date of commercial use or by registration with the trademark office. In cases of infringement, registered trademarks enjoy a higher level of legal protection with the courts, as compared to a non-registered one.

The United States Patent and Trademark Office may be accessed online at www.USPTO.GOV. This is a great place to start to discover if the desired trademark is available, and then to actually register the mark.

Reasons to Apply for Trademark
There are numerous reasons why an Artist needs to trademark and register their name and/or logo. First of all, a trademark plays a central role in preventing the use of the Artist's name by another Artist or other musical groups. Trademark law states that an Artist or band with a registered trademark cannot use a name that is similar to another Artist or band. There have been many cases where bands have ended up changing their names just because they used a name similar to another group. That's why it's important to create a unique name of the Artist or band name in the first place.

It is recommended to come up with a unique name that does not sound or seem similar to another group, and trademark it as soon as possible to preclude other groups from using it. Trademarking a band name also allows an Artist to legally distribute merchandise, sell records, and carry out music industry dealings with the trademarked logo on it.

Advantages of a Trademark

1. **Proof of Use and Ownership**
   In case a common law trademark is registered by a person who is not the first user of the mark, that person gets the right to use it and the original user of the common law mark loses all rights. Hence it is best if the trademark is registered.
2. **Right to Use it Nationwide**
   The trademark can accompany goods or services distributed throughout the nation where it is registered.
3. **Showing Legitimacy**
   Every music business professional such as record label executives and publishers will want to know that the Artist that they are about to collaborate with has a trademark on their name. Can you image a record label signing an Artist to the label and then put in lots of time and money to make the product: the recording, the mixing, the mastering and the CDs, then the record company releases the product, and three days later, they get a cease and desist letter from someone who has trademarked that Artist's name? The record label will demand that the Artist's name is trademarked before they ink a deal with them.
4. **Settling of Disputes**
   A registered trademark is helpful in settling any disputes in a federal court of law, regarding the use or infringement of the trademark by others.
5. **Preventing Counterfeit Products**
   A business can prevent the import of counterfeit products by registering the mark with the U.S. Customs Department.
6. **Foreign Country Trademarks**
   A Federally registered trademark can be used in order to expedite the process of obtaining a trademark from a foreign government. This is necessary in case the products of the Artist are exported, because a trademark only has national validity.
7. **Selling the Business**
   In case of selling the business, it would be helpful if the owner has registered trademarks. Trademarks result in increasing the worth of a business, by helping to distinguish the products of a particular Artist or business from others. This is important if an Artist owns their recordings and releases them on their own record label. The Artist may eventually sell their record label to another person or business.

According to legal provisions, the product engraved with a trademark cannot be imitated. A fake product of same quality cannot be produced and sold under the same name and logo. If done, it is considered to be a violation of trademark rights. Those rights are held by the producer of original product.

It is evident that registering a trademark is a necessity rather than a convention. The benefits of registering clearly outweigh the cost involved in registering the mark. Every business, however small, should protect its right to use its mark by registering it with the United States Patent and Trademark Office..

Trademark Categories & Classes
When registering a trademark, an Artist must identify a category for their mark. Class 35 is for advertising and business. For example, you could have a new soft drink produced and the owner could call it Toyota because it's a soft drink and not a car. So you have to have a category of where you're going to go. So, if you're advertising a business, the Artist's category 35.

Class 41 is education and entertainment. Many Artists use this category because Class 41 includes singers, dancers and musicians.

****

12.04 Task

For this section of the Artist Business Plan, write about the plan for trademarks of the Artist's company.

****

Discography

12.05 Discography

A part of an Artist's Intellectual Property is their discography; their ownership and control of their sound and video recordings. This is in addition to their ownership of intellectual property such as copyrights, trademarks and patents.

When an Artist performs on a sound or video recording, they are either recording it them self or someone else is producing it. If the Artist hires someone to record their performance, then perhaps the person doing the recording is not claiming their ownership of the recording. In this case, the person doing the recording may be working as a "work-for-hire" situation and the owner of the recording would be the Artist. If the Artist does not own the recording of the song, they may be receiving royalties for their artistic contribution. If the Artist is the owner of the recording, then they should include each one in their list of products identified in the Artist Business Plan.

Many Artists who own their own recordings, use this as a potential income source. They may decide to duplicate the recording on a compact disc or make it available as a download on the World Wide Web. In addition, the Artist may choose to license the recording for use in a movie or television show.

An Artist's discography is the collection of their recordings. It essentially is a catalog of all the Artist's audio and video recordings. This catalog of the Artist's recordings may reap income every year in royalties. For this reason, it's important for Artists to keep this section of their business plan up to date.

There may be two types of discography catalogs that an Artist may have: published and un-published. The recordings that are published are ready for licensing. They are also listed on the Artist's Product List as well as addressed in the Artist's Product Development Plan.

The unpublished recordings may be works-in-progress or demos. Many times an Artist will record a rough version of a new song. This recording may not ever be released to the public. If an Artist is focusing on releasing quality works, to create a quality brand, it's important to focus on releasing only the best recordings possible. Artists rushing to get their recording to the public may be losing fans in the long term.

For ease of discography cataloging, Artists should put their song-list on an electronic spreadsheet or database and label columns with specifics about each song such as: musical genre, names of the musicians involved, the time and place of the recording, the title of the piece performed, release dates, chart positions, and sales figures.

****

12.05 Task

For this section of the Artist Business Plan, write about the discography plan for the products of the Artist's company.

****

Performing Rights Organizations

12.06 Performing Rights Organizations

There are many types of intellectual properties that an Artist may have to deal with. It would be very difficult for a songwriter to monitor all the radio stations in his/her state, much less the entire country, in order to get compensated for their song being used by radio stations to attract listeners, sell ads and make a profit. This is where Performing Rights Organizations step in.

In addition to this section being addressed here, it is also found the Artist Development Plan of the Artist.

Since the 1909 Copyright Act, copyright holders in the United States hold the exclusive right to the public performance of their works. Enforcing the copyright holder's right presents a problem. To truly police this right, the holder must monitor a range of performance venues from strip malls to strip clubs. How could one individual, or a small group of owners, hope to enforce their rights against impermissible use across the entire United States?

In the United States, there are three Performing Rights Organizations:

ASCAP, BMI and SESAC. A fourth, similarly functional organization is SoundExchange. These are the organizations that do the police work and collect payments for Artist-Songwriters as well as their publishers.

Performing rights are related to copyright. It should be treated with similar consideration for those wishing to use material protected by content creator's rights and to those wishing to enforce their rights.

Performing rights are granted to users of artistic works in a few ways.

1. Broadcasting and recording live performances;
2. Copying, distribution, renting and lending of recordings of performances;
3. Broadcasting, and other communication to the public by electronic transmission; including on-demand services of sound recordings of performances;
4. Playing in public sound recordings of performances.

In the music industry, copyright holders are able to employ a type of collective rights administration called Performance Rights Organizations (PRO) or Performance Rights Societies (PRS). Composers, lyricists and publishers join together as part of one of these entities which can negotiate licenses, extract royalties and monitor the enforcement of each member's copyright when performed in public venues, TV and radio.

PROs issue blanket licenses to such businesses as venues and radio stations. A blanket license grants a licensee the right to perform any or all the works in the PRO's repertory. Each PRO monitors various public venues to seek out new licenses and enforce existing ones. Based upon the copyright statute, these public venues include any business that uses music as a part of its customer relations. This includes restaurants, bars, clubs and hotels. It also includes venues where live or recorded music is played such as shopping malls and stores. The license also may cover trade shows; conventions; dance studios; skating rinks; private clubs or "music on hold" for telephone customers.

An important part of an Artist's Business Plan is how the Artist will enforce and collect fees for their intellectual property. Artists who are composers, lyricists or songwriters should join a performing rights organization. In the United States, there are three: ASCAP, BMI and SESAC. They are free to join for songwriters. If a Artist-Songwriter does not belong to a P.R.O., they may not, and probably won't, get paid when their songs are used in public.

****

12.06 Task

In this section of an Artist Business Plan, and if the Artist is also a songwriter, describe the Performing Rights Organization that the Artist is affiliated.

****

Registration

12.07
Registration

In this section of the Artist Business Plan, the Artist must understand that their new song, logo or invention is not protected under U.S. law unless it is officially registered. Although a copyright is valid as soon as the work is in tangible form, it is not officially protected until registered with the US Copyright Office. The same holds true with trademarks or patents which are protected by the U.S. Patent and Trademark Office.

Copyright Registration

The purpose of copyright registration is to place on record a verifiable account of the date and content of the work in question, so that in the event of a legal claim, or case of infringement or plagiarism, the copyright owner can produce a copy of the work from an official government source. In the U.S., this government source is the U.S. Copyright Office.

Before 1978, in the United States, federal copyright was generally secured by the act of publication with notice of copyright or by registration of an unpublished work. The Berne Convention largely superseded this internationally. It now provides rights synchronized at an international level without a requirement for national registration. However, the U.S. still provides legal advantages for registering works of U.S. origin.

In the United States, the United States Copyright Office accepts registrations. Content creators may file online or offline. To file online, visit the US Copyright Office at www.copyright.gov. To file offline, send all registration materials to Copyright Office, Library of Congress, Washington, DC 20559. It's cheaper and easier online.

Online Registration: Visit their website and complete the online application form. The US Copyright office offers instructions there to make it easy for those to make a copyright registration. They also have an electronic PDF form that can be filled out, printed and then mailed via Offline Registration.

Offline Registration: To register a copyright offline, request their forms via the US Postal Service or complete the PDF download online as described above. Take printouts and mail it, along with their fees.

Trademark Registration

As with other intellectual properties, a formal registration is recommended for trademark protection. In the United States, an application to register a trademark should be filed with the United State Patent and Trademark Office, the same office that handles patent registration.

The United States Patent and Trademark Office (USPTO) accepts online applications for trademark registration through the Trademark Electronic Application System (TEAS). Before choosing a particular word, phrase or logo as a trademark, an Artist should go through the USPTO database in order to ensure that the mark is not already in use. A detailed description of the goods and services provided by the Artist's business should accompany the application, since the mark is intended for use or is already being used with those goods or services.

Online applicants receive a serial number immediately after applying for registration. The entire process of registering the trademark can take anywhere between 6 months and 1 year, depending on the complexity of the situation and the legal issues involved. If the Artist is uncomfortable filing their own trademark, trademark lawyers are available to help with the process of registering a trademark. The details on the fee for registering the mark can be obtained from the USPTO website. The application for a trademark has to be filed by the person who controls the use of the mark.

Registration entails completing an application form and attaching a copy of the trademark. If filing an application in a country which is not that of the inventor then an address in that country must be given or that of someone holding power of attorney for the applicant. Other formalities are often required such as the payment of a fee or authentication by a public notary. Finally, the applicant should list the goods or services for which the mark is to be registered.

The application is then examined by attorneys at the USPTO. During this process third parties are given the opportunity to contest the trademark's registration through the 'opposition procedure'. If there is no opposition, then the office may agree to grant the trademark a certificate. It is issued to the owner of the trademark registration stating that the exclusive rights exist from the date of registration. Trademarks may be registered by individuals or companies.

Patent Registration

There are a series of steps to take in order to register a patent. The U.S. Patent and Trademark Office recommend that inventors use a registered patent agent or attorney to complete the application process. However:

The first step in the patent application process is to request a Patent Search Study.
   a. Patent Search: Search the Patent Office records for evidence of prior "art." Prior art is anything published before the filing date of the patent which may describe the same or a similar invention.
   b. Analysis and Recommendation: Based on the characteristics of the invention and preliminary search findings, the attorney in charge of the search will present an analysis and recommendation regarding the probability of obtaining a patent grant. The report will include copies of patents relevant to the invention if a similar patent exists.

Patent applications must be accompanied by a detailed technical description of the patent as well as drawings. This important step in protecting the inventions, the patent shows technical specifications and the drawings.

****

12.07 Task

For this section of the Artist Business Plan, write about the plan for registration of intellectual property for the products of the Artist's company.

Content Development

12.08
Content Development

Although Content Development is discussed in an Artist's Development Plan, there is no question that an intellectual property strategy for content development should be aligned with Artist's business strategy as well. As a member of the arts community, creation is the crux of what Artists do. From Artists who improvise to Artists who plan every note, the development of content comes with constant practice and consideration.

Intellectual property, especially songs, actually drives strategic considerations in an Artists organization. For example, Artists have to consider the content to perform or record. Some content is better performed live and some is better recorded and sometimes, both. An Intellectual Property Strategy for an Artist's content should definitely be a part of an Artist Business Plan.

Property of original material must be categorized and protected.

When Artists consider that 80% of the value of their business is in its intangible assets, then it makes sense that the framework of the Artist's organization is based around those assets and associated intellectual property issues. This is much better than trying to dovetail an Intellectual Property strategy into a less than effective Business Plan.

However in the real world most Artists have grown organically rather than through ruthless planning, so this part of an Artist Business Plan should take into account the existing DNA of the Artist's art when developing an intellectual property strategy through a step-by-step approach.

An intellectual property strategy must include a publication policy, an ownership policy and associated template agreements. Everyone on the Artists team should understand who owns what. This includes ownership of the Artist's name, logo, trademark, recordings, songs and other Intellectual Property.

Intellectual Property Bookkeeping
As an Artist grows their Intellectual property and more uses are found for their art, a good bookkeeping system of ownership, inventory and licenses issued is imperative. Artists with a lot of content need a way to manage that content. Are there recordings of any of the Artist-Songwriter's songs? Who owns those recordings? Where are those recordings licensed? Who is collecting the royalties? Is the Artist-Songwriter being compensated properly? Is the Artist-Musician also being compensated for their performance on the recording? A good bookkeeping system of the Artist's catalog will help.

When an Artist does an audit of their

intellectual property, it identifies a few items:
1. Gaps in protection
2. Risks, particularly in terms of internal systems, ownership and conditions of use
3. Opportunities for the use of the content that may have not been apparent before

Involving the right people at the genesis of intellectual property can save a lot of heartache later on. If the Artist does any collaboration with another songwriter, it's a good idea to recognize their agreement early in the process. A good intellectual property strategy is to insure that every person who is a content developer understand their role and their part of ownership.

Important Steps when Developing an Intellectual Property Strategy

1. Register the Copyright of all the Artist-Songwriter's songs.

2. Check trademark databases to avoid using an existing trademark and protect trademarks before launching a new product or service with a new brand name.

3. Make sure that content in development such as a songwriter's unfinished song, are kept confidential.

4. For export-oriented Artists make sure intellectual property is protected in all potential export markets.

5. Leverage the Artist's intellectual property portfolio when seeking sources to finance upcoming projects.

6. When co-writing, make sure that there is sufficient clarity on who will own any potential intellectual property generated from the project.

7. Monitor the market and make sure that the Artist's intellectual property assets are not being infringed. If violation of the Artist's intellectual property rights is detected it may be advisable to contact a lawyer to help resolve possible infringement issues.

8. Conduct an intellectual property audit in order to identify all of the Artist's songs and creations.

The checklist is by no means exhaustive. These are some of the basic strategies that have been successfully pursued by Artists that have fully integrated intellectual property rights into their business strategy.

****

12.08 Task

For this section of the Artist Business Plan, write about the plan for content development for new products and services of the Artist's company.

****

Content Clearances

12.09
Content Clearances

There are two types of content clearances that an Artist may have to investigate. One may make the Artist money. The other is will cost the Artists money.

The Golden Rule of Licensing: if you don't own or control it, you likely need a license to use it. There are a few exceptions (such as public domain compositions), though the golden rule is a common sense guideline that can help determine when licenses are needed.

Income from Content Licenses
One important step in the success of any Artist is the content of their intellectual property. For an Artist, this intellectual property could come from a number of sources. Songs are one type of content and recordings of songs are another type of content. Owning and/or controlling content is the money tree in the entertainment industry.

An Artist needs a plan when a third-party comes knocking for some of their intellectual property content. This is usually done in the form of a license. For example, a Artist-Songwriter grants a license to a record company for use of their song that a record label want to record and release to the general public. A movie director needs a license to use a recording in a film. In addition, the movie director may also need a license for the song used in the recording. Yes, two licenses: one for the song and one for the recording of the song: two copyrights = two licenses.

Fees for Content Licenses
In most cases an Artist-Performer does not need a license to perform or record material that they do not own. However, if the Artist is more than a performer, then perhaps they may. As mentioned in the above section, there are two copyrights with every recording: one for the song (the Circle-C) and one for the recording of the song (Circle-P). The copyright of the song may be owned by the songwriter or the songwriter's publisher. The recording of the song is typically owned by the record company. If the songwriter records the song then the songwriter is also the record company. In this case the songwriter owns all the rights. So, where I am going with this?

If the Artist is using copyrights other than their own, they need the clear the license with the copyright owner(s) prior to any work being done with that copyright. This includes sampling as well as creating derivative works. A sample may require two licenses: one for the song on the recording and one for the recording of the song.

"Sampling" refers to taking a pre-existing recording or musical composition and using it within a new musical piece. Unless permission is granted from the copyright owner(s) to use that piece of music, known as "clearing" the sample, then legal infringement on the copyright owner's exclusive right to approve/refuse the creation of derivative works has been committed.

The two most common forms of sampling are using a piece of a master recording, or re-recording a version of a piece of the musical composition. What's the difference? When sampling a master recording, permission must be obtained from both the owner of the recording, such as a record label and publisher(s) with a copyright interest in the song. Remember, there are actually two copyrights in music: one for the sound recording (typically owned by the record label), and one for the underlying musical composition (the actual song itself), owned by the publisher(s).

In addition to clearing copyrights for recordings, if the Artist is promoting their own event, concert or festival, they are now wearing the promoter "hat." As an event promoter, they may need to obtain a copyright license from each of the three Performing Rights Organizations (PRO). These organizations have been given the authority by songwriters and publishers to collect royalties from promoters using their songs publicly. However, if the Artist is performing in a venue that already has a blanket license for the year, a new license would not need to be obtained. If there are questions about performance licenses, it would be best to contact one of the three Performing Rights Organizations: ASCAP, BMI or SESAC.

Clearing Samples: Step-by-Step

Step #1: Gather information about the song on the sample:

1. What is the name of the original composition about to be sampled? Identify the song name, the composer(s) of the original composition, and the publisher of the song.
2. Who owns the recording of the song to be sampled? Identify the record label or the owner of the recording, and the name of the Artist on the recording.

   Need help finding this information? Check out these resources:
   a. All Music Guide – http://www.allmusic.com/
   b. Discogs – http://www.discogs.com/
   c. Music Brainz – http://musicbrainz.org/
   d. Who Sampled – http://www.whosampled.com/

3. Timing: Know the length of the sample you are planning to use. Include minutes: seconds time/number of measures Example- 1:04/18 bars of music.
4. Usage: a description of the Artist's use of the sample include minutes: seconds time/number of measures, how many times it will

be used in the new version Example- :35/15 bars of music, hook from the original chorus will be used in two choruses of the new version.

Step #2: Prepare the recorded works and paperwork to send to Copyright Owner:

1. Prepare a copy of the new recording using the sample to send to the copyright holder(s).
2. Have a copy of the original recording to send as well; if the copyright holder, such as a publisher, controls many works, they may not be familiar with the original song.
3. Engage in clearance correspondence.

Clearance Correspondence

- Are you sampling the master recording? Clearance is necessary with both the record label and publisher(s).

- Are you sampling the musical composition only? You only need to correspond with the publisher(s).

- Find the address and phone number of the record label and/or publisher. Use resources such as performing rights organizations, music industry directories, company websites, etc. - All Music Guide - ASCAP - BMI - SESAC

- Write to the record label and/or publisher requesting permission to sample, including: - all gathered information from Step #1 - the Artist's contact information - how many units you expect to initially release - the prospective release date of the Artist's new version

1. **Some companies provide sample clearance forms** instead of requiring written requests.

2. **Send the written request or form to the Licensing Department or Business and Legal Affairs Department of the record label and/or publisher.** - Call each company or check company websites for the name of the person to whom you should address the request. Send the copies of the new recording and of the master recording sampled.

Note: Always ensure the record label and publisher(s) have the authority to grant permission for use of the sample, meaning they are the current copyright holders of the work. Also make sure the grant of rights extends to future owners of the Artist's new version (such as future publishers). If permission has been given to sample the original composition, then getting permission to obtaining a license is easier, but not guaranteed. Since sampling is not governed by statutory law, it is up to you and the record label and/or publisher to determine the terms of the Artist's individual agreements. The following are important negotiation points of clearing a sample.

Points of Negotiation

1. **Ownership** of the new version and royalties split - Determine the extent of the copyright share the record label and/or publisher will have in the Artist's new version: partial, whole, or

none at all. - If the copyright will be shared, determine the royalties and how they will be split.

2. Extent of usage - Determine the use of the sample in the recorded version, or if use extends to remixes, live performances, or other possible applications.

3. Payment options - There are no standard rates for samples, so the figures vary widely. These are different payment options that can be negotiated:
- **Flat Fee** Example: one-time payment of $400 with no further payment due
- **Rolling Fee Paid Over Time** Example: $150 initial payment, $150 upon release, and $100 after 50,000 units sold
- **Ongoing royalty fee** Example: 15% of the statutory mechanical rate for every unit sold

4. Crediting the original composition - Determine the extent of crediting the original composition for press, advertisements, on the song or album, etc. - Determine who will be included in the credits such as composer(s), Artist(s), publisher(s), record label, etc.

Music Supervisors / Synch Licenses

Music supervisors work in the film, television and video industry. It's their job to obtain licenses for the songs and/or recordings used in connection with video. These agreements between the video company and the copyright owner of the song are call synchronization licenses.

Music Supervisors clear two sides of the copyright: the Circle-C Copyright for the music and lyrics as well as the Circle-P Copyright for the master recording.

Music Supervisors must be chameleon-like in their business dealings, and develop an ability to adapt their methods to the needs of every new production environment. For that, it is essential that every project be well documented, especially as regards the parties in every transaction: the composer and song title, the publisher, and the record label.

Many times, the licensing process starts after the spotting session in the video production process. During the spotting session, the music supervisor, producer, director, music producer, and music editor go through the script and highlight areas that require music. A license is needed when the picture is "locked" to the music in a final version. A quote request is sent to the publisher, who returns information about the credits used, their stake in the work, and the rate charged. The Music Supervisor then sends a confirmation of the terms and includes a grant of rights, the fee, and contact information.

The Publisher, who holds the rights to the Performing Arts Copyright (Circle-C), i.e. music and lyrics, is contacted first because without permission to use the song, the recording of the song has no use.

Next, the Music Supervisor would approach the copyright owner of the sound recording (Circle-P), usually the record label. Once the publisher approves the request for the use of the song and the record label approves the request for the use of the recording of the song, the music supervisor creates a formal synchronization license for the publisher and a master use license for the record company with additional standard contract terms.

> **Two Licenses used by Music Supervisors**
>
> **Synchronization License for Songs**
>
> **Master Use License for Recordings of Songs**

***

12.09 Task

For this section of the Artist Business Plan, write about the plan for clearing content for new products of the Artist's company.

***

> **Digital Rights Management**

12.10
Digital Rights Management

Used by Artists, record labels, publishers and copyright holders, Digital Rights Management (DRM) is a type of technology which intends to control the use of digital content and devices after sale of a recording to control copying. With second-generation DRM, the intent is to control executing, viewing, copying, printing, and altering of works or devices. The term is also sometimes referred to as copy protection, copy prevention, and copy control.

In 1998, the Digital Millennium Copyright Act (DMCA) was passed in the United States to impose criminal penalties on those who make available technologies whose primary purpose and function is to circumvent content protection technologies.

Although not universally accepted, some content providers claim that DRM is necessary to fight copyright infringement. They content that it can help the copyright holder maintain Artistic control or ensure continued revenue streams. These proponents argue that digital locks are necessary to prevent "intellectual property" from being copied freely, just as physical locks are needed to prevent personal property from being stolen.

Those opposed to DRM contend there is no evidence that DRM helps prevent copyright infringement, arguing instead that it serves only to inconvenience legitimate customers, and that DRM helps big business stifle innovation and competition. Furthermore, works can become permanently inaccessible if the DRM scheme changes or if the service is discontinued.

Digital locks may also restrict users from exercising their legal rights under copyright law, such as backing up copies of CDs or DVDs, lending materials out through a library, accessing works in the public domain, or using copyrighted materials for research and education.

With that in mind, some Artists are for it and other against it. Most record labels are for DRM because they feel it protects their P-Circle copyright of their recordings from possible infringement,

****

12.10 Task

For this section of the Artist Business Plan, write about the plan for managing the digital rights of the Artist's products.

****

Notes

Notes

Chapter 13
Business Plan for Artists
Technology

As a part of an Artist's Business Plan, the technology section explains the strategies and plan to build and maintain current and future technologies.

Technology Overview

13.01 Technology Overview

Technology strategy is the overall plan which consists of objective(s), principles and tactics relating to use of technologies for the Artist. Most Artists will utilize various technologies during the course of their career. A good example would be the Artist's instrument, cell phone, laptop computer, stage gear and studio gear. In addition, many Artist companies own trucks, vans, PA systems and light production systems.

Technology for Artists

Office Technology
Promotion Technology
Recording Technology
Equipment Technology
Software Technology

****

13.01 Task

For this section of the Artist Business Plan, write about the technology overview for the products and services of the Artist's company.

****

Office Technology

13.02
Office Technology

If an Artist is interested in incorporating technology into their business then there are actually a lot of ways on how to do just that. One major technology that an Artist may use for their business is a computer. This will assist the Artist to process the different tasks involved in their business, including maintaining an electronic database of contacts, bookkeeping of their budgets and expenses as well as utilizing online social networks for promotion of their products and services.

Some Artists have a business which deals with the selling and licensing of different products such as CDs and T-shirts. They may use a manual Point of Sale system at their merchandise table during their gigs. Perhaps they should consider upgrading their current system into a computerized Point of Sale system. This way, they will be able to save more time in processing every transaction. Also, the Artist will be able to reduce the chance of having errors thus increasing their business accuracy. This is true especially when it comes to the accounting of each transaction.

Another way that Artists can incorporate technology in their business is by using computers to create, edit, copy, save, and print documents. Instead of having a file cabinet to store and archive for all the business' files. Documents can be saved in a secured location on a computer. This way, Artists will be able to save not only time when it comes to retrieving the said files but also space in the office itself. Since Artists may not need a file cabinet anymore, they will no longer need to rent a place which will actually accommodate file cabinets. With this, Artists can then potentially rent a smaller place to do their business.

Advances in technology have empowered Artists to work from outside the office, as long as they have the right tools and systems in place. Many Artists take their office with them on the road.

For an Artist to consider office technology, they determine many of the technologies and systems that may be needed such as a lap-top computer, a printer-scanner, a Wi-Fi adaptor, as well as dependable software for word processing and accounting. This allows Artist to keep a low overhead, increasing their profit.

Another technology that is beneficial to Artists is cloud-based products. This allows the Artist to have instant collaboration possibilities. Even when team members are in different locations, they can still work together on projects through virtual conferencing or document management systems.

****

13.02 Task

For this section of the Artist Business Plan, write about the plan for office technology of the Artist's company.

****

Promotion Technology

13.03
Promotion Technology

For most struggling Artists, any expense for promotion may be too much. In today's world of promotion both offline and online, technology has come to the rescue. There are many ways for Artists to promote their brand, music, performances or projects without a big corporate budget behind them.

By using many of the new technologies, amazing things can be accomplished. In fact, these new technologies have placed so much opportunity into the hands of Artists that it amounts to a virtual revolution against the dominance of mega-record companies.

The Internet
The first and most obvious promotion technology is the World Wide Web, aka the Internet. In the recent past, record companies controlled all access to fans, customers and audiences. With the exception of performing live in small venues, Artists had to rely on "getting signed" to become "stars." Now for just a few dollars a month, Artists can make their work available all over the world.

Web Sites
The Artist's web site is their front to door to the world. Fans and potential fans can peruse, review, watch and listen to an Artist and their music long before they buy, or steal. However, it is vitally important for an Artist to establish a quality web presence and they do this with their own website.

What products is the Artist offering on the web site and what is the benefit? Is there an electronic press kit area with the Artist's bio and photos, gig listing history and contact information? Is there separate areas for the industry professionals and the general public?

Does the Artist have a general news area? Is there a section for people to sample the Artist's music? Is there an area for people to e-mail the Artist, does the Artist offer a link to join and e-mail list? Does the Artist have a general info area that provides a bio/history on the band, band photos, tour dates, etc.?

Is the Artist's genre/audience well-suited to a web site? Will the talent buyers that the artist needs to work with enjoy moving around this site?

Is there an e-commerce area? Is the Artist selling CDs through their site? How will that process work and who is going to manage it?

How is the Artist promoting the web site and how does that fit into the rest of the Artist's strategy? Will the Artist have any contests/promotions for the general public on the web site? What are the Artist's online sources to promote the web site? Are there key links, partnerships, and/or sponsors that will be attached to the web site?

Appendix: If you want to include samples of the web site, please only reference and include in an appendix.

Online Services
There are a variety of online services that Artists may utilize for their business. Companies like CafePress.com lets the Artist upload their artwork, and then are able to manufacture and sell t-shirts, mugs and mouse pads on a per order basis. This service is free until an item is sold. In addition, Konaki.com does the same thing for CDs.

There are many other opportunities on the Internet There are many companies such as MP3.com that allow Artists (free of charge) to create a band web page and upload MP3 files of their music on their site. Many of these companies pay the Artist a few cents each time one of their songs is played. Since MP3.com is one of the Internet's most popular sites, quite a lot of people surf in and explore new music.

Search Engines
With the Artist's web site in place, an important next step is to get people to come to the site. Fans and customers need to find the Artist, other than through word-of-mouth or from the Artist's business card. Artists should be found on every search engine. Submitplus.com helps Artists by getting their site listed to numerous search engines.

MP3 S
Currently, the easiest and best way for fans and customers to listen to and appreciate an Artist's music is through the use of MP3 S. This music storage format takes little computer storage and easily transferrable. Music file sharing is often done with MP3 S.

Video
Every Artist should utilize the technology of video. With video, Artists can visually reach new customers and fans as a picture paints a thousand words. Many Artists place video cameras in their rehearsal space while others utilize it for on-stage presentations.

The Final Barriers
Thanks to new technologies it is now possible for Artists to create their own work and market it directly to the public. The only real hurdle for Artists to overcome is that the media still lives in the old world where the only commercially viable Artists are those backed by big corporations.

New technologies are definitely going to change the entertainment industry. No one is quite sure how things will end up, but change is constantly taking place. With the good comes the bad. With limited barriers to entry into this industry and the amount of money that can be generated, many more Artists will enter as competitors. Traction will become more difficult and only quality will shine.

****

13.03 Task

For this section of the Artist Business Plan, write about the plan for promotion technology of the Artist's products and services and of the Artist's company.

****

Recording Technology

13.04 Recording Technology

Of all the technology utilized by an Artist, the recording technology is probably the most developed and refined. Sound recording and reproduction started with Thomas Edison and has historically been an electrical or mechanical inscription and re-creation of sound waves. These sound waves, such as spoken voice, singing, instrumental music or sound effects are captured by one of two main classes of sound recording technology: analog recording and digital recording.

Analog Recording

Acoustic analog recording is achieved by a small microphone diaphragm that detects small changes in atmospheric pressure (acoustic sound waves) and then records them as a graphic representation of the sound waves. These are captured on a medium such as a phonograph in which a stylus senses grooves on a record. Another type of analog recording is completed with magnetic tape. These sound waves vibrate the microphone diaphragm and are converted into a varying electric current. The current is then converted to a varying magnetic field by an electromagnet. The electromagnet makes a representation of the sound as magnetized areas on a plastic tape with a magnetic coating on it. Historically, this type of recording technology was the primary means of capturing sound. Then came digital recording.

Digital Recording

Digital recording and reproduction converts the analog sound signal picked up by the microphone to a digital form by a process of digitization, allowing it to be stored and transmitted by a wider variety of media. Digital recording stores audio as a series of binary numbers representing samples of the amplitude of the audio signal at equal time intervals, at a sample rate high enough to convey all sounds capable of being heard. Digital recordings are considered higher quality than analog recordings not necessarily because they have higher fidelity (wider frequency response or dynamic range), but because the digital format can prevent much loss of quality found in analog recording due to noise and electromagnetic interference in playback. Analog recording also has mechanical deterioration and potential damage to the storage medium. A digital audio signal must be reconverted to analog form during playback before it is applied to a loudspeaker or earphones.

****

13.04 Task

In this section of the Artist Business Plan, write the technology that the Artist plans to use when they are recording audio. If the Artist also has specific recording studios that they plan to use, this would be a good place to post that information.

****

Equipment Technology

13.05 Equipment Technology

For today's Artist, the technological possibilities are almost limitless. Although, many Artists strive to maintain a sense of realism through their use of purely acoustic instruments, the fact remains they use microphones, recording equipment and computers play an important role with their exposure of their art.

Types of Equipment for Artists
1. Musical Instruments
2. Office Equipment
3. Recording Equipment
4. Performance Equipment
5. Manufacturing Equipment

Musical Instruments & Equipment

Obviously each Artist needs to own or rent the instrument(s) they play. We all know that each instrument has its own feel and sound. Quality musicians know the effect that he/she is trying to achieve and will select an appropriate instrument to achieve that goal.

For most Artists, a basic setup will suffice in the beginning. For example, a guitar player may start with just one acoustic guitar and expand to multiple acoustic, electric, and bass guitars over time. A drummer might start with just a basic 'kit', including a bass, snare, and tom; adding additional components as the need arises and the budget allows.

Office Equipment

As previously described, a small office may be a home office or a business with just a few employees. The needs across all types of offices are similar in terms of equipment, but many decisions will come down to the specific needs and goals of the business. The basics include desks, chairs, computers and peripherals, including monitors and printers.

1. **Power:**
   Electronic equipment works best when it has a clean, steady supply of power. Artists will need power at different times for different purposes. The office may require enough power outlets to run a computer, printer, scanner, and perhaps a video / audio playback system. When the Artist is rehearsing, there must be enough power for amplifiers and electric instruments. If the Artist has their own studio for recording, they may need isolation transformers and power conditioners for each studio component.

2. **Computers**
   Computers are key pieces of equipment for any small office. One of the biggest decisions is whether to go with desktops, laptops or a combination of the two. Artists and

business users that need to go out on the road should consider laptops for themselves or for any employees that need to travel. When shopping for computers, look for machines that will last for several years before needing an upgrade. Check into small business-class laptops and desktops from major manufacturers. These often include more rugged components and the option for longer warranties than most consumer computers.

3. **Peripherals**
Peripherals include technology items, such as monitors, keyboards, mice, copiers and printers. Flat panel displays are the standard. Consider investing in larger screens or dual monitors for jobs that require extensive work with databases, multimedia or multitasking with multiple programs. All-in-one laser printers can be a smart purchase for a small office. These handle copying and scanning along with printing in a compact, low cost package. For offices with multiple computers and employees, invest in a network printer that can accommodate the size of the business.

4. **Photocopies**
The technology of photocopying has been around for many years but still very useful for promotion and office use. Artists utilize photocopies for flyers, posters, set lists and even lyric sheets.

5. **Networking**
Networking equipment is what connects a small office to the Internet and computers within the office to each other. The most popular option for small and home offices is wireless networking. A small office can easily hook up multiple desktop and laptop computers to a single DSL or cable connection. Be sure to turn on wireless security and password protect the network to safeguard the Artist's business data as well as recordings.

Recording Equipment

If the Artist is working in a studio, they will need comfortable chairs for everyone. This is often overlooked but should be the first thing on the list of equipment for a recording session. That's it. Huh? What? Think about it. If the Artist is uncomfortable in the recording session, is there reason to believe that the recorder should be the first priority. The Artist's uncomfortable seat will show in the Artist's work.

There are numerous sources of magazines offering options for Artists and their home studios. Very basically, a home studio will require a simple computer-based system, a couple of good mikes and a set of studio reference speakers as the playback system.
Another option is to consider standalone digital recording consoles that include inputs for mikes and instruments, a mixing panel, and a hard-drive storage system which puts most of the equipment into one package.

1. **Digital Recording Software**
Digital recording software programs allow producers to shape songs without paying for costly studio time. Two of the more popular options is Fruity Loops and Pro-Tools. This type of software allows producers to

download snippets of songs -- or samples -- and special effects from files stored in a laptop computer. Within minutes, the producer can use the program to create a rhythm track, and then add many effects or sounds on top of it.

2. **Rhythm Machines**
In the late 1970 S, the emergence of programmable drum machines offered audio loops that a producer can compress, edit or lengthen as necessary. These machines can create unusual rhythmic patterns that a human drummer can't produce.

3. **Multi-track Recorder**
Multi-track recorders allow producers to capture individual performances at different times. One of the most popular options is the 24-track digital recorder -- which the producer can use as a standalone unit, or connect with his computer, where work can be downloaded and prepared for a final mix. One notable disadvantage of this approach is that some multi-track recorders aren't equipped with CD burners, which forces the producer to buy a standalone device to handle that job.

4. **Synthesizer**
Many producers incorporate synthesizers to reproduce bass lines, brass parts and even string sections, as needed. Getting a more contemporary sound requires investing in digital synthesizers that also function as portable sound libraries and workstations.

Performance Equipment

When an Artist gets to the point of performing publically, they may find the need for public performance equipment. There are minimum requirements that are needed from day one and a lot of optional equipment, depending on the performance venues where the Artist may be performing.

At some point, performing Artists will need a PA (Public Address) system when they play live shows to more effectively balance their sound. If the Artist plays in venues that schedule a lot of live music, the venue will generally provide the sound equipment that makes up a PA system. If, however, the Artist plans to perform in venues such as coffee shops, parties, and parks that do not come equipped with a PA, the Artist may need to invest in some basic sound equipment for use in these types of venues. PA systems can be rented or owned.

For acoustic sets, the Artist may have a small sound system consisting of two 12" powered speakers, a 4-channel mixer and a small monitor that sits on one of the microphone (mic) stands. For a full band, the concept is the same (main speakers, amps, mixer, microphones, and monitors.) It's just on a larger scale.

At a bare minimum, Artists will need mic stands and a PA system. The PA system may include a mixer that's big enough to plug everyone into.

Note: Most live performance venues provide their own PA and mics, but smart Artists know that it's good to have a basic one of their own. They may need it for rehearsals anyway.

Minimum Components of a Public Address (Sound) System for a Full Band

In order to play live gigs in venues where the Artist has to supply the sound equipment, here are the minimum sound equipment that they may need.

1. **Main Speakers** – ("Mains") At a minimum, a pair of speakers is required: one for the left and one for the right. Many speaker systems have a combination of speakers with a large speaker for the mids and a tweeter for the highs. If the Artist is in need of a big, full bass sound, they should use a sub-woofer. There are powered as well as unpowered speakers.
2. **Amplifiers** – Amps boost the outputs of a mixer to a level that can be reproduced by the speakers. Artists will need amplifiers to power their speakers unless the speakers are already powered. Amplifiers need to have enough wattage to drive the speaker as well as the correct load rating, which is measured in ohms.
3. **Mixer** – The mixer/sound board is used to feed all of the microphones and instrument lines into one place where their sounds can be balanced and mixed to the desired levels and then output to the amplifiers. Typically performers use at least 4 channels for the drums, 1 or 2 channels for electric guitars, 1 channel for each vocalist and the bass guitar as well as any acoustic guitars.
4. **Microphones & Stands** – Mics for each singer and straight or boom stands for each mic to allow 'hands-free' usage. Wired mics are generally less expensive.
5. **Monitors** – Unless the venue is small, a PA system should include monitors for each singer and musician. Monitors are small speakers that are either placed on the floor or on a mic stand. Monitors are placed at the front of the stage facing the performers so they can hear how they sound to the audience.

Of course, Artists can expand on these basics of a PA system and may add all kinds of other equipment to enhance their sound. Don't forget cases.

Video Recording Equipment

Beyond the obvious fact that an Artist will need a video camera to create a video, there are a multitude of optional video equipment components that can be used to help an Artist create a video production.

1. **Digital Editing Workstation**
   A Digital Editing Workstation is nothing more than a normal desktop or laptop computer. All editing workstations are computers, but not all computers are editing workstations. Even the most rudimentary, basic computer models can be purchased for a couple hundred dollars, and will be sufficient to be used as a workstation.

   Both digital audio and digital video will benefit from manipulation after they are captured from their original source. There are tons of options for video software.

2. **Portable Audio Recorder**
   In addition to a video recorder, it may become apparent to Artists that

they will need a portable audio recorder as well. There are some small multi-track audio recorders with video interfaces. This may be a good option to capture quality audio for an Artist's video.

3. **Microphones**
Since actual movie film is a series of photographs taken at high speeds, film cameras don't usually have the capability to record audio. So the way major filmmakers' record sounds during filming is by using a shotgun microphone on a boom pole.

A shotgun is a long, slender, highly sensitive directional microphone. It records sounds in stereo and tends to pick up the greatest volume of sound from the direction it is pointing. While filming a scene in which two people are talking, for example, the shotgun mic is suspended above and between them, pointing downward so that it picks up their dialogue.

4. **Muffs / Windscreens**
Shotgun mics are sometimes fitted with a muff or windscreen. The windscreen/muff covers the mic entirely and keeps breezes from blowing directly into the filaments. When this happens, a noise is created which tends to cause an annoying, scratchy sound. A windscreen muffles other audio before it reaches the mic.

5. **Boom Pole**
A boom pole is an extendable rod that holds the shotgun mic at the far end and allows it to be hung over the action in a scene, close to where the bulk of the sound is taking place.

In this way a louder, clearer sound signal can be recorded from afar without any interference, even if the shot is framed widely.

6. **Lighting**
While the sound design and camera work set the tone of videos, it's the lighting that sets the mood. Lighting a scene with multiple subjects and/or people requires a three-point lighting setup.

Manufacturing Equipment

In addition to the equipment that an Artist may need to perform or record, many Artists also use equipment to burn their own compact discs, print t-shirts or distribute their recordings online. Each of these requires a full analysis by the Artist to determine their specifics needs.

****

13.05 Task

For this section of the Artist Business Plan, write about the plan for equipment technology of the Artist's company.

****

Software Technology

13.06

Software Technology

The music business is constantly evolving and every day there is new software technology that Artists use for their business. There is software for performing and recording as well as software to help Artists run their business or to promote their new creation. As a part of an Artist's Business Plan, the identification and implementation of computer software will help the Artist build and maintain a successful business.

Software for Performances

Many Artists use computers in their live performances. From laptops, to sound boards, to lighting systems to in-ear monitor systems, there are numerous possibilities for Artists to utilize the latest technology for their live performances.

In many instances, it's the Artist's collaborators, such as the sound and light technicians, who use computer software in the course of their job. However, the instrument that an Artist chooses to use for performances may be electronic and have pre-set software applications as well as effects for their instrument.

Software for Recording

In the digital world of recording, there are numerous software programs to help capture the performance of an Artist. From Reaper to Reason, the ease of digital tracking and editing is thousands of times easier for producers. Smart Artists may not know how to run a recording session, but are well versed in the possibilities of software enhancements.

Home Replication

Many Artists create their own compact discs on their home computer CD recorder. In addition, they can design the covers in Photoshop and print them on an inexpensive printer. Artists should keep in mind that burning CD's is inferior quality to pressing them.

Software for Management

Management software is abundant and easily accessible. Spreadsheets, word processing and relational databases are packaged to work together. Of all the possibilities for electronic management, there are a few that are specific to the logistics of the touring or recording Artist.

Since the music business is full of projects, a good project management software program could be the most beneficial. Many Artists develop their own spreadsheets of tasks involved with each upcoming performance or promotion.

Software for Promotion

In addition to having a clean and active database, the number of software applications available for promotion is endless. Many Artists use a merge application from their database to a newsletter to fans. Others use graphic software to design CD covers. In addition, the vast amount of online social networks forms a good ways for promotion of the Artists upcoming performances as well as recordings.

Shopping Cart

An important part of any Artist's website is a store with a shopping cart where Artists may expose and sell their recordings, t-shirts, compact disc and downloads. With a shopping cart function of their website, Artists are able to accept credit / debit cards for their sales. This money can then be transferred directly into the Artist's bank account.

****

13.06 Task

For this section of the Artist Business Plan, write about the plan for software technology used in the Artist's company.

****

Online Software Ideas for Artists

Analytics & Business Tools
1. Artist Growth – Manage the Artist's gigs, finances, schedule and more.
2. Bandbook – Online community connects bands, fans, managers and venues.
3. BandCentral - Management tools for music professionals.
4. Bandize – Organize the Artist's band from the ground up.
5. Buzzdeck – Advanced analytics for the music business.
6. Musicmetric - Powerful Artist analytics platform.
7. Next Big Sound - Actionable intelligence for the music industry.
8. RockDex - Track buzz, find fans, spot trends.
9. TourIntel – Concert business intelligence.
10. Zenph - Transform music into data.

Collaborate
1. Bandlink – Connecting local musicians.
2. Dopetracks- Hip-Hop/Rap based forum where Artists can join forces musically
3. Gobbler – High-speed file transfer and backup for pro audio.
4. Indaba Music - A place for musicians to network and make music together.
5. Kompoz – Online music collaboration.

Direct-to-Fan
1. Bandcamp – Sell the Artist's music and mercy directly to fans.
2. Bands.com – Keep 100% of the Artist's music and merch sales.
3. Guguchu – Promote music, only better.
4. LiveJam HD – Direct-to-fan video distribution.
5. Nimbit – Reward fans. Sell recordings
6. Topspin Media – Spread content anywhere, increase fan connections
7. Tracks.by – A new way for Artists to release new music and videos.
8. VibeDeck – Sell and promote the Artist's music. Free to use. Keep 100% of sales.

Distribution
1. INgrooves – Digital distribution and marketing.
2. IODA – Independent online distribution alliance.
3. ONErpm – Sell music on iTunes, Facebook and more.
4. Spotmeup – Simple Spotify distribution.
5. Tunecore – Music and video distribution.

Marketing & Promotion
1. Artists.MTV- MTV has a database full of information, videos and pictures
2. Champion Sound – E-mail marketing and all-in-one promotion tools.
3. FanBridge – Fan growth and marketing made simple.
4. FanMail Marketing – Tools to find, know and reach fans
5. Haulix – Create digital promos, mange media contacts, protect releases
6. Instagram- Share pictures
7. OurStage- Share and promote music while networking
8. OurWave- Use this site as a promotion tool
9. ReverbNation – One stop shop for online tools.
10. Sonicbids – Social music marketing.
11. SoundCloud- Share sounds
12. Voxbloc – Engage and reward the Artist's fans.
13. YouTube- Share videos

Music Industry News and Blogs
1. Digital Music News – News authority for music industry and tech execs.
2. Hypebot – Music. Technology. The new music business.
3. Make It In Music – The ultimate guide to help you succeed in the music business.
4. Music Ally - Music business information and strategy.
5. Topspin Tips – Tips, tricks and tutorials for Topspin users.

Music Listening
1. 8tracks- Expand the Artist's listening horizons when it comes to music
2. Last.fm- Last.fm introduces Artists and recommends others
3. MOG- Listen and organize music
4. Pandora – Online radio station
5. Spotify- Create playlists

Performing Rights Related
1. ASCAP – The American Society of Composers, Authors and Publishers
2. BMI – Broadcast Music, Inc
3. Harry Fox – Song Clearances
4. SESAC – Performing Rights Og4ranization
5. SoundScan – For royalty collection of non-interactive, streaming music online.

Playing Live
1. Eventful- If you have an event, post it here and people will find you
2. Eventric - Software and services for the professional live entertainment industry.
3. GigMaven - Free online gig booking for musicians.
4. GigsWiz - Artist powered ticketing service.
5. Musigigs - Book gigs online. Bands apply to venues, venues manage shows.
6. OnTheAir - Live personal encounters happening online.
7. Show Kicker - A new way to book and get booked.
8. SplitGigs - Easy way to find more gigs. A gig exchange.
9. Ticketometer - Increase attendance at the Artist's events. Incentivize ticket sales.

10. Weiv - Revolutionize the way you interact with live visuals.

Re-Define "Record Label"
1. Oocto – Collective action for musical projects.
2. PledgeMusic – Fan funded music platform.
3. Rockstar Motel – Fans are the record label.
4. SonicAngel – Crowd funding. Music powered by the fans.
5. TuneRights – Social music platform to share in royalties.
6. Tunezy – The social record label. Bring power back to musicians.

Social Networks
1. Facebook- Facebook has "like" feature for fans
2. MP3.com- a site for fans to discover new music
3. MySpace- Good online format allows the Artists to post photos & upload songs
4. Tumblr- Express the Artist using the Artist's words, a picture, or a video
5. Twitmusic- An extension of Twitter specifically geared towards musical acts
6. Twitter- 140 characters to tell the world what you're about

Websites, Social Media and Apps
1. ArtistData - Update all the Artist's band profiles at once.
2. BandPage - Powering 500k musicians on Facebook every day.
3. Bandstand - A new media and content management system for bands.
4. Bandzoogle - Band website platform.
5. CASH Music – Doing for musicians what WordPress did for bloggers.
6. FanRx - Customize the Artist's Facebook page and timeline.
7. Gigaboxx - Create the Artist's own direct-to-fan mobile app.
8. Headliner.fm - Reach new fans without having to be liked or followed first.
9. Onesheet - Build a beautiful, maintenance free websites and mobile apps.
10. Songpier - Create the Artist's free Artist app.
11. Viinyl – Showcase the Artist's music with song-based websites.

Miscellaneous
1. 1band1brand.com – Seeking and connecting emerging music and fashion.
2. Bandmix – Search local musician classifieds.
3. DIY Music Platform - Empowering social commerce.
4. Dropcards - Custom music download cards.
5. Link-Busters – Professional anti-piracy solutions.
6. Menyou – "Fair play" music.
7. Mixeeba – Monetize the Artist's music content with deep affiliate links.
8. Moontoast - Advanced social commerce platform.
9. Radar – Commission, promote and broadcast music videos.
10. Sponsorfied - Event sponsorships, simplified.
11. The Echo Nest - The intelligent music application platform.
12. Tunipop - Connecting merchandise with digital music.

Chapter 14
Business Plan for Artists
Finance Plan

A financial plan for every Artist is a document that describes their current financial status, financial goals, the target achievement date for those goals and the strategies to meet them. Artists can use their finance plan as a benchmark to measure the progress they're making and update the plan as their goals and time frames change.

Finance Plan Overview

14.01
Finance Plan Overview

Is this a hobby or a business?

In simple terms, if an Artist can't deliver significant returns, it may not be worth the risk for them, and they have to ask them self if it is worth continuing with their business. In this scenario Artists should complete a reverse income statement. Start by defining how much profit the Artist wants to see at the end of a certain time period. Then determine the amount of revenues needed to generate that profit and the costs to deliver that profit. Do the numbers add up and make sense? The goal here is to be objective. If the expected revenue is not sufficient to generate an Artists required profit at the end, based on an estimate of costs, they shouldn't simply fudge the numbers and assume they can reduce costs or increase revenues. Artist should be diligent in their assessment.

This plan is a summary of an Artist's financial needs or goals for the future and how they are going to achieve them. Financial planning involves deciding what projects to start and the investments and activities most appropriate to fulfill them. All things being equal, short-term financial planning involves less uncertainty than long-term financial planning because, generally speaking, market trends are more predictable in the short term. Likewise, short-term financial plans are more easily amended in case something goes wrong.

Although an Artist sales and costs are estimates, they should be basing it on past successes or a really thought out formula. Look closely at what other Artists are selling and then consider if the Artist is really being realistic? Call to ensure that the costs that the Artist has set out for them self actually make sense.

If the Artist has been around for a while and have kept track of their past financial information, they should be including it in this section.

Artists should always know their current financial situation.

As well, Artists should be making future projections on their projects. Artists can also do a high, low and medium sales scenario in this area.

The most common forms of financial reports are the Balance Sheet, Income Statement and Cash Flow / Budget. These do not need to be included specifically in the business plan (they can be put in the appendices); however, they should be summarized in their financial section. What are their costs, sales and do they know when they will need the most money? What is the Artist's actual financial request?

Finally, some institutions / investors will require that the Artist provide a list of collateral that will go towards any loan that the artist may request.

The Finance Plan is especially important for traditional investors. Artists should be stating what their assumptions they are basing their success and financial statements on.

How did the Artist estimate their sales? What formula did they use? How did they estimate their costs?

Who key people are necessary to the Artist's success? What events / actions are key in their marketing plan to be successful?

As importantly, Artists should indicate what alternatives they have considered if their assumptions fall through in order to ensure success.

****

14.01 Task

For this section of the Artist Business Plan, write about the finance plan overview for office technology of the Artist's company.

****

Start-Up Summary

14.02
Start-Up Summary

This section of the financial plan of an Artist Business Plan shows how much capital the Artist is seeking and the uses they'll put it to for startup. It typically precedes all other financial tables, and sits in the business plan immediately after the end of the Artist's Executive Summary. The start-up summary gives an Artist or one of their investors a quick look on how the Artist will allot their initial funding and what the ratios are of loan to investment.

Traditionally, startup expense categories will include all of the following:

> Musical Instruments
> Artist Development issues
> – copyrights, trademarks
> Legal fees
> Stationery
> Consultants
> Insurance
> Rent for rehearsing
> Advertising/Marketing

Use of Funds

The start-up summary should also lists the assets that the Artist will need to purchase (computers, instruments, equipment, furniture, etc.) and the inventory of songs, bookings and recordings they need to acquire. The table should also demonstrate the total amount of cash on hand they need to begin operations. Most start-up summaries will show start-up funding and start-up expenses as well as the amount coming from different sources. While this is a vital piece of the financial pro forma, it is only the first component in an integrated 3-year of 5-year plan.

Total of Start-up Expenses
+ Total of Start-Up Assets
= Total of Start-Up Funding Needed

Total Investment
+ Total Loans
= Total Capital + Liabilities

****

14.02 Task

For this section of the Artist Business Plan, write about the start-up summary for the Artist's company.

****

14.03
Use of Funds

Every business, whether large or small, will need to consider their use of funds. As a part of the Finance Plan, an Artists use of funds includes all the financial resources, such as cash in hand, bank balance, and accounts receivable. Any change in these resources is reflected in the Artist's financial position.

Since the entertainment industry is project based, Artists regularly need to determine their desired project based on the project's actual cost. In order to begin proceeding with any project, Artists will need to know how they are going to fund it. This is where all cash inflows and cash outflows from all sources must be reflected in the Artists Finance Plan and / or Project Plan.

By evaluating a Use of Funds statement, Artists can see one indication among many of their company's financial health. A business activity may be reported as income if a company has agreed to a contract, even if no money has actually changed hands; a cash flow statement seeks to avoid this by showing how much cash the company has on hand. It is also called an application of funds statement.

Because many companies tend to use accrual accounting, the income statements they generate each quarter may not necessarily reflect changes in their cash positions. For example, if an Artist lands a major contract, that contract will be recognized as revenue (and therefore income), but the Artist's company may not yet receive the cash from the contract until a later date. Although the Artist may be earning a profit in the eyes of accountants (and paying income taxes on it), the company may, during the quarter, end up with less cash than it had when it started. Even profitable companies can manage their cash flow inadequately. That is why the cash flow statement is important: It helps Artists and their managers see if their company is having cash troubles.

****

14.03 Task

For this section of the Artist Business Plan, write about the sue of funds for the Artist's company.

****

Important Assumptions

14.04
Important Assumptions

Important assumptions as shown in the Artist's Business Plan should show accepted cause and effect relationships, or estimates of the existence of a fact from the known existence of other fact(s). Although useful in providing a basis for action and in creating "what if" scenarios, assumptions can be dangerous when accepted as reality without thorough examination. Many Artist are delusional about their future and this part of their business plan may help them focus on reality.

Assumption-based planning in project management is a post-planning method that helps Artists to deal with uncertainty. It is used to identify the most important assumptions in their company's business plans, to test these assumptions, and to anticipate and accommodate unexpected outcomes.

Financial assumptions and projections are critical components of all business plans and Artist Business Plans are no exception. Three universal financial presentations are expected in all business plans. There must be a projected income statement, balance sheet and a cash flow statement for the coming three to five years. Along with the numbers, many Artists include a narrative that explains the assumptions and how the line items were computed.

Income Statement Assumptions

Assumptions on an Artist's income statement should be on a month-to-month basis for the first one to two years. After that, Artists can then switch to quarterly projections for years three through five. One key item dominates this presentation. Artists should base their income and expense assumptions on factual, verifiable information. For example, if an Artist's service of performing at a concert venue competitively sells for $500 to $1000 per gig, Artists should refrain from using a $5000 selling price to craft their sales projections. Also, Artists should base their sales volume assumptions on realistic statistics which may be easily verified by a quick market analysis.

Balance Sheet Assumptions

Assumptions for balance sheet presentations should be conservative and based on reasonable expectations of asset acquisitions in the coming five years. Of particular concern to Artists and their business are inventory and accounts receivable. Both are functions of sales. Therefore, Artists should carefully match their inventory assumptions with their gross income projections. Unless accounts receivable are typically large in certain projects that the Artist may be involved, they should not project high balances. Cash is usually in short supply for Artists and their small businesses. Tying up this precious resource in excessive inventory or accounts receivable can be damaging.

Cash Flow Statement Assumptions

If an Artist or their small business needs financing or investment, the projected Cash Flow Statement may be the most important financial assumption they make. While both lenders and investors want an Artist's small business to generate solid net income and have a strong balance sheet, cash flow is more important. It is from cash flow that Artists can repay loans or distribute cash to investors from profits.

Warnings about Assumptions

Making financial projections based on solid assumptions is wonderful but Artists must explain the derivation and calculations to give their business plan readers' confidence in their data. Artists shouldn't commit newer entrepreneur mistakes. Many spend hours evaluating data and create reasonable financial projections. However, newbies often forget or feel inadequate to explain their assumptions in text format. Artists are smart to assume that loan officers are experts in reading business plans, however, assuming they are experts in the entertainment industry is a mistake. Artists need to write as detailed a narrative as possible for their financial assumptions, with references that can be verified.

****

14.04 Task

For this section of the Artist Business Plan, write about important assumptions for the Artist's company.

****

Key Financial Indicators

14.05
Key Financial Indicators

To help Artists evaluate the financial condition, or health, of their company, they need to understand the use of Key Financial Indicators. These criteria include both financial ratios and other signs that point to the health - or sickness

- of their company.

- Liquidity and financial stability
- Balance sheet and capital structure
- Turnover of assets
- Cash Flow
- Operating performance
- Return on assets
- Return on equity
- Benchmark to industry standards
- Sales trends

When Artists, and/or their collaborators such as bankers or investors, are concerned about the accuracy and reliability of financial statements provided by a company, they often consider other indicators. These include:

- Track record of meeting sales goals and objectives
- Cash balances
- Credit history and terms that suppliers are offering
- Supporting evidence that tax payments and payroll obligations are current
- Sales prices and trends, especially for live performances
- Sales pace and trends
- Reputation among competitors, creditors, and within industry

****

14.05 Task

For this section of the Artist Business Plan, write about the key financial indicators for the Artist's company.

****

Break-Even Analysis

14.06
Break-Even Analysis

The break-even point represents the sales amount in either unit or revenue terms that is required to cover total costs (both fixed and variable) of a project or product of an Artist. Profit at break-even is zero. Loss at break-even is zero. Break-even is only possible if an Artist's prices are higher than its variable costs. If so, then each unit of the product sold will generate some "contribution" toward covering fixed costs.

In economics & business, specifically cost accounting, the break-even point is the point at which cost or expenses and revenue are equal: there is no net loss or gain, and one has "broken even." A profit or a loss has not been made, although opportunity costs have been "paid," and capital has received the risk-adjusted, expected return. In short, all costs that need to be paid are paid by the Artist but the profit is equal to zero.

For example, if an Artist sells fewer than 200 compact discs each month, it will make a loss; if it sells more, it will make a profit. With this information, the business managers will estimate if they expect to be able to make and sell 200 compact discs per month.

If they think they cannot sell that many, to ensure viability they could:

1. Try to reduce the fixed costs (by renegotiating rent for example, or keeping better control of telephone bills or other costs)

2. Try to reduce variable costs (the price they pays for compact discs by finding a new supplier)

3. Increase the selling price of their compact discs.

Any of these would reduce the break-even point. In other words, the Artist's business would not need to sell so many recordings to make sure it could pay its fixed costs.

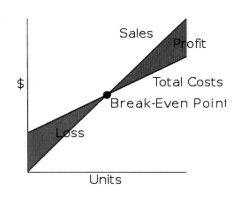

****

14.06 Task

For this section of the Artist Business Plan, write about the break-even analysis for the Artist's company.

****

Projected Profit & Loss

14.07
Projected Profit & Loss

An income statement or profit and loss statement (P&L), revenue statement, statement of financial performance, earnings statement, operating statement, or statement of operations are part of the financial statements of an Artist's company and shows the company's revenues and expenses during a particular period. It indicates how the revenues (money received from the sale of products and services before expenses are taken out) are transformed into the net income (the result after all revenues and expenses have been accounted for) also known as "net profit."

It displays the revenues recognized for a specific period, and the cost and expenses charged against these revenues, including write-offs (e.g., depreciation and amortization of various assets) and taxes. The purpose of the income statement is to show Artists, managers and potential investors whether the Artist or Artist's products made or lost money during the period being reported. One important thing for an Artist to remember about an income statement is that it represents a period of time much like their cash flow statement. This contrasts with the balance sheet, which represents a single moment in time.

The income statement can be prepared in one of two methods. The Single Step Income Statement takes a simpler approach, totaling revenues and subtracting expenses to find the bottom line. The more complex Multi-Step income statement (as the name implies) takes several steps to find the bottom line, starting with the gross profit. It then calculates operating expenses and, when deducted from the gross profit, yields income from operations. Adding to income from operations is the difference of other revenues and other expenses. When combined with income from operations, this yields income before taxes. The final step is to deduct taxes, which finally produces the net income for the period measured.

****

14.07 Task

For this section of the Artist Business Plan, write about the projected profit and loss for the Artist's company.

****

Projected Balance Sheet

14.08
Projected Balance Sheet

In financial accounting, a balance sheet or statement of financial position is a summary of the financial balances of an Artist's business organization. Assets, liabilities and ownership equity are listed as of a specific date, such as the end of the Artist's financial year. A balance sheet is often described as a "snapshot of a company's financial condition." Of the three basic financial statements, the balance sheet is the only statement which applies to a single point in time of a business' calendar year.

Assets = Liabilities + Equity

A standard company balance sheet has three parts: assets, liabilities and ownership equity. The main categories of assets are usually listed first, and typically in order of liquidity. Assets are followed by the liabilities. The difference between the assets and the liabilities is known as equity or the net assets or the net worth or capital of the company and according to the accounting equation, equity (net worth) must equal assets minus liabilities.

Another way to look at the balance sheet equation is that total assets equals liabilities plus owner's equity. Looking at the equation in this way shows how assets were financed: either by borrowing money (liability) or by using the owner's money (owner's or shareholders' equity). Balance sheets are usually presented with assets in one section and liabilities and net worth in the other section with the two sections "balancing." That's why it's called a Balance Sheet.

A business operating entirely in cash can measure its profits by withdrawing the entire bank balance at the end of the period and add any cash in hand. However, many Artists are not paid immediately; they build up inventories of goods and they acquire equipment. In other words: businesses have assets and so they cannot, even if they want to, immediately turn these into cash at the end of each period. Often, these businesses owe money to suppliers and to tax authorities, and the proprietors do not withdraw all their original capital and profits at the end of each period. In other words, businesses also have liabilities.

****

14.08 Task

For this section of the Artist Business Plan, write about the projected balance sheet for the Artist's company.

****

Goodwill

14.09
Goodwill

The value of an Artist is the total of all sales during the year. It is also the earning potential of the Artist.

As discussed in other sections of the Artist's Business Plan, an Artist may own subsidiary companies such as their own record label, publishing company or booking agency. Eventually, they may want to sell one of these companies. The status of these company's intangible assets may be defined in the Goodwill section of their Finance Plan.

As an example of goodwill, an Artist's company may have net assets (consisting primarily of miscellaneous equipment and/or property, and assuming no debt) valued at $1 million, but the company's overall value (including brand, customers, and intellectual capital) is valued at $10 million. Anybody buying that company would book $10 million in total assets acquired, comprising $1 million physical assets and $9 million in goodwill. In a private company, goodwill has no predetermined value prior to its acquisition. A publicly traded company, on the other hand, is subject to a constant process of market valuation, so goodwill is always apparent.

While an Artist can invest to increase its reputation, by advertising or assuring that its products are of high quality, such expenses cannot be capitalized and added to goodwill, which is technically an intangible asset. Goodwill and intangible assets are usually listed as separate items on a company's balance sheet.

Early in an Artist's career, it may be difficult to establish their goodwill in their Finance Plan. If this is the case, Artist's should acknowledge that goodwill is not yet considered as a part of their financial attributes but that it is likely to be a part of it as the Artist's becomes more successful.

****

14.09 Task

For this section of the Artist Business Plan, write about the goodwill for the Artist's company.

****

Accounting

14.10 Accounting

Accounting, or accountancy, is the measurement, processing and communication of financial information about the economic status of the Artist and/or Artist's company. Accounting measures the results of an organization's economic activities and conveys this information to a variety of users including investors, creditors, management, and, of course, the Artist. Practitioners of accounting are known as accountants. Many Business Managers of Artists are accountants.

Accounting can be divided into several fields including financial accounting, management accounting, auditing, and tax accounting. Financial accounting focuses on the reporting of an Artist's financial information, including the preparation of financial statements. Accounting focuses on the measurement, analysis and reporting of information for internal use by management. The recording of financial transactions, so that summaries of the financials may be presented in financial reports, is known as bookkeeping, of which double-entry bookkeeping is the most common system. No, this does not mean two sets of books. Double-entry refers to credits and debits.

Financial Accounting

Financial accounting focuses on the reporting of an Artist's financial information. It measures and records business transactions and prepares financial statements for external users such as managers, distributors, investors and collaborators.

Financial accounting produces past-oriented reports, for example the Financial Statements prepared in 2016 reports on performance in 2015, on an annual or quarterly basis, generally about the organization as a whole.

Management Accounting

Management accounting is the measurement, analysis and reporting of information that can help managers in making decisions to fulfill the goals of the Artist. In management accounting, internal measures and reports are based the analysis of cost verses benefit.

Management accounting produces future-oriented reports. For example the budget for 2016 is prepared in 2015 and the time span of reports varies widely. Such reports may include both financial and nonfinancial information, and may, for example, focus on specific products and/or projects of the Artist.

Auditing

Auditing is the verification of the bookkeeping and assertions made by others regarding the financial statements of the Artist's business.

****

14.10 Sample

14.10 Task

For this section of the Artist Business Plan, write about the plan for accounting for the Artist's company.

Independent Accountant's Report

14.11 Independent Accountant's Report

Smart Artists know that their estimates and their forecasts are just that: estimates and forecasts. Hiring a professional with a background in finance and accounting is one way to bring their "hopes" into focus. In addition, many Artists use the services of a certified public accountant to help review the bookkeeping of their collaborators such as record labels and publishers.

A Certified Public Accountant (CPA) should examine the financial records and business transactions of an Artist's company that he/she is not affiliated with. An independent auditor is typically used to avoid conflicts of interest and to ensure the integrity of the auditing process. When an audit is performed, it is the financial auditor's job to make sure that records are examined in an honest and forthright manner. Independent auditors are sometimes called external auditors.

An accountant's opinion statement can either be qualified or unqualified. When the opinion is qualified, the accountant is questioning the accounting principles and/or scope of the information provided. An unqualified opinion is given when the accountant sees that the given information in the financial statements is sound. In other words, an unqualified opinion is desirable whereas a qualified opinion is not.

14.11 Task

For this section of the Artist Business Plan, write about the independent accounts report for the Artist's company.

Forecasted Financial Statements

14.12 Forecasted Financial Statements

Forecasting the income or expenses of an Artist's business may help the Artist determine if their efforts to survive with their art is viable. A financial forecast is based on income statements, balance sheet and/or cash flows. Often, revenues will provide the initial groundwork for the forecast, while expenses and other income statement items will be calculated as a percentage of future sales.

A financial statement (or financial report) is a formal record of the financial activities of an Artist, their business and/or each of their projects or products. Relevant financial information is presented in a structured manner and in a form easy to understand. They typically include basic financial statements, accompanied by a management discussion and analysis:
1. A balance sheet reports on a company's assets, liabilities, and ownership equity at a given point in time.
2. An income statement or profit and loss report, reports on a company's income, expenses, and profits over a period of time. A profit and loss statement provides information on the operation of the Artist. These include sales and the various expenses incurred during the stated period.
3. A statement of cash flows reports on an Artist's cash flow activities, particularly its operating, investing and financing activities.

These statements may be complex and may include an extensive set of notes to the financial statements as well as management discussion and analysis. The notes typically describe each item on the balance sheet, income statement and cash flow statement in further detail. Notes to financial statements are considered an integral part of the financial statements.

Purpose of Financial Statements

Financial statements provide information about the financial position, performance and changes of an Artist's business that is useful to a wide range of users in making economic decisions. Financial statements should be understandable, reliable, relevant, and comparable. Reported assets, liabilities, equity, income and expenses are directly related to an Artist's financial position.

Financial statements may be used for various purposes:
- As business owners, Artists require financial statements to make important business decisions that affect its continued operations. Financial analysis is then performed on these statements to provide the Artist and their management with a more detailed understanding of the figures. These statements may also be used for Artists to understand the success (or failure) of the Artist and when they can quit their day job.
- Prospective investors make use of financial statements to assess the viability of investing in an Artist's business or individual projects such as a new recording or an upcoming tour. Financial analyses are often used by investors and are prepared by professionals (financial analysts), thus providing them with the basis for making investment decisions.
- Financial institutions (banks and other lending companies) use them to decide whether to grant a company with fresh working capital or extend debt securities (such as a long-term bank loan or debentures) to finance expansion and other significant expenditures.

****

14.12 Task

For this section of the Artist Business Plan, write about the forecasted financial statements for the Artist's company.

****

Forecasted Balance Sheet

14.13 Forecasted Balance Sheet

A balance sheet is a financial statement that summarizes a company's assets, liabilities and owners' equity at a specific point in time. These three balance sheet segments give Artists, their managers and investors an idea as to what the company owns and owes, as well as the amount invested by the owners.

The balance sheet must follow the following formula:
Assets = Liabilities + Owners' Equity

It's called a balance sheet because the two sides balance out. This makes sense: a company has to pay for all the things it has (assets) by either borrowing money (liabilities) or getting it from the owners.

Each of the three segments of the balance sheet will have many accounts within it that document the value of each. Accounts such as cash, inventory and property are on the asset side of the balance sheet, while on the liability side there are accounts such as accounts payable or long-term debt. The exact accounts on a balance sheet will differ by company and by industry, as there is no one set template that accurately accommodates for the differences between different types of businesses.

Balance Sheet
Definition: A financial statement that lists the assets, liabilities and equity of an Artist's company at a specific point in time and is used to calculate the net worth of the business. Total assets (what a business owns) must equal liabilities plus equity (how the assets are financed). In other words, the balance sheet must balance. Subtracting liabilities from assets shows the net worth of the business.

The top portion of the balance sheet should list the company's assets in order of liquidity, from most liquid to least liquid. Current assets are cash or its equivalent or those assets that will be used by the business in a year or less. They include the following:
- Cash is the cash on hand at the time books are closed at the end of the fiscal year. This refers to all cash in checking, savings and short-term investment accounts.
- Accounts receivable is the income derived from credit accounts. For the balance sheet, it's the total amount of income to be received that's logged into the books at the close of the fiscal year. This might include royalties from publishers or record labels.
- Inventory is derived from the cost of goods table. It's the inventory of a product not yet sold.

"Total current assets" is the sum of cash, accounts receivable, inventory and supplies.

Other assets that appear in the balance sheet are called long-term or fixed assets because they're durable and will last more than one year.

"Total long-term assets" is the sum of capital and plant, investments, and miscellaneous assets.

"Total assets" is the sum of total current assets and total long-term assets

After listing the assets, Artists then have to account for the liabilities of their business. Like assets, liabilities are classified as current or long term. Debts that are due in one year or less are classified as current liabilities. If they're due in more than one year, they're long-term liabilities. Here are examples of current liabilities:
- Accounts payable include all expenses incurred by the business that are purchased from regular creditors on an open account and are due and payable.
- Accrued liabilities are all expenses incurred by the business that are required for operation but have not yet been paid at the time the books are closed. These expenses are usually the company's overhead and salaries.
- Taxes are those payments still due and payable at the time the books are closed.

"Total current liabilities" is the sum of accounts payable, accrued liabilities and taxes.

Long-term liabilities include the following:
- Bonds payable is the total of all bonds at the end of the year that are due and payable over a period exceeding one year.
- Mortgage payable is loans taken out for the purchase of real estate that are repaid over a long-term period. The mortgage payable is that amount still due at the close of the fiscal year.
- Notes payable are the amounts still owed on any long-term debts that won't be repaid during the current fiscal year.

Total long-term liabilities" is the sum of bonds payable, mortgages payable and notes payable.

"Total liabilities" is the sum of total current and long-term liabilities.

Once the liabilities have been listed, the owner's equity can then be calculated. The amount attributed to owner's equity is the difference between total assets and total liabilities. The amount of equity the Artist has in the business is an important yardstick used by Artists and their managers to evaluate the company. Many times, it determines the amount of capital they feel they can safely invest.

****

14.13 Task

For this section of the Artist Business Plan, write about the forecasted balance sheet of the Artist's company.

****

Forecasted Statement of Cash Flow

14.14 Forecasted Statement Of Cash Flow

Cash comes in from sales, loan proceeds, investments and the sale of assets and goes out to pay for operating and direct expenses, principal debt service, and the purchase of assets. A cash flow budget highlights the following figures:
- Sales/revenue
- Development expenses
- Cost of goods
- Capital requirements
- Operating expenses

An Artist's cash flow projections are based on the past performance of their business. To project cash flow, Artists need to start by breaking down projected sales over the next year according to the percentage of business volume generated each month. Divide each month's sales according to cash sales and credit sales. Cash sales can be logged into the cash flow statement in the same month they're generated. Credit sales aren't credit card sales, which are treated as cash, but rather invoiced sales with agreed-upon terms such as royalties.

The next item on a cash flow statement is "other income." Other income refers to any revenue derived from investments, interest on loans that have been extended, and the liquidation of any assets. Total income is the sum of cash sales, receivables and other income. In the first month of an Artist's cash budget, it will usually consist of cash sales, other income and any receivables from the previous budget that have aged to a point of collection during the first month of the current budget.

Also tied to the breakdown of sales is cost of goods and direct labor. For an Artist to sell their products or services, they must first produce it. If the Artist has already broken down sales by month, they need to determine the cost in material and labor to produce those sales. They should refer to the cost of goods table in the Artist Business Plan. Artists need to determine how much direct labor will be for the year to produce their products and services. Divide that number by the percentage breakdown of sales. Direct labor can be logged into cash flow during the same month in which it is accrued.

Material costs, on the other hand, are a little different. Artists need to include the material cost in cash flow using a time frame that allows them to convert the cost of raw material in cash flow into finished goods for sale. Therefore, if it requires 60 days to convert raw material to finished goods, and the Artist's payable period is 30 days after delivery, then enter the cost of goods under material in cash flow 30 days before sales are logged.

Working capital can be determined from operating expenses. All personnel and overhead costs are tied to sales. Artists can figure out their working capital and payroll requirements by dividing marketing and sales, general and administrative, and overhead expenses by the total projected operating expenses. Divide that total by the percentage breakdown of sales for each month and apply that amount to the appropriate line items in the cash flow statement.

Capital equipment costs are accounted for under the heading "capital." If an Artist can service additional debt or purchase the equipment from operating expenses, then it's best to have the equipment purchased and installed at the beginning of the business year or quarter closest to the time when they actually need the equipment. If the Artist's cash flow is tight, then they might want to wait and purchase and install the needed equipment at a point during the year where additional volume warrants the expenditure, thereby assuring sufficient cash flow to handle the additional debt service or the outright purchase of the equipment.

In addition to the preceding costs, Artists should include their tax obligations and any long-term debt or loans. These figures are readily available on loan schedules and tax charts used to project these costs.

Once all these costs have been entered in the cash flow budget, add them up to produce total expenses. When total expenses are subtracted from total income, the result is the Artist's cash flow--either a surplus or deficit. If it's a deficit, determine the minimum cash balance that the Artist wishes to maintain, then calculate the difference between the minimum cash balance and the cash-flow deficit. This result is the amount required for financing purposes.

When forming a cash-flow budget, any amounts financed within a given month need to be included in the cash flow under a projected repayment schedule. Artists should consult with their accountant or banker when developing this repayment schedule.

****

14.14 Task

For this section of the Artist Business Plan, write about the forecasted statement of cash flow of the Artist's company.

****

Forecasted Operating Expenses

14.15
Forecasted Operating Expenses

Operating expenses are expenses incurred by an Artist when carrying out their daily activities. Operating expenses consist of things such as payroll, rent, utilities, repairs and taxes. Manufacturing costs of compact discs or t-shirts are not included in operating expenses.

The Artist's income statements typically separates operating expenses from other expenses such as manufacturing expenses. An income statement shows the Artist's company's revenues, expenses and profits. To calculate operating expenses for an income statement, the Artist's general ledger accounting records are needed.

Steps to Forecast Operating Expenses

1. Gather the general ledger accounting records. The general ledger is used by Artists for recording all financial transactions occurring within their business. The ledger lists all the accounts used by the Artist and are listed in a specific order. The ledger lists assets first, then liabilities, equity accounts, revenues and expenses. The ledger also contains a running balance for each account.

2. Find the expense section in the ledger; usually listed last on a general ledger. These expense accounts are considered nominal accounts. This means they are temporary accounts and are used for tracking amounts spent in each category. For example, an Artist may have an expense account for instrument maintenance, jewel boxes, or band bus repair. These accounts begin the year with a zero balance, and entries are made into the accounts all year. At the end of the year, the Artist can see how much was spent in each category.

3. Investigate the expense accounts listed. Normal income statements contain five different categories into which expenses are broken.
   A. Cost of goods sold is an expense related to the production of goods such as compact discs, t-shirts, etc.
   B. Cost of services sold is an expense related to live performances or pitching songs for publishing.
   C. Extraordinary items are expenses from unusual transactions as this business is project based.
   D. Operating expenses from selling
   E. Operating expenses from general and administration

4. Determine which accounts are considered operating expense accounts. Any expense relating to the Artist's day-to-day operations are considered operating expenses. To calculate the Artist's operating expenses, all payroll accounts should be listed. These include commissions, employee benefits, pension contributions and travel reimbursements. Other expenses to include in operating expenses are depreciation expenses, rent, repairs, utilities, taxes, software contracts and advertising costs.

5. Add all operating expenses. Each expense that fits into these categories is written down and added up. This gives a total of how much the Artist spent on expenses relating to the operations of the business.

****

14.15 Task

For this section of the Artist Business Plan, write about the forecasted operating expenses of the Artist's company.

****

Forecasted Assumptions

14.16
Forecasted Assumptions

Every year is different so Artists need to note any changing circumstances that could significantly affect their sales. These factors - known as the sales forecast assumptions form the basis of their forecast.

Remember, there are two types of customers for Artists: fans and music industry professionals such as talent buyers and publishers. It might be easier to forecast sales assumptions based on which customer is being targeted.

Wherever possible, put a figure against the change. Artists and their managers can then get a feel for the impact it will have on their business. Also, give the reasoning behind each figure, so that other collaborators can comment on whether it's realistic.

Typical Assumptions:

1. **The Market**
   A. The performance market that the Artist sells into will grow by 5 per cent.
   B. The Artist's market share will shrink by 5 per cent, due to the success of a new competitor.

2. **Resources**
   A. The number of regional agents will increase from two people to four people, halfway through the year.
   B. The Artist will spend 50 per cent less on advertising, which will reduce the number of enquiries from potential customers.

3. **Overcoming Barriers to Sale**
   A. The Artist is moving to a better location, which will lead to 30 per cent more talent buyers booking their show next year.
   B. The Artist is raising prices by 10 per cent, which will reduce the volume of bookings sold by 5 per cent but may result in a 4.5 per cent increase in overall revenue.

4. **The Artist's Products**
   A. The Artist is launching a range of new products. Sales will be small this year and costs will outweigh profits, but in future years, the Artist will reap the benefits.
   B. The Artist has products that are newly established and that have the potential to increase sales rapidly. The Artist has established products that enjoy steady sales but have little growth potential. The artist has some markets that face declining sales of bookings, perhaps because of a competitor's superior products and/or services.

For new Artists, the assumptions need to be based on market research and good judgment.

Developing the Artist's Forecast

The Artist should start by writing down their sales assumptions.

They can then create their sales forecast. This becomes easy once they've found a way to break the forecast down into individual items.

Can the Artist break down the Artist's sales by product, market, or geographic region? Are individual customers important enough to the Artist's business to warrant their own individual sales forecast?

Can the Artist estimate the conversion rate - the percentage chance of the sale happening - for each item on the Artist's sales forecast? Selling more of the Artist's product or service to an existing customer is far easier than making a first sale to a new customer. So the conversion rates for existing customers are much higher than those for new customers.

Artists may want to include details of which product each customer is likely to buy. Then they can spot potential problems. One product could sell out, while another might not move at all.

By predicting actual sales, Artists are forecasting what they think will be sold. This is generally far more accurate than forecasting from a target figure and then trying to work out how to achieve it.

The completed sales forecast isn't just used to plan and monitor an Artist's sales efforts. It's also a part of the cash flow.

Avoid Forecasting Pitfalls

1. **Wishful Thinking**
   It's all too easy to be over-optimistic. Every Artist thinks that everyone will love their music or performance if only they see it or hear it. It's a good idea for an Artist to look back at the previous year's forecast to see if their figures were realistic. New Artists should avoid the mistake of working out the level of sales they need for the business to be viable, then putting this figure in as the forecast.

   Artists also need to consider if it is physically possible to achieve the sales levels they're forecasting. For example:
   - A band can only perform a certain number of gigs each day.
   - A booking agent can only reach a certain number of customers each week.

2. **Ignoring the Artist's own Assumptions**
   Artists should make sure their sales assumptions are linked to the detailed sales forecast. If not, Artists can end up with completely contradictory information. For instance, if they assume a declining market and declining market share, it's illogical to then forecast increased sales.

3. **Moving Goals**
   Make sure the forecast is finalized and agreed within a set timescale. If an Artist spends a lot of time refining the forecast, it can distract them from focusing on their targets. Artists should avoid making excessive

adjustments to the forecast, even if they discover it's too optimistic or pessimistic.

4. **No Consultation**

An Artist's sales people probably have the best knowledge of the Artist's customers' buying intentions, therefore:
- ask for their opinions
- give them time to ask their customers about this
- get the sales team's agreement to any targets that will be set

5. **No Feedback**

After an Artist has built their sales forecast, they need someone to challenge it. Get an experienced person - the Artist's accountant or a manager or agent - to review the whole document.

The assumptions an Artist uses are critical to their profit & lost and cash flow forecasting. Artists should base their assumptions on factual, verifiable information. For example, revenues and cash flow for next year should be based on either last year's performance or a three year average of performance. Along with the numbers, it's important to include a narrative that explains the Artist's assumptions and how each line item was computed.

Assumptions

Assumptions for balance sheet presentations should be conservative and based on reasonable expectations of bookings or recordings in the coming two years. Of particular concern should be inventory and accounts receivable. Both are functions of sales. Therefore, Artists should match their inventory assumptions with the gross income projections.

Because cash is usually in short supply for many Artists, tying up this precious resource in excessive inventory or accounts receivable can be damaging. The most important forecast for a new business is a cash flow statement.

While both Artists and their managers want their small business to generate solid net income and have a strong balance sheet, cash flow is more important. It is from cash flow that an Artist can repay loans or distribute cash from profits.

Making valid financial assumptions and explaining them clearly, can make the difference in receiving the funds an Artist needs or suffer the prospect of folding their business.

****

14.16 Task

For this section of the Artist Business Plan, write about the forecasted assumptions sheet of the Artist's company.

****

Forecasted Revenue

14.17
Forecasted Revenue

When starting out, financial forecasts for Artists may seem overwhelming. Forecasting revenue and expenses during the startup stage is really more art than science. Many entrepreneurs complain that building forecasts with any degree of accuracy takes a lot of time-- time that could be spent selling rather than planning. But smart Artists know that thoughtful forecasts mean more potential profits. More important, proper financial forecasts will help Artists develop operational and staffing plans that will help make their business a success.

Here's some detail on how to go about building financial forecasts when an Artist is just getting their business off the ground and don't have the luxury of experience.

Forecasted Expenses

Start with expenses, not revenues. In the startup stage, it's much easier for an Artist to forecast expenses than revenues. So Artists should start with estimates for the most common categories of expenses as follows:

Fixed Costs/Overhead
- Rent for rehearsals and office space
- Utility bills
- Phone bills / communication costs
- Accounting / bookkeeping
- Legal / insurance / licensing fees
- Postage
- Technology
- Advertising & marketing
- Salaries

Variable Costs
- Cost of Goods Sold
  - Materials and supplies
  - Packaging
  - Gas

- Direct Labor Costs
  - Technicians – sound & light
  - Direct sales – agents
  - Direct marketing

Here are some rules of thumb that Artists should follow when forecasting expenses:
1. Double the Artist's estimates for advertising and marketing costs since they escalate beyond expectations.
2. Triple the Artist's estimates for legal, insurance and licensing fees since they're very hard to predict without experience and almost always exceed expectations.
3. Keep track of direct sales and customer service time as a direct labor expense even if doing these activities the during the startup stage. This forecast this expense when the Artist has more clients.

Forecasted Income
Forecast revenues using both a conservative case and an aggressive case. If the Artist is like most entrepreneurs, they'll constantly fluctuate between conservative reality and an aggressive dream state which keeps them motivated.

Rather than ignoring optimism and creating forecasts based purely on conservative thinking, build at least one set of projections with aggressive assumptions. Artists won't become big unless they think big. By building two sets of revenue projections (one aggressive, one conservative), Artists will force themself to make conservative assumptions and then relax some of these assumptions for their aggressive case.

For example, the Artist's conservative revenue projections might assume:
- Low price point
- Two marketing channels
- No sales staff
- One new product introduced each year for the first three years

An Artist's aggressive case might have the following assumptions
- Low price point for base performances, higher price for premium gigs
- Three to four marketing channels managed by the Artists and a marketing manager
- Two agents paid on commission
- One new product (compact disc) introduced in the first year, five more products introduced for each segment of the market in years two and three

By unleashing the power of thinking big and creating a set of ambitious forecasts, Artists are more likely to generate the breakthrough ideas that will grow their business and their success.

Key Ratios

Key ratios make sure the Artist's projections are sound. After making aggressive revenue forecasts, it's easy to forget about expenses. Many entrepreneurs will optimistically focus on reaching revenue goals and assume the expenses can be adjusted to accommodate reality if revenue doesn't materialize. The power of positive thinking might help an Artist grow sales, but it's not enough to pay the Artist's bills!

The best way to reconcile revenue and expense projections is by a series of reality checks for key ratios. Here are a few ratios that should help guide.

Gross Margin. What's the ratio of total direct costs to total revenue during a given quarter or given year? This is one of the areas in which aggressive assumptions typically become too unrealistic. Beware of assumptions that make the Artist's gross margin increase from 10 to 50 percent. If direct sales expenses are high now, they'll likely be high in the future.

Operating Profit Margin. What's the ratio of total operating costs--direct costs and overheard, excluding financing costs--to total revenue during a given quarter or given year? Artists should expect positive movement with this ratio. As revenues grow, overhead costs should represent a small proportion of total costs and the Artist's operating profit margin should improve. The mistake that many Artist-Entrepreneurs make is they forecast this break-even point too early and assume they won't need much financing to reach this point.

****

14.17 Task
For this section of the Artist Business Plan, write about the forecasted revenue sheet of the Artist's company.

****

Risk Reduction

14.18
Risk Reduction

Artist-Entrepreneurs face typical business risks but can reduce these risks and their personal liability through focusing on specific risk-reduction measures. Businesses of all sizes face risks regarding development of products, manufacturing them, selling them, earning a profit on these operations and managing growth. If the Artist-entrepreneur is a sole proprietor, he or she faces additional personal liability risks and financial risks from the actions of their company. Risk management techniques include risk reduction, risk transfer and risk avoidance. An entrepreneur can apply these techniques to the business and personal risk they face.

Risk Reduction 1
Artists should select a business structure that limits personal liability. Artists may want to change their business structure from a sole proprietorship or partnership in which they are personally liable for any and all business operations, to a corporation or limited liability company where the Artist has limited liability. This is an easy solution for a very real use.

Risk Reduction 2
Transfer risk to insurance companies by insuring against major risks such as damage to the Artist's instruments, rehearsal facilities, product liability, and possible injuries to fans at the Artist's performances. In addition, insurance can be obtained against the death or incapacity of one or more members of the Artist's group.

Risk Reduction 3
Perform a risk analysis by evaluating the consequences of risky activities, the likelihood of the consequences occurring and the benefits of the risky activities. Avoid risk by not carrying out activities that have severe and likely consequences and low benefits. One big error that may young Artists make while attempting to tour their first time is not having enough money to get home. This example of a potential risk can be avoided if planned properly.

Risk Reduction 4
Transfer the risk of activities with severe and likely consequences but high benefits to other parties. Create a new, independent company to carry out these activities or assign them to suppliers or partners. Many Artists own a company that only supplies the tour bus to the Artist. If the bus company gets into an accident or kills someone, the Artist may not be liable. In this scenario, perhaps the Artist's bus company is at risk but not the Artist.

Risk Reduction 5
Reduce risk from product failure and warranty claims by implementing a quality assurance program. Develop a system of reporting from customer service to identify problems. Structure the quality assurance program to document production tasks

and product testing. Link the problems reported by customer service to specific failures in production or testing procedures and then institute corrective action. Many times, the sound quality of a recording does not transfer well to compact disc. Before releasing recordings to fans, Artists may want to randomly select copies to listen to and review. This reduces the risk of releasing inferior products.

Risk Reduction 6
Reduce risk of surprises in operating results by keeping accurate records and instituting effective controls. Put in place a system that limits who can authorize specific actions and how much they can spend. Implement a reporting system that gives the Artist key information about company performance. Evaluate the controls and reporting system by comparing actual practice and performance to the control procedures and the reported information.

Risk Reduction 7
Reduce financial risk by managing the Artist's accounts receivable. Artists may want to check with other Artists who have performed at a new venue where the Artist just got a booking. Does the venue manager ever not pay? Does the venue manager skim profits? How trustworthy is the venue manager or talent buyer? Artists need to minimize potential headaches and identify booking choices long before problems occur. Artists should evaluate music industry customers and ask for advance payment from customers who don't meet the standards. Either that, or don't take the gig.

Risk Reduction 8
Artist can reduce financial risk by keeping outstanding loans and financing needs to a minimum. Artists need to control growth at a rate that their company can finance internally. If the company can't pay off some loans, Artists may want to replace short-term credit with long-term, fixed-rate loans.

Reminders for Artist Entrepreneurs
- Always be aware of how others perceive the risk of the Artist's business. If the Artist is performing in a venue that is located in an unsafe area of town, perhaps the fans will not attend the show.
- Take advantage of low-cost, or no-cost, ways to reduce the perceived risk. A good example is the Artist-guitarist who brings additional guitar strings to the gig. The risk of breaking a string and not having a replacement can easily be avoided.
- Be cautious and careful when using outside professionals with whom the artist hasn't worked before. Smart Artists get references.
- Artists should surround them self with professionals, mentors, and advisors who can help them level the playing field. Their advice may show the Artist potential risks and potential solutions.

Other Risk Considerations:
- How loud is the band? Is there potential to blow a fan's eardrum? There has been more than one lawsuit based on the loudness of a band.
- How fresh is the Artist's new song? Before releasing it, check to see if it's really original.
- Is attitude a risk? A negative attitude will certainly hurt an Artist. Therefore, it is a risk.
- Focus or the lack of focus is certainly a risk for all Artists. Smart

Artists know their niche and their market. They are not everything to everyone. They do not spread themselves too thin. Perhaps after much success in the chosen niche, an Artist may consider "crossing-over" to a new market while keeping their older, most established fans.

****

14.18 Task

For this section of the Artist Business Plan, write about the plan for risk reduction for the Artist's company.

****

Risk Management

14.19 Risk Management

Everything in the entertainment business is a project. One of the things a project manager needs to do when developing a project is to create a risk management plan. A project of any size can face risks: financial, physical or even legal. Having a risk management plan in place before the project even begins can help Artists anticipate these risks and minimize or eliminate them before they can damage the project.

- Make a list of the potential risks. Start by making a list of the categories of the project, and then assess each category for risks. For example, the Artist might have a budget category for a new recording; determine what factors might increase the budget and list them.

- Determine the high-priority risks. Prioritize the risks: list them in order of their likelihood and how much of an impact on the project that risk will have if it happens.

- List the actions that must be taken if a risk occurs. Have plans in place that can reduce the chances of a risk happening as well as actions that can ease the damage of a risk should it occur.

- Assign tasks to specific people, collaborators or departments to undertake the planned actions in the event the project runs into one of these risks. Create a timeframe to complete these actions.

- Create a clearly-defined risk management process that the Artist can implement should the project become at risk. Explain how the Artist can apply the actions and timeframes that were created earlier. Make sure all those involved in the project understand the risk management plan, how it's utilized and each person's function in the risk management process.

Risk management should be part of every organization's ongoing business planning process. Artist businesses and businesses of all sizes are now exposed to many more risks than in the past in the form of legal risk, technology risk and economic risk. Understanding the potential impact of these risks is a necessity in today's business environment.

What do we mean by "risk?" Risk is the chance that an action or event will adversely impact the Artist and/or the Artist's company. Risk management is a systematic process that the Artist puts in place to help minimize the consequences of any adverse event. It's a way of identifying, analyzing, monitoring and managing activities or occurrences that have the potential to damage the Artist's operations.

It's important to develop a concrete risk management process as part of the business's day-to-day operations. This usually starts with the Artist's Business Plan. Most business plans contain a SWOT (strengths, weaknesses, opportunities and threats) analysis. The SWOT analysis identifies risk and is the first step in any risk management framework. Once a risk has been identified, Artists can develop a risk profile. A risk profile outlines potential risks to which the business is exposed. Businesses can't completely eliminate risk - for example, it's impossible to completely avoid computer risk. But what Artists can do is work out which risks they are prepared to expose their business to, and what the Artist can do if these dangers become reality.

This is why managers need to work out the risk tolerance zone or the extent to which the business is prepared to be exposed to danger.

When an Artist knows their potential risks, they can start developing risk minimization strategies. This might involve things like ensuring that the Artist has strong firewalls in place to reduce the chance of their computers being exposed to viruses and hackers.

It might also include ensuring that the Artist has the right insurance coverage if, for example, the business was destroyed by fire. A written action plan including a timetable of activities that will help reduce risk is usually part of a risk minimization strategy.

Developing a culture that encourages team members to report potential business risks also goes a long way in helping to reduce risk. Every person on the Artist's team should be aware of potential risks as well as report any risks perceived in their normal line of duty.

The smart move for an Artist is to nominate someone to be the champion of the risk management process and encourage other team members to go to this person if they believe the company is at risk in any way. Also put in place clear reporting frameworks so that the risk management system is clearly documented.

Bogged down in the day-to-day, it's easy for small business owners to ignore risk management. In reality, most businesses can't afford NOT to have a risk management strategy.

****

14.19 Task
For this section of the Artist Business Plan, write about the plan for risk management of the Artist's company.

****

Exit Strategy

14.20 Exit Strategy

Definition: The planned exit of an owner from their business

Many Artists think their art and their business will continue indefinitely. That may be so for a solo Artist, but bands break-up every day. Just as Artists need a plan to get into business, they need a plan to get out of it as well. Exiting from a business requires some forethought, strategizing and careful implementation. In some ways, it's a little more complicated than starting a business. For instance, while there's really only one way to start a company, there are at least three primary methods for entrepreneurs to leave the businesses they founded: selling, merging and closing.

Three Ways of Exiting a Business

Selling
Merging
Closing

Deciding to sell the business that an Artist has worked so hard to grow is rarely an easy decision. However, it may be the right one under some common circumstances. Selling may be preferable to owning if:

- The Artist is ready to retire and have no heir to continue the company
- Partners who co-own the business decide to dissolve their partnership
- One of the owners dies or becomes disabled
- One of the owners get divorced and need cash for a settlement
- The Artists wants to do something more challenging, more fun or less stressful
- The Artist doesn't have enough working capital to keep going

****

14.20 Task

For this section of the Artist Business Plan, write about the exit strategy of the Artist's company.

****

Spending Strategy

14.21 Spending Strategy

Creating long term financial strategies is very important when developing an Artist's finance goals. This means developing a financial plan that includes planning for upcoming recording projects, promotion, and performances as well as creating a monthly budget and establishing funds and financing from investors, collaborators and banks.

For Artists of all kinds, an effective monthly budget will include both how to pay monthly bills as well as how to save for the future. There are many budgeting software systems available; however, many Artists develop an effective budget with nothing more than a pencil and paper.

Savings should be included as with any effective budget. Whether the Artist is saving for a new recordings or tour, it is vital that they remember the importance of saving for the future and include it in their budget.

One of the most effective ways to help develop savings strategies is to track spending habits. To begin, gather receipts and write the information down into a composition notebook or software program. Label each receipt into appropriate categories such as rent, recordings, new gear, promotion, entertainment, gas. By incorporating this system into an Artist's budget, Artists will be able to curb excess spending which will result in substantial savings.

One of the easiest ways to save for the future is to develop a spending strategy. Artists should always live within their means. By only spending what they have, will they be able to save for their future.

Artists should pay off credit card debt as quickly as possible. Using this tactic will allow an Artist to save money by avoiding the interest associated with credit card debt. The fastest way to pay credit card debt off is to pick the smallest balance and work to pay it off. Once that credit card is paid off, begin paying off the next lowest balance. Many people who owe their credit card companies, first pay off the one that has the highest interest rate. Either way, avoid credit card debt.

Keep good records. By keeping good records, Artists will be ready when tax time arrives to receive every deductible item that they are entitled to. Build a file system that will separate each receipt into its proper category. These categories might include project receipts, utility receipts and receipts for promotion and entertainment.

There are a number ways to help Artists develop long-term financial strategies that will help them achieve their goals. Keep in mind, financial planning is a long-term commitment that must be carried out with consistency and commitment.

****

14.21 Task

For this section of the Artist Business Plan, write about the spending strategy of the Artist's company.

****

Return on Investment

14.22
Return on Investment

Return on Investment (ROI) is a performance measure used to evaluate the efficiency of an investment or to compare the efficiency of a number of different investments. For Artists to calculate ROI, the benefit (return) of an investment is divided by the cost of the investment; the result is expressed as a percentage or a ratio.

The return on investment formula:
In the above formula "gains from investment," refers to the return from the time and money spend in making the Artist successful. Return on investment is a very popular metric because of its versatility and simplicity. That is, if an investment does not have a positive ROI, or if there may be other opportunities with a higher ROI. An Artist who does not evaluate their true value may only have a hobby and not a business. This is a difficult value to determine for most Artists.

Keep in mind that the calculation for return on investment and, therefore the definition, can be modified to suit the situation: it all depends on what an Artist includes as returns and costs. The definition of the term in the broadest sense just attempts to measure the profitability of an investment and, as such, there is no one "right" calculation. If an Artist records a new album but sells none, is that a waste of time and resources? Maybe yes, and maybe no for an Artist.

For example, an Artist may compare two different products by dividing the gross profit that each product has generated by its respective marketing expenses. A financial analyst, however, may compare the same two products using an entirely different ROI calculation, perhaps by dividing the net income of an investment by the total value of all resources that have been employed to make and sell the product.

This flexibility has a downside, as ROI calculations can be easily manipulated to suit the Artist's purposes, and the result can be expressed in many different ways. When using this metric, Artists make sure they understand what inputs are being used.

Return on investment (ROI) is the concept of an investment of some resource yielding a benefit to the investor. A high ROI means the investment gains compare favorably to investment cost. As a performance measure, ROI is used to evaluate the efficiency of an investment or to compare the efficiency of a number of different investments. In purely economic terms, it is one way of considering profits in relation to capital invested by the Artist.

Calculation
For a single-period review, divide the return (net profit) by the resources that were committed (investment):

Return on Investment (%) = (Net Profit / Investment) × 100

****

14.22 Task

For this section of the Artist Business Plan, write about the return on investment of the Artist's company.

****

Budgets

14.23
Budgets

A sub-section of the Artist's Business Plan is the Financial Plan. Within the Financial Plan is a section about budgets. The entertainment business is all about projects and each project needs a budget. It's a plan within a plan within a plan.

An Artist's budget is a quantitative expression of a plan for a defined project or period of time. It may include planned sales volumes and revenues, resource quantities, costs and expenses, assets, liabilities and cash flows. It expresses strategic plans of business units, projects, activities or events in measurable terms.

Budgets also help to aid the planning of actual operations and projects by forcing Artists to consider how the conditions might change and what steps should be taken now. Having a budget encourages Artists to consider problems before they arise. It also helps co-ordinate the activities of the Artist by compelling them to examine the cost versus benefit between none project and another.

Budgets are used to:
1. To control resources
2. To communicate plans to various project managers
3. To motivate and strive to achieve budget goals
4. To evaluate the performance of managers
5. To provide visibility into the company's performance
6. For accountability

A good budget provides a valuable tool to any Artist's business.
1. It provides a forecast of revenues and expenditures. It constructs a model of how an Artist's project and/or business might perform financially if certain strategies, events and plans are carried out.
2. It enables the actual financial operation of the Artist's project and/or business to be measured against the forecast.
3. It establishes the cost constraint for a project, program, or operation.

Business Start-Up Budget
The process of calculating the costs of starting a small business for an Artist begins with a list of all necessary purchases including tangible assets (for example, equipment, instruments,

costumes and inventory) and services (for example: rehearsal, travelling, writing, pre-production and insurance), working capital, sources and collateral. The budget should contain a narrative explaining how the Artist decided on the amount of this reserve and a description of the expected financial results of business activities. The assets should be valued with each and every cost. All other expenses such as labor, overhead all start-up expenses are also included into business budgeting.

Company Budget
The budget of a company is often compiled annually, usually requiring considerable effort. Artists typically have multiple projects that are planned for each year. For a yearly budget, Artists need to compile all their projects and estimate the total budget for the year. Expected revenues and expenses for the Artist are listed in the final budget.

Project Management Budgets
A budget is a fundamental tool for an Artist to predict with a reasonable accuracy whether the project will result in a profit, a loss or will break-even.

There are two basic philosophies, when it comes to budgeting. One approach is based on mathematical models, and the other on people.

The first school of thought believes that financial models, if properly constructed, can be used to predict the future. The focus is on variables, inputs and outputs, drivers and such. Investments of time and money are devoted to perfecting these models, which are typically held in some type of financial spreadsheet.

The other school of thought holds that it's not about models, it's about people. No matter how sophisticated models can get, the best information comes from the people in the business. This is true for many Artists. The focus is therefore in engaging the project managers more fully in the budget process, and building accountability for the results. Project managers develop their own budgets.

Budget Types
1. Sales budget – an estimate of future sales, often broken down into both units and currency. In the entertainment industry, units may be defined as the number of performance gigs, compact discs, music licensed and/or downloads. It is used to create sales goals of the Artist's company.
2. Production budget – an estimate of the number of performances that must be completed or compact discs to be manufactured to meet the sales goals. The production budget also estimates the various costs involved with producing those performances or compact disc units, including labor and material.
3. Capital budget - used to determine whether an Artist's long term investments such as new equipment, replacement instruments, new promotions, new products, and research development projects are worth pursuing.
4. Cash flow/cash budget – a prediction of future cash receipts and expenditures for a particular time period. It usually covers a period in the short term future. The cash flow budget helps the Artist's business determine when income will be sufficient to cover expenses and when the company will need to seek outside financing.
5. Marketing budget – an estimate of

the funds needed for promotion, advertising, and public relations in order to market the Artist's product or service (recordings or performances.)
6. Project budget – a prediction of the costs associated with an Artist's particular company project. These costs include labor, materials, and other related expenses. The project budget is often broken down into specific tasks, with task budgets assigned to each. A cost estimate is used to establish a project budget.

****

14.23 Task

For this section of the Artist Business Plan, write about the budget of the Artist's company.

****

Financial Ratios

14.24
Financial Ratios

A financial ratio (or accounting ratio) is a relative magnitude of two selected numerical values taken from an Artist's financial statements. Often used in accounting, there are many standard ratios used to try to evaluate the overall financial condition of an Artist's company. Financial analysts also use financial ratios to compare the strengths and weaknesses of each of the Artist's projects.

Ratios can be expressed as a decimal value, such as 0.10, or given as an equivalent percent value, such as 10%. Some ratios are usually quoted as percentages, especially ratios that are usually or always less than 1, such as earnings yield, while others are usually quoted as decimal numbers, especially ratios that are usually more than 1, such as the Price to Earning (P/E) ratio; the latter are also called multiples. Given any ratio, one can take its reciprocal; if the ratio was above 1, the reciprocal will be below 1, and conversely. The reciprocal expresses the same information, but may be more understandable: for instance, the earnings yield can be compared with bond yields, while the P/E ratio cannot be: for example, a P/E ratio of 20 corresponds to an earnings yield of 5%.

Values used in calculating financial ratios are taken from the balance sheet, income statement, statement of cash flows or (sometimes) the statement of retained earnings. These comprise the Artist's "accounting statements" or financial statements. The statements' data is based on the accounting method and accounting standards used by the Artist.

Purpose and types of ratios
Financial ratios quantify many aspects of an Artist's business and are an integral part of the financial statement analysis. Financial ratios are categorized according to the financial aspect of the business which the ratio measures.
1. Profitability ratios measure the assets and control expenses to generate an acceptable rate of return.

2. Liquidity ratios measure the availability of cash to pay debt.
3. Activity ratios measure how quickly non-cash assets are converted to cash.
4. Debt ratios measure the ability to repay long-term debt.
5. Market ratios measure investor response to owning a company's stock and also the cost of issuing stock. These are concerned with the return on investment for shareholders, and with the relationship between return and the value of an investment in company's shares.

> **Financial Ratios Allow for Comparisons**
>
> - between companies
> - between industries
> - between various projects of the Artist
> - between different time periods for one company
> - between a single company and its industry average

Ratios generally are not useful unless they are benchmarked against something else, like past performances or past projects. Thus, the ratios of an Artist's projects, which face different risks, new fans and customers, capital requirements, and competition, are usually hard to compare.

Accounting Methods and Principles
Financial ratios may not be directly comparable between companies that use different accounting methods or follow various standard accounting practices. Most public companies are required by law to use generally accepted accounting principles, but private companies, partnerships and sole proprietorships may not use accrual basis accounting.

Abbreviations and Terminology
Various abbreviations may be used in financial statements, especially financial statements summarized. Sales reported by an Artist are usually net sales, which deduct returns, allowances, and early payment discounts from the charge on an invoice. Net income is always the amount after taxes, depreciation, amortization, and interest, unless otherwise stated.

Artists who are primarily involved in providing performance services do not generally report "Sales" based on units. These Artists tend to report "revenue" based on the monetary value of income that their services provide, such as performances.

Shareholders' Equity and Owner's Equity are not the same thing, Shareholder's Equity represents the total number of shares in the company multiplied by each share's book value; Owner's Equity represents the total number of shares that an individual shareholder owns (usually the owner with controlling interest), multiplied by each share's book value. It is important to make this distinction when calculating ratios.

Financial Ratios

Profitability Ratios
Profitability ratios measure the Artist's use of its assets and control of its expenses to generate an acceptable rate of return.

Gross profit margin or Gross Profit Rate
Gross Profit / Net Sales or Net Sales – COGS / Net Sales

Operating Income Margin, Operating Profit Margin or Return on Sales
Operating income is the difference between operating revenues and operating expenses, but it is also sometimes used as a synonym for EBIT and operating profit. This is true if the firm has no non-operating income. (Earnings before interest and taxes / Sales)

Profit Margin, Net Margin or Net Profit Margin
Net profit / Net Sales

Return on Equity (ROE)
Net Income / Average Shareholders' Equity

Return on Assets (ROA)
Net Income / Average Total Assets

Return on Assets (ROA)
Net Income / Total Assets

Return on Net Assets (RONA)
Net Income / Fixed Assets + Working Capital

Return on Capital
EBIT (1-Tax Rate) / Invested Capital

Risk Adjusted Return on Capital (RAROC)
Expected Return / Economic Capital

Return on Capital Employed (ROCE)
EBIT / Capital Employed
(This is similar to (ROI), which calculates Net Income per Owner's Equity

Cash Flow Return on Investment (CFROI)
Cash Flow / Market Recapitalization

Efficiency Ratio

Non-Interest Expense / Revenue

Basic Earning Power Ratio
EBIT / Total Assets

Liquidity Ratios
Liquidity ratios measure the availability of cash to pay debt.

Currents Ratio (Working Capital Ratio)
Current Assets / Current Liabilities

Acid-Test Ratio (Quick Ratio)
Current Assets − (Inventories + Prepayments) / Current Liabilities

Cash Ratio
Cash and Marketable Securities / Current Liabilities

Operation Cash Flow Ratio
Operating Cash Flow / Total Debts

Activity Ratios (Efficiency Ratios)
Activity ratios measure the effectiveness of the firm's use of resources.

Average Collection Period
Accounts Receivable / (Annual Credit Sales / 365 Days)

Degree of Operating Leverage (DOL)
Percent Change in Net Operating Income / Percent Change in Sales

DSO Ratio
Accounts Receivable / (Total Annual Sales / 365 Days)

Average Payment Period
Accounts Payable / (Annual Credit Purchases / 365 Days)

Asset Turnover
Net Sales / Total Assets

Stock Turnover Ratio
Cost of Goods Sold / Average Inventory

Receivables Turnover Ratio
Net Credit Sales / Average Net Receivables

Inventory Conversion Ratio

365 Days / Inventory Turnover

Receivables Conversion Period
(Receivables / Net Sales) X 365 Days

Payables Conversion Period
(Accounts Payables / Purchases) X 365 Days

Cash Conversion Cycle
Inventory Conversion Period + Receivables Conversion Period − Payables Conversion Period

Debt Ratios (Leveraging Ratios)
Debt ratios quantify the firm's ability to repay long-term debt. Debt ratios measure financial leverage

Debt Ratio
Total Liabilities / Total Assets

Debt to Equity Ratio
Long-Term Debt + Value of Leases / Average Shareholders' Equity

Long Term Debt Ratio
Long-Term Debt / Total Assets

Times Interest Earned Ratio
EBIT / Annual Interest Expense
Or
Net Income / Annual Interest Expense

Debt Service Coverage Ratio
Net Operating Income / Total Debt Service

Market Ratios
Market ratios measure investor response to owning a company's stock and also the cost of issuing stock. These are concerned with the return on investment for shareholders, and with the relationship between return and the value of an investment in company's shares.

Earnings per Share
Net Earnings / Number of Shares

Payout Ratio
Dividends / Earnings

Dividend Cover (the inverse of Payout Ratio)
Earnings per Share / Dividend per Share

P/E Ratio
Market Price per Share / Diluted EPS

Dividend Yield
Dividend / Current Market Price

Cash Flow Ratio
Market Price per Share / Present Value of Cash Flow per Share

Price to Book Value Ratio
Market Price per Share / Balance Sheet Price per Share

Price / Sales Ratio
Market Price per Share / Gross Sales

PEG Ratio
Price per Earnings / Annual EPS Growth

****
14.24 Sample

****
14.24 Task

In this section of an Artist's Business Plan, Artists should evaluate their income and their expenses. By compiling this information, Artists can see the profits and losses of their business. They will be able to estimate budgets based in current and past performances and productivity. It is suggested that Artists utilize the services of a professional accountant to ensure accuracy of their financial ratios

****

Accounts Receivable

14.25
Accounts Receivable

Accounts receivable are a legally enforceable claim for payment to a business by its customer / clients for goods supplied and/or services rendered in execution of the customer's order. In the entertainment business this includes payments by promoters to Artists for performances, as well as payments due from Online Music Distributors (OMD) such as I-Tunes for sale of downloadable recordings. These claims are generally in the form of invoices raised by the Artist's business and delivered to the customer for payment within an agreed period of time. Accounts receivable are shown in the financial balance sheet as an asset. It is one of a series of accounting transactions dealing with the billing of a customer for goods and services that the customer has ordered.

Accounts receivable represents money owed by entities to the Artist on the sale of products or services on credit. Usually Artists are compensated directly after a live performance. However, this is not as easily completed for each download sold by an Online Music Distributor. In this case, a credit is due the Artist. Accounts receivable is typically executed by generating an invoice and either mailing or electronically delivering it to the customer, who, in turn, must pay it within an established period of time, called credit terms or payment terms.

Artists determine their accounts receivable through their sales ledger, because a sales ledger normally records:
1. The sales that the Artist's business has made.
2. The amount of money received for the Artists products or services.
3. The amount of money owed at the end of each month

Payment Terms
An example of a common payment term is Net 30 days, which means that payment is due at the end of 30 days from the date of invoice. The debtor is free to pay before the due date and many businesses offer a discount for early payment. Other common payment terms include Net 45, Net 60 and 30 days end of month. The creditor may be able to charge late fees or interest if the amount is not paid by the due date.

Booking a receivable is accomplished by a simple accounting transaction; however, the process of maintaining and collecting payments on the accounts receivable subsidiary account balances can be a full-time proposition. Very often, Artists are cash-strapped and cannot allow their account receivable ledger to extent very long. Usually, Artists need the cash and they need it now. However, if an Artist is utilizing a brick-and-mortar record store to sell their compact discs, they may often have to leave their merchandise with the retailer "on consignment." When the retailer sells the Artist's product, they owe the Artist for the sale. Collecting these fees can be a daunting task.

Since not all customer debts will be collected, businesses typically estimate the amount of and then record an allowance for doubtful accounts. This appears on the balance sheet as a contra account that offsets total accounts receivable. When accounts receivable are not paid, some companies turn them over to third party collection agencies or collection attorneys who will attempt to recover the debt via negotiating payment plans, settlement offers or pursuing other legal action.

On an Artist's balance sheet, accounts receivable are the money owed to them by entities outside of their company. Account receivables are classified as current assets assuming that they are due within one calendar year or fiscal year. This includes royalties owed by publishers and record companies. To record a journal entry for a sale on account, Artists must debit a receivable and credit a revenue account. When the customer pays off their accounts, the Artists debits cash and credits the receivable in the journal entry. The ending balance on the trial balance sheet for accounts receivable is usually a debit.

If an Artist is trying to obtain a loan for a new project, they may be able to use their accounts receivable as collateral. This is true only if there is an agreement from the purchaser to pay. Artists may also sell these receivables through factoring or on an exchange.

****

14.25 Task

For this part of an Artists Business Plan, write down the process for anticipated Accounts Receivable. If the Artist has none; then all the better. However, as a part of the plan, what happens "if." Write it down. Put it in the plan.

****

Accounts Payable

14.26
Accounts Payable

Accounts payable (A/P) is money owed by a business to its suppliers and shown as a liability on an Artist's balance sheet. It is distinct from notes payable liabilities, which are debts created by formal legal instrument documents.

An accounts payable is recorded in the Account Payable sub-ledger at the time an invoice is issued for payment. This is the same as receiving a bill in the mail for a service or product already received such as cell phone usage or power & light utility. The A/P sub-ledger is an outstanding, or open, liability because it has not been paid.

Payables are often categorized as Trade Payables which are payables for the purchase of physical goods, and Expense Payables, which are payables for the purchase of goods or services that are expensed. Common examples of Expense Payables are advertising, travel, entertainment, office supplies and utilities. Accounts Payables are a form of credit that suppliers offer to their customers by allowing them to pay for a product or service after it has already been received. An example is a printing business that prepares and prints flyers and posters for an Artist and then bills them for their work.

Commonly, a supplier will ship a product, issue an invoice, and collect payment later, which describes a cash conversion cycle, a period of time during which the supplier has already paid for raw materials but hasn't been paid in return by the final customer.

In accounts payable, a simple mistake can cause a large overpayment. A common example involves duplicate invoices. An invoice may be temporarily misplaced or still in the approval status when the vendor calls to inquire into its payment status. After the Artist looks it up and finds it has not been paid, the vendor sends a duplicate invoice; meanwhile the original invoice shows up and then gets paid. When the duplicate invoice arrives, it may inadvertently get paid as well, perhaps under a slightly different invoice number.

Audits of Accounts Payable

An Artist's financial auditor often focus on the existence of approved invoices, expense reports, and other supporting documentation to support checks that were cut. The presence of a confirmation or statement from the supplier is reasonable proof of the existence of the account.

****

14.26 Task

In this section of an Artist's Business Plan, write down the procedure for dealing with the Artist's accounts payable. This information goes into the finance section of the plan.

****

****

Notes

_____

_____

_____

_____

_____

_____

_____

_____

Chapter 15
Business Plan for Artists
Resources

Depending on the goals and objectives, an Artist will determine types of resources needed to attain those goals. There are many and some are easy to find and some not so much. Music industry resources for Artists can help indie bands, garage bands, local bands, musicians, and songwriters get to where they want to be with their music career. There are resources for promotion tips, band resources, music industry articles, music jobs, band press kit tips, recording studios, and CD DVD duplication listings and many more.

Music industry resources for Artists may include how to get gigs, how to sell CDs, digital distribution ideas, music careers, online music distribution (OMG), and band promotion tactics.

Resources Overview

15.01 Resources Overview

Resources for Artists

15.01 - Resources Overview
15.02 - Related Statistics
15.03 - Industry Involvement
15.04 - Legal Resources
15.05 - Web Related Resources
15.06 - Research Statistics & Demographics
15.07 - Trade Publications
15.08 - Databases

****

15.01 Task

For this section of the Artist Business Plan, write about the overview of resources of the Artist's company.

****

Related Statistics

15.02 Related Statistics

Whether Artists are establishing their business or designing new products, today's small business managers face greater complexities than ever before. Running a business that deals with the arts cannot be run on instinct alone. Statistics provide Artists with more confidence in dealing with uncertainty in spite of the flood of available data. This enables Artists and their managers to more quickly make smarter decisions and provide more stable leadership to their team.

Statistics can be found in multiple resources including trade publications, online social networks and local entertainment magazines. Smart Artists know to use an electronic database to help them manage their contacts, and therefore massage the statistics used to assist in finance, marketing and performance logistics.

Here are some useful government resources for locating business-related statistics.

This website from the U.S. Census Bureau includes business and industry statistics.

- U.S. Economic Census - http://www.census.gov/econ/census/

This website from the U.S. government includes business and economic statistics.

- USA.gov Data and Statistics - http://www.usa.gov/Topics/Reference-Shelf/Data.shtml

This resource includes statistics relevant to business, economics, finance, and many other areas.

- Statistical Abstract of the United States - http://www.census.gov/compendia/statab/

****

15.02 Task

For this section of the Artist Business Plan, write about the related statistics of the Artist's company.

****

Industry Involvement

15.03 Industry Involvement

The entertainment industry is all about networking and relationships. For Artists who understand that this business is also about project management, they understand the importance of being involved with the industry.

Early in an Artist's career, they may begin their networking possibilities by participating in open-mics at local coffee shops or nightclubs. As they move up the ladder, they will network and get more involved by attending music industry conferences and seminars.

Participating in the business side of the entertainment industry opens many possibilities for Artists, because frankly, many opportunities for new projects are discovered because somebody was in the right place at the right time. If a producer is looking for talent to perform on an upcoming recording project, they often turn first to the people they know. This same idea extends to a talent buyer who books Artists whom he or she already knows as opposed to taking a risk on an unknown act.

****

15.03 Task

How involved is the Artist with the local, regional and national industry? As a part of the Artist's 12 month calendar, identify and plan how and where the Artist will become more involved with the music and entertainment industry.

****

Legal Resources

15.04
Legal Resources

The entertainment business is gaga about agreements. There are agreements for every conceivable project of an Artist. Some of these legal issues could dramatically impact an Artist's business. In addition to the section about legal issues as described in the Artist Development Plan, the Artist Business Plan also addresses some of the same concerns. Smart Artists protect them self and their business by knowing what legal resources are available to them.

For any business, whether an Artist's or not, It makes good sense to know how to handle legal issues that may impact the business. Not all legal matters require a lawyer, but they do require understanding. Sometimes the best way for an Artist to protect them self and their business is to know where to go for assistance. In addition to the attorney of the Artist there are other sources to help Artists.

- The American Bar Association's (ABA) guide on legal help for the consumer.
- ABA Lawyer Referral Service
- The State Bar Association
- SCORE
- Plain English Guide To Contracts

When utilizing legal resources, Artists should be aware of potential fees and expenses. All individuals have a right to know how they will be charged, how much the case is likely to cost, and when they have to pay. Additionally, it is important to get a fee agreement in writing. Typical fee arrangements include: hourly fees calculated by multiplying the amount of hours an attorney works on the case by an agreed upon hourly rate, a fixed predetermined rate for the attorney's work, and a percentage of any judgment amount awarded to the individual.

****

15.04 Task

For this section of an Artist's Business Plan, write down the resources that an Artist may use for their business. Include the names of attorneys that are already on the Artist's team or that the Artist may want on their team. Be specific. Write it down.
****

Web Related Resources

15.05
Web Related Resources

Information is the key to good business decisions. There is a great deal of good information freely available on the Web. This part of an Artist's Business Plan, show which web resources are being utilized by the Artist and which site may eventually be a part of the Artist's business.

The following websites provide a starting point for the Artist's business research activities. They are arranged in categories to help you expedite the Artist's search.

Associations – Directories
ASAE & The Center for Association Leadership - www.asaecenter.org
This page allows you to search for an association by name, interest area, or geographic location. You also can search using a combination of fields.

Internet Public Library - www.ipl.org/div/aon/
A collection of over 1100 Internet sites providing information about a wide variety of professional and trade associations

Associations – Business
American Marketing Association - www.marketingpower.com
The world's largest and most comprehensive professional society of marketers

American Society of Composers, Authors and Publishers (ASCAP)
www.ASCAP.com
One of the three Performing Rights Organizations in the United States

Broadcast Music Inc. (BMI) –
www.BMI.com
One of the three Performing Rights Organizations in the United States

National Retail Federation - www.nrf.com
The world's largest retail trade association

SESAC – www.SESAC.com
One of the three Performing Rights Organizations in the United States

Software & Information Industry Association - www.siia.com
The principal trade association for the software and digital content industry

Benchmarking
Biz Stats - www.bizstats.com
Compare the Artist's company performance to others in the same industry

Fintel Scorecard - www.fintel.us/products/BusinessScorecard.html
Compare the Artist's company to others in the industry based on 9 core ratios

Business Plans
American Express - www.openforum.com/idea-hub/topics/managing/article/how-to-write-a-small-business-plan/
How to write a Business Plan

BizPlanIt - www.bizplanit.com/free.html
BizPlanIt's Virtual Business Plan is an online Business Plan resource based on real-world business planning advice.

Carnegie Library of Pittsburgh - www.clpgh.org/subject/business/bplansindex.html
Guide to business plans by type of business

Entrepreneur Magazine - www.entrepreneur.com/businessplan
Articles and resources for creating the Artist's Business Plan

SBA Business Plan Basics – www.sba.gov/smallbusinessplannernesspplanner/plan/writeabusinessplan/index.html
Step by step instructions for creating a Business Plan from the SBA

SCORE Business Plan Template - http://www.score.org/node/803280
Easy to follow template for creating a Business Plan, preferred by counselors

Competitive Intelligence
Fuld & Company - www.fuld.com
Specialist in competitive intelligence

Investigators Toolbox - www.virtuallibrarian.com/research/ci.html
Tools for performing a competitor search

Competitive Intelligence - www.llrx.com/features/ciguide.htm
Articles on competitive intelligence

Securities & Exchange Commission - www.sec.gov
Search for required filings of publicly traded corporations

Society of Competitive Intelligence Professionals - www.scip.org
Provides education and networking opportunities to business and competitive intelligence professionals (including marketing, market research, strategy, and information.

Demographics / Psychographics
American Fact Finder - www.factfinder2.census.gov
Ongoing data collected by the Census Bureau

FreeDemographics - www.freedemographics.com
Free demographic market analysis reports

Melissa Data - www.melissadata.com
Free address information for businesses and individuals

NC Rural Databank - www.ncruralcenter.org/databank/index.html
Statistical information on North Carolina's rural counties

Economic Development
EconData - www.econdata.net
Regional Economic Data

Entertainment Industry
Billboard Magazine – www.Billboard.com
A weekly magazine servicing the entire music and entertainment industry

CD test - http://www.realtraps.com/test-cd.htm
CD Test review the audio frequencies of a compact disc and makes recommendations of its improvement.

Gracenote - http://www.gracenote.com/
Gracenote is a database for software applications to look up audio CD (compact disc) information over the Internet.

Freedb - http://www.freedb.org/
FreeDB is an open source CD information resource that is free for developers and the public to use.

Music Brainz - http://musicbrainz.org/
MusicBrainz is a user-maintained community music meta-database

Entrepreneurship
Council for Entrepreneurial Development - www.cednc.org
A private, non-profit organization formed to identify, enable and promote high growth, high impact entrepreneurial companies and to accelerate the entrepreneurial culture of the Research Triangle and NC

Edward Lowe Foundation - www.lowe.org
To champion the entrepreneurial spirit by providing information, research and educational experiences that support entrepreneurship and the free enterprise system

Entrepreneur Magazine - www.entrepreneur.com
Small business tools; Business Plan guide; entrepreneur's databases for business opportunities and franchise information

Entrepreneurial Connections - www.entrepreneurialconnection.com/About.asp
Provides tools, tips and training for the self-employed and small business owners

Inc Magazine - www.inc.com
Provides small-business information, Web-based tools, products, and services

Kauffman Foundation - www.kauffman.org
Focuses its grant making and operations on advancing entrepreneurship and improving the education of children and youth.

Financing Resources
Capital Opportunities for Small Business

sbtdc.org/resources/publications/capital-opportunities/
SBTDC's online publication for finding capital resources for NC businesses

SBA-Financing - www.sba.gov/category/navigation-structure/loans-grants
Describes loan availability, eligibility, sources of grants

Government Resources – Federal
Internal Revenue Service - www.irs.gov/businesses/small
Tax information for small businesses
Laws & regulations by industry - business.usa.gov
Provides a single access point to government services and information to help the nation's businesses with their operations.

Securities and Exchange Commission - www.sec.gov
Corporate filings

US Patent & Trademark Office - www.uspto.gov
Search for patents and trademarks

US Small Business Administration website - www.sba.gov
An independent agency of the federal government to aid, counsel, assist and protect the interests of small business concerns

Legal
FindLaw - www.findlaw.com
Legal information for lawyers and general public, including case law, statutes, lawyer search

Martindale - www.martindale.com
Directory of lawyers

Market Research
Annual Reports - www.annualreports.com
Online access to annual reports

Marketresearch.com - www.marketresearch.com
Reports to purchase

Quirks - www.quirks.com
Magazine for market researchers

Valuation Resources - www.valuationresources.com/IndustryReport.htm
Free industry reports

Marketing
American Marketing Association - www.marketingpower.com
Resources for marketers and advertisers

M Plans - www.mplans.com
Choose from several free marketing plans or purchase others

****

15.05 Task

For this section of the Artist Business Plan, write about the web related resources of the Artist's company.

****

Research, Statistics & Demographics

15.06
Research, Statistics & Demographics

As a part of most Business Plans, there is a section in the Resources section that states where the Artist received the research, statistics and demographics used in the plan. This section is important as Artists grow their business because they will have the data at hand, when needed.

Finding information about a consumer is one of the most difficult aspects of marketing research. Some of the best resources are professional market research reports that companies contract when doing any new market analysis. These reports can be quite expensive. Alternatives to mainstream data, may professional Artists include trade associations as well as statistics resources.

Demographic Research

Demographics are statistics about people: how many people live in a specific area, where they work, what they buy, and how they live. Statistics can shape the delivery of a new recording or a new area of the country to market performances for the Artist.

Census

Every ten years, the U.S. Census Bureau attempts to count and categorize all of the people in the United States and Puerto Rico. Along with counting the people, the Census Bureau also collects certain economic and social characteristics about everyone. Rather than doing the long form every 10 years, the Census Bureau is now taking an annual American Community Survey which provides an estimated count of many socioeconomic characteristics. The questions asked are those that help federal and state agencies carry out the services they provide as mandated by Congress. This mandate is a benefit to business owners, social service agencies and others who need demographic information.

When an Artist is researching the viability of performing in a new market, they should investigate whether the new market is financially viable or not.

Information can be gathered about states, cities or towns, counties as well as zip codes.

Statistics are given for more than 40 variables and include:
- Population Characteristics
- By three age categories
- By racial/ethnic categories
- Family size
- Social Characteristics
- High school graduates
- College graduates
- Foreign born
- Married
- Speakers of other than English at home
- Housing Characteristics
- Owner occupied
- Rental occupied
- Vacant housing
- Average home value
- Average mortgage value
- Economic Characteristics
- Employed
- Average time traveled to work
- Average family income
- Average per capita income
- Families living below poverty level

- Individuals living below the poverty level

Other websites with statistical data:

Bizstats.com
Financial ratios, business statistics and benchmarks.

Click Z Stats.com
The Web marketer's guide to online facts, Internet research, trends, and analysis. The ToolBox is divided into sections on Internet Traffic, Advertising Stats, Demographics, E-Commerce and Internet access.

EconStats.com
A compilation of domestic and international statistics and release dates for items such as the GDP, Industrial capacity and industrialization, new orders and shipments inventories, manufacturing and trade inventories, U.S. housing and pricing index, construction spending, retail sales, consumer credit, jobless claims, interest rates, etc.

Statistics by Zip Code
Resources that have been compiled by a librarian from California State University at Northridge. Statistics are gathered from a variety of government departments and independent organizations.

U.S. Dept. of Labor - Bureau of Labor Statistics
Consists of profiles of 12 industry super sectors. Each profile contains a variety of facts about the industry sector, and includes links to additional statistics, which include items such as employment hours, wages, and trends.

Zapdata.com
This site provides market analysis reports of industries and companies by metro area and state.

****

15.06 Task

For this section of the Artist Business Plan, write about the research, statistics and demographics used for the Artist's company.

****

Trade Publications

15.07
Trade Publications

Definition: Trade publication is a term for a specific kind of publication -- usually a magazine -- that is geared to people who work in a specific business or industry.

A trade publication, unlike a consumer publication, covers a specific industry for people who work in that industry. Trade publications therefore cover an industry in more minute details than a consumer publication might. The idea is that trade publications deliver information that's of value to those who work in a certain field, but might not be of as much interest to the general public.

For example, someone who likes music might read a consumer publication like

Rolling Stone because it covers entertainment. But someone who works in the music industry will probably be reading publications like Billboard, Pollstar or the College Media Journal, three trades that cover deals and other things happening on the music charts more closely.

The Advantages of Advertising in Trade Directories

In order for the Artist's business to get effective publicity, it is important that they advertise in some media as theirs budget dictates. Artists can advertise in newspapers, on the Internet or by other means.

An excellent way of advertising is to advertise in trade directories. Below are some of advantages of doing so.

1. **Advertising Hits the Target**
   By advertising in trade directories, Artists are assured of reaching out specifically to the Artist's target audience. This ensures that the Artist's advertising budget is put to its full use. This move also ensures that the Artist gets the right inquiries and orders from people that they intend to serve. This is in contrast to newspapers or other media, where an Artist may get a lot of time-wasting inquires.

2. **Meet New Suppliers**
   By advertising in trade directories, Artists not only get new customers, but they will be able to reach out to new wholesalers or manufacturers that can supply the Artist with products at lower rates. This will provide the Artists with a wider variety of suppliers, and also give them a chance to expand the Artist's product range.

3. **Costs Can Be Quite Reasonable**
   Advertising in newspapers or on television requires a lot of money in order to have a sustained campaign. However, just a couple of advertisements in a reputable trade directory will give the Artist's advertising budget more mileage for a longer period of time. Normally, people tend to hold on to trade directories for at least a year.

4. **Respectability**
   By advertising in trade journals, the Artist's business will also get more respectability as compared to advertising in newspapers.

If an Artist can write articles related to the Artist's business for the same trade directory, then that will be all the more better for the Artist's business.

Artists should start advertising in trade directories if they have not yet done so, they may immediately meet new customers and suppliers, taking the Artist's small business to a new level.

****

15.07 Task

For this section of the Artist Business Plan, write about the plan use of trade publication and which ones for the Artist's company.

****

Databases

15.08 Databases

A database is information organized in a logical way. The phone book is an example you've probably seen and used many times. Names, addresses and phone numbers are organized alphabetically by last name or business name. Your own personal address book is a database too; one that you put together yourself.

Computers have allowed databases to be taken to a whole new level. The practical size of your phone book is limited by how large a book a person can store and use. A computer can store far more information, by orders of magnitude, in less space than a phone book. And you don't have to flip to the right page. You can pull information out of the database just by typing in the name (or even part of the name) you are looking for.

Computerization has also increased the flexibility of databases. What if you wrote down a phone number but don't remember whose it is? Or you know a first name, but not a last name? A standard phone book won't help you much with these problems. You could use a reverse look-up phone book to find the owner of a phone number, but this would necessitate a second book. On a computer you can search by the phone number or first name or last name, or any other piece of information the database contains.

Furthermore, computers have enabled adding dimensions to a database. What happens when you put a married couple who have different last names in your address book? Do you list them under both last names? Then, if they move, you have to enter the new address in both places. If you forget and only change the address in one place, you might find later that you have two different addresses and are not sure which is correct. By creating relationships, a computerized database can store the address in one place and the names in another and relate the two. When you look at the information, it all appears together, but you only have to change one address.

Well, you're probably already using more than one. There's your address book (whether in your Day Timer or on your Palm Pilot). If you're using accounting software, it's probably based on a database. Scheduling software, probably a database. Project or task management, database.

If you have information that fits into categories (like names, phone numbers, dates, locations, item names, etc.), it can be organized in a database. Sometimes you have this information organized in a spreadsheet or word processing program. Technically, those are databases, but they aren't the most efficient databases. They don't take advantage of the capabilities that software designed for databases provides, such as sorting, filtering, relationships, calculations and viewing the information in a variety of ways. If you want to look up that information later, without sorting through paper or scrolling down in a word processing or spreadsheet document, database software can be very helpful.

A database is essentially a way to organize information. Today, the volume of information that we keep and use and process is enormous. It can put a high administrative burden on individuals and organizations. A database is a way to manage that volume easily, efficiently, and without going crazy. Using the right database software can help you manage your information, and open up the time for you to devote your attention the things you really want to do.

The database is one of the four main tools utilized to insure a well promoted event. You need a database of area newspapers, magazines, radio stations, television and cable stations, and other avenues to help get the word out. This database should be in some format to properly execute mail merges. If you don't have a database, you have much more work to do.

Compiling Your Database
Think of two radio stations in the area. That's a good start. Now add their address, phone number, promotion manager's name, e-mail, website and any special comments. Now do the same with other area media outlets. The yellow pages works well for data.

You may be able to acquire a database from various sources such as the artists who are performing, the venue where the event is taking place, or a public relations firm you have hired to help with the promotion.

Assuming you already have a database, your first step is to filter the data. You may want to contact everyone in the world about the event but that would be highly impractical. Filter your list to your area. This may be done with postal codes, area codes, city or state names.

After the initial filter, you should now have a list of all the people, businesses and contacts you may need to contact or be a part of your team. If you haven't done so already, create a column for contact type. For example, a magazine should be identified differently than a record store. A magazine may receive press releases as well as flyers from you where a record store may only receive the flyers. You may want to define some of your database a media and some as drop points for your street team.

****

15.08 Task

For this section of the Artist Business Plan, write about the databases used in doing business within the Artist's company.

....

Notes
_____
_____
_____
_____
_____
_____
_____
_____
_____
_____

Chapter 16
Business Plan for Artists
Appendix - Overview

The major sections of the Artist's Business Plan should only contain summarized findings and highlights for the Artist's business. To avoid information overload by including every piece of information about the Artist such as gas receipts and old recording templates. The reader may determine if reading the entire plan is worth the effort. Instead, include detailed research, sources, and other related information about the Artist and the Artists' business in the appendix.

Appendix Overview

16.01 Appendix Overview

Artists may want to consider including the following information in the appendix of their Artist Business Plan:

- Management resumes
- Pictures of Artists, products, Compact Disc covers
- Copies of purchase orders
- Tour plans
- Marketing materials
- Contracts & Agreements
- Market research surveys and results
- Other supporting documents

****
16.01 Task

For this section of the Artist Business Plan, write about plan for documents in the appendix of the business plan for the Artist's company.

****

Forward Looking Statements

16.02 Forward Looking Statements

Forward Looking Statements are statements made that are not historic and are thereby predictive. When writing a forward-looking statement, use words such as 'believe', 'expect', 'anticipate', 'intend', 'estimate', 'assume', 'project' and other similar expressions. This statement as a part of an Artist's Business Plan predicts or indicates future events and trends or that do not relate to historical matters. Such forward-looking statements involve known and unknown risks, uncertainties and other factors. These statements may cause actual results, performance or achievements to be materially different from any future results, performance or achievements expressed or implied by such forward-looking statements.

Investors and owners often want to know about what they believe will happen in future time periods. While it is clear to everyone that no one can predict the future, management is often in the best position to see new trends that may be occurring and to speak about what the Artist has planned.

Despite the implicit understanding that certain statements are speculation, the SEC requires public companies to include a disclaimer on all management discussions with investors in order to emphasize this point. This includes Artists who sell shares in their LLC. When properly emphasized, stockholders generally may not take legal action against company management for forward looking statements which proved to be inaccurate. In the U.S., the Private Securities Litigation Reform Act of 1995 provides certain safe harbor provisions against fraud claims dealing with forward looking statements.

Hypothetical Examples of Forward-Looking Statements:
- The Artist plans on expanding their geographic performance area to 5 new cities within the next year.
- The Artist anticipates the value of their brand to continue to rise for over the next few years, increasing dividends for shareholders.
- The Artist predicts that their new recordings will revolutionize the music niche they have chosen; expanding their niche to a new audience of over 1 million new fans.

****

16.02 Task

For this section of the Artist Business Plan, write about the plan for forward looking statements used in the business plan for the Artist's company.

****

Personal Income Statement

16.03
Personal Income Statement

A personal financial statement tells an individual about how 'healthy' their financial position is. Similar to an Artist's business, the personal financial statements of an individual Artist includes the importance of assets and liabilities.

If the Artist is more than one individual such as a band, ensemble or orchestra, each person may want to know and learn from understanding of their personal financial statement. Firstly, it enables individuals to organize their assets allocation is in terms of assets and liabilities. Assets for an Artist may include the any investments or personal ownership of things that are generating income and profit such as musical instrument or copyrights. In addition, it can include stocks, vehicles (if owned), their businesses and real estate. Liabilities for Artists are expenses and things owned that does not generate income for the individual.

The significant factor here is assets are things owned that brings in the income and increase the individual Artists net worth. A personal net worth tells the individuals how rich the individual is in terms of his personal finance positioning. For example, if an Artist with personal expenditures of $10000 a year and a net worth is $50,000, then the Artist will take five years before his net worth reaches $0.

Another significant lesson that an Artist can learn is awareness of positive or negative cash-flow in the financial statement. Cash flow here is the amount left after deducting the expenses from the income earned. Positive cash-flow management enables the Artist to develop good management skills in his finance especially in developing wealth for long term.

****

16.03 Task

For this section of the Artist Business Plan, write the personal income statement of each of the owners of the Artist's company.

****

Resumes of Team Members

16.04
Resumes of Team Members

In this section of the Artist Business Plan, include resumes of each of the team members of the Artist's business. Include their background and musical history.

****

16.04 Task

For this section of the Artist Business Plan, provide the resumes of each owner and member of the Artist's company.

****

Notes

Business Plan for Artists Forms

DISCLAIMER
This article is offered as an educational and informational tool only, and should not be relied on as legal advice. Applicability of the legal principles discussed may differ substantially in individual situations. The sample contract is for illustrative purposes only, and has not been verified for compliance with the law of any particular state. If you have a specific legal problem or concern, you should consult an attorney.

Band Member Agreement Sample

For _____(Insert band name)

AGREEMENT made this _____ day of _____, 199_, by and between the undersigned Artist and the undersigned Musician(s).

This Agreement is entered into in the City of _____ and County of _____, State of _____ and is guided by and governed by the laws of that state.

The undersigned parties hereby agree to the following responsibilities:

1. Show up for practice as agreed upon failure to do so can void contract and end any future agreements. UNLESS there is an emergency or other uncontrollable circumstances out of the Musician(s) control. (Example: Death of family member, illness, accident, act of God.) If there is a problem notify Artist within _____hours before rehearsals were to commence.

2. It is the Musician(s) responsibility to keep their equipment in good working condition, and upgrade appropriately when the revenue is available.

3. There should be no drinking/smoking on stage, always maintaining good showmanship/ quality as deemed by management and myself.

Musician(s) will follow the instructions of the Artist and management team.

Other Provisions

4. Under no circumstances is a band member (Musician(s)) allowed to talk to club owners, record labels, radio stations, etc. in regards to setting up anything for the band, in which promises are made or money is mentioned, etc.. The band members (Musician(s)) should direct all inquiries to myself and then I can pass it along to management, or hand out business cards with our managements contact info on it.

5. Any other outside performing with another band or engagement that interferes with the schedule of Artist will void the contract if necessary.

6. Understanding that the band members (Musician(s)) main job objective is bring to life songs that are in the Artist format and 100% attention, enthusiasm and dedication is needed to make things happen. Lack of any of the above can void contract if it is detrimental to our success.

7. The Artist makes no promises or guarantees about Rewards and compensation but every effort will be in achieving the goals and payment will be made to the Musician(s) when possible.

The following conditions are in effect only as long as the contract is valid.

2. Live performances, bandmember (Musician(s)) will receive 20% of the performance fee.

3. In regards to royalties from any independent release that a band member plays on (examples would be cd's, cassettes, EP.'S.' singles, etc., that has been financed by myself and/or management team. The bandmember (Musician(s)) will receive a percentage of 15% after the cost of manufacturing and distribution, production has been made back. Example - I spend 1500 to record and manufacture 2000 cd's, after the 1500 is made back from the sales of the item, royalty checks will go out in accordance to what was agreed upon. In the event of signing with a major or Indie label the royalty rates may be renegotiated at that time.

4. There will be specific pay days, and dates for all compensation. Band member should not expect payment right after a gig or a sale of a cd.

Merchandising

5. Merchandising (T-shirts, hats, etc.), Musician(s) will receive a percentage after the cost is made back. The percentage will be in the 2-10% range, due to the fact that this money will be used to finance upcoming events for the band-tour support, recording, etc.

6. When and if the Artist is signed to a label or any other organization that handles booking, distribution, etc. than what is in place presently, then contract will need to be renegotiated to exact out new figures.

7. This contract is an open agreement voided at such time the Artist or Musician(s) deems necessary.

Touring

Musician(s) should meet to discuss all touring and gigs before the actual date. A plan will be made then in the event of prolonged touring to ensure all Artists and Musician(s) are in essence in the right place at the right time. Equipment checklists will be made and followed as well as set lists for shows. Musician(s) are responsible for things such as personal leaves from day jobs for touring etc. Musician(s) will meet with the Artist on specific days and times to discuss issues pertaining to the tour work. Band members will not leave the tour group unless they have let other parties know where they are going. This is only a protection for the band as a whole should an accident or other uncontrollable circumstance arise.

Complaints

All complaints will be handled in an orderly manner. If Musician(s) feel they are being treated unfairly outside the realm of this agreement they may contact the management team and the complaint will be addressed and remedied in an efficient manner.

(Omit or replace with your management information) Management

You may also contact managers' assistants.

_____

Artist

_____

Musician(s)

Notes

DISCLAIMER
This article is offered as an educational and informational tool only, and should not be relied on as legal advice. Applicability of the legal principles discussed may differ substantially in individual situations. The sample contract is for illustrative purposes only, and has not been verified for compliance with the law of any particular state. If you have a specific legal problem or concern, you should consult an attorney.

Artist / Personal Management Agreement Sample

The signatories hereof warrant to each other that each has taken the professional advice of a solicitor specializing in such agreements before their signature hereof.

Artist Name:-
Stage Name:-
Address:-

Managers Name:-
Address:-

Agreement Date:-

Dear Sir/Madam:-

We confirm our Management Agreement whereby we appoint you to represent us as our sole and exclusive manager under the provisions of this agreement as follows:-

1. This agreement relates only to my professional activities and confers the right to represent me as a solo artist. (Bands/groups/duo's etc. need to specify that only the band as a whole is represented and any solo activity requires separate consent).

2. Both you and I warrant by our respective signatures that there are no existing restrictions that prevent either party from entering into this agreement or performing any of our obligations.

3. This agreement relates solely to activities as a musical artist and in no way confers the right to represent or hold yourself as representing me in any other field of entertainment or area of work not connected with the music business without prior written consent.

4. During the Term of this agreement defined below you shall have the following obligations:

    a) To use your best endeavors to promote and develop my career as a musical artist and provide me with regular reports on your work.

    b) To ensure all monies due to me are promptly collected and remitted directly to me by the parties from which they are due.

c) To refer all enquiries connected with our work in areas which you are not permitted to act directly to me.

d) You shall not have the right to assign or transfer obligations to any other person or company without prior written consent, any such act shall immediately and retrospectively terminate your appointment and this agreement.

5. The following are the obligations I agree to:

a) To be available and comply with your reasonable requests to undertake activities pertaining to my career at my sole discretion.

b) Not to attempt to negotiate agreements with 3rd parties directly which relate to activities which you are responsible for and to refer all such third parties to you.

c) To refer all Press enquiries to you.

d) To notify you of any changes in address or contact numbers.

6. During the term of this agreement I shall reimburse any expenses directly relating to your activities as my manager upon request by you, with the exception of office expenses i.e., telephone, staff etc., which will be your sole responsibility.
Expenses in excess of $_____ for any single item must have been approved in writing prior to being incurred or will not be reimbursed.

7. If you are permitted to manage other artists then I require you to submit written details in respect of expenses that are related solely to your activities as my manager and not as manager of other artists.

8. During the Term of this agreement you shall not be entitled to manage other artists without my prior knowledge and/or consent and you shall ensure that management of said artists does not adversely affect your obligations set out within this agreement.

9. You shall be entitled to charge for your services a commission of 15% (maximum 20%) of the (gross or preferably net) income received by myself in respect of the activities the subject hereof during the Term and Commission Period (excepting that following termination of the Term the commission payable shall reduce to 10% of the (gross/net) income and will be subject to the limitations on the source of such income set out below). Commission shall be payable based on net income received by myself for live work during the Term and for the avoidance of doubt during the Commission Period you shall only be entitled to you commission in respect of income derived from recordings and compositions made in whole during the Term. You shall be solely responsible for meeting your own income tax, insurance, and business tax.

10. The Term of this agreement shall be 2 years from the Agreement Date with the provision that I shall be entitled at my sole discretion following the expiry of 6 months from the Agreement Date to terminate the Term in the event that you have not procured the

signature of a publishing or recording agreement by such date. The Commission Period following the expiry or termination of the Term whereby you are still entitled to receive commission as set out in Clause 10 shall be 2 years from the date of termination, however in the event that I have exercised the right to terminate the term after 6 months you shall not be entitled to receive commission on future income derived from recordings or compositions made during the Term.

11. The Territory governed by this agreement shall mean the _____. (United States, World, whichever country you reside and/or any countries you designate)

12. You shall be entitled to appoint another person as my manager in certain countries or territories of the Territory provided I grant consent to such appointment and the identity of such person and provided that such appointment shall not discharge you from any of your managerial obligations as set out in this agreement.

13. Nothing within this agreement shall be deemed to create a partnership or joint venture between the signing parties.

14. This agreement shall be governed by the laws of _____.

Please indicate your acceptance of the terms hereof by signing and returning the attached copy to me.

Yours faithfully

Names and dated signatures of artist/s

Read and Agreed

Name and dated signature of the manager

Notes

DISCLAIMER
This article is offered as an educational and informational tool only, and should not be relied on as legal advice. Applicability of the legal principles discussed may differ substantially in individual situations. The sample contract is for illustrative purposes only, and has not been verified for compliance with the law of any particular state. If you have a specific legal problem or concern, you should consult an attorney.

Artist / Producer Agreement Sample

Date:_____

This shall serve as the sole agreement between _____ (hereinafter referred to as "Producer") for services in producing Master Recordings, (hereinafter referred to as "Masters") for and of the recording artist(s) professionally known as _____ (hereinafter referred to as "Artist").

1. The term of this agreement shall commence as of the date hereof and shall continue until the completion of Producer's services.

2. (a) Recording sessions for the Masters shall be conducted by Producer under this Agreement at such times and places as shall be mutually designated by Artist and Producer. All individuals rendering services in connection with the recording of Masters shall be subject to Artist's approval. Artist shall have the right and opportunity to have Artists representatives attend each such recording session. Each Master shall embody the performance by the Artist of a single musical composition designated by the Artist, and shall be subject to Producers approval as technically satisfactory for the manufacture, broadcast and sale of phonorecords, and, upon Artists request, Producer shall re-record any musical composition or other selection until a Master technically satisfactory to Artist shall have been obtained, provided additional production costs will be paid by Artist. Producer agrees to begin preproduction, rehearsals, and recording on _____, 20____.

(b) Producer shall deliver to Artist a two-track stereo tape suitable for duplication and manufacture of phonorecords for each Master. All original session tapes, rough mixes and any derivatives or reproductions thereof shall also be delivered to Artist, or, at Artists election, maintained at a recording studio or other location designated by Artist, in Artists name and subject to Artists control.

3. All Masters produced hereunder, from the inception of the recording thereof, and all phonorecords and other reproductions made therefrom, together with the performances embodied therein and all copyrights therein and thereto, and all renewals and extensions thereof, shall be entirely Artists property, free of any claims whatsoever by Producer or any other person or person engaged in the production of the Masters. (It being understood that for copyright purposes Producer and all persons rendering services in connection with such Masters shall be Contractors for hire).

4. (a) Conditioned upon Producer's full and faithful performance of all the terms and provisions hereof, Artist shall pay Producer, as an advance recoupable by Artist from any and all royalties payable by Artist to Producer hereunder, the sum of $ _____ DOLLARS payable upon commencement of recording, and the balance upon the delivery to you of the Masters.

(b) Notwithstanding anything contained in (a) above to the contrary:

(i) in the event the Masters are released on any label other than _____ or its subsidiary or affiliate label or labels, Producer shall not receive a royalty in connection with the sale of such records;

(ii) in the event the Masters are released on the _____ label or a subsidiary or affiliate label, Producer shall be paid in respect to the sale of such phonorecords a royalty rate of three percent (3%) of the suggested retail price of each phonorecord sold and paid for in the United States. Payments of royalties from foreign sources shall be ONE HALF of the United States royalty rate. All fees paid to Producer hereunder shall constitute recoupable advances which shall be recouped prior to further payment of royalties.

5. Producer has agreed to assist Artist in presenting the Masters to major record companies in pursuit of a record production agreement with a major label. Producer understands that Artist will also be presenting the Masters to major labels and that Producer will not be Artists exclusive representative. Therefore, Producer agrees to notify Artist prior to making any formal contact with representatives of any major record company on Artists behalf in order to coordinate respective efforts and agrees to contact on Artists behalf only those companies mutually agreed upon. In the event Artist enters into a record production agreement with a major label for the Masters recorded hereunder and the further services of Artist as a result of substantial efforts and negotiations by Producer with such company within the period of ONE YEAR following the completion of the Masters Artist agrees to pay Producer a commission of six percent (6%) of the actual cash advances (exclusive of recording budgets) received by Producer upon execution of said agreement. A major record company as defined herein shall be a company or corporation with gross sales of one million (1,000,000) units in the current calendar year.

6. Producer hereby warrants, represents, and agrees that he is under no disability, restriction, or other incumbency with respect to his right to execute and perform the services described in this Agreement.

7. Artist shall have the right, at Artists election, to designate other producers for recording sessions with the Artist, in which event Producer shall have no rights hereunder with respect to the Masters produced at such other recording sessions.

8. Artist shall have the right, at Artists election, to assign any of Artists rights hereunder, in whole or part, to any subsidiary, affiliated, or related company, or to any person, firm or corporation acquiring rights in the Masters produced hereunder.

9. (a) This contract sets forth the entire understanding of the parties hereto relating to the subject matter hereof. No amendment or modification of this contract shall be binding unless confirmed in writing by both parties.

(b) Artist shall not be deemed to be in breach of any of Artists obligations hereunder unless and until you have given Artist specific written notice of the nature of such breach and Artist have failed to cure such breach within thirty (30) days after Artists receipt of such notice.

(c) Nothing herein contained shall constitute a partnership or joint venture between Artist and Producer.

(d) This contract has been entered into in the State of _____, and its validity, construction, interpretation, and legal effect shall be governed by the laws of the State of _____.

(e) This contract shall not become binding and effective until signed by Artist and Producer.

Agreed and Accepted:

_____
PRODUCER

_____
ARTIST

Notes

DISCLAIMER
This article is offered as an educational and informational tool only, and should not be relied on as legal advice. Applicability of the legal principles discussed may differ substantially in individual situations. The sample contract is for illustrative purposes only, and has not been verified for compliance with the law of any particular state. If you have a specific legal problem or concern, you should consult an attorney.

Single Song Publishing Agreement Sample

AGREEMENT DATED __th day of _____, 201_ (Hereafter called "Agreement Date").

SINGLE SONG AGREEMENT: The Writer and _____ Music Publishing Company, hereafter called Publisher, do hereby agree to the terms of this Agreement under the following terms and conditions:

1. Publisher agrees that if the song by Writer now entitled _____ is not assigned a mechanical license to be recorded and released to the general public on phonorecords within 24 months of agreement date, the Writer may request, in writing, that the Publisher relinquish and return all rights and copyrights to the Writer.

2. If Publisher does not receive a written request for reversion of rights prior to the expiration date above, this agreement will self-renew for 12 months, and continue to do so every 12 months, indefinitely. A reversion request received at any time after the initial expiration date will be honored at the end of the current 12 month renewal period, or immediately, at Publisher's discretion.

3. The Writer shall not be held responsible for any payment to the Publisher regardless of the amount Publisher may have spent on the recording, development, promotion, or any other expense incurred by Publisher relating to this song.

4. In the event Publisher is responsible for the placement of said musical composition on phonorecords released to the public, Writer hereby agrees to affiliate with BMI, ASCAP, SESAC, or SOCAN, if not already so affiliated, and to sign a standard clearance form from such organization, listing Publisher as owning 100% of the publishing rights for said musical composition. This will be either submitted to Publisher for approval before filing, or may be supplied by Publisher.

5. Writer agrees that this agreement shall be in force and binding during the original specified period and during any self-renewal period, and will not assign the rights to the aforementioned song to any other until this Agreement has expired AND not been self-renewed, without the song being recorded on phonorecords for the public.

6. During the Agreement period, and any renewal periods, Publisher shall not be required to defend Writer against any legal action against Writer for copyright infringement, or any other proprietary right.

7. Writer grants permission for Publisher to play and freely copy all submitted demo material, for promotional purposes only, for the life of this agreement and any renewals thereof.

If any part of this agreement shall be held invalid or unenforceable, it shall not affect the validity of the balance of this Agreement.

We the undersigned do hereby acknowledge and agree to the terms of this Agreement.

Date: _____,_____.   PAU Number: _____

BY_____   BY_____
PUBLISHER   WRITER

DISCLAIMER
This article is offered as an educational and informational tool only, and should not be relied on as legal advice. Applicability of the legal principles discussed may differ substantially in individual situations. The sample contract is for illustrative purposes only, and has not been verified for compliance with the law of any particular state. If you have a specific legal problem or concern, you should consult an attorney.

Record Label / Artist Agreement Sample

1. AGREEMENT made this _____ day of _____, _____, between _____ (herein called "the Company") and _____ (herein called "the Artist") for the tendering of personal services in connection with the production of Commercial Sound Records.

2. This agreement shall remain in effect for a period of _____ from the date hereof, and during that period you will, at mutually convenient times, come to and perform at the Company's recording studios for the purpose of recording _____ _____ selections or more than this number if the Company so desires.

In consideration of this Agreement and without further payment than as herein provided for yourself, you grant to the Company, its associates, subsidiaries and nominees (1) the right to manufacture, advertise, sell, lease, license or otherwise use or dispose of in any or all fields of use, throughout the world, or to refrain therefrom, throughout the world or any part thereof, records embodying the performances to be recorded hereunder, upon such terms and conditions as the Company may approve; (2) the right to use your name and photograph if desired, in connection with the exploitation of said records; and (3) all rights in and to the matrices and records, and the use and control thereof, upon which are reproduced the performances to be recorded hereunder.

3. The Company will pay you for the rights granted herein and the services to be rendered hereunder by you a royalty of _____ cents for each double-faced record manufactured and sold throughout the world by the Company or its associates or subsidiaries, on both faces of which are embodied any of the selections recorded hereunder. In case of records manufactured and sold by the Company on only one face of which is embodied a selection recorded hereunder, the amount of royalty shall be one-half of the amount set forth above, excepting in cases where the recording shall be of full length on one side (in such case as a Compact Disk).

4. Payment of accrued royalties shall be made semi-annually on the first day of _____ __ for the period ending _____, and on the first day of _____ for the period ending _____ of each year. The Company, however, shall have the right to deduct from the amount of any statements, or accounts of royalties due, the amount of royalties previously paid to you or records subsequently returned, either as defective or on exchange proposition.

5. You agree that during the period of this Agreement you will not perform for any other person, firm or corporation, for the purpose of producing commercial sound records, that after the expiration of this Agreement you will not record for anyone else any of the musical selections recorded hereunder, and that in the event of a breach of this covenant, the Company shall be entitled to an injunction to enforce same, in addition to any other remedies available to it.

6. The Artist hereby warrants that he has no oral or written obligations contracts, or agreements of whatever nature entered into prior to the signing of this agreement which are now in force and binding and which would in any way interfere with carrying out this agreement to its full intent and purpose.

7. If any instrumental musicians whose services are engaged hereunder are members of the American Federation of Musicians, the following provision shall be deemed to be a part of this agreement:
"As the musicians engaged under the stipulations of this contract are members of the American Federation of Musicians, nothing in this contract shall ever be construed as to interfere with any obligation which they owe to the American Federation of Musicians as members thereof."

8. It is mutually understood and agreed that in the event the license issued to the Company by the American Federation of Musicians, and pursuant to which the Company engages the services of Federation members as instrumental musicians, should be revoked or terminated, with or without cause, and in the event you or any of the members of the Musical Organization are members of the Federation, the Company may, at its option, terminate and cancel this agreement without liability to you.

9. The Company shall have the privilege and option to extend this Agreement from the date of its expiration for a period equal to the terms of this Agreement by giving to you notice in writing of its exercise of such option and its election to continue. Such notice shall be given to you personally or be mailed to your last known address not less than ten days prior to the expiration of this Agreement. Upon the giving of such notice this Agreement shall be continued and extended for such further period upon the same terms as those above set forth.

IN WITNESS WHEREOF, the parties hereto have hereunto set their hands and seals this day and year first above written.

By_____
Record Company Executive

By: _____
Artist

BUSINESS PLAN – ARTIST
GLOSSARY
Music Industry Definitions

You gotta know what you're talking about.

360 Deals - An increasingly common major label deal structure in which the label not only earns income from the sale of recorded music of their artists but also gets a cut of other artist income, including money generated by touring and merchandise sales.

7" / 10" / 12": The diameter of vinyl records. 7" items are usually singles that play at 45 rpm, 10" items could be a single or an EP, and 12" items could be a single (45 rpm) or an album (33 1/3 rpm

A&R is the person or group of people who sign new acts to a record label. (They used to select material from publishers for artists signed to their label, hence Artists and Repertoire.)

Acetate In sound recording an acetate disc is a reference audio disc used during production of a gramophone record (e.g. an LP record). The acetate disc is created as one of the initial stages of record production and used to determine how a given recording will transfer to disc.

Advance – In the field of intellectual property licensing, an advance against royalties is a payment made by the licensee to the licensor at the start of the period of licensing (usually immediately upon contract, or on delivery of the property being licensed) which is to be offset against future royalty payments.

Advance the Show – A telephone call to a promoter from a road manager to go over specifics of an upcoming performance.

Aftermarket: For the purposes of the discography, this term describes any item that contains material being resold in a secondary fashion, usually by a company not normally associated with the artist or the record label. The best examples are box sets; most of the time the CDs are regular copies of albums or singles that are easy to find, but have been repackaged with miscellaneous trinkets (e.g., a book, poster, postcard, shirt, or button). Even though some of a box's contents may be official, the box itself is not.

AFM - (AF of M) American Federation of Musicians. The musicians' union sets minimum wages and working conditions for American artists. The majority of performance contracts are drawn up using the AF of M standard contract format. The AF of M also provides a variety of services to its members, including health insurance, legal aid, etc.

Agent - A person who seeks employment for artists, actors, musicians, actors and other people in the entertainment business and negotiates performance contracts. An Agent gets the artist the gig. Agents make their money by making a percentage of the money that their client is paid. There are different regulations that govern different types of agents that are established by artist's unions and the legal jurisdiction in which the agent operates. There are also professional organizations that license talent agencies.

Aggregator - A digital music aggregator collects music from a number of different sources such as musicians and labels and then distributes them to online music distributors. By doing so, iTunes and Amazon don't need to worry about dealing with the time consuming job of getting content to populate their music store. Music aggregators can offer additional services such reconciliation on behalf of the artist from the store, making the process very easy for any unsigned or indie label.

Album - A collection of songs, regardless of format.

All In - the total licensing price of a song and master use combined - OR the two licensing rights- both combined--(as in " is the total fee --ALL IN -for both rights").

Area of Dominant Influence ADI - ADI or Area of Dominant Influence is the geographic area or market reached by a radio or television station. It is used by advertisers and rating companies to determine the potential audience of a station.

Artist - Music industry contract term for musician or performer.

ASCAP - American Society of Composers, Authors, and Publishers. One of three organizations that grants licenses for performances of a given songwriter or publisher's music.

Assignment - Copyright can be assigned to a label or publisher, or a third party such as a royalty collection society. This allows them to act on behalf the copyright owner to issue licenses and collect royalties within the terms of the assignment.

Avails or Availabilities – Term used to identify the availability of artists for performances or appearances.

Axe – a musician's instrument

Backline - Instruments and everything needed onstage to put on a concert, with the exception of some sound and lights. This includes drum kits, base rigs, amps, etc.

Bar Code - A bar-code is a machine readable number (e.g. UPC code) used for various purposes in manufacture, retail and commercial use of a CD. Bar-codes don't just identify CDs at the sales counter, they are also used for chart returns. Some distributors and retailers insist on bar-coding.

Bean Counters - Slang for those who count the money and keep track of sales.

Bill – A list of performers on a show

Blister pack: A Blister Pack is a stiff plastic molding surrounding the case of a CD. The term is borrowed from the marketers who originally made the packaging. Blister Packs were mainly used on 3" CDs so that they could be hung on shop displays. 3" CDs with the original Blister Packs have a slightly higher value than those without; however there is no accurate record as to which releases had this packaging and which did not.

Blanket License - "Blanket license" is a license which allows the music user to perform any or all songs in the Performing Rights Organization's repertory as much or as little as they like. Licensees pay an annual fee for the license. The blanket license saves music users the paperwork, trouble and expense of finding and negotiating licenses with all of the copyright owners of the works that might be used during a year and helps prevent the user from even inadvertently infringing on the copyrights of the P.R.O's members and the many foreign writers whose music is licensed in the U.S.

BMI - Broadcast Music Incorporated. One of three organizations that grants licenses for performances of a given songwriter or publisher's music.

Bogart-Bacall Syndrome - (Also called Lauren Bacall Syndrome) Condition in which improper vocal technique while speaking results in a gravelly-sounding voice. Common in women.

Book – A band is "booked" at a club if they are scheduled to play there.

Booking Agent – A person who solicits work and schedules performances for entertainers.

Bootleg: these are the unauthorized recordings of live or broadcast performances. They are duplicated and sold - often at a premium price - without the permission of the artist, composer or record company.

Box Set: - A set of items that are packaged together.

Break – An artist is about to "break" when he or she is on the verge of becoming very well known - this usually happens after some serious radio airplay or publicity is taking place and the expectations are high for great sales and visibility.

Bridge - In a song, a bridge is usually of different length than the verse or chorus and usually has different music accompaniment. A bridge usually will "sum up" a songs message, or flash forward or backwards in time or often give a different perspective or surprise twist to a song.

Broadcast - the replaying of pre-recorded works to multiple listeners through various media or in a 'semi-live' setting such as a bar or bookstore, and including radio, TV, webcasting, podcasting, etc.

Business Manager - Keeps track of an artist's finances and is usually a CPA who specializes in the entertainment industry.

Buzz - There is a "buzz" about a particular band if people are talking about them and saying positive things.

Buyer - (Talent Buyer, Purchaser, Concert Promoter, Promoter) Makes offers of employment to artist through the artist's agent.

Cap – slang for capacity

Capacity - The number of audience members a concert venue will legally hold.

Card Price – The Card Price is the cost of a CD for a retailer. Often, major labels give a retailer 5 percent discount of the Card Price.

Cassette - A sealed plastic unit containing a length of audio or video tape wound on a pair of spools, for insertion into a recorder or playback device.

Catalog Number - Also known as order number or issue number. 1. The number(s), letter(s), and/or other symbols assigned to a publication by the publisher to establish a unique control of a particular publication. 2. The number, usually different from the matrix- or master-number(s), assigned by the publisher under which an item appears listed in catalogues, leaflets, and other publicity material issued by the company owning the rights to the recording. Usually common to all parts of the published item, appearing generally on each part of a multipart package as well as on the container for the multiple parts. This number may change when, or if, one or more of the parts are re-published again at a later date. Recordings have from time to time been published with the same catalogue number, both inadvertently and deliberately. Dubbings are sometimes assigned the original catalogue number, but frequently with a variant prefix or suffix

Chorus – The chorus is a section of lines that generally contain the catchiest part of the song. Usually the chorus contains a songs hook.

CO Copyright Form - This is the registration form from the Library of Congress that you use to register a song online. It protects the copyright in and to the words and music of the song.

Collective Work - A work, such as a periodical issue, anthology or encyclopedia, in which the Work in its entirety in unmodified form, along with a number of other contributions, constituting separate and independent works in themselves, are assembled into a collective whole. A work that constitutes a Collective Work will not be considered a Derivative Work (as defined below) for the purposes of this License.

Composite Card - An 8x10 photograph containing images of artists in varied "looks" or angles. These are used to obtain modeling, television ad, and acting gigs, but having one doesn't hurt for live tour auditions.

Comps – slang for complimentary tickets

Concert Promoter - Makes offers of employment to artist through the artist's agent.

Copy Protection - Record labels use a number of different (so-called) copy-protection techniques for certain releases. These are formatted in a non-standard way to stop them playing normally in PCs.

Copyright - the exclusive rights granted to the author or creator of an original work, including the right to copy, distribute and adapt the work. Copyright lasts for a certain time period after which the work is said to enter the public domain. Copyright applies to a wide range of works that are substantive and fixed in a medium. Some jurisdictions also recognize "moral rights" of the creator of a work, such as the right to be credited for the work. Copyright is described under the umbrella term intellectual property along with patents and trademarks.

Copyright Exemption and/or Exceptions - A provision in the *Copyright Act* which permits the use of a copyright-protected work, without the payment of license fees, by religious, educational or charitable organizations, when the use of such work is in furtherance of a religious, educational or charitable object.

Copyright infringement - Violation of the exclusive rights of a copyright owner (e.g., publicly performing a copyright-protected musical work without the copyright owner's consent).

Corporate Date - A private show an artist plays for a corporation's convention, party, or retreat.

Cover - (Cover Tune, Cover Song) A song that has been released before by another artist.

Cover Band - A band that plays only cover songs. Sometimes a band chooses to cover only one artist. In this case, a band that only performs songs written by the Grateful Dead would be considered a Grateful Dead cover band.

Cut Outs - Product titles discontinued by the record label, usually due to lack of sales. Often purchased in large amounts by another company and sold dirt-cheap in discount bins.

DAT Master - means to have a DAT master mixed down recording -for dubbing into the film/ or TV production

Deadwood - Unsold tickets at a concert.

Demo - A recording made to demonstrate how a song should sound. Could be done by a songwriter to pitch a song to a recording artist, by an artist to work out the arrangement and production of a song before entering the studio for final recording, or by an artist for use in a promo package to attract labels and Talent Buyers.

Derivative Work - A work based upon the Work or upon the Work and other pre-existing works, such as a translation, musical arrangement, dramatization, fictionalization, motion picture version, sound recording, art reproduction, abridgment, condensation, or any other form in which the Work may be recast, transformed, or adapted, except that a work that constitutes a Collective Work will not be considered a Derivative Work for the purpose of this License. For the avoidance of doubt, where the Work is a musical composition or sound recording, the synchronization of the Work in timed-relation with a moving image ("synching") will be considered a Derivative Work for the purpose of this License.

Diamond Record – Units Shipped of over 10 Million units

Digipak - Digipak is a proprietary range of CD (and DVD) packaging.

Digital Distribution means "moving music files electronically". It normally refers to the online equivalent of traditional distribution (shifting downloads instead of CDs).

Distribution - Traditional distribution is about moving CDs (or other physical recordings) from record labels to retailers. Distributors do more than carry boxes of CDs, they also promote and invest in releases.

Distribution Deal - to obtain a record distributor - to manufacture and mass reproduce stock, sell and distribute a CD or film to the public throughout the retail commercial marketplace. Some record distribution companies may also be record companies as well that commercially distribute other record label's product.

Door Deal – A financial arrangement to pay an artist from the proceeds generated by sales at the door. The artist typically would not receive a guarantee. A door deal may be structured as a percentage of the admission charge before or after expenses such as production, security or certain staff such as a sound technician.

Downstage - The part of the stage closest to the audience.

DRM - Digital Rights Management is a kind of copy-protection. It is a hardware or software device that forces users to comply with copyright owners' conditions.

Dramatic Rights - While the line between dramatic and non-dramatic is not clear and depends on the facts, a dramatic performance usually involves using the work to tell a story or as part of a story or plot. Dramatic performances, among others, include:

(I) performance of an entire "dramatic-musical work." For example a performance of the musical play Oklahoma would be a dramatic performance.

(II) performance of one or more musical compositions from a "dramatic-musical work" accompanied by dialogue, pantomime, dance, stage action, or visual representation of the work from which the music is taken. For example a performance of "People Will Say We're In Love" from Oklahoma with costumes, sets or props or dialogue from the show would be dramatic.

(III) performance of one or more musical compositions as part of a story or plot, whether accompanied or unaccompanied by dialogue, pantomime, dance, stage action or visual representation. For example, incorporating a performance of "If I Loved You" into a story or plot would be a dramatic performance of the song.

(IV) performance of a concert version of a "dramatic-musical work." For example, a performance of all the songs in Oklahoma even without costumes or sets would be a dramatic performances.

The term "dramatic-musical work" includes, but is not limited to, a musical comedy, opera, play with music, revue or ballet.

Performing Right's Organizations have the right to license "non-dramatic" public performances of its members' works - for example, recordings broadcast on radio, songs or background music performed as part of a movie or other television program, or live or recorded performances in a bar or restaurant.

Dramatic and grand rights are licensed by the composer or the publisher of the work.

Draw - A band has a "draw" if they can generate a live audience at a live concert. On the flipside, a band that doesn't attract an audience has "no draw."

Emancipated Minor - Person under the age of 18 who has been legally declared an adult and is no longer under his or her parents' control. Obtaining emancipated minor status, which gives a minor the legal rights of an adult, is common with teens in the entertainment industry because it enables them to enter into legal agreements such as contracts on their own behalf, work longer hours, and gives them control to make financial decisions for themselves.

EP - Extended Play. Record containing at least 3 songs (2 songs per side is usual), but not as many songs as an LP.

EPK – Electronic Press Kit

Equity - Slang for Actors Equity, the union representing theater actors and stage managers.

Fair Use - A limitation and exception to the exclusive right granted by copyright law to the author of a creative work, is a doctrine in United States copyright law that allows limited use of copyrighted material without acquiring permission from the rights holders. Examples of fair use include commentary, criticism, news reporting, research, teaching, library archiving and scholarship. It provides for the legal, non-licensed citation or incorporation of copyrighted material in another author's work under a four-factor balancing test.

Fingerprinting - A way of recognizing digital files by patterns in their data. The fingerprint is a short code, which can be read by special software to reliably identify the title and other details of a particular track.

First Right – After completing a song, a songwriter has the right of FIRST USE. This is the period where they essentially hold a monopoly on the song. These means that songwriters own the monopoly to record the song first, or they may grant the first right to someone else to record the work. If a big name artist wants to use your song on their next CD, you can give them a temporary exclusive.

Fly - To suspend equipment (or people) above the stage via a system of trusses and cables. Riggers are the crew members in charge of doing this.

F.O.H. – Slang for Front of House.

Format - 1. Type of music or programming on a radio station (CHR, AOR, Talk Radio, etc.). 2. Less commonly, the type of playback media music is available on (CD, MP3, etc.)

Front of House - (F.O.H.) 1.The area around the main sound console, in the audience portion of the venue. 2. The audience area of the venue, nearest the stage. 3. Slang for the crew member who mixes sound for this part of the venue.

Four-Walling - Producing a show at a location that is rented out for a single evening, is called "four-walling," as it entails renting a venue and receiving no additional services or technical equipment other than the space itself.

Gig – a live performance

Gold Record – In the USA, units shipped of over 500,000 units. In Uruguay, a Gold Records indicates units shipped of over 2000 copies.

Harry Fox - The Harry Fox Agency (HFA) represents music publishers for their mechanical and digital licensing needs. They issue licenses and collect and distribute royalties for their affiliated publishers. This includes licensing for the recording and reproduction of CDs, ringtones, and Internet downloads. HFA does not issue synchronization (or synch) licenses for the use of music in advertising, movies, music videos, and television programs. HFA also conducts royalty examinations, investigates and negotiates new business opportunities, and pursues piracy claims.

Head Shot – a photograph of an artist's face & head

Headliner – One or more artists who are the primary reason why a performance ticket is sold.

Hook – A hook in a song is a phrase of words or music that catches the listener's ear. If the listener remembers anything of the song, it's usually the hook.

House - The audience portion of a concert venue.

IFPI - The International Federation of the Phonographic Industry is the international trade body for major labels and large independents.

In-Ears - In-ear monitor system that makes it easier for musicians to hear each other onstage than with traditional wedges.

Independent - Independent normally means record labels that are not majors.

Indie - A broad term with many general meanings. It refers to independent record labels, several ways of doing business, various styles of music and a number of philosophies.

Intellectual property - A form of creative endeavor that can be protected through a copyright, trademark, patent, industrial design or integrated circuit topography.

ISRC - International Standard Recording Codes identify recordings (tracks).

ISWC - International Standard Musical Works Codes identify compositions.

J-Card - The front insert for a slim jewel case.

Jewel Case - A standard plastic CD case.

Kill Seats - (sometimes called "kills") Concert tickets held from sale until after stage set up for seats expected to be unusable ("killed") due to staging elements or the sound board being in the way. The number of kill seats is usually overestimated, and after the stage is set, any seats not eliminated are put on sale. (Those with "partially obstructed views" are marked as such). In the past, kill seats could often be bought at the venue box office close to show time, but the advent of more online ticket sellers have virtually eliminated their availability at the venue.

Label Code - The Label Code (LC) was introduced in 1977 by the IFPI (International Federation of Phonogram and Videogram Industries) in order to unmistakably identify the different record labels for rights purposes.

License – A License is simply the permission to use something. It is the right, granted by the copyright holder, for a given person or entity to broadcast, recreate, perform, or listen to a recorded copy of a copyrighted work. A License is the right, granted by the copyright holder, for a given person or entity to broadcast, recreate, or perform a recorded copy of a copyrighted work. Types of licensing contracts can include: 1) A flat fee for a defined period of usage, or 2) Royalty payments determined by the number of copies of the work sold or the total revenues acquired as a result of its distribution. Most music licensing agreements include some form of compensation of the copyright owner when the work in which it is included (i.e. movie, play) is financially successful.

Licensee - the person or entity to whom the work is licensed.

Licensing or Clearance Houses - To clear a piece of material is to obtain the legal rights necessary to use it. The agents for licensing for the film/ TV shows who obtain (by contracting in writing) (i.e. to obtain licenses) all the necessary legal rights in the show for all the music usages. Licensing houses may also sometimes supply music for productions.

Licensor - the owner of the licensed work and offers the Work under the terms of a License.

Line-Up - The bands that are supposed to play a particular show together make the "line-up. " Also known as The Bill

List - If you're on "the list," your name is on the list of people who do not have to pay to get into the show. People who put names on "the list" include: someone who works at the venue, the artist, the record label, the concert promoter, or the publicist.

Literary work - Work consisting of text, which includes novels, poems, catalogues, reports tables and translations of such works. It also includes computer programs.

Live Nation – A concert promotion company which was spun off from Clear Channel Communications.

Load-In – A term used to describe the process of moving equipment into a venue.

Load-Out – A term used to describe the process of moving equipment out of a venue.

Long-box - An oversized cardboard package that CDs used to be sold in, a form of exterior cardboard packaging for CD's in widespread use in North America in the 1980 S and early 1990 S. When compact discs first began to appear in the retail stores, the long-box packaging served a transitional purpose, allowing shops to file new compact discs in the same bins originally used for vinyl records. Long-boxes are 12 inches tall by almost 6 inches wide, and capable of containing two separate discs when necessary. Most long-boxes were full color, with details about the compact disc on the back, and artwork that was frequently taken from the original square album cover art, reworked for the new shape and size.

Loop - A piece of music that is repeated in a song.

L.P. – Long Play – more than 4 songs on an album. Longer than an E.P.

Major - A major record label. The major record labels are the biggest members of record industry trade bodies (e.g. RIAA in America and BPI in the UK). There isn't a fixed definition—the majors are just the labels that sell most records.

Manager - Business Manager, Personal Manager, Tour Manager, Stage Manager

Market - 1. Audience which can be identified through demographic research and/or preference analysis. 2. Group of buyers or consumers. 3. Sometimes, slang for a market city.

Market City - Area of a state or country large enough to support an arena or stadium concert. Often the capitol. Some states and countries have several market cities.

Master Rights (Master Use Rights) - The right to use a Master Recording of a song. This means the Album, CD, DAT that the song is embodied on.

Master Use Licensing - the licensing of the recording of a musical work to be performed as a soundtrack, bumper, lead-in or background to a motion picture.

Master Use License - A master use license is a phonographic copyright license to pay recording owners for music used in film, video, or TV soundtracks. There is no fixed fee for master use licenses.

Mastering - The final engineering stage in audio production, normally for duplication. It is a skilled, genre-specific job. Mastering is completed after tracking, editing, and mixing.

Mechanical Rights - This is the right to record a song to sell it on a record, MP3, laser disc, mini disc, video, CD rom, etc. The "MECHANICALS " are the SALES MONIES from the sales of the record or above medium. Compulsory Mechanical Royalties are 9.1 cents per song per sale for songs up to 5 minutes. Mechanical Royalties get larger for longer songs for longer songs. The present statutory rate for songs between five minutes and six is 10.5 cents per copy made. It's 12.25 cents if the song is over six minutes long, and you get 14 cents a copy for songs longer than 7 minutes, and so on.

Mis-pressings: A mis-pressing is when a record or CD is pressed with different music to what is stated on the label. Mis-pressings are actually quite common, particularly on CD. If the labels are simply stuck on the wrong sides of a record it is not strictly a mis-pressing. I.e. the labels should denote a different release to the music that is actually on the record. Some vinyl records by famous artists sell for extra if mis-pressed but with CDs there is almost no added value.

Monitor - A speaker or in-ear system that lets musicians hear each other onstage. (See also, in-ears, wedges.)

MP3 - A popular music file format used for downloading and digital music players. File sizes are generally about a tenth of the original size. MP3 was invented in 1987 and available publicly from 1995. MP3 is an MPEG standard.

Music Sup – slang for Music Supervisor. One who make decisions on which songs are used in TV, film or commercials.

Neighboring Rights – The rights granted for the use of a song in a recorded format. A Circle P copyright is a neighboring right.

Non-Routed Date - A show that does not fall in the natural path of travel between two other shows that were previously booked. They are usually either private gigs on a night off or special "one night only" performances when the artist is on a break from touring.

One Sheet – A promotion item that provides a picture, bio and other information on one sheet of paper.

Opener – A term used to describe an artist who does not have the draw of a headliner and is used to prime the audience before the headliner's performance. An opening act.

Option - An option is normally an option to extend the term of a contract but it doesn't mean everybody has options. Sometimes only the label has the option and it may be automatic.

Original - (Original Songs) 1. A song not previously recorded by another artist. 2. Song written by the artist who performs it.

OSHA - Occupational Safety and Health Administration. US Government Agency that regulates job-related safety and health issues. OSHA's mission is "to prevent work-related injuries, illnesses, and deaths."

PA - 1. "Public address system". Delivers sound into the concert venue so that the audience can hear the band. 2. Slang for Production Assistant or Personal Assistant.

PA Copyright Form - This is the registration form from the Library of Congress that you use to register a song. It protects the copyright in and to the words and music of the song.

Paper - Slang for tickets given away to fill seats and give the appearance of a full concert venue.

Papering the House - The act of giving tickets away to fill seats and give the appearance of a full concert venue.

Per Diem - Money allotted to the artist and each crew member for daily living expenses on the road.

Per Program License - A "per program" license is similar to the blanket license in that it authorizes a radio or television broadcaster to use all the works in the Performing Rights Organization's repertory. However, the license is designed to cover use of music in a specific radio or television programs, requiring that the user keep track of all music used. Also, the user must be certain to obtain rights for all the music used in programs not covered by the license.

Performance - the live performance of a musical piece, regardless of whether it's performed by the original artist or in the manner it is best known.

Performance Rider - (see also Technical Rider or Rider) Part of the artist's contract that details production requirements and staging for the artist's show. The rider also outlines details pertaining to the care and feeding of the artist and touring personnel.

Performing Rights Society - (AKA Performing Rights Organization) Organization that grants licenses for performances of a given songwriter or publisher's music. In the United States, there are three: ASCAP, BMI, and SESAC.

Personal Assistant - (AKA PA) Assists an artist or executive with day to day personal tasks such as scheduling, travel arrangements, correspondence, picking up dry cleaning, hiring domestic help, coordinating meetings, shopping for gifts or personal necessities, etc. Usually travels with the artist.

Personal Manager – A Manager who oversees the artist's career. He or she does big picture, long-range planning and acts on the artist's behalf.

Platinum Record - In the USA, units shipped of over 1,000,000 units.
In Uruguay, units shipped of over 4,000 units.

Podcast - A podcast is a download through podcasting software such as iPodder. Podcasting software finds new downloads using RSS and adds them to playlist software for automatic transfer to a music player

Points - A point is a percentage point (one hundredth, or a penny in the pound). It normally applies to royalties. The total amount (100%) is not always what it appears to be.

PR - Technically means "press relations" but is also used in a slang way to refer to a person who works in press relations. PR is also known as "publicity." PR companies/PR people are usually hired to work on a campaign basis to promote a new album, single or tour. Some PR people only promote to print media, some only to websites, some only to TV and some to a combination of mediums. Some PR people also work in radio plugging, but often radio is treated as a separate entity.

Pre-Cleared Music - music that has been pre-negotiated for price, distribution and legal use, generally through licensing for film, video, television (commercials and programs), Internet, events, video games and multimedia productions.

Press Kit - A professional folio containing your resume and/or bio, photograph, CD, list of venues you have performed, press clippings, recommendations, posters and mementos from concerts (especially those with your name listed,) lyric samples, and other materials to support your professional viability.

Private Date - A show an artist plays that is not open to the public, such as a wedding, private party, invitation-only fundraiser, or corporate convention. Sometimes it is called a corporate date.

PRO - Performing Rights Organization is a general term for publishing rights societies like ASCAP, BMI, SESAC or PRS in the UK

Product - Label speak for CD's, cassettes, etc. Retail term for inventory.

Production – usually means sound and light equipment.

Production Manager - In charge of the technical equipment for the artist or venue. Rents the staging and equipment, keeps the mechanical stuff working.

Promo Package - (Promotional package, Promo Kit, Promo) A package of materials assembled to attract labels or talent buyers. Contents may vary depending on the purpose of the promo package but typically include a CD of the artist's music, a bio, a photo, and press clippings.

Promoter - Slang for concert promoter. Makes offer of employment through artist's agent.

Promotion Manager - Person at radio station in charge of the stations promotions.

Public Domain - Not copyright. This happens when copyright expires or the owner explicitly puts the material in the public domain.

Public Performance - A public performance is one that occurs "in a place open to the public or at any place where a substantial number of persons outside of a normal circle of a family and its social acquaintances is gathered." A public performance also occurs when the performance is transmitted by means of any device or process (for example, via broadcast, telephone wire, or other means) to the public. In order to perform a copyrighted work publicly, the user must obtain performance rights from the copyright owner or his representative.

Publish - Publishing used to refer to the availability of printed sheet music. Today it refers to the public availability of copyright material in any form.

Publisher - for the purposes of copyright, a publisher is the owner of the copyrighted work.

Publishers Share - (The following example given is @ 100% Publishing) If you divide 100% of The Song in Half -- the remaining 50% is the Publishers Share -It is then referred to as 100% Publishers Share.

Publishing Administration - is limited to royalty collection. The publisher will not get additional customers for the compositions. The rate for administration is normally about 10%.

Purchaser - Music industry contract language for the talent buyer or concert promoter. Purchasers make offers of employment to artists through the artist's agent.

Pyro - Slang for pyrotechnics. Fireworks or sparkler type effects used at a concert are considered pyro and requires a highly skilled licensed pyro technician.

Q - Rating Research product of the Long Island-based research company Marketing Evaluations, used to rate the "liability" and appeal of various celebrities on TV on a scale from 0-50. Good looking and personable celebrities typically get the highest Q ratings. www.qscores.com

Radio Plugger - Also sometimes simply known as a plugger, radio pluggers promote releases to radio. Pluggers usually work with specific singles and go around to radio station playlist meetings, playing the singles they are representing and trying to get them placed on a playlist. In some cases, pluggers may work with full albums, letting the stations themselves decide what the single is.

Record Label - A record label (or record company) makes, distributes and markets sound recordings (CD's, tapes, etc.) Record labels obtain from music publishers the right to record and distribute songs and in turn pay license fees for the recordings.
A record label was originally a company that made recordings (their company or imprint label was stuck on the centre). Today few if any record labels make records themselves. Now, record labels invest in artists, promote recordings and collect earnings from phonographic copyrights.

Recoupables - Expenses charged by a label against an artist's royalties. Recoupables are deducted before the artist sees any money, so a tight rein should be kept on the recording and promotional budgets. (See charge-backs.) Can also refer to expenses a manager covers for the artist which will be paid back at a later date.

Red Book - The technical rule book for standard audio CDs is known as the Red Book.

Reflux - Laryngitis Throat condition caused by acid reflux in which stomach acid rises to the throat area and causes hoarseness and other throat symptoms.

Region – Label or radio speak for a geographical section of the country or world.

Release - The release of physical (vinyl, cassette, CD) records to radio and retail was always coordinated and formal. The release of a big record was staged like the premiere of a major film. This still happens in the mainstream but the delivery of content on an independent artist's site is normally much less formal.

Resonance - Full, pleasing sound, determined by vibration and or echo of tone.

Retransmission - A transmission of a performance is one that is sent by any device or process (for example, radio, TV, cable, satellite, telephone) and received in a different place. A retransmission is a further transmission of that performance to yet another place.

Reversion is when a copyright assignment ends. Assignments are normally limited to a period of time or some other condition depending on the circumstances of the original rights owner.

RIAA - Recording Industry Association of America. Trade association that represents the labels and certifies albums "Gold," "Platinum," and "Diamond" all of which are trademarks of the RIAA.

Rider - (see also Technical Rider or Performance Rider) Part of the artist's contract that details production requirements and staging for the artist's show. The rider also outlines details pertaining to the care and feeding of the artist and touring personnel.

Rigger - Tour or venue personnel who "fly" lights and other staging equipment above the stage.

Roadie - Dated term for a member of the road crew. In some circles, a derogatory term. When in doubt use "crew member" or "tech." (See Tech.)

Road Manager - See Tour Manager.

Rotation - Frequency of radio or video airplay in a 24-hour period. Heavy rotation is many plays per day, light rotation is few.

Routed Date - a show that falls in the natural path of travel between two other shows that were previously booked. It's often a private gig on a night off.

Routing - The route a tour takes across the country or around the world. Tours are usually routed by the artist's agent with input from the artist's management, usually 6-9 months in advance. Most major tours are routed to follow the sun as much as possible in order to avoid weather-related travel problems and ensure best attendance; warm climates in Winter, cooler climates in Summer.

Royalties - fees paid to rights owners (normally record labels, publishers, writers and performers) for the use of their work.

RSS – Rich Site Summary (originally RDF Site Summary, often dubbed Really Simple Syndication) is a family of web feed formats used to publish frequently updated works—such as blog entries, news headlines, audio, and video—in a standardized format. [An RSS document (which is called a "feed", "web feed", or "channel") includes full or summarized text, plus metadata such as publishing dates and authorship.

Runners - Local crew members who run errands during the time the artist is in town. May also shuttle the touring party to and from the airport, hotel, and venue.

Runs - Aguillera-esque vocal tricks in which the singer sends each note up and down like a multi-hilled rollercoaster. Runs have existed in R&B and gospel music for decades, but were made popular in the mainstream by such artists as Mariah Carey and Christina Aguillera.

Sampling - requires record label and publishing clearance. There is no fixed rate for clearance. Sampling may be allowed under the terms of a blanket MCPS assignment to pay the writer mechanical income. If the work is not assigned to MCPS the sample should also be cleared through the publisher.

Scalpers – Persons who buy tickets with the intent to sell them for a higher amount.

SCMS - The Serial Copy Management System stops controlled digital media from being copied on certain machines by setting a marker on new recordings. Recordings with the marker cannot be copied again in these machines. SCMS is part of the Sony/Philips Digital Interface (S/PDIF) format.

Secular Music - Non-religious music.

SESAC – One of three organizations that grants licenses for performances of a given songwriter or publisher's music.

Session Musicians – Musicians who are paid a one-off fee (which should not be less than the Musicians' Union rate) for playing at recording sessions.

Set - A group of songs performed by an Artist. An artist may perform more than one set with a break in between.

Settlement - The completion of paperwork, deduction of expenses, and payment of the artist after the show.

Silver Record - In the USA, units shipped of over 100,000 units.

Song Hold - The process in which an A&R Rep, Manager, or Producer claims "first dibs" on a song to prevent another artist from recording and releasing it. A typical hold is 90 days with first rights, but 30-day and 60-day holds are also common.

Song Plugger - Person at a publishing house who tried to get record labels or artists to record their songs. In the days before demo tapes, the songs were presented live by singers hired just for this purpose by the song plugger.

Song Shopping Agreements - This is a letter of intent from Writer to Publisher (or vice versa) spelling out the terms and conditions and time limit the publisher has to get the song placed. These agreements can be extremely specific with percentages of Publishing granted when the Publisher gets a cut (or placement) in the set time period specified. It will most likely contain further options.

Song Shopping Agreements - This is a letter of intent from Writer to Publisher (or vice versa) spelling out the terms and conditions and time limit the publisher has to get the song placed. These agreements can be extremely specific with percentages of Publishing granted when the Publisher gets a cut (or placement) in the set time period specified. It will most likely contain further options.

Sound Exchange – a non-profit performing rights organization that collects royalties on behalf of sound recording copyright owners and featured artists for non-interactive digital transmission, including satellite and internet radio.

Sound and Lights - Contract term pertaining to stage equipment for sound and lighting needed for a concert. Term also referred to as "production."

Sound Recording - A sound recording refers to the copyright in a recording as distinguished from the copyright in a song. The copyright in the song encompasses the words and music and is owned by the songwriter or music publisher. The sound recording is the result of recording music, words or other sounds onto a tape, record, CD, etc. The copyright encompasses what you hear: the artist singing, the musicians playing, the entire production). The sound recording copyright is owned by the record label. The copyright in the musical work itself is owned by the music publisher, which grants the record label a "mechanical" license to record and distribute the song as part of the record.

SoundScan - SoundScan is the official method of tracking sales of music and music video products throughout the United States and Canada

Spider - A small piece of plastic that holds CDs in a card case.

Soundman – A technician who operates the sound production at a performance.

Split Point – The point negotiated between Promoter and Agent where percentages of income are split. This point is usually determined after expenses and a reasonable return on investment.

SR Copyright Form - This is the registration form from The Library Of Congress that you use to register the sound recording only (that the song is embodied on) i.e.-The master recording as its embodied on the Cassette, Record, CD that you enclose for deposit materials.

Stage Left - The side of the stage on the artist's left as he/she looks out at the audience from the stage. (Stage Left is the audience's right as they look up at the artist.)

Stage Plot - A map of where the artist's equipment goes onstage. Part of the technical rider.

Stage Right - The side of the stage on the artist's right as he/she looks out at the audience from the stage. (Stage Right is the audience's left as they look up at the artist.)

Standing Waves - An acoustic phenomenon in which a reflected signal intersects the original signal and there's a halving or doubling of frequencies in that area. You can hear this for yourself by going into a narrow hallway with hard surfaces on both sides and no thick floor coverings. Clap your hands. The sounds will seem to "collide" with each other.

Stanza – A stanza in a song is similar to a paragraph in a book. A stanza is a section of grouped lines. Usually a song will have multiple verses and a chorus. A verse is a stanza.

Sync Rights (Synchronization Rights) - A synchronization or "synch" right involves the use of a recording of musical work in audio-visual form: for example as part of a motion picture, television program, commercial announcement, music video or other videotape. Often, the music is "synchronized" or recorded in timed relation with the visual images. Synchronization rights are licensed by the music publisher to the producer of the movie or program.

Synchronization Licensing - the licensing of musical works to be synchronized with moving pictures as background in a motion picture, television program, video, DVD, etc.

Talent Buyer - (Purchaser, Concert Promoter, Promoter) Makes offers of employment to artist through the artist's agent.

Tech - (Technician) Member of the crew. Often specializes in one area of production, such as lights, pyro, drums, etc. Formerly known as "roadies."

Tech Rider - (Technical Rider) Part of the artist's contract that details the technical aspects of the artist's production requirements, including equipment, its placement on the stage, and local personnel needed.

Technical Rider - (Tech rider) Part of the artist's contract that details the technical aspects of the artist's production requirements, including equipment, its placement on the stage, and local personnel needed.

Throat Coat - Tea Popular with professional singers. Manufactured by Traditional Medicinals.

Ticket Buys – a term used for the number of tickets a record label purchases for one of their artists shows. Usually ticket buys are used a giveaways on the radio.

Tip Sheet - Newsletter which lists various music opportunities and jobs for songwriters and composers.

Tour Manager - (Road Manager) The artist's representative on the road and works closely with the Personal Manager. A tour manager may have many functions, depending on the size of the tour. On very large tours, there may be both a Tour Manager, who oversees the entire tour, as well as a Road Manager, who represents the artist in day-to-day activities on the road on behalf of the Personal Manager.

Tour Support – Financial support provided by a record label to an artist to help the artist with their promotion while on a performance tour. This is done in coordination with the release of a current album.

Trademark - The legal protection of a trademark is about misuse of the business asset, passing off and confusing potential customers. It isn't an exclusive right to the trademarked name.

U -Card - The paper CD tray or back insert for a jewel case.

Upstage - The part of the stage farthest from the audience.

Upstream – When an Independent Record label encourages their artist to sign with a larger label.

Venue - Place where a concert is held.

Wedges - Wedge-shaped monitors.

Business Plan for Artists
INDEX

Accounting 322	Company Structure 21, 22, 24, 26
Accounts Payable 351	Company Summary 8
Accounts Receivable 349	Competition 217
Administrative 62	Competition Industry Analysis . . 218
Advertising Budget 195	Competition Summary 11, 17
Advertising Mix 196	Competitive Comparisons 222, 223
Advertising Objectives 192	Competitive Research 221
Advertising Offline 200	Competitive Strategy 225
Advertising Plan 187	Content Clearances 291, 292
Advertising Plan Summary 11	Content Development 290
Advertising Potential 194	Content Licensing 272
Advertising Strategy 190, 191	Contingency Planning 44
Advertising Summary 17	Co-Op Advertising 197, 198
Agents 56, 57	Co-Op Promotions 157
Annual Update 5	Copyrights 277
Appendix - Overview 365	Cover Letter 6
Appendix Summary 13, 18	Creative Talent 198
Artist / Personal Management Agreement Sample 373	Credibility 112
Artist / Producer Agreement Sample 377	Customer Demographics 144
Artist Summary 32	Customer Niches 141
Assessing Your Company's Potential 4	Customer Profiles 142
Band Member Agreement Sample 369	Customer Service Plan 145
Branding Strategy 109, 111	Customer Summary 10
Break-Even Analysis 318	Customers Overview 135
Budgets 342	Databases 362
Communication Strategy 155	Determine Objectives 2
Company Description 19, 20	Digital Rights Management 296
Company Layout 27	Direct Mail 203
Company Location 25	Discography 285
Company Objectives 28	Distribution Overview . . 262, 263, 264, 266
Company Overview 19	Distribution via Brick & Mortar . 268
	E-Mail Advertising 212

405

Equipment Technology	304	Marketing Goals & Objectives	98
Executive Summary	7, 15	Marketing Mix	107, 108
Exit Strategy	339	Marketing Plan	97
Expiration of copyright	279	Marketing Plan Overview	95
Fan Customers	137, 138	Marketing Plan Summary	9
Finance Plan	313	Marketing Summary	17
Finance Plan Summary	12	Mastering	82
Finance Summary	18	Merchandise Sales Strategy	250
Financial	5	Merchandising	91, 92
Financial Ratios	344, 345	Milestones	43
Financing Goals	3	Mixing and Editing	81
Forecasted Assumptions	330	Monitoring & Evaluating Plans	132
Forecasted Balance Sheet	325	Music Industry Customers	139
Forecasted Cash Flow	327	Music Industry Definitions	385
Forecasted Financial Statements	323	Musicians	53
Forecasted Operating Expenses	328	Newsletters	205
Forecasted Revenue	332	Office Technology	299, 300
Forward Looking Statements	365	Online Advertising	208
Future Products & Services	92	Online Distribution	269
GLOSSARY	385	Online Marketing Plan	126
Goodwill	321	Online Sales Strategy	252
Growth Strategy	246	Operations Plan	23
Important Assumptions	316	Organizational Structure	21
Income Sources	32	Packaging Process	89
Independent Accountant's Report	323	Packaging Strategy	125
Industry Involvement	354	Patents	280
Industry Participants	220	Performance Promotion	181
Intellectual Property	275	Performing Rights Organizations	286
Intellectual Property Summary	12, 18	Personal Income Statement	366
Key Financial Indicators	317	Pressing Vinyl	88
Keys to Success	40	Pricing Policy	121, 122, 123
Legal Resources	355	Pricing Strategy	234
Lifestyle	5	Producers	55
Live Performances	76	Producing Audio	78
Main Competitors	224	Product & Services	9
Management & Personnel	8	Product Development	71
Management Summary	16	Product Mix	74
Management Team	50, 51	Product Strategy	71
Managing the Major Revisions	6	Product Testing	114
Manufacturing	86	Products & Services Overview	69
Market Analysis	100	Products & Services Summary	16
Market Potential	101	Profit Sources	235
Market Segmentation	105	Projected Balance Sheet	320

Projects profit & Loss 319	Sales of Performances Strategy 257
Promotion Analysis 150	Sales of Recordings Strategy . . 255
Promotion Objectives 151	Sales Plan 227
Promotion Plan – Overview 147	Sales Plan Summary 11
Promotion Plan Summary 10	Sales Programs 248
Promotion Potential 152	Sales Strategy 233
Promotion Strategy 153, 154	Sales Summary 17
Promotion Summary 17	Short-Term Plan 47
Promotion Technology 301	Singers 54
Publicists 58	Single Song Publishing Agreement Sample 381
Publishers 60	Social Media Plan . 129, 130, 131
Publishing Sales Strategy 260	Social Network Advertising 210
Radio Promotion Plan 159	Software Technology 308
Record Label / Artist Agreement Sample 383	Songwriters 54
Recorded Audio 78	Sourcing Professional Services . 63
Recorded Video 83, 84	Spending Strategy 339
Recording Technology 303	Start-Up Summary 314
Registration 288	SWOT Analysis 105, 106
Related Statistics 353	Target Marketing Strategy 119
Research, Statistics & Demographics 359	Technology 299
Resources Summary 13, 18	Technology Summary 12
Resumes of Team Members . . . 367	Tickets Sales Strategy 273
Return on Investment 340	Trade Publications 361
Risk Management 337	Trademarks 281
Risk Reduction 334	Use of Funds 315
Sales Affiliates 249, 250	Use Your Plan 4
Sales Forecasts 243	Video Promotion 177
Sales Management 230	Web Related Resources 356
Sales Objectives 232	Writing and Producing Music . . 279